The Morning Chronicle's

LABOUR AND THE POOR

VOLUME III

THE METROPOLITAN DISTRICTS

The Morning Chronicle's

LABOUR AND THE POOR

VOLUME III

THE METROPOLITAN DISTRICTS

HENRY MAYHEW

Edited By
Rebecca Watts & Kevin Booth

Ditto Books
www.dittobooks.co.uk

First Published by Ditto Books 2020

© Ditto Books 2020

A catalogue record for this book is available
from the British Library

ISBN 978-1-913515-03-4 (hardback)
ISBN 978-1-913515-13-3 (paperback)

Cover Image:
The "Rookery," St. Giles's
From "Old & New London"
George Walter Thornbury & Edward Walford
Published 1878
Image courtesy of The British Library

"Bond-street an't no good now. Oxford-street, up by Old Cavendish-street, or Oxford-market, or Wells-street, are all favourite pitches for Punch. We don't do much in the City. People has their heads all full of business there, and them as is greedy after the money an't no friend of Punch's."

Contents

i

List of Illustrations

Preface

This work attempts to be a faithful reproduction of the "Labour and the Poor" letters as printed in *The Morning Chronicle*. Only obvious typographical errors and omissions have been corrected. Variations in the spelling and hyphenation of words have largely been retained. We hope any such inconsistencies prove to be of some historical interest to the reader.

As much as possible we have tried to recreate the original layout and styling of the text and all factual tables have been reproduced as closely to the originals as possible with only minimal alterations made where necessary to improve readability.

Not all letters were titled. Where missing we have added titles to the Table of Contents to assist navigation and explanation of content. The letters themselves are as per the originals.

A handful of illustrations have been added to each volume. These did not appear in the original text but hopefully provide added interest.

R. W.
K. B.

Introduction

In 1849 a leading London-based newspaper, *The Morning Chronicle*, undertook an investigation into the working and living conditions of the poor throughout England and Wales in the hope that their findings might lead to much needed change.

The reputed catalyst for their "Labour and the Poor" series was an article written by Henry Mayhew recording a journey into Bermondsey, one of the most deprived districts of London, which was printed in September 1849. Following this it was proposed that an in-depth investigation be carried out and "Special Correspondents", the investigators, were selected and distributed around the country. The first article or "Letter" appeared on the 18th of October 1849 and the series would run for almost 2 years and 222 letters.

The well-known and respected writers and journalists recruited for the task included Henry Mayhew who was assigned to the Metropolitan districts, Angus Bethune Reach to the Manufacturing districts, Alexander Mackay and Shirley Brooks to the Rural districts and Charles Mackay to investigate the cities of Birmingham and Liverpool. The author of the letters from Wales is as yet unknown.

The "Labour and the Poor" letters were extremely popular at the time, being widely read throughout the nation and even abroad. The revelations in them caused quite a stir amongst the middle and upper classes of Victorian society. *Letters to the Editor* poured in with donations for specific cases of distress that appeared in the letters and also for the general alleviation of the suffering of the poor. A special fund was set up by *The Morning Chronicle* to collect and distribute these donations.

These *Letters to the Editor* have been included in this series, predominantly in the Metropolitan district volumes whose letters elicited the majority of responses. They provide a unique window into the thoughts and sentiments of the Victorian readership as they react to the incredible accounts of misery and desperation being unveiled.

The Morning Chronicle's extraordinary and unsurpassed "Labour and the Poor" investigation provides an unparalleled insight into the people of the period, their living and working conditions, their feelings, their language, their sufferings and their struggles for survival amidst the poverty and destitution of 19th century Britain. An investigation of such magnitude had never before been attempted and the undertaking was truly of epic proportions. Its impact at the time was profound. Its historical importance today is without question.

LABOUR AND THE POOR.

—◆—

THE METROPOLITAN DISTRICTS.

[FROM OUR SPECIAL CORRESPONDENT.]

LETTER XXXVII.

It was my intention to devote the present Letter to the subject of Prison Labour; but, before doing so, it is necessary that certain statistics and accounts be obtained; these require some little time to prepare, and I am therefore compelled to postpone the inquiry for a few days. In the meantime I have turned my attention to the state of the metropolitan Toy-makers; for they, being a limited class, do not demand a long investigation, and are, consequently, well fitted to fill up the interval.

I shall, then, in this and the following Letter, seek to give as comprehensive a view as possible of the condition and earnings of the London manufacturer of toys. First, however, let me endeavour to impress the reader with some faint idea as to the variety of arts and sciences which are brought into operation in the construction of the playthings of the young. Some ten or a dozen years ago there was an elaborate article on the subject of toys in the *Westminster Review*, which at the time was currently attributed to an eminent writer on political economy. This, with Dr. Paris' celebrated little book, entitled "Philosophy in Sport made Science in Earnest," constitute, so far as I know, the only scientific treatises on the subject.

Mr. McCulloch, in his *Commercial Directory*, thus speaks of Toys. "They include," he says, "every trifling article made expressly for the amusement of children. How frivolous soever these articles may appear in the estimation of superficial observers, their manufacture employs hundreds of hands, and gives bread to many families in London, Birmingham, &c. The greatness of the demand for them may be inferred from the fact that a manufacturer of glass beads and articles of that description has received a single order for £500 worth of dolls' eyes!" (Fourth Report, Artisans and Machinery, p. 314).

A toy is, then, a trifling object, constructed for the amusement of the young. Contemptible, however, as the child's plaything may appear—it is at least a purely æsthetical object—conferring upon us our first taste of mental enjoyment. In toys we shall find expressed almost every form and source of ideal pleasure. Thus, imitation—perhaps the first rude aim of all the fine arts—is largely drawn upon as a means of delight; and accordingly we have horses, dogs, and donkies—carts, windmills, and houses—dolls and theatres, and a long catalogue of other wooden, waxen, and *papier maché* configurations, which please merely from their fancied resemblance to the objects that they are intended to represent. Other toys, again, are made to yield an additional delight, not only by their similarity of form, but by their repetition of the same sounds, or their performance of the same acts, as some living creature. Hence composition dogs are made to bark, wooden cuckoos to cry, birds to sing, carved monkeys to climb up a pole, puppets to move their limbs, and dolls to open and shut their eyes. Some toys, on the other hand, are exercises of dexterity, appealing to that universal principle of human nature—the love of success. The delight which the grown man feels in overcoming any difficulty, or in excelling a rival, is thus made to contribute to the amusement and the manual or intellectual skill of the youth. This we observe in the different games more especially, as in marbles, draughts, chess, cards, cricket, cup and ball, and an infinity of others of a similar kind. Other toys, however—such as the more scientific ones—are amusing on account of the wonder they excite. Thus the magnetic swan and fish that swim after the loadstone in water, the magic-lantern with its unreal figures on the wall, the microscope, the balloon, the thaumatrope—all appeal to that pleasurable feeling which we experience on the perception of any circumstance which is out of the common order of events in nature. Jack-in-the-box, crackers, detonating-balls, leaping frogs, are toys of mere surprise. The kaleidoscope, accordions, and musical glasses, are, on the other hand, toys of visual and audible beauty, pleasing by the combination and succession of harmonious forms and sounds.

The sciences which are laid under contribution in the construction of toys are almost as multifarious as the arts which are employed in the manufacture of them. Optics gives its burning-glass, its microscope, its magic lantern, its stereoscope, its thaumatrope, its phantasmascope, and a variety of others; electricity, its Leyden jars, galvanic batteries, electrotypes, &c.; chemistry, its balloons, fireworks, and crackers; mechanics, its clock-work mice—its steam and other carriages; pneumatics contributes its kites and windmills; acoustics, its Jew-harps, musical-glasses, accordions, and all the long train of musical instruments; astronomy lends its orreries; in fine, there is scarcely a branch of knowledge which is not made to pay tribute to the amusement of the young. Nor are the arts and artists that are called into play in the manufacture of toys less numerous. There is the turner, to turn the handles of the skipping-ropes, the ninepins, the peg, the humming, and the whipping tops, the hoop-sticks; the basket-worker, to make dolls' cradles, and babies' rattles, and wickerwork carts and carriages; the tinman, to manufacture tin swords and shields, peashooters and carts, money-boxes, and miniature candlesticks; and the pewterer to cast the metal soldiers, and dolls' cups, and saucers, and fire-irons, and knives and forks, plates and dishes, chairs and tables, and all the leaden furniture of the baby-house; the modeller, to make the skin and composition animals; the glassblower, to make the dolls' eyes; the wig maker, to manufacture the dolls' curls; the tallowchandler, to mould miniature candles for the dolls' houses; the potter, to produce dolls' cups and saucers. Then there are image-men, conjurors, cutlers, cardmakers, opticians, cabinetmakers, firework-makers, and, indeed, almost every description of artisan—for there is scarcely a species of manufacture or handicraft that does not contribute something to the amusement of the young.

Such, then, are the characters of toys and toy-makers in general. Of the latter there are in Great Britain, 1,866 toy-makers and dealers. The distribution of these throughout the country is as follows:—

ENGLAND.
COUNTIES.

Berks	1
Bucks	1
Cambridge	2
Chester	11
Cornwall	3
Cumberland	2
Derby	5
Devon	8
Dorset	6
Durham	2
Essex	9
Gloucester	20
Hertford	3
Huntingdon	1
Kent	23
Lancaster	35
Leicester	5
Lincoln	5
Middlesex	359
Monmouth	6
Norfolk	14
Northumberland	3
Nottingham	4
Salop	2
Somerset	8
Southampton	10
Stafford	53
Suffolk	3
Surrey	93
Sussex	21
Warwick	942
Westmoreland	2
Wilts	1

Worcester	9
York, East Riding	3
City and Ainsty	1
North Riding ..	4
West Riding ...	23
Total	1,814

WALES.
COUNTIES.

Carmarthen	1
Carnarvon	2
Denbigh	1
Glamorgan	1
Total	5

ISLANDS IN THE BRI-
TISH SEAS ...   4

SCOTLAND.
COUNTIES.

Aberdeen	4
Ayr	3
Clackmannan	1
Edinburgh	13
Fife	2
Forfar	2
Haddington	2
Lanark	7
Perth	2
Renfrew	2
Ross and Cromarty ..	5
Total	43
Great Britain, grand total	1,866

Of this number there were—Males above 20, 1,174; females (ditto), 417; males under 20, 197; females (ditto), 78. Hence we see that there are more toy-makers in the county of Warwick than in any other part of England. After Warwick, the greater number is to be found in Middlesex and Surrey—the two metropolitan counties. In the metropolis there were 553 toy-makers, of whom 320 were males above 20, and 163 females beyond the same age; and 48 were males under 20, and 22 females below the same age.

Let me now endeavour to arrive at some rough estimate as to the total earnings of the toy-makers of Great Britain, as well as the sum expended, in one year, in this country upon foreign and English toys:—

According to the Occupation Abstract, there were in the metropolis, in 1841, 407 toy-makers, and 146 toy-merchants and dealers. The number of toy-makers and dealers in Great Britain was 1,866; therefore we may calculate that about 1,373 of these individuals were toy-makers. Now, supposing that these earn each, upon an average, from 10s. to 15s. (say 12s. 6d.) per week, this would give the sum of £858 2s. 6d. for the weekly earnings of the collective toy-makers of Great Britain, or

per annum	£44,622	10	0
The cost of material would be about the same as for labour—thus ..	£44,622	10	0
And the interest for capital another third	44,622	10	0
Making together for the total cost of the toys produced annually in Great Britain	£133,867	10	0
The amount of toys imported into Great Britain in the same year was valued by the Customs at ..	22,130	0	0
Hence the total value of the toys sold in one year in Great Britain will be	£155,997	10	0

This sum, divided amongst the population of Great Britain under twenty years of age—which in the year above-mentioned amounted to 8,602,647 individuals—would give an average for each child, or young person, to spend in the year upon toys, of 4¼d.

I will now add an account of the different countries from which our foreign toys are imported. I am indebted for the information here given to the courtesy of a toy-dealer, in a large way, in High Holborn.

"The foreign toys," he said, "are made chiefly in France, Germany, and Switzerland; but I ought to characterise those from France as more fancy goods than mere toys—for what may properly be called toys from France may be termed mechanical toys. None, in my opinion, can be compared to the French in the ingenuity of their toys: they surpass the skill of the English workman. I am convinced, indeed, that the English toy-maker can hardly so much as repair a broken French toy. Few watch-makers here can repair a clock-work mouse; they will generally charge 2s. 6d. for repairing a mechanical mouse which I sell new for 3s. 6d. Such a mouse could not be made here, if it could be made at all, for less than 15s. I consider that the reduction of the duty on foreign toys is a decided benefit to the trade, and an advantage to the purchaser. They get toys cheaper so; but the cheaper they get them, the cheaper they want them. They're never satisfied. Those in this counter are German toys. Box toys are all German. Noah's arks, and boxes of cavalry soldiers, and of children's skittles, and of desserts, and of railroads (all sizes, up to 20s. a box), farm-yards, sheepfolds, and tea sets—and, in short, sets of almost everything. English toys are well made—such as rocking-horses and large things; but in smaller things the English workmen can't pretend to vie with the Germans. And those large things can't be imported, if they could be as well made in Germany, on account of the bulk. These box toys are the staple of the German trade. Nuremberg, Frankfort, and the vicinity of the Black Forest, are the principal places in Germany where these toys are made. Women, children, and poor people, with hardly food to eat, make them and take them to merchants, who export them, just as the people who work in garrets in the outskirts of London do with the toyshops here. They cut one another's throats for want of combination. I know the workmen do. I tell them so. They starve in trying to outdo one another in cheapness, which injures them, and is no benefit to the tradesman. The rosewood boxes which I used to sell at 15s., twenty years back, I now sell at 3s.—all owing to competition. The makers don't live, but starve by it. The French toys are ingeniously mechanical—moving figures of all sorts, often in glass cases; small china toys, tea and dinner services; fancy glass boxes—an immense trade done in them. The Swiss toys are the white wood toys—carved animals, and Swiss cottages and farms. I have often been told by travellers in Switzerland that they have bought toys of the Swiss peasants whom they saw at work in their cottages, in most parts of Switzerland; and they often tell me they have cost them more there than I should charge them, besides the bother of bringing them over. The Swiss make the wooden long figures, jointed, for the study of artists, sometimes 6 feet high. They are beautifully made. They can be placed and kept in a position that a living model cannot sustain sufficiently long for the artist's study or sketch. The cost of a six-foot lay-figure is about 9 guineas, and a very reasonable price. Barking dogs and musical toys are generally German. The English excel in the invention of games—round games for children; we excel greatly in dissected puzzles, geographical and such like. The foreign articles of that kind are so slight as to be useless. What the English workmen do, they do well, solidly and enduringly—it hasn't the tinselly look of the foreign, but it's not flimsy, and is useful. Toys have their fashions and runs. A month's fashion is not a bad average. These elastic faces (German) called gutta percha, but made of some composition, had a great run; the inventor, when they first came out, could have got any price for any quantity. The inventions in the toy trade are generally the work of men in the business. Scientific men have sometimes suggested to me a new toy, but not frequently. I never adopted any of their suggestions; they were attended with too much bother. I have often suggested things to the makers. I sell more of magic-lanterns and conjuring tricks than all the other houses. There is a very great demand for them. In such things we beat the foreigners all to nothing. Their magic-lanterns are as rubbishy as ever magic was, but they're sold wonderfully low. We can't sell low to sell good—not English magic-lanterns. There is decidedly a greater demand for scientific toys. My customers say, 'Let me have something instructive as well as amusing.' Panics and such like crises affect my trade considerably; indeed the trade is a sort of pulse of the nation's prosperity; for when people haven't money they can't buy their children toys."

To the above statement I subjoin a table of the rates of duty upon foreign toys at the different alterations of the tariff, and it is followed by an account of the amount of duties levied at the Custom-house, as well as of the estimated value of the toys imported.

Rate of duty from 1787 to 1818 inclusive, 33 per cent.
Rate of duty from 1819 to 1825 inclusive, 50 per cent.
Rate of duty from 1826 to 1841 inclusive, 20 per cent.
Since . . . . 1842 . . . . . . 10 per cent.

Amount of Custom-house Duties on Toys imported, from
1820 to 1848, and their estimated Value.

Year	Amount of Duty levied.	Value of Article imported.	Year	Amount of Duty levied.	Value of Article imported.
1820	£2,874	£ 5,748	1835	£4,284	£21,420
1821	2,819	5,638	1836	4,544	22,720
1822	3,569	7,138	1837	3,265	16,325
1823	4,361	8,722	1838	3,343	16,715
1824	4,744	9,488	1839	3,793	18,965
1825	5,197	10,394	1840	4,628	23,140
1826	1,949	9,740	1841	4,426	22,130
1827	2,303	11,515	1842	2,826	28,260
1828	2,944	14,720	1843	2,677	26,770
1829	3,152	15,760	1844	3,072	30,720
1830	3,578	17,890	1845	3,822	38,220
1831	3,769	18,845	1846	4,007	40,070
1832	3,479	17,395	1847	3,304	33,040
1833	3,826	19,130	1848	2,994	29,940
1834	4,819	24,095			

The London toy-makers are divided into several classes—such as
the toy-turner, the Bristol or green wood toy-maker, the white wood
toy-maker, the fancy toy-maker or modeller, and the doll-maker—of
which there are two grand branches, viz., the makers of the wooden
and of the sewed dolls. Then there are the tin toy-maker, the lead
and pewter toy-maker, the basket toy-maker, the detonating firework
maker, the drum and tambourine maker, the kite maker, and an infinity of others. The principal division, however, is into the toy-makers
for the rich, and those for the poor. I shall deal in the present article with those who principally supply the children of the working
classes with toys. These are not sold in the arcades and bazaars, but
are chiefly vended in the street markets, from barrows and stalls. One
toy stall keeper, I am told, clears 30s. a week by the sale of the cheap
penny toys. Occasionally they are sold in the chandlers' and sweet-
meat shops in the suburbs and the country, but the principal marts
are the fairs and street markets. The toys sold by these people consist
of either white or green wood—the latter being called Bristol toys. I
shall give a specimen of each; and first of the *White Wood Toy-maker.*
He lived at a cottage at the back of the Bethnal-green-road. In front
was a little square patch of ground railed in. This was laid out in
small flower beds, garnished with borders of white shells. Where the
flowers should have been, however, lay the bodies of defunct swings.
Under a rude shed stood a new velocipede—one worked with treadles

and hand levers, and brilliant with brass and bright colours. Beside this, reared high on end, was the body of a large unfinished locomotive, intended to carry as many as six, and to be moved in the same manner as the velocipede; but the works had yet to be affixed to it, so that in its present state it looked more like the seat of a huge swing than the body of a carriage. On one side of this was a small cart, originally made to carry the toy-maker himself (for he was a cripple), but now filled with gravel, intended for the pathway of the garden. Against the little cottage were small beams of timber, ready for use in the manufacture of penny carts or money-boxes, and on the ground lay the poles of an abandoned exhibition. These, with a sprinkling of old flower-pots, and a heap of paving-stones that had been dug up to convert the front yard into a garden, constituted the whole of the external appurtenances of the toymaker's house, and they were highly indicative not only of the ingenuity and enterprise of the occupant, but of the affliction that had deprived him of the power of using his limbs like the rest of mankind. The objects inside the house were equally suggestive of the character and occupation of the inmate. On a table in the centre of the room stood a yellow pie-dish filled with a thousand springs for penny mousetraps, and behind the door was a coil of wire that twanged as it closed after me. In the little square room adjoining the parlour, and which served the poor man for both bed-room and workshop, sat the toy-maker himself, making penny mouse-traps in the bed that he seldom or never quitted. On the counterpane in front was placed a small stool, and this served for his bench. He was half dressed, having only his coat and waistcoat over his night-gown. Close within his reach hung three small square bird-cages—one on one side his bed, and two on the other— and in them frolicked his favourite goldfinches, that seemed to bear their lifelong confinement as cheerfully as their master. Beside the bed stood a bench littered with tools of all kinds, boxes of wire hasps, and small pieces of cut wood ready to form the sides and triggers of the mouse-traps on which he was busied. The walls of the little room were hung with peep-shows and toys, the hoop of an old tambourine, tiny models of ships, and wooden swords that he had made for his boy in his over-time. Over the head of the toy-maker, on the top of the bedstead, were a heap of patterns in paper and wood of the various articles he made, and part of the works of a new locomotive carriage to be worked by hand, which he purposed getting up for himself when he could find leisure. The works, he told me in the course of conversation, a man whom he had taught when a youth had promised to make for his cripple master for nothing. On the stool that stood on the bed was piled a small stack of the same oblong pieces of thin deal as those on the carpenter's bench beside him, and these he was busy in cutting by means of a gauge from larger pieces of the same material. His story was another of the many evidences of the sterling worth and independence of the working classes of this country. I have often, in the course of my investigations, had to record the virtue, the honest pride, and the innate nobility of the artisans of London. I have told of the heroism of the young stockmaker who sat for three weeks without rest, labouring to keep her father from the workhouse. I have registered the deep patience and pervading faith of the dying husband of the poor tape-seller. I have described the contentment of the half-starved chickweed and groundsel dealer. I have spoken of the benevolence of the man who made soldiers' trowsers at 4d. per pair; and, more recently, of the starving painter, who shared his bare room with the homeless shoebinder. Indeed, in no class have I seen such patience in sufferings, such generosity in poverty, such heroism, such charity, as I have found in the working classes of this country. Their virtues, I repeat, are the outpourings of their simple natures— their vices mainly arise from the uncertainty of their work, and their occasional want of employment, followed by the long labour when their trade again becomes brisk to make up for loss of time. But of all the many bright examples that I have given of the virtues of the English workpeople, none has excelled the one I have now to record. The man shall tell his story himself:—

"I am a *white-wood toy-maker in a small way*—that is, I make a variety of cheap articles—nothing beyond a penny—in sawed and planed pine wood. I manufacture penny and halfpenny money-boxes, penny and halfpenny toy bellows, penny carts, penny garden-rollers, penny and halfpenny dolls' tables, penny washhand-stands, chiefly for baby houses; penny dressers, with drawers, for the same purpose; penny wheelbarrows, penny bedsteads, penny crossbows, and the penny mousetraps, that I am about now. I make all the things I have named for warehouses—for what are called the cheap 'Birmingham, Sheffield, and toy warehouses.' I am paid all the same price for whatever I make, with the exception of the mousetraps. For the principal part of the penny articles that I make I get 7s. for twelve dozen—and for the halfpenny articles, 3s. 6d. for the same quantity. For the penny mousetraps, however, I am paid only £1 for thirty-six dozen, whereas I get one guinea for an equal number of the rest. For the penny money-boxes, though, I have only 6s. for twelve dozen. You will please to look at that, sir" (he said, handing me his account-book with one of his employers for the last year); "you will see there that what I am saying is perfectly correct, for there's the price put to every article, and it is but right that you should have proof of what I'm a telling you. I took of one master, for penny mousetraps alone, you perceive, £36 10s. from January to December, 1849. But that is not all earnings, you'll understand. Out of that, I have to pay above one-half for material. I think altogether my receipts of the different masters I worked for last year came to about £120. I can't lay my hands on the bills just now. Yes, it's about £120, I know, for our income is about £1 to £1 2s. every week, and calculating rather more than one-half what I take to go for the expense of material, that will bring it just about to what I state. To earn the 22s. a week, you'll understand, there are four of us engaged—myself, my wife, my daughter, and my son. My daughter is 18, and my son is 11. That is my boy, sir; he's reading the *Family Friend* just now; it's a little work I take in for my girl for her future benefit; there's many useful receipts in it concerning cooking and household medicines, and good moral instruction in it besides. My girl is as fond of reading as I am, and always was. I should take in a number of periodicals myself, only I can't afford to spend a penny on myself in that way; but I think it's my duty to take in some good work or other for my girl. My boy goes to school every evening and twice on a Sunday. I am willing they should find as much pleasure from reading as I have. In my illness I found books often lull my pain—yes! I have, indeed, for many hours and days. For nine months I couldn't handle a tool, and my only comfort was the love of my family and my books. I can't afford them. I have no wish to incur any extraneous expense, while the weight of the labour here lies on my family more than it does on myself. Over and over again, when I have been in acute pain with my thigh, a scientific book, or a work on history, or a volume of travels would carry my thoughts far away, and I should be happy in all my misery; I shouldn't know that I had a trouble, a care, or a pang to vex me. I always had a love of solid works. For an hour's light reading I have often turned to works of imagination, such as Milton's 'Paradise Lost' and Shakespeare's Plays; but I prefer science to poetry. I think every working man ought to be acquainted with the general sciences. If he is a mechanic, let his station be ever so simple, he will be sure to find the benefit of it. It gives a man a greater insight into the world and creation, and it makes his labour a pleasure and a pride to him, when he can work with his head as well as his hands. I think I made about 106 gross of penny mouse-traps for the master whose account I have given you, and as many more for other employers in the course of last year. I calculate that I made more than thirty thousand mousetraps altogether, from January to December, '49. There are three or four other people in London making penny mousetraps besides myself. I reckon they may make among them near upon half as many as I do, and that would give about 45,000 or 50,000 penny mousetraps made in London in the course of the year. I myself brought out the penny mousetrap in its improved shape, and with the improved lever spring. I have made no calculation as to the number of mice in the country, or how soon we shall have caught them all if we go on at this rate; but I think my traps have little to do with that. They are bought more for toys than for use, though they are good for mice as well as children, let me tell you. The railway people say I send more traps down to Yarmouth than there are mice in the place; but you see farmers now set them round their fields and gardens when they sow their seed crops, to catch the field mice. Though we have so many dozen mousetraps about the house, I can assure you we are more troubled with mice here than most people. The four of us can make twenty-four dozen of the traps in a day, but that is a very close day's work; about eighteen dozen we can get through comfortably. For eighteen dozen we get about 10s. at the warehouse, and out of that I reckon our clear gains are near upon 4s., or a little less than a shilling a head. Take one with the other, we can earn about a penny an hour; and if it wasn't for my having been a tailor originally, and applying some of my old tools to the business, we shouldn't get on so quick as we do. With my shears I can cut 24 wires at a time, and with my thimble I thread the wires through the holes in the sides. I make the springs, cut the wires, and put them in the traps. My daughter planes the wood, gauges out the sides and bottom, bores the wire holes, and makes the doors as well. My wife nails the frames ready for wiring, and my son pulls the wires into the places after I have entered them. Then the wife springs them, after which the daughter puts in the doors, and so completes them. I can't form an idea as to how many penny and halfpenny money-boxes I made last year. I might have made altogether eight thousand—about five thousand halfpenny and three thousand penny ones. I'm satisfied there are a

great many more money-boxes made than I make. You see I make
the most mouse traps of any one in London, but perhaps the least
number of money-boxes. I should say that there were from 25 to 30
thousand penny and halfpenny white wood money-boxes made every
year in this town. How many papered and tin penny money-boxes
are made besides the white wood ones I can't exactly say, but they
must be a great many more than the white wood—the papered ones
particularly. The tinman, you see, won't make the tin ones if he can
help it, the material is so expensive. I should say there must be at least
100,000 of the different sorts of cheap money-boxes manufactured
in London in the course of the year. I'm very apt to think that the
money-boxes don't save much more than they cost. May be, taking
one box with the other, each of the cheap money boxes is the cause
of one penny being saved by the children of the poor, and 100,000
pence is nearly £450—so that we money-box-makers may say that
we are the means of saving some hundreds of pounds to the poor
people every year, for all the articles that we manufacture are sold to
their children only. Of penny garden rollers and carts, I don't think
I make more than 1,000 of each. I calculate that there may be about
10,000 of each produced in the metropolis. Such articles are made
entirely in London, I believe. If anything, there would be rather
more penny carts made than garden rollers, because the idea of a
carriage is more pleasing to a child. Let the little thing go where it
will in town, it will see a real cart, but very few children in London
ever saw a real garden-roller, and of those to whom our goods are
sold very few ever saw a garden either I take it—pent up in the close
courts they are, poor things! I am sure, of all the toys sold, dolls and
carts and horses are the greatest number—the dolls are for the girls,
and the carts and horses for the boys. The first toy is a doll for a girl,
and a halfpenny horse and a farthing whip for a boy—mind, I am
speaking of the children of poor people, who buy at the stalls in the
street. The penny and halfpenny bellows now have no run. Six or
seven years ago there was a great rage for them. Then I made about
12,000 in one year; but you see they were dangerous, and induced the
children to play with the fire, so they soon went out of fashion. I was
originally brought up to the tailoring business, but my master failed,
and my sight kept growing weaker every year; so, as I found a good
deal of trouble in getting employment at my own trade, I thought I
would take to bird-cage making. I had been doing a little at it before,
as a pastime. I was fond of birds, and fonder still of mechanics, so

I was always practising my hands at some craft or other. In my over-time at the tailoring trade I used to make dissected maps and puzzles—and so, when standing for employment, I used to manage to get through the slack of the year, or while waiting for orders from my master. I think it is solely due to my taste for mechanics, and my love of reading scientific books, that I am able to live as comfortably as I do in my affliction. After I took to bird-cage making I found the employment at it so casual that I could not support my family at it. My children were quite young then, for I have been ten years away from my regular trade at least. This led me to turn my mind to toy-making, for I found cheap toys were articles of more general sale. Then I got my children and my wife to help me, and we managed to get along somehow, for you see they were learning the business, and I myself wasn't much in a position to teach them, being almost as inexperienced at the trade as they were—and besides that we were continually changing the description of toy that we manufactured, so we had no time to perfect ourselves. One day we were all at work at garden rollers—the next, perhaps, we should be upon little carts—then, may be, we should have to go to dolls, tables, or wheelbarrows—so that, with the continual changing from one thing to another, we had a great difficulty in getting practised in anything. While we were all learning you may imagine that, not being so quick then as we are now, we found a great difficulty in making a living at the penny-toy business. Often we had merely dry bread for breakfast, tea, and supper; but we ate it with a light heart, for I knew repining wouldn't mend it, and I always taught myself and those about me to bear our trials with fortitude. At last I got to work regularly at the mouse-traps, and having less changing we learnt to turn them out of hand quicker, and to make more money at the business. That was about four years ago, and then I was laid up with a strumous abscess in the thigh; this caused necrosis, or decay of the thigh bone, to take place; and it was necessary that I should be confined to my bed until such time as a new thigh bone was formed, and the old decayed one had sloughed away. Before I lay up I stood to the bench until I was ready to drop, for I had no one who could plane the boards for me, and what could I do? If I didn't keep up I thought we must all starve. The pain was dreadful, and the anxiety of mind I suffered for my wife and children made it a thousand times worse. I couldn't bear the idea of going to the workhouse, and I kept on my feet till I could stand no longer. My daughter was only fifteen then, and I saw no means of escape. It was my office to prepare the boards for my family, and without that they could do nothing. Well, sir, I saw nothing but ruin and starvation before us. I took to my bed, knowing that it would take four years before a new bone could be formed and I capable of getting about again. What was to become of us all in the meantime I could not tell. Then it was that my daughter, seeing the pain I suffered both in body and mind, came to me and told me not to grieve, for that she would do all the heavy work for me, and plane up the boards and cut out the work as I had done. But I thought it impossible for her to get through such hard work, even for my sake. I knew she could do almost anything that she set her mind to, but I little dreamt that she would be able to compass that. However, with the instinct of her affection—I can't call it anything else, for *she* learnt at once what it had taken me *months* to acquire—she planed and shaped the boards as well as I myself could have done it after years of practice. The first board she did was as cleanly done as she can do it now; and when you think of the difficulties she had to overcome—what a mere child she was—and had never handled a plane before—how she had the grain of the wood to find out—to learn the right handling of her tools, and a many little niceties of touch that workmen only can understand—it does seem to me as if some superior power had inspired her to aid me. I had often read of birds building nests of the most beautiful structure without ever having seen one built before, and my daughter's handiwork seemed to me exactly like that. It was a thing not acquired by practice, but done in an instant, without teaching or experience of any kind. She is the best creature I ever knew or heard tell of on earth—at least, she has been so to me all her life—aye! without a single exception. If it hadn't been for her devotion I must have gone to the workhouse, and perhaps never have been able to get away from it, and had my children brought up as paupers. Where she got the strength to do it, too, is as much a mystery to me as how she did it; for though she was then but a mere child, so to speak, she did the work of a grown man, and I can assure you the labour of working at the bench all day is heavy, even for the strongest workman, and my girl is not very strong now—indeed she was always delicate, from a baby. But she went through it, and would stand to the bench the whole of the day, and with such cheerful good humour that I cannot but see the hand of the Almighty in it all. I never knew her to complain of fatigue, or ever go to her work without a smile on her face. Her only anxiety was to get it done, and afford me every comfort in my calamity that she could. For three years and two months now have I been confined to my bed; and for two years and a half of that time I have never left it, even to breathe the fresh, open air. Almost all that period I was suffering intense and continued pain from the formation of abscesses in my thigh, previous to the sloughing away of the decayed bone. I have taken out of the sores in my limb at least 200 pieces, some as small as needles, and some so large as to be an inch and a half long, and to require to be pulled out with tweezers from the wound. Often when I was getting a bit better, and able to go about in the cart outside there with the gravel in it (I made that on this bedstead, so as to be able to move about on it—the two front wheels I made myself, and the two back were old ones that I repaired here—I made the whole of the body, and my daughter planed up the boards for me)—well, often when I could just get about in that, have I gone out with a large piece of decayed bone protruding through my thigh, in hopes that the jolting would force it through the wound. The pain before the bone came away was often intense, especially when it had to work its way through the thick of the muscle. Night after night have I laid awake here. I didn't wish of course to distress the minds of my family any more than I could help—it wouldn't have been fair, so I bore all with patience. Since I have been here I have got through a great deal of work in my little way. In bed, as I sit with my little bench, I do my share to eight dozen of these traps a day—and last August I made a thaumascope for a young man that I had known since he was a lad of twelve years of age. He got out of work and couldn't find anything to turn his hand to; so I advised him to get up an exhibition—anything, I said, was better than starving. He had a wife and two children, and I can't bear to see any one want—let alone the young ones; so, cripple as I was, I set to work here in my bed and made him a large set of magic circles (I painted all the figures myself in this place, though I had never handled a brush before), and that has kept him in bread up to this time. I did it to cause him to exert himself, but now he's got a situation and is doing middling to what he has been. There's one thing though, a little money with care will go farther than a great deal without it. I shall never be able to get about again as I used, for you see the knee is set stiff, sir, and the thigh-bone is arched at the hip, so that the one leg is three inches shorter than the other. The bone broke spontaneously like a bit of rotten wood while I was rubbing my hand down the thigh one day, and in growing together again it got arched. I am just able now to stir about with a crutch and stick. I can sometimes treat myself with a walk about the house and yard, but that's not often. Last Saturday night I *did* make a struggle to get out in the Bethnal-green-road, and there, as I was coming along, my stick tripped against a stone, and I fell and cut my hands and face. If I had not had my crutch, I might have fallen on my new bone and broken it again; but, as it was, the crutch threw me forward and saved me. My doctor tells me the new bone would bear a blow, but I shouldn't like to try it after all I have gone through. I shan't be about again till I get my carriage, and that I intend to construct so as to be driven with one hand, by means of a new ratchet lever motion."

He here showed me the model, in wood, of the apparatus he proposed using. It was exceedingly ingenious, and was so arranged that either with a backward or forward motion of the lever the ratchet, by means of deacons and escapement, was always in power, and the axle made to rotate forwards.

The daughter of the toymaker then said that she "couldn't describe how it was that she had learnt to plane and gauge the boards. It seemed to come to her natural like," she said. She thought it must have been her affection for her poor father that made her take to it so quick. "I felt it deeply," she added, "to see him take to his bed, and knew that I alone could save him from the workhouse. I never feel tired over it, because I know that it is to make him comfortable." It is but right I should add, that I was first taken to this man by the surgeon who attended him during his long suffering, and that gentleman not only fully corroborated all the man told me, but spoke in the highest possible terms of both father and daughter.

A worker in green wood is termed a "Bristol toymaker." The quality and nature of the *Bristol toys* are detailed in the following narrative given to me by one of the makers of those articles. In the room where I conversed with him two boys were at work, making the wheels of scratch-backs—toys used by frolicsome people at fairs, the fun consisting in suddenly "scratching" any one's back with the toy, which gives a sudden, whirring sound. One boy was an apprentice, a well-grown lad; the other was a little fellow, who had run away from a City institution at Norwood, to whom the toymaker gave employment, having known his mother. It was curious enough, and somewhat melancholy, to observe the boy working at that which constitute other boys' play. Toys were piled all over the workshop. It was not very easy for a stranger to stir without the risk of upsetting a long line of omnibuses, or wrecking a perfect fleet of steam-boats. My informant, while giving his statement, was interrupted now and then by the delivery of orders, given, of course, in the usual way and tone of business, but sounding very grandiloquent—"A dozen large steamers," "Two dozen waggons;" and then a customer had room left in his sack for "half-a-dozen omnibuses with two horses." My informant said:—

"The Bristol toys are the common toys made for the children of the poor, and generally retailed at a penny. They were first made in Bristol, but they have been manufactured in London for the last 50 years. I believe there is still one maker in Bristol. Bristol toys are carts, horses, omnibuses, chaises, steamers, and such like—nearly all wheel-toys. We make scratch-backs too—that has a wheel in it. To make the toys we boil the wood—green and soft, though sometimes dry; alder, willow, birch, poplar, or ash are used. When the wood has been boiled, the toy is cut with a knife, and fixed together with glue, then painted. Trade is very bad at present, for when the labouring people are out of employ I feel it in my business. They cannot then buy toys for the children; unless they have decent earnings, children must go without—poor things! As all my goods go to the poor, and are a sort of luxury to the children, I can tell what's up with working and poor people by the state of my trade—a curious test, isn't it? but a sure one. When weaving is bad, Bristol toy-making is very bad. [He lived in the neighbourhood of Spitalfields.] When things are not so bad in Ireland, it's a rare time for my trade; they are so fond of them there. No cheap toys, at least in my way, are made in Ireland. When the big horses, the spotted fellows on wheels, that you must have seen, went out of fashion, it was a blow to my business. Steamers which have come up rather lately—though they have grand names painted on them, you perceive, Fire Flies and Dash Alongs, and such like—don't go off as the old horses did. Every child has seen a horse, but there's numbers never see a steamboat, and so care nothing about them; how can they? The men employed at journey work in the Bristol toy trade can earn 3s. and 3s. 6d. a day. But when work is slack, they just earn what happens to turn in in the way of work."

Of a description of toys differing little from those known as Bristol toys, I had the following account from a toymaker, who had been acquainted with the business many years. In addition to what he manufactured, he supplied his customers with a variety of low-priced toys, and the way in which these were distributed in the two spacious rooms of his ground-floor was striking, from its heterogeneous admixture. There was a great heap on a large table or counter; guns were over-ridden by brewers' drays, and drums rested with Noah's arks. Cats over-strode soldiers, and lambs [they were "called lambs," my informant explained] strayed amongst green forests, with trees of uniform height. In the course of conversation with this toymaker, he expressed an opinion to me that fashion, or change, affected cheap toys less, speaking generally, than any other article. This may be accounted for by the necessity of supplying them at the lowest rate, and by the anxiety of a mother, who has a penny to spare, causing her to buy a toy for her child such as pleased her own childhood, regardless of its want of novelty. My informant said:—

"I make the *common toys*, such as are *sold to the poor*—carts and horses chiefly. I am a white-wood toy maker, and work only on toys. My toys are made out of the deal as it comes from the timber yard—not boiled, as the Bristol toy makers do. The carts are shaped, and then the parts are fitted together with glue; the horse is cut out with a knife. I always feel the benefit of poor people being in good earnings, for then there is a better demand for my toys. Trade is very slack now, but the weather is against us—for mine, being good-sized horses and carriages, are used for children in the open air; they're thought too big to drive about a room. Prices are cut down greatly in my trade. The introduction of French and foreign toys, at the reduced rate of duty, has affected me a wonderful sight. They can undersell us; we can't at all work with those countries. This lamb here can't be made in London for a penny, but it's brought from Germany and sold here retail at a penny. If people, even girls and boys, are paid anything abroad for making such toys, it must be next to nothing. How they who depend upon such work live at all, is a puzzle to me. This foreign accordion, here, costs me 5s. 6d. a dozen wholesale—why it couldn't be made in England for four times the price, though there's so much talk now about music. You hear the four keys are perfect; and all for 5½d. There has been no change in the fashion of the articles I make for many years—I wish there was, it might bring better employment. I employ only my own family; but journeymen, when in work—that's it, you see, sir, it's the want of work that's the evil—earn 3s. and 3s. 6d. a day."

Toy-turning is a branch of the art on which I may have more to say, as to its nicer applications, hereafter. As I have devoted this letter to what a toymaker very well designates "popular toys," I give at present the statement of a turner, whose general employment was on goods not of the highest price; in fact, his trade, as will be seen, was confined to "popular toys." The process observed is that of other turners, and requires, therefore, no especial detail. He said:—

"I am a toy-turner. The principal articles made by the toy-turners, in my way, are humming and other tops, and skipping ropes. The humming tops are generally made of willow or alder: a block is hollowed by a tool made for the purpose, and the top is fitted to the hollowed block. We paint them ourselves, but we can't lay a picture on them, as it won't lay on account of the roundness—so the landscape, or whatever it is, is all done by a camel's-hair pencil. The French have not directly affected my trade (they may indirectly), nor the Germans either. It's heavy work, sir, making humming tops, and foreigners like light work best, I can tell you. Business is middling now; when the manufacturing districts are very prosperous, I feel an impulse given to my trade. When bread is very dear, children must do without toys, and then there's a slack. There is no great demand for toys in country villages, as I know from my experience in the north of England. They know nothing about humming tops. Immense numbers of skipping ropes and humming tops are shipped off to America. They won't go to high-priced goods, the Yankees; the best tops and ropes are sold at home. The home trade is far the best, though it's the custom, in many cities of the United States, to make presents of toys at Christmas time. Toy-turning is all piece-work. There may be twenty men working at toy-turning in my branch; they can average 20s. a week. It is a nice art; a humming top is turned according to the judgment of the workman, who must carry the pattern in his eye. Another branch of my business is the turning of boxes—puff-powder, tooth-powder, salve, and pill-boxes. There is a change in the painting of humming-tops, which is all the change I remember. Landscapes are now painted on them; before that, they were merely striped or flowered, but, as I have said, the globular shape prevents you giving a picture at a view. Pretty well off, do you ask, sir? Middling—middling—but *well* off, if compared with the poor Spitalfields weavers here—a man's heart may bleed to think of it." I may add that my informant's wife, in a tone of kindly feeling, detailed to me some very distressing cases among the weavers. "Something must be done for them," she said, or "they'll die out."

The Morning Chronicle, Thursday, February 21, 1850.

We have to acknowledge the receipt of a Post-office order for 1*l.* 10s., for the Poor Modeller, from B. S., of H. We have also received 6s. from an Oxford M. A., for the same party.

Mr. H., of Upper Thames-street, has forwarded us 1*l.* for the Lady and her Daughters.

The Morning Chronicle, Saturday, February 23, 1850.

To THE EDITOR OF THE MORNING CHRONICLE.

SIR—I have read with deep interest, from time to time, the statements in your paper of the sufferings of various bodies of the working classes; still more interesting are the accounts of the patience and sympathy with each other exhibited by many of them. Plans for relieving this mass of evil appear to me somewhat delusive, and often impracticable; but I have hopes some well-devised measures for gradually though slowly preventing these evils arising, by lessening their causes, may be suggested.

This must in any case be a work of time and patience. Though any aid given by donation is but as a drop of water, I cannot refuse myself the pleasure of placing in your hands a trifle, part of it for the poor toymaker and his kind daughter mentioned in your paper of to-day. The rest to aid any other kind-hearted sufferer your Commissioner may think most deserving of it. Thanking you for your efforts in this good cause—

I remain, your obedient servant,

R. A. S.

University Club, Pall-mall East, Feb. 21.
[A cheque for 10*l.* was enclosed in the above.]

M. J. requests the Editor of *The Morning Chronicle* to add the enclosed sum of 3*l.* 10s. to the funds for the emigration of the distressed needlewomen.—Framlingham, Feb. 21.

C. L. L. begs to enclose 1*l.*, which she will feel obliged by the Editor forwarding to the distressed modeller, whose case is mentioned in *The Morning Chronicle* of the 15th.—Feb. 20.

We have to acknowledge the receipt of a sovereign from P. C., to be applied for the benefit of the unfortunate Needlewomen who are disqualified from benefiting by the proposed emigration plan.

G. P. encloses 1*l.* for the poor shoebinder whose case lately appeared in this paper.

W. J. has forwarded us a half-sovereign for the white-wood toy-maker, with a diseased thigh.

The Editor of *The Morning Chronicle* is requested to be kind enough to convey the enclosed 10s. to the "White-wood Toy-maker;" or if inconvenient, to devote it as he pleases.

CANTABRIGIENSIS.

University Club, Feb. 21, 1850.

M. A. W. presents her compliments to the Editor of *The Morning Chronicle*, and requests he will give the enclosed 1*l.* to the poor widow (shoebinder) mentioned in the letter dated February 14, on "Labour and the Poor."

Thursday, Feb. 21.

LABOUR AND THE POOR.

—◆—

THE METROPOLITAN DISTRICTS.

[FROM OUR SPECIAL CORRESPONDENT.]

LETTER XXXVIII.

I continue my inquiries among the Toy-makers. In my last Letter I dealt chiefly with the makers of playthings for the children of the poor. In the present one I purpose dealing with those who manufacture the superior description of articles, such as are seen principally in the arcades and bazaars.

One among those whom I visited was a celebrated publisher of penny theatrical characters and maker of toy theatres. He is the person to whom the children of the present generation are indebted for the invention. I found him confined to his room with asthma. He sat in a huge armchair, embedded in blankets, with a white nightcap on his head. He evidently was very proud of having been the original inventor of the toy theatres, and he would insist upon presenting me with the earliest prints in connection with the mimic stage. He was a little spare man whose clothes hung loose about him.

"I am a maker of children's theatres, and a theatrical print publisher. I have been in the line ever since 1811. The first time I began to publish anything of the kind was when the pantomime of Mother Goose was performing. I was the first in the line. I think I had the business all to myself for two years. Mrs. J——, who lived in Duke's-court, Bow-street, took to it after that. She sold my prints at first, and then she began to print and publish for herself. Now, I think, there's about six in the line. I was originally in the circulating library and haberdashery line. My mother was in the haberdashery way, and I continued it. We had a glass case of toys as well, and among the toys we sold children's halfpenny lottery prints—common things that were done in those days, sir. Well, you see, my parents used to be at Covent-garden Theatre, and I took it in my head to have a print done of *Mother Goose*. I can show you the old original print by me. You shall see, sir, the first theatrical print ever published. [He here produced a bundle of impressions.] He's the third cheap the-atrical print ever published. It's numbered up here, you see—but I brought 'em out so fast after that I left off numbering them very soon. I brought out one a day for three years. The print consisted of eight characters in as many separate compartments. The first was the elder Grimaldi as Clown, the second Bologna as Harlequin, the third was the Columbine of that day. Oh dear," said the publisher, "what was her name?—she was a werry excellent Columbine at Covent-garden Theatre." The other compartments were filled with other characters in the piece. "You'll see, sir," continued the old man, "there's a line of foolish poetry under each of the characters. I made it myself to please the children. It runs:—

> 'The Clown, Joe Grim,
> John Bologna, the Harlequin;
> Gay and merry Columbine,
> With her lover, Spaniard fine;
> Demon of Interest, fiend of gold,
> Don Alvaro very old;
> A poor Chinese man,
> And Mr. Raymond, as Magician.'

The first theatrical print published was not very different from the third in the character of its art or poetical descriptions. There was, however, a spirit and freedom of touch about the execution that was far superior to what might have been expected.

The lines under the eight distinct characters were as follows:—

> 'The golden egg and Mother Goose—
> Prime, bang-up, and no abuse.
> Here's Harlequin as feather light,
> And Zany's antics to please you with delight;
> Here's Mr. Punch you plainly see,
> And Joan, his wife, both full of glee.
> In woman's habits does Harlequin
> Deceive the clown, by name Joe Grim.'

"I brought out this print, you'll understand, to please the children. The lottery things was so bad, and sold so well, that the idea struck me that something theatrical would sell. And so it did—went like wild-fire among the young folks. Shopkeepers came to me far and near for 'em. Bad as the drawing of these here is, I can assure you it was a great adwance on the children's halfpenny lotteries. These two figures here in the corner, you see, a'n't so bad, but they're nothing to what we do now. This plate was done by a 'prentice of the name of Green, who worked at Mr. Simkins', an engraver in Denmark-court. He used to do them in his overtime. He was obliged to have something to look at to copy. He was no draughtsman himself, you know. This here pictur of Mother Goose he took from a large print of Mr. Simmonds in that there character published by Ackerman, and sold in Covent-garden at 2s. 6d. plain, and 5s. coloured; the others was all copied from large prints of the day. I dare say I sold right off as many as 5,000. It was printed many times over, and every edition I know was a thousand. We don't do so many now. It was sold at a penny plain, and twopence coloured. You had better take that there impression with you. It's a curiosity, and a bit of the history of one's country—yes, that it is, sir. Why it's 39 years ago. I think I must have been about 24 when it was published—I'm 63 in June. The success of the theatrical prints was so great, I was obliged to get three presses to print them fast enough. I brought out a new one every day, as I told you before. We only did the characters in the pantomime at Christmas time. The small ones wasn't likenesses—they was merely characters to give the costumes. We didn't make likenesses till very late. The wardrobe people at the minor theatres and masquerade people used to buy a great many to make their dresses from. Young Green only did me two plates. He was such a bad draughtsman he couldn't do anything without a copy, and I was forced to get permission of the better printsellers for all he did. I gave Green 30s. or £2 for each plate he did for me. He was very dear, 'cause he was so slow over the engravings. Well, I think I had done about seven prints—they were bad-uns—only cop-ies, and badly done too—all by apprentices, when Mr. Hashley, of the Hamphitheayter, sent young —— with a drawing to show me. It was uncommon well done; oh, such a beautiful picture! he got on to be one of the first-rate artists arterwards, and drawed half-crown ca-ricatures; he did all the battle-pieces of them times—all Bonaparte's battles and Nelson's shipping. Well I gave him an order directly for the whole of the characters in the *Blood Red Knight*, wot Hashley was performing at that time. I can show you the print on it—you must see it, for it was a great adwance in my purfession, sir. I should like you to look at it, sir, cause I considers it as a matter of history like." He here brought out another brown parcel of prints. "Look here, sir," he said, as he turned over the impressions—"here's one of the stage fronts we do now—it's only part of it, you'll understand. It's done by a real architectural designer—but *he's* dead too: I suppose I shall go next. —— did this here stage-front of Drury-lane as it was after the fire; and he did Covent-garden for me as well, but he wasn't good at architect. This here, sir, was the first stage front we begun to make. It's the large impression; we had a small one out as well. The date, you see, is 1812—and it wasn't quite a year after I published my first print. I got liberty from the master carpenter to go and make the drawing of the front as soon as ever it was up after the fire. This here print," he continued as he turned over the different copies before him, "was done for me by a Royal Academician of the name of Mr. ——; it's Ducrow in the scene of 'the Ingun and the Vild Oss.' You see, sir, Mr. Ducrow paid for it being done by my man, and guv it away on his benefit night, and I had the plate of him afterwards. This is a late production, so you can see the improvement. There's the first plate —— did for me. It's the principal characters in *The Lady of the Lake*, as produced at the Surrey, and a great advance you see it is on the others. After that he did the *Blood-red Knight*. Here's one of his first prints of osses. It's *Baghvanho*, as performed at Hashley's. Here's the first battle he ever drew. He did it unbeknown to me on a copper of mine, thinking I would like it; but it was quite out of my line. It was that there as got him all J——'s battles to do. He showed it to him, and J—— guv him an order directly. After that he had ten pound a week from J——, and ten pounds a week from me too. He had 30s. a plate, and never did less than six in the week; and for the larger ones he had more. I found the copper. Why, I used to pay my copper-smith £70 and £80 a year for plates only. ——, the artist and scene painter, did a great many for me, and he was the only one as turned out grateful to me. All the others got such great men they wouldn't look on me. At first, you see, we didn't do any but the principal char-acters in a piece, 'cause we didn't think of making theayters then, and went on as we begun for two years. After that we was asked by the customers for theayters to put the characters in, so I got up the print of a stage front, thinking that the customers would get the woodwork done themselves. But after the stage front they wanted the theaytres themselves of me more than ever, so I got some made, and then the demand got so great that I was obliged to keep three carpenters to make 'em for me. One was a horgan builder and could make any-thing in machinery. I turned out the first toy theayter for children as ever was got up for sale, and that was in the year 1813. You see my father was the under property-man at Covent Garden Theatre, and I had a sister a dancer there, and another sister belonging to the fruit-office in the boxes—so we was all theatrical; and when I was about seven year old, I got my father's 'prentice in the shop to make me a wooden theayter—he was uncommon clever at carpenter work, and the painters and carpenters of Covent Garden used to come and see it when we exhibited in our one-pair back three times a week. We used to charge 2d. a piece. It was thought a great thing in those days; and so many people used to come to see it, that father and mother wouldn't allow it after a time; so it was put up as a raffle, and it was won by a young man, who took it with him to Scotland. It was that as gave me the hidea of making toy theayters for sale. After I made a few I was hobligated to make scenery, and to do the sets of charac-ters complete. Nobody but me made toy theaytres for a long while; nor did they do the scenery. One man used to do me three dozen theayters a week; and another man did me a dozen more of the small. The larger theayters took longer time, and I don't think I made more than a dozen of them in a year. I used to make, I think, about fifty toy theayters a week. I always had a room full of them up stairs, ex-cept at Christmas, when we couldn't turn them out fast enough. I think I must have sold about 2,500 every year of 'em. Some theayters I made came to as much as £20 a piece. I have made about four of them, I think, in my life time. They was fitted up with very handsome fronts—generally 'liptic harch fronts, built all out of wood, with or-naments all over it—and they had machinery to move the side wings on and off; lamps in front, to rise and fall with machinery, and side lamps to turn on and off to darken the stage, and trick sliders to work the characters on and change the pantomime tricks; then there was machinery to make the borders rise and fall as well, and cut traps to open for the scenery to go up and down through the stage. 'The Miller and his Men' has sold better than any other play I ever published. I wore out a whole set of copper plates of that there. I must have sold at least five thousand of that play, all complete. It's the last scene, with the grand explosion of the mill, as pleases the young 'uns, un-common. Some on 'em greases the last scene with butter—that gives a werry good effect with a light behind; but warnish is best, I can't abear butter. Some of them explosions we has made in wood work, and so arranged that the mill can fly to pieces; they comes to about 4s. 6d. a piece. The next most taking play out of my shop has been 'Blue

Beard.' That the boys like for the purcession over the mountains—
a coming to take *Fatima* away—and then there's the blue chamber
with the skelingtons in it—that's werry good too—and has an uncommon pretty effect with a little blue fire, though it in general sets
all the haudience a sneezing. The next best arter that was the 'Forty
Thieves'—they likes that there, for the fairy grotto and the scenery is
werry pretty throughout. Then again, the story pleases the children
uncommon—it's a werry good one I call it. I'll give you the date of
the first likeness as ever I did; I've got it here handy, and I should like
you to see it, and have it all correct, 'cause you see, as I said before,
it's a matter of history, like. Here's all my large portraits—there's 111
of them. This here's one of ——. It's Liston, as *Moll Flaggon*, you see.
That there one is done by Mr. ——, the royal academician. It's Mr. H.
Johnston as *Glaffier*. I think the part was in a tragedy called the 'Hil-
lusion.' That was the werry first portrait as I published. Here's one by
——, done about the same time. That's Mrs. Egerton, as Hellen Mac-
gregor. The portraits I have just been showing you are 2d. plain, and
4d. coloured—but they don't sell now, the penny has quite knocked
them up. Then there's other people wot makes as low as a halfpenny,
but they a'n't like the performance at all. You see the cheap shops
makes up the dresses with silk, and tinsel, and foil, but I never did.
My customers used to do some; but, to my mind, it spoilt the figures,
and took away all the good drawing from 'em. Formerly they used
to cut out the parts of the figures, and stick pieces of silk, and tinsel,
and lace behind them. Then the boys used to make all their own dots
and ornaments themselves; and I used to sell punches expressly for
doing 'em, and arter that I sold the ornaments themselves. Now the
ornaments are sold in large quantities by these halfpenny printsellers.
They are punched out by children I think—they make them as low as
a halfpenny a packet. I haven't published a new set of characters for
this seven year. You see they began to make halfpenny plates—they
used to copy my penny ones and sell 'em at half-price, so I thought
it high time to give over. I had come down in my large portraits
from 2d. to 1d., and I wasn't going to reduce to halfpenny—not I.
It seemed like lowering the purfession to me—besides, the theaytres
themselves couldn't make a do of it, so I gave over publishing. The
decline of the drama is hawful, and it's just the same with the toy
theaytres as it is with the real ones." [He then showed me his books.
They were all indexed alphabetically.] First came the small characters
under A—"Aladdin;" then came those in B—"Blue Beard," "Battle of

Waterloo" (of this nearly 10,000 had been printed), and "Bottle Imp;" under C were "Comus" and "Coriolanus;" under F was the "Forty Thieves;" under H "the High-mettled Racer," "Hamlet," and "Harlequin Brilliant;" under I came "Ivanhoe;" under M the "Miller and his Men," "Maid and the Magpie," "Montrose," and "Midsummer Night's Dream;" under O was the "Old Oak Chest" and "Olympic Revels;" under R, "Robinson Crusoe" and "Rob Roy;" and under T, "Timour the Tartar." Then came the index of the scenes in the same plays, arranged in a similar manner, with the number of impressions attached.

I remarked that he had printed a great many portraits of Mr. Bradley? He said that gentleman was such a great favourite with the children—he made himself up so murderous looking—and then he was such a fine swordsman with T. P. Cooke, you'd think they were going to kill one another. It was quite beautiful to see 'em—people used to go on purpose. He told me he had printed more portraits of Huntley, Bradley, and Blanchard, than of any other members of the theatrical profession—with the exception of Kean in Richard. He hadn't done anything particular with the others. He had made upwards of 1,000 pantomime tricks. He was fond of doing them for the children. Now he has scarcely any call at all for them. This Christmas had been a little better—he didn't know why. He showed me also an account of the expense of making a toy theatre that he had made to be sent out to Australia. It was for the children of the Chief Judge there. He had made two for the same party. The second was the best, and came to £16 12s. 6½d. He told me that his receipts used to be in his best time as much as £30 a week for theatres and penny and twopenny plates of characters only. Now he only takes about 3s. 6d. or 4s. 6d. a day, or from £1 to £1 5s. a week.

I now give the statement of a man employed in the making of rocking-horses for the toy-shops. The place where he worked presented a curious appearance; it was in an off street from a great thoroughfare. At the door lay the *torso* of a rocking-horse, discoloured from age, earless and legless, and battered apparently from hard usage. Near it, in startling contrast, was a newly-made horse of dazzling whiteness, placed out to dry. The interior of the workshop was crowded with timber, but on every side the staple of the place was horses, and these in all stages. Horses' trunks, heads, legs, tails, and manes, of all hues and sizes, huddled on the floor, piled on the shelves, or swinging from the ceiling; horses in the rough, and horses awaiting the last polish—for the rocking-horse makers make also all the smaller quadrupeds demanded in the trade. The latter, after the block has been prepared, are shaped with a sharp knife, like an ordinary pocket-knife, used very quickly. The workman at one cut makes precisely the incision or curvature he requires. The body is of pine, and the head and legs (generally) of beech. My informant remembered no change in the fashion of rocking-horses. He thus described the manufacture:—

"The first process is to take a pine plank, and form it, by jointing and glueing it, into a block. It used to be made out of solid timber, old 'girters' (beams of houses pulled down), or ship masts. The jointing is the better process. The block prepared is reduced by the drawing-knife and the plane (a chopper is used only when solid timber is worked), to the shape of the horse's body. It is then what we call bevilled and morticed, to make the holes into which the legs of the horse are placed. This manufacture, I assure you, requires considerable art, the eye being almost the only guide. We make the body by measurement—the formation and proportion of the several parts is made entirely by eye. The head is shaped out of solid wood (pine), after a pattern cut out of strong pasteboard or thin plank, but we have merely the outline supplied by the pattern; what may be called the anatomy, with the eyes, the nostrils, teeth, and the several parts of the face, are carved out, the skill of the workman being directed, as I have said, altogether by his eye. To make a good head is looked upon as one of the most skilled portions of the workmanship required in the trade. The legs are shaped without pattern, the skill of the workman having again no guide beyond his eye; and the 'tenant' is then cut in the leg—the 'tenant' being a portion of wood left on the top of the leg to be fitted into the mortice hole, made for that end in the body. Next, the head is affixed, being jointed, by a great nicety in adjustment, to the body of the rocking-horse, and then the toy in its rough state is complete. After that it is what we call 'worked off'—that is, each part has to be duly shaped, so that all may be in accordance, head, body, and legs—without that there would be no symmetry. The 'working off' is a four hours' process (taking the average sizes), and very hard work. The first layer of composition is then applied and left to dry, which takes from eight to ten hours. The rasp is then used all over the article, and then another layer of composition is applied, and then a third; this is done to get a smooth, level surface. The last application is rubbed down with glass paper. In these several processes there must be delays, at which the workman goes to other labours. No one can make a single rocking-horse, except at a loss; it's impossible, for half his time he would have to stand idle. The horse is then painted, and the legs are screwed and fitted to the 'rocker,' or frame, which is made before the horse is finished. It is then 'harnessed'—we do the saddler's work ourselves; after that the mane and tail are affixed, and then the rocking-horse is complete, unless glass eyes have to be put into the head, as is often the case. Some gentlemen are very particular about the shape and colour of their rocking-horses. They often say, 'That thing's more fit for the plough than for a parlour'—'It's a donkey and not a horse'—and such like. We divide the horses into two classes, 'gibbers' and 'racers;' a 'gibber' seems to be inclined to 'gib,' a racer is represented as at the very top of his speed. Gibbers have as much call as racers. The good journeyman averages say 18s. a week. At the present time, business is middling. The men are very seldom paid by the job, unless it be something for overtime; the wages are 3s. a day. I only know two women employed in making the harness in all London; they never meddle with the manufacture of the rocking-horse. I think there is not one apprentice to the trade at present. We have no union. I have not found the slightest difference in my trade in consequence of the reduction of duties on foreign toys by the tariff of '42. We make the 'roundabouts' for the fairs; once in five years there is a demand for them. I cannot tell how many rocking-horses may be yearly made in London. Perhaps it may be calculated this way: there are 30 men employed in making rocking-horses, and each man can make two a week. That gives 3,120 a year; but as we are employed in making horses of all kinds, as well as rocking-horses, you may reduce the number by one-half, yes I think 1,500 may be about the mark."

The statement I now publish is that of a man whose room presented an accumulation of materials—paper, paste, wires, gilding, wood, pasteboard, leather, and other things, mixed up with instruments for nice admeasurement. The *fancy toy maker's* appearance was that of a hearty, jovial man, and I was referred to him as being a workman alike humorous, trustworthy, and intelligent. He said:—

"I am a fancy toy maker. Fancy toys are mechanical and moving toys. To describe the whole would tire you. I invent them, all that I make, even to the casting line. I can go from the clay of the model to the perfect toy. I make the model. I model the toy myself. These are all my own models." [My informant showed me several. They were remarkable for their nice art and ingenuity.] "I was out on the world" (he continued) "young, and brought up to no business—and so, having confidence in my ingenuity, I took to the toy trade, and have carried it on for 35 years on my own account, working for the warehouses. My toys, though well known in the trade for their ingenuity, are not of great cost, but are chiefly within reach of the middle classes. They include animals of all descriptions—donkeys, horses, cows, cats, elephants, lions, tigers (I could make giraffes, but they're not in demand), dogs and pigs. Here is a toy of my own invention. This boy is flying a kite, and you see how, by the cranks and wires, the boy appears to advance and the kite takes the air. Here is a boat. These model men fix on here. By movements which I have contrived, they row the boat. I forget many of my inventions; the inventions in my calling are generally made in a slack time, when we have leisure to devote to the subject. It's slack now. Any man going into my trade must have great readiness as well as ingenuity—be quick as well as inventive. A man who hadn't those qualities would have as good a chance of succeeding in my trade, as a man who wrote badly and spelt worse would have in yours, sir. We are all working men, sir—you'll not be offended by my saying that. I started the figures on the donkeys, and the donkeys had a good run for a good while, and I hope they'll not leave off running for a good while longer, especially if they've good masters on their backs—I mean employers like Mr. G———. The boats with the men rowing in them had as good a run as the donkeys. The donkeys beat, though. There are very curious phrases in my trade. A boy who looked in at my workshop window, said, 'I'm blessed if I know what trade they are, but I heard them talk about cutting off three dozen donkeys' heads.' Donkeys' heads, you see, are made of papier-maché [I was shown a very good specimen], and the head is affixed so as to move—so are the ears, and the tail too, if demanded. I invented that donkey. The ass is made entire, and then the head is cut off to be refitted, with the faculty of moving. Here's an elephant—he moves his tail as well as his trunk. If I think of inventing a new toy, I often can't sleep from thinking of it. I assure you I have actually *dreamed* the completion of a new toy—of one that required great thought. I went to bed with the plan working in my brain, and that led to the dream. I talk about it in my sleep. I consider that I am not at all well paid for my labour. No toy-maker is *well* paid for his mere labour, let alone his ingenuity. I can't state my average earnings, there is such a casualty about the work; it is often a speculation. I have to pay for so many things for my experiments, and for colours and varnishes, that my earnings are really very low. Two pound a week, do you ask if I make? Not one, sir, though I'm the top of the trade. My trade is a sort of individual thing; a man finds he has a turn for it, and so he takes a turn at it. There are no women in the trade that I'm aware of, except a young woman known as 'the mechanic' for her remarkable taste and ingenuity. The introduction of French toys at a lower rate of duty (in 1842 I think it was) affected my trade. I had far fewer orders after that, and prices fell. I should say it has made fifty per cent. difference to me generally. Many of the inventions or patterns that I have originated have been copied in Germany. Sometimes I get a hint from them, in return for all they borrow, so to call it, from me. They rob me, and I take from them. The fashion in penny toys is very variable; but toys of twenty years back often come into fashion again. It's so with mechanical toys—chiefly such as I make—moving figures. Some things that I invented long ago have recently come into fashion again—the working blacksmiths and sawyers, for instance. They say that 'luck's all;' in my trade 'fancy's all.' "

A statement was given to me by a man whose workshop, as he explained, had one peculiar characteristic; *for copper toys of the better sort*—or perhaps, he added, of any sort—it was the workshop of the world. He bears an excellent character, and the appearance of his wife and children was highly creditable to an artisan of his limited means. He worked in a small room on a ground floor, devoted to the purposes of his trade. He said:—

"I have known the trade in copper and brass toys since I was a child. I am only 23, but when I was four or five years old, my father, who was in the trade, and indeed invented it, set me to work to clean the toys off, or punch holes, or do anything I could. We knew nothing but industry, and so were never driven to the streets; but my father might have made a fortune, with steadiness. At present I make chiefly copper tea-kettles, coffee-pots, coal-scuttles, warming-pans, and brass scales (toy scales); these are the most run on, but I make besides brass and copper hammers, saucepans, fish kettles, stewpans, and other things. I am now, you see, making copper tea-kettles and saucepans. There are sixteen pieces in one copper tea-kettle—first the handle, which has three pieces, seven pieces in the top and cover (lid), one piece for the side, two in the spout, one for the bottom, and two rivets to fix the handle, in all sixteen. That's the portion of the trade requiring the most art. Copper toys are the hardest work, I consider, of any toy-work. The copper is this dull sheet copper here, eight square feet in a sheet of it. I use generally a four-pound sheet, costing 13d. a pound. I make six dozen tea-kettles out of one sheet. The copper you see must be 'planished,' that is, polished by hammering it with a steel-faced hammer on a steel-faced 'head,' four inches square, to make it bright. I make, on the average for the year, eight dozen tea-kettles every week; that is, 4,992 a year. I make all that are made in London—yes, in the world. Here's the world's shop, sir, this little place, for copper toys. My father and I (when he worked at the trade) had it all to ourselves; now *I* have, for my father is on other work. He is now helping to fit up a ship for California, belonging to a gentleman who is going to send out his son to settle there as a bottled-porter merchant. An uncle of mine once *did* make a few. I make as many scuttles in a week as I do tea-kettles, for I'm always at it, and as many coffee-pots; altogether, that's 13,976 teas, scuttles, and coffees. Of the other sorts, I make, I know, as many as I do of teas, coffee-pots, and saucepans. They're all fit to boil water in, cook anything you like—every one of them. You can make broth in them. They are made on exactly the same principles as the large kettles, except that *they* are brazed together, and mine are soft-soldered. Altogether, then, I make 27,952 of copper toys in a year. I sell my copper toys—all sorts, take one thing with another—at 36s. a gross. All my toys are retailed at 6d. each. I think I can earn 20s. a week, if my wife and I work early and late, which we do when we've call, there's so much work in those things. Sometimes we earn only 10s. I calculate it as an average of 15s. the year through. That's but little to keep a wife and two children on—one only just born a month ago last Monday, and another is only just buried. It's little to earn for making all the copper toys, as far as I know, in the world. I think I could do well in New York, where my trade is not known at all. I have all the art of the trade to myself. It was very good once, but now it's come down very bad in this country, and I should like to try another. People here haven't got money for toys; besides, mine last too long; they ought to break quicker. What my father once had 20s. for, I now get 5s. When these toys first came up, an Irishman cleared £1,400 in five years by selling them in the streets. That's twenty years ago; and he's now thriving in America." "If my husband wasn't steady, good, and careful," said the wife who was present, "my children and I might see the inside of the 'large house.'" "Things get worse," resumed the husband. "Almost every time I go to the warehouses they say, you must work cheaper; but it's not possible if a man must live, and see his family living."

I visited a *pewter toy-maker*, a man who explained to me that he could account for the bareness of the room in which I saw him (and which was, he said, beyond the cobbler's stall in the song—for it served him for bed-room, and parlour, and workshop, and kitchen, and all) by too sad a cause. The illness and death of a child, lately buried, had compelled him to part with many of his things. It is not difficult to describe the contents of his room. A bed occupied a sort of recess, and the other contents (I avoid the word "furniture") of the garret were—pewter. There were trays of bright pewter tea-cups, ready for the final "working off;" trays of tea-pots, and of other articles of the "tea service," which he manufactured. Pewter was everywhere. He had the pale and subdued look which I have often seen in mechanics whose earnings are limited and uncertain. I may add, that he worked for the pewter toy-makers, whose "statistics" (as he called them) I give from him, and he took time and pains to state them with correctness.

"I am a pewter toy-maker," he said, "and make only toys, sets of tea services, such as these I show you, sir, which consist of twenty-three pieces—six cups, six saucers, six spoons, sugar tongs, milk-pot, tea-pot and lid, and sugar basin. I make only tea services, and can make three dozen sets in a day, that is 828 pieces—that's not a few, and that would require ten hours' good work. Each piece is cast in a mould, and I will show you how. Here I sit before the fire, with the melted pewter in this pan on the fire before me. I hold the mould in my hand, and dip my ladle into the melted pewter, and fill the mould with it. The mould, of course, is different for each piece. I often scald my fingers and hands—here is an old burn, and here another. I mix my own pewter—tin, and lead, and spelter. The spelter is to give it a colour. The commonest pewter would not answer my purpose. The mould is all brass, and, when filled with the metal, is at once dipped into water to cool; then the metal is turned out, and it has to be pared and trimmed ready for use afterwards. To make one set by itself would take me full two hours. You may cast a number before you even get the right heat. As it is, I cast one lot by itself—go on casting teapots, and then any of the other parts of the service. As fast as they are cast, I apply this knife as if opening an oyster, and open the mould, and out comes the article. Last year I made, one week with another, six dozen sets a week, or 3,744 in the year, that is 86,112 pieces, reckoning them singly and by the year. I think you'll find that right. The set is retailed at 4½d. and 6d., according to the prices of the shopkeeper. I get 3s. for a dozen sets—sometimes only 2s. 6d. Reckon that I make six dozen sets a week, and that's 18s.; but the material, including coal, costs me nearly 9s. out of that 18s.—so that I have but 9s. for myself. My trade is bad, and is generally bad for awhile after Christmas. I think it's improving. Easter and Whitsuntide are the grand times for us, on account of the fairs. There is another man in the trade who, with the help of eight men he has, can make three gross of tea or dinner services a day. He makes largely for shipping—to America and Ireland principally, where I've heard they're not up to toy-making. I suppose that, one week with another, the year through, he may turn out a gross and a half of tea and dinner services. He makes other things, but in the tea services that's 216 sets a week, or 11,016 sets a year, which is—mind, sir, we don't drop a few thousands—303,358 single pieces a year. There is another worker in pewter toys, or rather a family, who may make half as many as the person with the eight men, so that those two and myself turn out 551,149 pieces in a year— over half a million; as many farthings as it's over, would make me a happy man. I reckon there are twice as many (in pieces) made of the other pewter toys—such as gridirons, fire sets, kitchen sets, carts, horses, omnibuses, steam-engines, soldiers, sailors, drummers, milk-maids, cats and kittens, dogs with baskets in their mouths, shepherds and shepherdesses, and some more. So, if you'll calculate—and it's as near the mark as a man may come, and nearer than it often comes— for I know it all by practice—it comes to 1,102,298 pieces a year in my trade in London—quite within the mark, shepherdesses and all included. I haven't got full work, or anything like it, and can't get. I reckon my earnings last year—a clear 9s. a week—to have been less by 3s. than the other workmen in my way. My wife is a reel winder, and she earns as much, or nearly as much, as I do. There was an acquaintance of mine—a joking sort of man—said to me last week, 'Well, will you pewterers show anything at the Grand Exhibition of Industry, next year?' 'I don't know much what it's about,' I said, 'but mine's too small a way.' 'So,' says he, 'I hope something will be done for the honour of the toy trade.' 'Good earnings, I think, sir, would honour it best,' was my reply."

A basket toy-maker gave me the following information. His room was very poorly furnished, and was chiefly noticeable for its heterogeneous admixture of trades. The twigs used in basket-making lay on shoemakers' lasts; a bird-cage rested on a sieve; half-made toy-baskets were mixed with scraps of leather. All told of a dreary poverty: but the basket-maker's tone was cheery, and he told me he had felt the folly of repining uselessly.

"I was bred and born to basket-making," he said, "my father's and my uncle's trade. I've known the basket toy making for seventeen years. I follow it in the summer. There is little chance of selling basket-toys in the streets in bad weather. But in summer the children are walking out with their mothers, and the children are our best friends, for they tempt the mothers to buy of us. Besides, as to summer and winter, the country travellers (hawkers) don't go out in the winter. My goods are chiefly for fairs. I was very fortunate for a time. No one at all interfered with my trade in small baskets with pincushions in them. The pincushions are made of crimson velvet and sawdust; a few times I have used pink velvet, but that soon fades, so I stick to crimson. In the winter I take a turn at shoemaking, which I learned from an acquaintance. I myself am the only man in all the world who makes the penny pincushion-baskets. It's just a pincushion in a little basket, you see; but I started it. I sell it for a penny now with the cushion. Sixteen years ago I could sell more—ah! that I could, a great deal, and the same size—without the cushions, than I can now sell with them. But in that time a penny article of a nicer sort was a rarity, and so it went off. But now there's penny books, and penny papers, and penny numbers, and penny everythings, and nothing's so scarce that way as the pennies themselves. When I first made my baskets they was little things. Oh! here I've found a little basket, one of what I may call the first generation. But now this is the size. [The 'first generation,' as he called it, was about half the size of the 'present generation.'] My wife and I can make eight dozen a day; we made no more of the little ones, only the bigger ones take rather more time. That's a good day's work is 8 dozen—6 dozen is a fair day's work, what I call a 12 hours' day—as much as any man ought to work; but shoemakers must work 18 hours. It's no matter if we can make ourselves happy in our lot. Last year, from June to the end of October, I made three gross a week, that is, I did with my wife's help, she assisting at the cushions; that's 15 weeks at 432 a week, or 9,072 for the 21 weeks of the season. That's correct. The warehouses have the regular profit; they screw down. I can only get 7½d. a dozen, or rather 7s. 6d. a gross, for baskets with pincushions. Formerly warehouses laid in a stock of my baskets before Easter. Now they don't until they are asked for. There is such a change in fashion that shopkeepers is afraid to lay in. For all that, if I had capital I would now make a stock of them,

and take my chance; but what capital can I raise, working for 1s. to
1s. 6d. a day on slop shoes, and with a family. I have made every
kind of basket toys. Penny wicker carts, which pay the worst, go off
the best. I can't make 1s. a day at long hours at them, or I would
be carting now. The cushion-baskets was my regularest trade—the
pennies; but I have made them of very fine basket work. They were
sent out to Jersey, and to the repositories at the fashionable bathing
places in England, and indeed all over the country. They were 6d.,
and some higher, according to the work, to shops. In the last season
I only got 1s. 9d. clear profit on six dozen, or 10s. 6d. a week. It's
an awful trade. My only chance is at a fair, anyways handy, but that's
only a shilling or two extra, and fairs is few and far between, and then
there's travelling expenses to come out of that and fatigues to stand.
I wish I knew where I could get a few velvet cuttings cheap—that's a
great advantage to me."

A person to whom I was referred as a very ingenious workman,
gave me the following information concerning kites:—

"I am alone in the trade," he said, "the only man in the world who
makes kites after my peculiar scientific principles. This kite here, you
see, folds up and will go into a case like an umbrella case, so that you
can carry it in your hand. Instead of paper it is of fine cloth, as it is
called in the trade—but it is fine glazed calico. By the management
of the strings attached to the frame, the kite can be altered so as best
to suit the wind as ascertained previous to flying, just as a sail on
board ship is regulated. The tails of my kites have a series of 'cups,'
or 'cones,' also of glazed calico. I hook them on or off, and there is
no time lost. The introduction of the peculiar tails of my kites trebled
their sale. I have made kites 12 feet high, which have drawn a four-
wheeled chaise holding two persons. Such kites (12-foot kites) are
mostly used in drawing boats along the Rhine and other rivers. They
have amazing power. A pocket-handkerchief even, when held up in
a wind, will be found to influence the motion of a boat. I have known
even a 5-foot kite go to the full extent of the string, which was 1,700
yards, a few yards short of a mile. We calculate that two miles is the
greatest distance a kite can be made to fly, but that is only when one
kite is attached to the string of another already high in the air. No
one could hold a kite flown so high; a post, or something of that kind,
must be used. I have made kites for carrying meat into the air to test
the state of the atmosphere during the rage of the cholera. I made
5,000 kites last year, but mine is a peculiar trade. Numbers take up

kite-making without any instruction in the art. I suppose there are not above 25 kite-makers in London. Each, I should think, may make on the average a gross of kites in a day, which is 864 a week, which is 17,280 each man for the 20 weeks the season lasts, or altogether 432,000, and with more 437,000; of the farthing kites a man may make two or three gross a day, but some require labour, and a gross is a fair average. Average the cost of the kites to the public at 4d.; and my best 12-foot kites sell at £2, and a good 6-foot kite is fairly worth 6s. without the tail. I sell no kite under 1s. 6d. with the tail, and that will give £7,283 6s. 6d."

A woman who had known the *fancy ball business* for "well on to thirty years," she said, gave me the following information:—

"I make only the better sort. Here is one; made of different coloured cloths, you perceive, in diamonds of different lengths and widths. The joinings are covered over with this light gilt wire. That toy, sir, is my own invention, I may say. I invented it with six quarterings, and now it has thirty-six. I make such like in velvet. They are really beautiful. They're stuffed with the softest and finest seal's hair; so soft, the best hair is, that with a child's strength it wouldn't break a window, unless it was very bad glass, even if flung right against it. They're drawing-room balls. I work, sir, sometimes, for the Royal Family. The order comes to me through a warehouse, but I supply the article direct. I charge the warehouseman the same as usual; what he charges is no concern of mine. I look at it this way: if a shopkeeper pays a fair wage to let workpeople live decently, and not be beat out by the first rainy day, why, let him get as good a price as he can. These balls, you see, are coloured leathers, without gilt wire, but well made. Each diamond is cut out according to a nice iron pattern. These are common things which I'm forced to make for the low shops. They won't wear. As to the cheap shops, I myself have seen ——, in the ——, mark balls, that he had paid 4d. a piece to me for, at 2½d. in his window, before I'd left the place. He must make it up somehow, that's clear. What my returns in this business are, I can't tell; for my husband, who cuts out and such like, has another trade, and all the money goes together; we keep no separate accounts at all: but I do very well. We sell, I think, about a gross and a half a week, fancy balls. There are two other persons carrying on the trade, and the two together may make as many balls as I do. That's three gross a week, or 22,464 balls a year? Very likely. I pay no regular wages, as the trade is carried on by my own family; occasionally we have a little help. You

can, if you like, reckon what the toys I make amount to this way:—
Say 1s. a dozen in the lump, for though I only get 5d. a dozen for
some, I get 30s. for others. That's £561 12s. a-year. The other makers
together may take half that. The two sums added together come to
£842 8s. A good deal of money that, to be spent every year in fancy
balls."

I had the following statement from a Frenchman, who took no
little pride in his art. He is the only person who carries on the making
of *papier-maché toys* (as they have been called), which are covered—or,
more properly, and that was my informant's word, *clothed*—with fur
or hair. These toys display great taste and ingenuity. Some rabbits
were as large as life—he brought different specimens to show me—
and they looked natural enough, the body of the animal being made
of paper formed by an art and a process (according to his own account) peculiar to my informant. A French accent was perceptible
throughout the entire conversation, but was only very remarkable in
rapid speech or in a dash of excitement. He said:—

"Papier-maché was made before my father was born, or before my
father's grandmother, but improvements took place twenty-five year
ago. I can make you, if you please, the biggest animal in the world, wa-
terproof, and that nothing can never break, of paper or papier-maché.
Anything may be done with the paper, but I now use a composition as
well—it is my secret of what he is made. I make only animals. I make
them both way, for the ornament of the chimney and the amusement
of the children. I make every domestic. There is none but I manufacture him with natural hair and wool. French poodle dogs have the
call; rabbits is good; lambs go very well; goats is middling. All the
world can be supplied, from 3d. up to £5, with the French poodles.
I do not make the lions, nor the tigers, nor those creatures—I make
only in domestic animals, but I *could* make the lions and the tigers as
well. I make forty dozen domestic animals a week. Why you come
here to ask? Lately my trade has been bad. I employ women and girls
only, at so much on the dozen. I do not like to tell at what. It cannot
be necessary. I cannot tell what relates to my secret. I will not. The
skins for the poodles and the lambs I dress myself, or they would be
stink. The cost—oh, I will not tell, they cost too much. I have been
here for twenty-one years. I get the stink-lambs for skins. Last year I
used 4,800 lamb skins, and 5,000 some year. I employ eight English
women. The dogs is all lamb skins—their outsides. I use nearly as
many rabbit skins. I do not never admit persons into my work-room.

It is a very artful ingenuity. I can beat the French—indeed, I have beat my countrymen at home, for I have exportation to Paris; but the Germans come in cheap, cheap, and ruin the trade. This is a barking dog. I have made him, his bark and all—you see; yes, and you hear. The penny barks is no good; what barks can you expect for a penny? There's no get fat about him at 9d. This rabbit, you see, has a different skin to this other—the skin is the great cost with me. He have, too—the spring in his ears and tail, so that he lift them when the wheels go round. The earnings of my women? Oh! never mind; but I am not ashamed to tell. They earn 7s., and 9s., and 11s. a week, and never not less than 4s. My late wife could earn twenty and two shilling a week in this trade; but then she had the talent. Oh, no, none can now earn like that—they have not the talent—they have not the art in it—the nature—the interest. The work can only be done best by a relative of the master, one that has the interest in the making. The toys are not exactly papier-maché, which is fluid for mouldings, they are paper, common paper, in a solid form. The *how* it is made is my secret. None other persons are in my trade. I cannot open the secret any further. Pardon my reserve, for which I have account to you. How you say, sir, four dozen domestic animals a week, that's quite reasonable as to the arithmetic of it, and he makes 22,960 domestics a year. Yes, that at least and my women do not work hard. They might work harder. They work hard if they want new dresses for the Sundays. What will the twenty thousand and odd toys bring in in money? The price vary, you comprehend, according to sizes and qualities, and arts and beauties. Yes, you can say 1s. each. How much, £1,148 in a year for all the domestics. Yes; but I will not tell prices or secrets."

The Morning Chronicle, Monday, February 25, 1850.

STRONG SHOE TRADE.

To the EDITOR of the MORNING CHRONICLE.

Sir—I was sorry to see, by the report on the trade of the shoe-makers in your impression of the 18th inst., an error of some import-ance in regard to one of the statements there given, in mentioning the loss entailed on the closer in the strong trade by the use of the false size stick. In the 17th line in the second column of your letter, the price per pair should be 7d. by the fair measurement instead of 5d.—thus making the week's earnings 14s., and the loss to the closer, working by the false size stick, at 4½d. per pair, 5s. per week, or £13 per year. As I am thus writing to you on this subject, I think I may as well embrace the opportunity of letting the public know that your most useful exposures have already had a good effect in one instance. The employer referred to in the prior article (14th), has been com-pelled from sheer shame to put in somewhat better order the lodging den of his workmen. The room has just been washed out, as a nov-elty; and as a greater novelty still, clean sheeting has been supplied to their beds, and new quilts. So you see these people have at last a little shame.

Yours, &c.,

February 20. A STRONG HAND.

The Morning Chronicle, Tuesday, February 26, 1850.

We have to acknowledge the receipt of 20s. from "E. A. B." of Daventry, on account of Poor Fund.

FEMALE EMIGRATION SOCIETY.

This benevolent Association has practically commenced its oper-ations. The Female Emigration Society, it will be remembered, was called into being by that portion of the series of letters on "Labour and the Poor" devoted to the condition of the needlewomen of the metropolis. The object of the Association is sufficiently denoted by its title. It seeks to transplant to a new and rising country that species of labour for which there is least demand here, and that class of individuals which in our existing state of society are at once the most suffering and the most helpless. Yesterday the first party of female emigrants, sent forth under the auspices of the Society, proceeded down the river to the ship Culloden, lying at Gravesend. The Society have refrained from chartering a ship exclusively for their emigrants, believing it to be better policy to send them by small parties on board the ordinary class of vessels, so as to get rid, as far as possible, of invidious distinctions, and to merge the young persons sent out under their auspices in that general tide of emigration which is now setting in so fast from our shores to those of the Australasian continent. The Culloden sails from the river this day. She may touch at one of the Cape de Verd Islands, in case of being detained long in the Chops of the Channel; but the probability is, that the white cliffs once lost sight of, she will steadily hold on her unchanging course for her ultimate destination—Port Phillip.

The young female emigrants for whom the Association has provided berths on board the Culloden met yesterday, by appointment, at the Fenchurch-street Terminus of the Blackwall Railway. There also were collected several principal members of the committee, who had determined to see the first party of their *protégées* fairly off upon their long but hopeful voyage. The Right Hon. Mr. Sidney Herbert, the Hon. Mr. Arthur Kinnaird, the Hon. Mr. Littleton, Sir H. Verney, the Rev. J. Brown, the Rev. Mr. Sanger, and the Rev. Mr. Quekett were of the party, which was also graced by the presence of the Right Hon. Mrs. Sidney Herbert, and the Hon. Mrs. Wortley. Several gentlemen of literary celebrity were present, and amongst them we were rejoiced to recognise—looking none the worse, as the public will be glad to learn, from his recent long and severe illness—the author of "Vanity Fair."

Thirty-eight was the number of female emigrants who constituted the party destined for the Culloden. They assembled punctually to their time at the Fenchurch-street station, were regularly mustered, and answered to their names previously to the starting of the train. Their heavy luggage had been, of course, already stowed away aboard, but most of the girls carried parcels, or small bundles, and each was provided with a stout canvass bag of sand, to be used, as we understood, for drying the berth deck after scouring. The girls were, in a few instances only, accompanied to the railway by their friends and

relations. There were, of course, in these cases, touching and affec-
tionate farewells given and taken, but there were no manifestations
of that despairing grief, none of those painful outbreaks of emotion,
which we have more than once witnessed upon similar occasions. On
the contrary, although "some natural tears they shed," hope, buoyant
hope, was evidently in the ascendant in the breasts of the vast majority of the emigrants, and cheerful tones would ever and anon break
out amid sobs, and smiles shine forth through tears.

From Blackwall, the Satellite steamer conveyed the party down
the river, and in due time, by an ebbing tide, which almost counter-
balanced an easterly breeze, the steam-boat swept up alongside the
good ship Culloden, anchored off the Terrace-pier, at Gravesend, her
stout bulwarks dotted with anxiously peering heads, evidently watch-
ing with great interest for the advent of their *compagnons de voyage*.
The Culloden is a full-rigged ship of about 750 tons burden—a stout,
bluff-built, and serviceable merchantman—possibly not a very quick
craft in light breezes, but likely, in all probability, to be all the snugger
therefore when labouring over a mutinous sea—the scud flying fast to
leeward, and two reefs in the topsails.

Arrived alongside, the emigrants and their friends at once
proceeded aboard. The Culloden is a regular poop-ship, carrying
cabin passengers. The deck arrangements are of the usual class.
The launch—"Old Harney," as men-of-war's-men call the boat—
furnishes a convenient pen for the sheep, while the pigs are stowed
away beneath the shelter which she affords. A couple of life-boats are
suspended a little abaft, while the ship carries the usual quarter-boats
starboard and larboard. The arrangements on the berth-deck are
different from those adopted on board Government emigration
vessels, affording a greater degree of privacy; but, in the opinion of
very competent judges, not being by any means so advantageous in
respect to the supply of light and fresh air.

Let us briefly attempt to sketch the *coup d'œil* 'tween decks.
Imagine, then, running from the foremast right aft, a dim shadowy
corridor, illumined only by the square patches of light streaming
down the open hatchways. Right fore and aft extends a long narrow
table, with raised ledges, so as to avert, as far as possible, the chances
of smashed crockery in a rolling sea, while a frame-work above the
centre of the board, hung all along with mugs and jugs, shows that
the dining-table answers the purpose of a beaufet as well; on either
side a long range of what men at sea call bulkhead, and men on

shore partition, composed of white unpainted wood, screens off the sleeping berths—the humble state-rooms of the main deck—from what may be called the living and sitting room. The single men are bestowed for'ard, the married couples are disposed amidships, and the single women sleep aft. Let us push aside the sliding door, and glance into one of the many tiny chambers which, for four or five months, are to be the sleeping apartments of from five to ten young women. In the former case, imagine a "nook"—that is the most expressive word we can find—about seven feet by five. The seven feet are to be measured transversely from the bulkhead to the ship's side. Along them are four berths, two on either side, the berths being, in other words, shallow boxes without lids, fitted with beds and blankets, and not at all devoid of a certain air of compact snugness. Along the side of the ship, beneath the small air-hole, runs the fifth berth. The oblong patch of floor is principally occupied by a chest destined to contain the clothes to be worn on the voyage; and above it, and close to the fifth berth, is a curious extempore-looking washhand-stand, with a due allowance of tin basins. The larger "state-rooms" are of course fitted up on the same system of ingenious economy of space. Right aft—just inside the stern windows, and commanding an uninterrupted view of the wake—is disposed a labyrinth of berths, arranged so as to form quite a large sleeping-room, and laid out with curious ingenuity, so as not to leave a square inch of room unoccupied. It was pleasant to see how satisfied the emigrants seemed to be with their novel accommodation—how fussily each girl arranged her parcels upon her bed, and with what innocent importance she announced to all querists that that was to be *her* berth. After the first brush of sea-sickness is got over, we doubt not but that the Culloden will prove a comfortable and an orderly ship.

The thirty-eight young women despatched by the Female Emigration Society consist, we believe, of individuals selected with anxious and discriminating care; ample testimonials as to moral and industrial character having been exacted, and full inquiry instituted, in each case. The emigrants were plainly but comfortably and warmly clothed, and presented, I was assured, and can well believe, a very different appearance to that which they had exhibited on their first application to the committee.

On the voyage, educational training is, as far as possible, to be conjoined with needlework. The matron is to arrange her charge into classes, for the purposes of scriptural and general reading, with instructions in writing, arithmetic, and geography. A great quantity of calico has been put on board, supplied by a large City house at cost price, with models of the shirts generally used in the "bush," and the products of every girl's industry during the voyage will be delivered up to her on landing. In addition to the usual ship allowance, Mr. Sidney Herbert sent on board a quantity of "concentrated milk," to be used on high days and holidays throughout the voyage.

To one very hopeful feature of the day's transactions we must devote a special paragraph. Close to the Culloden, and bound to the same port, lies the fine ship Sir Robert Sale, freighted with a goodly company of agricultural emigrants. The surgeon of the latter vessel— a gentleman, we understand, well known and highly respected in the colony—came yesterday on board the Culloden, commissioned to offer engagements in the new households of the emigrating farmers to at least twenty of the society's *protégées*, while the rest were assured that they would find many homes eagerly opened to them.

After the emigrants had been finally mustered on the quarterdeck, the Rev. Mr. Quekett addressed a few words to them. They had in a body attended the reverend gentleman's chapel the Sunday evening before, when an address suitable to the occasion was delivered. Mr. Quekett merely took the last opportunity of recommending to them the strict observance of the rules of the ship, and entreated them to be in all things obedient to the matron and the other authorities placed over them.

This appeared to be the most trying moment. Many of the poor girls broke into open lamentations, others turned aside and wept silently, but the time was up—the steamer again alongside. There were hearty shakes of the hand, and fervently-expressed thanks and good wishes, and promises to write long and speedily, and then, to the shrill call of the boatswain's whistle, the bulwarks were crowded fore and aft, and, under three good hearty English cheers, the Satellite shot away up the river on her return.

So, as the old bills of lading had it, "May God send the good ship safe on her destined voyage!"

The Morning Chronicle, Wednesday, February 27, 1850.

We have to acknowledge the receipt of 5s., for the daughter of the lame toyman, named in Letter XXXVII.

LABOUR AND THE POOR.

—◆—

THE METROPOLITAN DISTRICTS.

[FROM OUR SPECIAL CORRESPONDENT.]

Letter XXXIX.

The manufacture of dolls employs many hands, being divided into many distinct branches. The two main divisions are the "wooden" and the "sewed" dolls—the former being the dolls of the poor, and the latter those of the rich. The wooden dolls are exceedingly primitive in their structure—there is little or no attempt at symmetry in the body—while the limbs are mere slips of lath jointed. The sewed dolls rank much higher as works of art. Whether this be the consequence or the cause of a greater division of labour, it is difficult to say; suffice it that, whereas the wooden doll is generally begun and completed by one hand (with the exception, perhaps, of the wig), the sewed doll has as many distinct branches of manufacture as it is divisible into distinct parts. In the first place, there is the doll sewer and stuffer—the calico integuments being generally cut out by the manufacturer, and given out with the sawdust, hair, or wool, with which the body is to be filled, to the same party. Then there is the dolls' head maker (wax and composition)—the dolls' arm and leg manufacturer—the dolls' wig maker—the dolls' eye maker—and the doll dresser. Each of these are separate branches of the trade. Occasionally some family may be met with where the whole of the branches (with the exception of making the eyes) are performed; but this is far from usual, especially with the better description of work.

And first concerning the *wooden dolls.* I called upon a maker whom I found ill in bed, suffering from rheumatism. In his room were piles of the bodies, and collections of the arms and legs of dolls; they caught the eye on every side. This doll-maker regretted the decline of art in some branches of his calling. A description of cheap wooden dolls that used to have their noses carved were now made, through the demand for lowness in price, with the nose but a little elevated on the countenance—"nothing to call a nose," he said; but, though the man was conversible enough, I did not think it proper to persevere in my inquiries with him in his sick state, and so visited another, whom I found at work, assisted by his daughter. He was an elderly person, who had known the trade many years, as his narrative shows. He said:—

"I make the jointed wooden dolls. The turned work (the body) is the work of the turner's lathe. I do it myself, and the faces of the commoner dolls are a composition put on afterwards. I go in for beauty as much as I can, even in the lower priced dolls. These dolls, now, are carved, after having been turned out of the wood. The 'carving' and 'drawing'—making the eyes, eye-brows, and lips in colours with a fine brush—are the fine touches of the trade. Nice lips and eyes set the article off. The lower-priced dolls have wooden joints at the middle, by which the legs are fastened to the body. We don't go in for symmetry in the commoner sorts of legs; nor, indeed, for any calves at all to them. They are just whitened over. The better ones have nice calves, and flesh coloured calves too. They are more like nature. The joints of the two sorts are made on the same principles. I buy their ringlets—it's generally ringlets, but, sometimes, braids or plaits, ready made—and have only to fit them on. That's not very different from human nature, I take it. The arms are stuffed leather, made by others. The best time for my trade was from 1809 to 1816. In every one year that I have named, I made 35 gross of dolls a week: but they were little creatures, some of them 4 inches long, dwarfs of dolls. I don't deal with the little creatures now. I'm in the larger line, as you see. A namesake of mine at that time made 100 gross a week. That's 1,060,880 dolls a year, is it? Look at that, now, for us two only. The little things I spoke of used to fetch a penny, now it's a farthing. I make now, I believe, two gross of dolls one week, and one another. The larger dolls require more time, which accounts, independent of the demand, for the difference. My dolls are sold to the public at 3s. and 4s.: that's the retail price, mind, and small are my profits. Wooden doll making is generally confined to families, so we can't speak of journeymen's wages. There are eight other doll-makers, and perhaps each may make twice as many as I do, but as they make so many more of the smaller sort, the cost (to the public) wouldn't be more than mine, perhaps about the same—but I can only guess. I have felt a great falling off in the demand since the last tariff—at least one quarter less is now made. When the duty was highest I knew a gentleman who now and then would venture £1,000 in buying foreign toys. It was, he said, a speculation, but he generally got £2,000 for his £1,000, and the toy trade was benefited, for variety and new fashions were seen, and there was a better demand for toys."

Now of the *sewed dolls.* The following statement will give the reader a slight insight into the earnings and condition of those who contribute so much to the pleasure of the young of the metropolis. It was given me by a man whose whole appearance showed grinding poverty. His cheeks were sunk more than I remember to have ever seen in any previous instance, and altogether he seemed, from grief and care, like a man half dead. His room, as well as I could see it by the light of the small candle—for it was late at night before I could visit him—was bare of anything to be called furniture, except only a very poor bed, a chair or two, and a table or bench at which he was at work with his paste and paper. In one corner was an oblong object, covered with an old quilt. It was a coffin containing the body of his child, a girl four years old, who had died of the hooping-cough. There were four living children in the room—all up, late as it was, and all looking feeble, worn, and sickly. A baby of four months old was asleep in the arms of a little girl of five or six. A baby of fifteen or sixteen months apparently, was in the arms of another girl, who in vain strove to quiet it. The mother was absent with some of her wares. The man's manner was meek and subdued, and he did not parade either his grief or his poverty. He merely answered my questions, and to them he said:—

"I make the *composition heads for the dolls*—nothing else. They are made of papier maché" ("paper mashed" he called it). "After they go out of my hands to the doll-makers, they are waxed. First, they are done over in 'flake' light (flesh colour), and then dipped in wax. I make a mould from a wax model, and in it work the paper—a peculiar kind of sugar paper. My little girl, fifteen years old (I have her besides these four young ones), and myself can only make twelve or thirteen dozen a day of the smallest heads. For them I get 4d. a dozen, 4s. the gross, and the material I reckon costs me 1s. 10d. If I make 2s. 6d. in a day, I reckon it a good day's work—and what is half-a-crown for such a family as mine? I pay 4d. per lb. for paper, and am so poor that I am forced to buy it all retail. I make, of all sizes, four gross of heads a week, the year through. That is 29,952 a year. I do not make 12s. a week on the average, take the year through. Besides, doll making is a precarious trade; and then there's fire and candle extra when you must work in a hurry. The dark must do when I'm forced to be idle. There are five more in the trade, and each may do more a year than I do, but I cannot tell. Some of the warehouses, moreover, get their heads made on their premises by boys at 5s. or 6s. a week, and that knocks us out altogether sometimes. They think only of cheapness—it's nothing what such as I may suffer. My poverty is grievous enough, as you see; and as you asked, I tell you. My wife makes a few dolls' arms of stuffed sheepskin; sawdust is used. She only gets seven farthings a dozen for them, and has very little employment. My trade was far better. Only two years ago I had from 1d. to 2d. a dozen better prices for my heads—a great difference to me—and my wife had 5d. a dozen for her arms some years ago. They get the bodies now stuffed with sawdust at 2s. 6d. a gross, and they did pay 5s. It's starvation work—stuffing 144 bodies for half-a-crown. Ah, sir, the children of the people who will be happy with my dolls little think under what circumstances they are made, nor do their parents—I wish they did. Awful circumstances in my room. Death there now (pointing to the coffin), and want here always." [This was really said most plaintively, because most naturally.]

The *doll's eye making* is a peculiar and interesting branch of doll manufacture. There are only two persons following this business in London, and by the most intelligent of these I was furnished with the following curious narrative:—

"I make all kinds of eyes," he said "both dolls' and human eyes; the birds' eyes are mostly manufactured in Birmingham. Of dolls' eyes there are two sorts—the common and the natural, as we call it. The common are simply small hollow glass spheres, made of white enamel, and coloured either black or blue (only two colours are made). The bettermost dolls' eyes, or natural ones, are made in a superior manner, but after a similar fashion to the others. You see this blue one: it has the iris correctly represented. I have been in the trade upwards of forty years, and my father followed it for sixty years before me. The price of the common black and blue dolls' eyes is 5s. for twelve dozen pairs of the small ones, and about 6s. for the same quantity of the large ones. We make very few of the bettermost kind, or natural ones. The price for those is about 4d. a pair, but they are only for the very best dolls. A man may make about twelve dozen pairs of the commoner, and about two or three dozen pairs of the better kind, in the course of the day. Average it throughout the year, a journeyman dolls'-eye maker earns about 30s. a week. There are very few journeymen in the trade. We employ only two men, and the other party in the trade has, I believe, six workpeople, three of whom are females. The common dolls' eyes were 12s. the 12 dozen pairs, twenty-five years ago—now they are only 5s. The decrease of the price is owing to competition; for, though there are only two of us in the trade in London, still the other party is always forcing his business by underselling us. Immediately the demand ceases at all, he offers his eyes at a lower price than in the regular season, and so the prices have been falling every year. There's a brisk and a slack season in our business, as well as in most others. After the Christmas holidays, up to March, we have generally little to do; but from that time the eyes begin to look up a bit, and the business remains pretty good till the end of October. Where we make one pair of eyes for home consumption, we make ten for exportation. Yes, I suppose we should be soon over-populated with dolls if a great number of them were not to emigrate every year. The increase of dolls goes on at an alarming rate every year. As you say, sir, the annual rate of mortality must be very high, to be sure, but still it's nothing to the rate at which they are brought into existence. They can't make wax dolls in America, sir, so we ship off a great many there. I make eyes for a French house at Havre that exports a vast quantity. The reason why they cannot produce dolls in America is owing to the climate. The wax won't set in very hot weather, and it cracks in extreme cold. I knew a party who went out there to start as doll maker. He took several gross of my eyes with him, but he couldn't succeed. The eyes that we make for Spanish America are all black. A blue-eyed doll in that country wouldn't sell at all. Here, however, nothing goes down but blue eyes. The reason for this is, because that's the colour of the Queen's eyes, and she sets the fashion in this as in other things. We make the same kind of eyes for the gutta percha dolls as for the wax. It is true, the gutta percha complexion isn't particularly clear, but our eyes are the natural tint; and if the gutta percha dolls look bilious, why we a'n't a going to make our eyes bilious to match. It is not true that an order was given for £500 worth of dolls' eyes. I know Mr. McCulloch says as much in his Commercial Dictionary, but it was contradicted at the time. The largest order I ever knew given at one time was for £50, and that was from the speaking dollmaker in High Holborn. We also make *human eyes.* Here are two cases—one black and hazel, and the other blue and grey." [He then took the lids off a couple of boxes that stood on the table; they each contained 190 different eyes, and so like nature that the effect produced upon a person unaccustomed to the sight was most peculiar and far from pleasant. They all seemed to be staring directly at the spectator, and occasioned a feeling somewhat similar to the bewilderment one experiences on suddenly becoming an object of general notice. The eyes of the whole world literally appeared to be fixed upon you, and it was almost impossible for the spectator at first to look at them without instinctively averting his head. The hundred eyes of Argus were positively insignificant in comparison with the 380 belonging to the human eye maker.] "Here, you see, are the ladies' eyes," he continued, taking one from the blue-eye tray; "you see it's clearer, and not so bilious as the gentlemen's. There's more sparkle and brilliance about them. Here's two different ladies' eyes—fine looking young women both of them. When a lady or gentleman comes to us for an eye we are obliged to have a sitting just like a portrait-painter. We take no sketch, but study the tints of the perfect eye. There are a number of eyes come over from France—but these are generally *misfits*. They are sold cheap, and seldom match the other eye. Again, from not fitting tight over the ball, like those that are made expressly for a person, they seldom move 'consentaneously,' as it is termed, with the natural eye, and have, therefore, a very unpleasant and fixed look— worse almost than the defective eye itself. Our artificial eyes move so freely, and have so natural an appearance, that one gentleman passed nine doctors without his false eye being detected. There is one lady who has been married three years to her husband, and I believe he doesn't know that she has a false eye to this day. The generality of persons take out their eyes when they go to bed, and sleep with them either under their pillow, or else in a tumbler of water beside their bed. Most married ladies never take their eyes out at all. Some people will wear out a false eye in half the time of others. This doesn't arise from the greater use of them, but from the increased secretion of the tears, which act on the false eye like acid on metal, and so corrodes and roughens the surface. This roughness produces inflammation, and then a new eye becomes necessary. The Scotch lose a great many eyes—why I cannot say; and the men lose more eyes than the women. A great many eyes are lost through accidents while shooting. We generally make only one eye, but I did once make two false eyes for a widow lady. She lost one first, and we repaired the loss so well for her that, on her losing the other, she got us to make a second for her. False eyes are a great charity to servants. If they lose an eye no one will engage them. In Paris, there is a charitable institution for the supply of false eyes to the poor; and I really think if there was a similar establishment in this country for furnishing artificial eyes to those whose bread depends on their looks—like servants—it would do a great deal of good. We always supply eyes to such people at half price. Our usual price is £2 2s. for one of our best. I suppose we make from three hundred to four hundred false eyes every year. The human eyes are part blown and part cast, and we are obliged to be very good chemists to know the action of the metallic oxides on the fire, so as to produce the proper colour of the iris. The great art of making a false eye is in polishing the edges quite smooth. The fire polish alone will do this. The French eyes are cut to fit the eye-ball by the lapidary in this country; the edges consequently, are left rough, and this causes great irritation. Of dolls' eyes we make about 500 gross of pairs of the common ones every year. I take it there are, of all sorts, near upon 24,000 dozen pairs of dolls' eyes made in London every year."

From the very ingenious inventor of the *speaking doll*, a tradesman in High Holborn, I had this statement:—

"I am the only person who ever made the speaking doll. I make her say 'papa' and 'mamma.' I haven't one in the house now to show you. I have sold the last. I sold one to be sent to St. Petersburg—it was damaged on the passage, and when landed couldn't say either 'papa' or 'mamma,' and the gentleman who bought it couldn't get it mended in all Russia. I could have told him that before. For the Exhibition of 1851 I believe there will be something equivalent to what I tell you of, but there will be something of everything. The invention of the speaking doll took me many experiments and much study. The thought first struck me one day on hearing a penny trumpet—why not make a doll speak? Science is equal to everything. Some time ago a ventriloquist came over from Dublin to me; he could imitate everything but a baby, and he came to consult me about a baby's voice. I put him in my show-room, and said 'You stand in the corner and hear it.' I made the doll speak, and he said 'that is the thing;' he gave the two guineas for the price of the machine (not a doll), and went away quite glad. I have taken the apparatus to a party and made him speak on the stairs; a young gentleman I did it to tease turned quite white, as he could not tell who or what was coming. After I determined to try and manufacture a speaking doll, I persevered day by day, thinking of it when doing other things, and completed it in three months. I often dreamed of it, but never got a hint of the speaking doll in my sleep, though I have in other discoveries. When I heard my first speaking doll call me 'papa'—which she very properly might—I said in a sort of enthusiasm—it was with feelings of the greatest gratification—'I've got her at last.' I sell rather more than a dozen in a year at £6 6s. each. Many a time in my show room have the children looked out for the baby when they heard my doll. I had a rascal of a parrot once who could say 'papa' and 'mamma' as well as my doll herself—the parrot learned it from the doll. Many doll-makers have dissected my speaking doll to get at my secret. I knew one clever man who tried twelve months to copy it, and then he put his work in the fire. I laugh—I don't care a fig. I have the fame and the secret, and will keep them; the profit is but small—and as for the fame, why that's not for me to talk about."

From a man and his wife who *knitted cotton dresses* for dolls, I had the following statement. The cotton dress is a doll's dress, covering the arms, and indeed the entire doll; with a cotton knit bonnet, and even a knitted muff and a knitted parasol if desired. The dress shown to me was neatly edged with a line of red cotton. One of its excellences was, I was told, that it could, in the process of knitting, be made to assume the fashion of ladies' "bustles." The following is the information given me:—

"Last year was a very bad year indeed for us. Take it all through, we hardly made half a dozen in a week, and they are retailed by us at 1s. a dress. The cotton used is of any sort, generally thick, and the way is that of the knitting practised by ladies." "Yes," said the wife, "with a few improvements invented by myself." "The badness of trade," resumed the husband, "has made us very poor; and, in spite of us, the rent has got into arrear. Here is my book—no payment since January 17! Such a thing never happened with us before. If it wasn't for a little fancy knitting in other things, and a little washing, we might starve. Three years ago we could and did make a dozen of these cotton dresses a day, by working long hours, and could clear full 30s. a week. We had better prices then. Perhaps it's a change in fashion that has made the trade so bad."

A *toy drum and tambourine maker* gave me the following account:—

"The first process in making a tin drum," he said, "is to cut the tin the size required, solder the ends together, and colour the body. We then paint the Royal Arms on it, or a crown and V. R. The hoops are then cut (they are beech) and coloured, and then what we call the 'twig' is cut, and the parchment for the top of the drum being sewn to it, the twig is fitted to the tin body, and attached to it by the strings, which are tightened or slackened by leather braces, for the weather affects the drum. A best toy drum goes thirty-five times through our hands before it is finished, as time must be given in the working for the parts to dry and set. I don't make the sticks, the toy turners do them. I and my four boys could make a gross of small wooden drums in a day, but only a dozen of the best large tin drums, highly ornamented. Of wooden drums, I make a gross a week, the year through—and 52 gross, at 3d. a piece (retail) gives £93 12s. There are other makers in London, who may make about as many as I do; giving altogether £187 4s. We make very few tin drums now to what were made—the foreign toys have affected us so. I may make half a gross of them a week through the year, and taking the average price at 1s. (the big ones making up for the sixpennies), it gives £185 14s., which you can calculate as with the wooden drums—double it for other makers—and it's £371 8s. for London-made drums. Tambourines are made after the same fashion, but have only a limited sale. I only make about three dozen a week, and the public may buy them (retail) say at an average of 9d.—that's £70 4s. I can hardly tell you what the other makers sell. Whether the same calculation as with the drums would be correct or not for the tambourines, I can't say. I *have* heard an uncle whom I succeeded say—and he employed eleven men where I have four boys at apprentices' wages—that the war time was the time for the toy drum trade."

A *gun toy-maker*, whom I found at work, his wife assisting him, gave me this statement:—

"I was born to the business of toy, gun, and pistol, as well as of tin toys, which consist of mugs and trumpets; but the foreigners have got all the trumpet trade now, what we got 30s. a gross for we now get only 7s. The other tin toys—such as horses and carts, got up by machinery for a penny—are made in Birmingham. None are made in that way in London; they're but *slop toys*. The tin toy trade at Birmingham is the factory system with children; think of children working hard at toys—poor little things to whom a toy is a horror! A gun is made in this manner. The wooden part, the stock, is made ready for the gunmaker's use by any carpenter; it is of pine. The next process is the making of the wire spring, then the barrel (tin). These different parts are then put to the stock, the lock is made by ourselves; they are of solder, and cast. The spring is placed inside the barrel, a ring is placed at the end by which it is drawn out, fastened to the pin (like the nipple of one of your deadly guns), and the weapon is ready for discharge. I make the week through three gross, which is 22,464.

There is one other toy gunmaker in London, and he may make as many as I do, which will be 44,928 made in London. Reckon a third retailed to the public at 4d. (called pistols), and reckon those retailed at 6d. in the proportion of 6 to 4 in number with those retailed at 1s., and you have the sum of £1,238 4s. The foreign trade has injured my business greatly, both as to quantity and price. I first felt the effect in 1844 and 1845, and my business has kept getting worse and worse until now. I do not make half so many guns as I did before the change in the tariff, and the price is worse to me by 3s. out of 21s.— that was the price formerly of a gross of such as these, now they are 18s. only. The trumpet trade's quite blown away from us—I may as well have my joke about it. Of tin mugs I make 10 gross a week the year round, which is 74,880. There are three other makers, who may turn out one-half as many as I do, the three of them together—that is 111,320 in all. They are all retailed at 1d. (I have 7d. a dozen), and so the public pay for tin mugs, made in London annually, £468 6s. 8d. In war time, bless you, that was the time for my business—there *was* a demand for guns then I can tell you! I sold eight, then, to one that I sell now, though the population's increased so. These pistols, which I get 1s. 6d. a dozen for now, I had 3s. 6d. a dozen for then. I remember the first botched-up peace in 1802. I can just recollect the illumination. My father (I heard him say so) thought the peace would do no good to him, but it didn't last very long, and the toy-gun trade went on steadily for years—with a bit of a fillip, now and then, after news of a victory; but the grand thing for the trade was the constant report that Bonaparte was coming—there was to be an invasion, and then every child was a soldier. Guns *did* go off briskly at that period—anything in the shape of a gun found a customer in those days. Working people could then buy plenty of toys for their children, and did buy them too. The men in the trade earn 12s. a week. The warehouses send out quantities of my guns and pistols to the colonies, especially to Australia—the duty keeps them out of the United States. The slop toy trade goes down here now."

An Italian gave me the following account of the *detonating cracker business*. His parlour, as well as the window of his workshop, presented an admixture sufficiently curious. Old foreign paintings, religious, mythological, or incomprehensible, were in close connection with unmistakeable Hogarth prints. Barometers (for these also were "made and repaired"), showed that it was "set fair," and alongside them were grosses of detonating crackers. Of frames and mouldings there was a profusion, and in all stages, from the first rough outline to the polished gilding. He said, in pretty good English with a strong Italian accent:—

"Yes. I make de detonating crackers, and am de only man in England skilful to make dem. It is a grand secret, mine art. It live in my breast alone—de full, entire secret. I will show you de pulling crackers. Dey go in wid de pastrycook's things at de parties of de rich. A gentleman say to a lady, so I have heard, in de pleasantness of de party, 'please to pull.' Yes, indeed, as they write above de bells. And so de pretty lady pull, and de cracker goes bang—a sudden bang—and de lady goes 'Ah-h-h!' quite sudden too, of course, dough she must have known before dat de crack was to come. Ah! sir, dey seldom tink of de Italian artist who make de pulling cracker dat has brought out her nice 'Ah-h-h!' for 3½d. de gross—dat is all we gets for de dozen dozen. I dare say de rich fashionable pastrycook get a great deal for dem. I don't know how much. Dey are sold at de retail shops, dat are not high shops, at a halfpenny a dozen. Den de detonatings—them what are trone down on de stones, and go bang, and make de people passing go start. Do dey cause many accidents do I tink? Bah, nonsense. It is de play of de boys: it keep dem out of mischief. I sell fifty gross, one week with another. I can make, if required, wid my boy, eighteen gross a day. All last year I sold, as near as I can tell, fifty of de pulling, and fifty gross of de detonating. Dat is—yes, no doubt—14,400 a week, or 748,800 a year. How curious! More dan seven hundred dousand bang-bangs made in dis little place. Dere is danger, perhaps, in de make to some, but no to de right artist. At a halfpenny a dozen, dat is £260 paid by de public—dat is only part of my business; but den de pastrycook charges may make de amount double, and double again, and more dan double dat again."

A very ingenious man, who resided in two spacious rooms at the top of a high house, gave the following statement concerning *camera obscura* making. I may here remark that I have always found the intelligent artisan—who could easily be made to understand the purport of my inquiries—ready to give me the necessary information, not only without reluctance, but with evident pleasure. Among the less informed class I am often delayed by meeting with objections and hesitations; these, however, are always obviated by having recourse to a more intelligent person. My present informant said:—

"I have known the camera obscura business for twenty-five years or so; but I can turn my hand to clock-making, or anything. My father was an optician, employing many men, and was burnt out; but the introduction of steam machinery has materially affected the optical glass grinder—which was my trade at first. In a steam-mill in Sheffield, one man and two boys can now do the work that kept sixty men going. I make bagatelle boards—there's no great demand for them—and targets—they go off very fair. The only improvement I remember in the making of the common cameras is this:—Formerly the object glass was a fixture in the wood of the box, and immovable, and of course could only take an object at a certain distance, whereas, by applying a movable brass tube, with the glass in it, you can command objects at any distance, adjusting it precisely on the principle of a telescope. Too much light obliterates your object, and too little light won't define it. Last year I think I made three gross. Here is the stuff of the box body, cedar; all blacked in the inside, so as to exclude any false light. The bottom is deal, and the natural colour of that or of the cedar would obliterate an object by giving false lights. The small cameras are 2s. 6d. (retail), the next size is 5s., and so by half-crowns, generally up to 20s. or 21s. I make more than one-half 2s. 6d. ones; they sell well in the summer season. I don't get more than 6d. a piece out of the 2s. 6d. ones. Perhaps I make two gross smaller, and the other sizes, of the third gross, in about equal proportions; altogether £126 19s. There is no other maker for the toy-shops in the camera obscura trade, to my knowledge, beyond myself. In making my cameras I test them from this door to objects at a distance. It gives every line of those tiles, every shape of those chimney pots, and every tumble of those tumbler pigeons. So I detect any error in the focus, and regulate it. I must test them at a good height, with a good light. A fog gives you only a fog—no defined object. The perfect adjustment of the focus, and, indeed, of every portion, is the nice art of my trade."

A very ingenious and intelligent man to whom I was referred, as the best in his trade, gave me the following account of magic lanterns. His parlour behind the shop—for he had risen to be a shopkeeper in some kinds of toys and other articles, known as the "fancy trade," was well furnished, and in a way that often distinguishes the better class of prosperous artisans. A fondness for paintings and for animals was manifested. On a sofa lay two very handsome King Charles's spaniels. On a chair were a fine cat and kitten. Outside his parlour window was a pigeon colony, peopled with fine large birds, a cross between those known as a "carrier" and a "horseman." Books, of no common class, were abundant enough, and his periodical was not wanting. He said:—

"I have known the business of magic lantern making thirty-five years. It was then no better than the common galantee shows in the streets, Punch and Judy, or any peepshow or common thing. There was no science and no art about it. It went on so for some time—just grotesque things for children, as 'Pull devil and pull baker.' This is the old style, you see, but better done." [He showed me one in which, to all appearance (for it was rather obscurely expressed), a cat was busy at the washtub, with handkerchiefs hanging on her tail to dry; Judy, with a glass in her hand, was in company with a nondescript sort of devil, smoking a pipe, and a horse was driving a man, who carried the horse's panniers.] "Bluebeards were fashionable then—uncommon blue their beards were, to be sure; and Robin Hoods—and Robinson Crusoes with Fridays and the goats, and the parrot, and the man's footmark on the sand—and Little Red Riding Hoods, as red as the Blue Beards were blue. I don't remember Ali Babas and Forty Thieves, there were too many of the thieves for a magic lantern—too many characters; we couldn't very well have managed forty thieves—it's too many. There were things called 'comic changes' in vogue at that period. As the glasses moved backwards and forwards, fitted into a small frame like that of a boy's slate, a beggar was shown as if taking his hat off, and Jim Crow turning about and wheeling about, and a blacksmith hammering—moving his hammer. There were no theatrical scenes beyond Harlequins and Clowns. About thirty years ago the diagrams for astronomy were introduced. These were made to show the eclipses of the sun and moon, the different constellations, the planets with their satellites, the phases of the moon, the rotundity of the earth, and the comets with good long tails. What a tail 1811 had! and similar things that way. This I consider an important step in the improvement of my art. Next, moving diagrams were introduced. I really forget, or never knew, who first introduced those improvements. The opticians then had the trade to themselves, and prices were very high. The moving diagrams were so made that they showed the motion of the earth and its rotundity, by the course of a ship painted on the lantern—and the tides, the neap and spring, as influenced by the sun and moon. Then there was the earth going round the sun, and, as she passed along, the different phases were shown, day here and night there. Then there were the planets going round the sun, with their satellites going round them. How wonderful are the works of the Creator! The comets, too; that of 1811, however, with a famous tail, as he deserved. His regular course—if you may call it regular—was shown. I saw him when a schoolboy in Wiltshire then. There has not been a comet worth calling a comet since. The zodiac made very pretty slides—twelve of them, each a sign. These things greatly advanced the art and the demand for magic lanterns increased, but not much for some years, until the dissolving views were introduced, about eighteen years ago, I think it was. But I should tell you that Dollond, before that, made improvements in the magic lantern; they called the new instrument the phantasmagoria. Mr. Henry, who conjured at the Adelphi Theatre some eighteen years ago, was one of the first—indeed I may say *the* first—who introduced dissolving views at a place of public amusement. Then these views were shown by the oil light only, so that the effect was not near so good as by gas, but even that created a great impression. From that period I date what I may call the popularity of magic lanterns. Henry used two lanterns for his views; but using them with oil, and not on so large a scale, they would be thought very poor things now. Then the Careys introduced the gas microscope, up in Bond-street. The gas microscope (the hydro-oxygen it's sometimes called) is the magic lantern, and on the principle of the magic lantern, only better glazed, showing the water lions and other things in a drop of stagnant water. Thames water may do. I now introduce insects and butterflies' wings in my lanterns—real insects and real wings of insects on the slides. I make such as fleas, bugs, pig-lice (an extraordinary thing, with claws like a crab, sir), and so up to butterflies—all between glasses, and air tight—they'll last for ever if necessary. Here's the sting, tongue, and wing of a bee. Here you see flowers. Those leaves of the fern are really beautiful—of course they are, for they are from the fern itself. This is one great improvement of the art, which I have given in a more simple form than used to be the fashion. You can magnify them to any size, and it's still nature—no disproportion and no distortion. Butterflies may be made as big as the wall of this room, through one of my magic lanterns with microscope power attached—but the larger the object represented, the less the power of the light. Gas, in some degree, obviates that fault. No oil can be made to give a light like gas. After this the question arose as to introducing views with the lime-light, but the paintings in the lanterns were then too coarse, for the light brought them out in all their coarseness. Every defect was shown up, glaringly, you may say. That brought in better paintings—

of course at a greater cost. The Polytechnic has brought the lime-light for this purpose to great perfection. For the oil-lights the paintings are bold, for the lime-light fine and delicate. Next the chromatrope was introduced, revolving stars chiefly—the hint being taken from Chinese fireworks. Mount Vesuvius was made to explode and such like. That's the present state of the art in London. The trade is five or six fold what I once knew it. Landscapes, Fingal's caves, cathedrals, sea views, are most popular now. In the landscapes we give the changes from summer to winter—from a bright sun in July to the snow seen actually falling in January. I make between 500 and 600 a year, say 550; I think I make one half of those made. The lowest price of a well-made lantern is 7s. 6d., and so on up to £20, dissolving and double lanterns. About a third of the lowest price are made, but people often go on from that to a superior article. I sold last year about 100 of the best of single lanterns, retailed at £10. Calculate a third at 7s. 6d., and 100 at £10, and the intermediate prices in—I think we may say—equal proportions—and you have the amount. Average the middle lot at 30s., suppose—that is £1,469 14s. I think that the other magic lanterns made, though they may be double my quantity, will not realize more, as so many lower-priced lanterns are made; so double the amount, and we have £2,939 8s. for London-made magic lanterns. I think I can, and shall, introduce further improvements. There are slop magic lanterns; they are slops, made, I believe, but I am not sure, in French Flanders; and I believe more of them are sold than of our own. What is worse than slop art, sir? These slop lanterns are generally retailed at 1s. 6d. each, with 12 slides. The tin part is neatly made; but, altogether, it is sad rubbish. I have been told by persons who bought them—and I have been often told it—that they could make nothing of them. The only good that they can do is, that they may tempt people to buy better ones—which is something. The admission of foreign toys at a low rate of duty has not injured the magic lantern business, but has rather increased it."

The Morning Chronicle, Thursday, February 28, 1850.

"S. S." encloses a five-pound note, and requests Mr. Jones to apply £1 10s. to the poor modeller, and the remainder to the poor shoemaker who wished to emigrate, and to the painter's family and poor widow who lodged with them; or to any case Mr. Jones thinks more deserving.

We have to acknowledge the receipt of a sovereign, for the toyman and his daughter, from "L. L. L."

"A. B." has handed us a sovereign, of which 15s. is to be given to the poor painter, and 5s. to the widow shoebinder living under the same roof.

We have received a sovereign from "E. H. B.," for poor needlewomen.

A Lady sends 5s., to be divided between the two cases mentioned in the *Bell's Weekly Messenger* of February 16, as having been copied from *The Morning Chronicle* of the previous Thursday.
Brighton, Feb. 21.

Miss Brown presents her compliments to the editor of *The Morning Chronicle*, and she takes the liberty to enclose five shillings' worth of letter stamps for the relief of the coalwhipper who broke his leg and afterwards hurt his hand, living in a court near the Shadwell entrance to the London Docks, mentioned in Letter XIX. on the Metropolitan Districts.

To the EDITOR of the MORNING CHRONICLE.

Sir—A number of very able articles have appeared in *The Morning Chronicle*, headed "Labour and the Poor," the purport of which appears to be to create sympathy for and to protect the poor working man from oppression and wrong. The intention is highly praiseworthy, but you will admit, sir, that where great talent is employed to advance a cause, or to enforce an argument, so much the more caution is necessary on the part of the advocate, when he states "the truth and the whole truth," that he should state "nothing but the truth." I believe the writer in question has no desire "to set down aught in malice;" one cannot imagine that he has any interest in doing so, but it may be admitted that when a man has a purpose to serve, even though it be a good one, his feelings or his prejudices will render him liable to accept evidence of a very questionable nature, and to deduce facts from it which he is not warranted in doing.

In his 34th letter, he has certainly done this; and I humbly pray you, sir, to permit one of your constant readers a small space in your valuable paper to defend himself and others of his class from what he must designate an unwarrantable and undeserved attack made upon them therein.

I am a shoe-factor or sale-master, in a large way of business—one of those whom the letter-writer in question, designates as "illegal," "scab," or "slaughter-shop keepers," as contradistinguished from "the legal or honourable trade," or in other words, the metropolitan bespoke shoemaker.

He says, "These men are a curse to the bespoke trade"—undoubtedly we are; if it were not for the Northampton manufacturers, and for us who sell their goods, the bespoke traders would be enabled to sell their Wellington boots at from 2*l.* 2s. to 2*l.* 10s. per pair, and their shoes at proportionate excessive prices. This would be desirable enough for them, but it would be a monopoly quite against the spirit of the times, and detrimental also to the public. The real truth of the matter is, sir, that the depreciation of wages is occasioned by first, the admission of foreign goods at very low duties; and secondly, by an excess of competition both among masters and operatives, occasioned probably by the rapid increase of population. Against this there is a material difference in the price of provisions; for as one of this writer's witnesses says, "two or three years ago 9s. would go for bread. Now, with the same number in family, I pay 4s.

3d. a-week for it." Relative to the introduction of French goods, the letter says:—

"In fact, there would be every week upwards of two thousand pairs to be made in this country more than there is now. That would occupy 220 men more every week than are now occupied in that particular labour. What I have said as to the admission of French goods, and the injury done to the English workman is, I am quite confident, the opinion of my class."

Now, sir, a Protectionist might say, "do not admit the goods of the foreigner," but surely the most bigoted Protectionist would not exclaim—"Do not admit the Northampton goods to compete with those of the metropolis," and yet here is the great grievance of the London bespoke masters and the London operatives. House rent and wages are lower at Northampton than in London, and so the manufacturers there can undersell the Londoner, and thus it becomes a question of free-trade and legitimate competition in business.

Again, an informant of the writer says:—

"I attribute the depressed earnings of working men more to the cupidity of the middle classes than to anything else; they cut each other's throats in competition, but the poor journeyman pays for it. By the change in the tariff, in 1842, I am quite certain, both from my own experience and from my knowledge of my fellow workmen, the working men in my trade were very materially injured."

Another witness says, and I trust you will admit his say—as it has reference to the question of Free Trade in general as well as my particular line of business:—

"I attribute the decline in the wages (I'm speaking of my own particular shop and my own particular branch, so as to confine myself to facts that have come within my own knowledge), to the introduction of French goods and the superabundance of labour in the market, produced by the employment of boys. I will give you an example of the effect that the lowering the duty upon the French goods had upon our wages. Immediately after the reduction of the duty in 1842 my employer went to Paris, and brought over 20 gross of French silk and satin goods. He showed a sample of these to the workmen employed upon similar kind of work, and produced the invoice to prove how cheap he could purchase such an article upon the Continent. He did not state that he purposed making a reduction of the wages, but strongly insinuated as much; and from that time to the present he has steadily lowered our wages at every slack season of the year."

One more extract, sir, and I will no longer trespass upon your kind patience, or that of your readers:—

"The system which has, I believe, the worst effect on the women's trade throughout England, is *chamber-mastering*. There are between 300 and 400 chamber-masters. Commonly the man has a wife and three or four children, ten years old or upwards. The wife cuts out the work for the binders, the husband does the knife-work; the children sew with uncommon rapidity. The husband, when the work is finished at night, goes out with it, though wet and cold, and perhaps hungry—his wife and children waiting his return. He returns, sometimes, having sold his work at cost price, or not cleared 1s. 6d. for the day's labour of himself and family."

And now, sir, have I not proved, or rather, has not the writer proved for me, that the real cause of the reduction in the wages of the London boot and shoe-makers is attributable to the admission of foreign goods, and to excessive competition; and this being admitted, is it not also proved that an unfair, unjust, and uncalled-for attack has been made upon the class to which I belong—namely, the sale-masters of the metropolis? Trusting you will find room for this letter, and by so doing confer a favour on myself and others, to whom reference has been made, I beg to subscribe myself, your obedient servant,

S.

The Morning Chronicle, Saturday, March 2, 1850.

A lady and gentleman enclose a Post-office order to the amount of 2*l.*, and they would be obliged to the Editor of *The Morning Chronicle* to apply 1*l.* for the benefit of the poor Shoemaker who wished to emigrate, mentioned in Letter 35 of *The Morning Chronicle* of Feb. 14; and 1*l.* for the crippled Penny Mouse-trap-maker and his daughter, whose history is related in Letter 37, in your paper of Feb. 21; or, if he should consider these two cases sufficiently provided for from any other sources, they would thank him to make what use of it he pleases in relief of the objects whose poverty and misery the letters have served to bring before the public. They cannot but express their cordial sympathy with the investigation into the hidden causes of the misery and crime so universally prevalent which has been so ably and indefatigably carried on by his Special Correspondents; and would sincerely hope that, by leading to the removal of those causes, their labours may effect not only the temporary but also the permanent alleviation of the evils, of which in so many cases they have disclosed the springs.

"F. A. E. A." has forwarded 10s. for the Dolls'-head-maker, whose child died, stated in *The Morning Chronicle* of Feb. 28.

The Morning Chronicle, Monday, March 4, 1850.

Miss S— has sent us 2s. 6d., by the hands of Mrs. H., for the Poor Modeller.

The Morning Chronicle, Tuesday, March 5, 1850.

"C. L. W." encloses to the Editor of *The Morning Chronicle* 1*l.*, to be equally divided between two cases mentioned in Letter 39 on "Labour and the Poor"—viz., the maker of knitted cotton dresses for dolls, and the maker of composition heads for dolls, who had lost a child in hooping-cough.

"T. C. G." encloses 1*l.* 10s. for the relief of the second case (the maker of composition dolls) named in Letter 39, which appeared in *The Morning Chronicle* on the 28th Feb.

The Morning Chronicle, Wednesday, March 6, 1850.

J. M. and E. have sent 5s. to be placed at the disposal of our Metropolitan Correspondent.

LABOUR AND THE POOR.

——◆——

THE METROPOLITAN DISTRICTS.

[FROM OUR SPECIAL CORRESPONDENT.]

LETTER XL.

I am again obliged to defer for a few days my investigation into the subject of Prison Labour. In the meantime I purpose occupying myself by inquiring into the condition, earnings, and treatment of the men belonging to the Mercantile Marine.

According to the Occupation Abstract of 1841 the number of British seamen at that period was as follows:—

Navy on shore	6,508
Merchant seamen on shore	45,915
Navy and merchant seamen on shore	52,423
Ditto ditto afloat	96,799
Total number of British seamen in 1841	149,222

I am informed, however, by the Registrar-General of Seamen, that the above statement is very defective and not to be depended upon.

The number of the last mariner's ticket issued at the office of the Registrar-General, up to Saturday, March 2, 1850, was 487,599. But this affords us no criterion as to the number of seamen. In the first place, all the ports have to be furnished with a sufficient store of tickets to meet demands. There are 120 such ports in the United Kingdom, and the average stock at each is about 150 tickets, amounting in all to 18,000. Moreover there are generally from 15,000 to 16,000 tickets kept on hand for the navy—so that the total number of tickets issued to seamen may be said to be always between 30,000 and 40,000 less than the number of the last ticket given out at the office of the Registrar-General. In round numbers, then, there are about 450,000 registered seamen; or, more correctly speaking, as many as 450,000 mariners have received tickets since the opening of the office on the 1st January, 1845. From this 450,000 a large number must be deducted for the deaths, shipwrecks, desertions, and other contingencies, which have occurred since that period. These, I am informed by Lieutenant Browne (to whose courtesy, experience, and intelligence I am indebted for a considerable portion of the statistical information contained in this letter), may be fairly said to amount to from 160,000 to 180,000. Hence the number of seamen belonging both to the navy and the merchant service, may be assumed to be between 260,000 and 280,000 individuals—

say 270,000
Of these, there are in the mercan-
    tile navy 200,000
In ships of war 25,000
In foreign service 45,000
                      ————— 270,000

I am informed by the same authority that no fewer than 102,000 lads have been apprenticed to the merchant service within the last 15 years.

In the present letter, and those immediately following, I purpose dealing with the *merchant seamen* alone. In order, however, to take a more comprehensive view of the maritime resources of the country, it may be as well, before treating specially of the mercantile marine, to lay before the reader a brief account of the *naval force of the kingdom;* for all admitted authorities, whether historians, statists, or political economists, agree in considering the elements of the naval power of a State to consist in the extent and quality of its "merchant service," which not only supplies the seamen necessary to man a fleet in seasons of war, but which maintains that fleet by repairing the casualties produced by conflict with the enemy or the elements.

According to the Government Report on the Army Navy, and Ordnance Estimates of 1848, there were 252 ships and vessels of war in commission on the 1st of January in that year. The following table, copied from that Report, shows us the number of vessels belonging to the different classes:—

THE NUMBER OF SHIPS AND VESSELS IN COMMISSION ON THE
1ST JANUARY, 1848, THE NUMBER OF HANDS COMPOSING
THEIR CREWS, AND THE NUMBER OF GUNS THEY CARRIED,
WAS AS FOLLOWS :—

  5 First Rates, carrying from 110 to 120 guns, and 950 men
     and upwards.

11 Second Rates, carrying from 80 to 110 guns, and 750 to
     950 men.

  1 Third Rate, carrying from 70 to 80 guns, and 620 to
     750 men.

  7 Fourth Rates, carrying from 50 to 70 guns, and 450 to
     620 men.

10 Fifth Rates, carrying from 30 to 50 guns, and 300 to
     450 men.

15 Sixth Rates (including all ships bearing a captain).

49 Sloops of war and brigs.

  9 Packets.

20 Surveying, troop, store, and hospital ships.

24 Cutters, schooners, yachts, and tenders.

78 Steam-vessels.

22 Mail packets.

  1 Steam guard-ship.

252 ships in commission.

Concerning the number of men belonging to the Navy, the Naval Estimates of the present year afford us the latest information. The "*Service Afloat*" is there calculated to consist of *twenty-six thousand* seamen and *two thousand* boys, the wages for whom are computed at £1,041,190. For an explanation of these items we are referred to the following:—

STATEMENT SHOWING THE NUMBER OF FLAG OFFICERS AND
THEIR RETINUE IN COMMISSION; OF OFFICERS SUPERIN-
TENDING HER MAJESTY'S DOCKYARDS; OF OFFICERS, PETTY-
OFFICERS, SEAMEN AND BOYS, COMPRISING THE FULL COMPLE-
MENTS (EXCEPT THE MARINES) OF ALL HER MAJESTY'S SHIPS
AND VESSELS IN COMMISSION ON THE 1ST OF DECEMBER, 1849.

NAVAL SERVICES.

RANK.	NO.	RANK.	NO.
FLAG-OFFICERS IN COMMISSION AND THEIR RETINUE.		CAPTAINS, PETTY OFFICERS AND MEN.	
Admirals	2	Captains { 1st Class	12
Vice-Admirals	3	Captains { 2d do	6
Rear-Admirals	4	{ 3d do	17
Commodores of the		{ 4th do	21
1st class	2	Commanders	81
Commodores of the 2d		Lieutenants	427
class	3	Inspectors of machinery afloat	2
Flag-Lieutenants	11	Masters	124
Secretaries to Flag-officers	14	Chief Engineers { 1st Class	9
		{ 2d do	18
Clerks and retinue	130	{ 3d do	40
		Chaplains	50
	169	Surgeons	127
Deduct Commodores included among the Captains	3	Paymasters and Pursers	106
		Naval Instructors	43
	166	Mates	388
		Assistant-Surgeons	203
		Second Masters	103
OFFICERS SUPERINTENDING DOCK YARDS.		Assistant Engineers	274
		Midshipmen	310
Rear-Admirals	3	Master Assistants	145
Commodore of the 2d		Clerks	221
class	1	Naval Cadets	140
Flag-Lieutenants	3	Gunners	
Secretaries	2	Boatswains }	822
Clerk and Retinue	18	Carpenters	
		Engineers	79
	27		
Deduct Commodore included among the Captains	1		3,768
		Petty Officers	5,949
	26	Able and ordinary Seamen, Landsmen and boys, including Kroomen	14,619

Total for effective Naval Service 24,528

There are, then, it may be said, 25,000 seamen in the British navy, whose united wages amount annually to £1,000,000.

It is, however, with the *Mercantile Marine*, and more especially with that part of it trading to and from the port of London, that I am at present concerned. In order to understand the relative importance of this particular branch of the merchant service, as compared with that appertaining to the other ports of the United Kingdom, it will be necessary that we first take a survey of the mercantile marine in general. I shall, therefore, present the reader first with a statement of the number of merchant vessels belonging to the British Empire, and then proceed to compare the strength of our "maritime resources" with that of France and the United States. After which, I propose giving an account of the number, tonnage, and crews of the vessels (foreign as well as British) that annually enter or quit the different ports of the kingdom. To this I shall subjoin a statement as to the countries whence they come and whither they go, so that we may understand the relative importance of our commercial transactions with various foreign countries—and, finally, I shall cite the gross yearly value of our imports and exports, in order that the public may form some idea as to the amount of property which is annually entrusted to the care of the Merchant Seamen of this country.

First, then, as to the number of vessels belonging to the British Empire. Subjoined is a statement distinguishing those belonging to the United Kingdom, from those appertaining to the Isles of Guernsey, Jersey, and Man, as well as the British plantations. This is done for a series of ten years, so that an estimate may be formed as to the rate at which our maritime commerce is annually increasing.

VESSELS BELONGING TO THE BRITISH EMPIRE.

Statement of the Number, Tonnage, and Crews of Vessels belonging to the British Empire during the undermentioned years:—

Date.	Vessels.	Tons.	Men.	Vessels.	Tons.	Men.	Vessels.	Tons.	Men.	Vessels.	Tons.	Men.
1839 ...	21,037	2,531,005	151,790	633	39,630	4,473	6,075	497,798	35,020	27,745	3,068,433	191,283
1840 ...	21,983	2,724,107	160,509	671	44,155	5,018	6,308	543,276	35,813	28,962	3,311,538	201,340
1841 ...	22,747	2,886,626	167,117	714	48,773	5,224	6,591	577,081	37,857	30,052	3,512,480	210,198
1842 ...	23,207	2,990,849	170,628	747	50,571	5,396	6,861	578,430	38,585	30,815	3,619,850	214,609
1843 ...	23,152	2,957,437	169,816	746	50,144	5,339	7,085	580,806	38,822	30,983	3,588,387	213,977
1844 ...	23,253	2,994,166	170,162	763	50,226	5,529	7,304	592,839	40,659	31,320	3,637,231	216,350
1845 ...	23,621	3,073,537	177,761	767	49,643	5,405	7,429	590,881	41,734	31,817	3,714,061	224,900
1846 ...	24,002	3,148,323	180,653	769	51,462	5,516	7,728	617,327	43,107	32,499	3,817,112	229,276
1847 ...	24,409	3,254,353	183,278	791	53,568	5,706	7,788	644,603	43,906	32,988	3,952,524	232,890
1848 ...	24,832	3,344,764	185,826	806	56,045	5,651	8,034	651,351	44,592	33,672	4,052,160	236,069

According to the above table, then, the increase in the vessels, tonnage, and crews belonging to the mercantile marine has, in the course of ten years, been as follows:—

INCREASE IN THE MARITIME RESOURCES OF THE UNITED
KINGDOM IN TEN YEARS.

Vessels 3,795
Tonnage 813,759
Men 34,036

INCREASE IN THE MARITIME RESOURCES OF THE BRITISH
ISLES IN TEN YEARS.

Vessels 173
Tonnage 16,415
Men 1,178

INCREASE IN THE MARITIME RESOURCES OF THE BRITISH
PLANTATIONS IN TEN YEARS.

Vessels 1,959
Tonnage 153,553
Men 9,572

INCREASE IN THE MARITIME RESOURCES OF THE BRITISH
EMPIRE IN TEN YEARS.

Vessels 5,927
Tonnage 983,727
Men 44,786

Hence we perceive that the merchant vessels of the British Empire increase at the rate (in round numbers) of 6,000 in 10 years, or 600 per annum; while the increase in the tonnage amounts to very nearly 1,000,000 in the same space of time, or 100,000 tons annually. Employment is thus found for 5,000 fresh hands every year. According to the rate of increase in the population of the kingdom, the mercantile marine ought to gain only 19,000 fresh hands in ten years; whereas it will be seen that the real increase in that time is very nearly 50,000. Hence, 30,000 individuals must, by the continual extension of our maritime commerce, be drafted from the overstocked handicrafts and manufactures of the country.

Let us now compare the increase of the vessels belonging to the British Empire with that of the French and American vessels. The following table will afford us the means of so doing:—

AN ACCOUNT OF THE TONNAGE AND NUMBER OF VESSELS BELONGING
TO THE PORTS OF THE BRITISH EMPIRE, THE PORTS OF FRANCE,
AND THE UNITED STATES, IN THE FOLLOWING YEARS.

Date.	Vessels.		Date.	Tons.		
	British Empire.	Ports of France.		British Empire.	Ports of France.	United States.
1828	24,095	14,447	1828	2,518,191	693,381	1,741,391
1829	23,453	14,952	1829	2,517,000	692,356	1,260,977
1830	23,721	14,852	1830	2,531,819	689,589	1,191,776
1831	24,242	15,031	1831	2,581,964	684,127	1,267,846
1832	24,435	15,224	1832	2,618,068	669,381	1,439,450
1833	24,385	15,025	1833	2,634,577	647,107	1,606,149
1834	25,055	..	1834	2,716,100	..	1,758,907
1835	25,511	..	1835	2,783,761	..	1,824,940
1836	25,820	15,249	1836	2,792,646	685,011	1,882,102
1837	26,037	15,326	1837	2,791,018	696,978	..

By referring to the above table, we shall see that the vessels belonging to the British Empire numbered, some few years ago, considerably above a third more than those belonging to France, whilst the
tonnage of the French vessels is less than one-fourth of that of the
shipping of the British Empire. On account of defective returns, we
cannot arrive at the number of vessels which belonged to the United
States in the above years, but it will be seen that their amount of tonnage was about a third less than that of the British ships, and nearly
three times as much as that of the vessels belonging to France.

Having shown the extent of our mercantile marine, it now remains for me to set forth the amount of foreign trade carried on by
its means between this and other countries. This I shall do first by exhibiting the number of vessels, British and foreign, that entered and
quitted the different ports of the United Kingdom:—

TABLE SHOWING THE NUMBER, TONNAGE, AND CREWS OF VESSELS (INCLUDING THEIR REPEATED VOYAGES), THAT ENTERED INWARDS AT THE SEVERAL PORTS OF THE UNITED KINGDOM, FROM AND TO FOREIGN PORTS, DURING EACH OF THE UNDERMENTIONED YEARS :—

Yrs.	British and Irish Vessels.			Foreign Vessels.			Total.		
	Vessels.	Tons.	Crews.	Vessels.	Tons.	Crews.	Vessels.	Tons.	Crews.
1839	17,635	3,101,650	170,339	10,326	1,331,365	79,550	27,961	4,433,015	249,889
1840	17,883	3,197,501	172,404	10,198	1,460,294	81,295	28,081	4,657,795	253,699
1841	18,525	3,361,211	178,696	9,527	1,291,165	73,634	28,052	4,652,376	252,330
1842	18,987	3,294,725	178,884	8,054	1,205,303	65,952	27,041	4,500,028	244,836
1843	19,500	3,545,346	191,326	8,541	1,301,950	69,791	28,041	4,847,296	261,117
1844	19,687	3,647,463	195,728	9,608	1,402,138	76,091	29,295	5,049,601	271,819
1845	21,001	4,310,639	225,688	11,651	1,735,079	91,787	32,652	6,045,718	317,475
1846	21,273	4,294,733	224,299	12,548	1,806,282	98,452	33,821	6,101,015	322,751
1847	24,017	4,942,094	252,808	14,789	2,253,939	118,326	38,806	7,196,033	371,134
1848	21,783	4,565,533	233,932	13,100	1,960,412	103,532	34,883	6,525,945	337,464

TABLE SHOWING THE NUMBER, TONNAGE, AND CREWS OF VESSELS (INCLUDING THEIR REPEATED VOYAGES), THAT CLEARED OUTWARDS AT THE SEVERAL PORTS OF THE UNITED KINGDOM, FROM AND TO FOREIGN PORTS, DURING EACH OF THE UNDERMENTIONED YEARS:—

Yrs.	British and Irish Vessels			Foreign Vessels			Total		
	Vessels.	Tons.	Crews.	Vessels.	Tons.	Crews.	Vessels.	Tons.	Crews.
1839	17,066	3,096,611	173,806	10,698	1,398,096	79,818	27,764	4,494,707	253,624
1840	17,633	3,292,984	181,580	10,440	1,488,838	81,672	28,073	4,781,872	263,252
1841	18,464	3,429,279	186,696	9,786	1,336,892	75,694	28,250	4,766,171	262,390
1842	18,785	3,375,270	186,816	8,375	1,252,176	68,493	27,160	4,627,446	255,309
1843	19,334	3,635,833	197,976	8,709	1,341,433	71,718	28,043	4,977,266	269,694
1844	19,788	3,852,822	212,924	9,816	1,444,346	77,109	29,604	5,297,168	290,033
1845	20,231	4,235,451	227,120	12,296	1,796,136	94,643	32,527	6,031,587	321,763
1846	21,079	4,393,415	233,562	13,323	1,921,156	103,201	34,402	6,314,571	336,763
1847	22,669	4,770,370	249,818	15,256	2,312,793	119,464	37,925	7,083,163	369,282
1848	21,177	4,724,027	244,971	13,645	2,056,654	106,822	34,822	6,780,681	351,793

The above table exhibits the following results:—

OUTWARDS (BRITISH VESSELS).
Increase in the number of British vessels in 10
years 4,111
Do.   tonnage of do.   do.   1,627,419
Do.   crews of   do.   do.   71,165

OUTWARDS (FOREIGN VESSELS).
Increase in the number of foreign vessels in 10
years 2,947
Do.   tonnage of do.   do.   658,558
Do.   crews of   do.   do.   27,004

INWARDS (BRITISH VESSELS).
Increase in the number of British vessels in 10
years 4,148
Do.   tonnage of do.   do.   1,463,883
Do.   crews of   do.   do.   63,533

INWARDS (FOREIGN VESSELS).
Increase in the number of foreign vessels in 10
years 2,774
Do.   tonnage of do.   do.   629,047
Do.   crews of   do.   do.   23,982

OUTWARDS (BOTH BRITISH AND FOREIGN).
Increase in the number of vessels in 10 years .. 7,058
Do.   tonnage of do.   do.   2,285,974
Do.   crews of   do.   do.   98,169

INWARDS (BOTH BRITISH AND FOREIGN).
Increase in the number of vessels in 10 years .. 6,422
Do.   tonnage of do.   do.   2,092,930
Do.   crews of   do.   do.   87,575

It appears, then, that from the year 1839 to 1849, the maritime commerce of this country has increased to the extent of upwards of 2,000,000 of tons, three-fourths of which has been confined to British vessels.

Such is the extent and rate of increase in the maritime commerce of the kingdom. In order, however, to complete the circle of our knowledge on the subject, it is necessary to set forth the particular countries with which this trade is carried on. This will be seen in the annexed statement:—

A RETURN OF THE SHIPPING EMPLOYED IN THE UNITED KINGDOM,
DISTINGUISHING THE TRADE WITH EACH COUNTRY, IN THE YEAR
1848.

INWARDS.

	British.		Foreign.	
	Ships.	Tons.	Ships.	Tons.
British North Colonies, America	2,279	886,696	—	—
Russia	2,274	488,156	288	77,148
France	3,848	461,998	4,127	350,987
Asia	708	341,675	12	4,726
Germany	1,593	314,991	1,257	130,148
United States, America	493	303,854	927	581,700
Holland	1,617	273,750	1,189	108,171
Prussia	1,343	201,590	671	129,855
British West Indies, America	704	199,589	—	—
Central and Southern States, America	557	169,006	33	7,927
Africa	575	168,869	10	1,974
Channel Islands	1,711	154,733	67	6,903
Belgium	817	113,080	651	93,442
Italian States	538	88,968	111	28,950
Portugal, Azores, &c.	754	77,424	89	8,397
Foreign West Indies, America	243	65,916	82	19,191
Turkey	272	54,242	3	1,088
Spain and Canaries	494	47,819	103	11,799
Denmark	260	29,720	1,966	146,589
Moldavia, &c.	171	26,402	33	6,871
Sweden	136	18,211	539	98,801
Whale Fisheries	55	15,476	1	113
Gibraltar	51	14,382	1	102
Mexico, America	28	14,346	1	150
Greece	88	13,520	9	2,731
Ionian Islands	83	10,874	—	—
Malta	53	7,785	2	315
Norway	34	1,979	928	142,334
Syria	4	482	—	—
Falkland Islands	—	—	—	—
Total	21,783	4,565,533	13,100	1,960,412

OUTWARDS.

	British.		Foreign.	
	Ships.	Tons.	Ships.	Tons.
British North Colonies, America	1,766	668,087	—	—
United States, America	942	523,444	890	573,938
France	3,316	445,541	3,863	332,133
Asia	780	398,129	23	10,779
Russia	1,661	348,222	255	56,040
Germany	1,491	308,775	1,211	116,614
British West Indies, America	798	237,258	—	—
Holland	1,369	219,759	967	77,700
Central and Southern States, America	694	215,413	106	25,909
Africa	619	187,263	84	17,042
Prussia	1,161	174,161	551	109,504
Italian States	817	156,449	216	50,532
Channel Islands	1,373	123,121	7	329
Denmark	794	117,630	2,793	245,806
Spain and Canaries	713	104,692	257	49,730
Belgium	570	83,653	551	77,572
Foreign West Indies, America	249	78,812	105	26,499
Turkey	348	77,090	58	16,382
Portugal, Azores, &c.	709	74,221	180	29,311
Malta	303	65,853	45	11,448
Gibraltar	170	30,163	18	3,796
Sweden	135	17,428	365	46,746
Whale Fisheries	49	13,292	—	—
Ionian Islands	74	11,614	2	555
Moldavia, &c.	68	9,717	1	255
Greece	58	9,708	6	1,519
Mexico, America	45	7,901	7	2,576
Norway	61	7,197	1,084	173,933
Syria	40	6,453	—	—
Falkland Islands	3	873	—	—
Total	21,177	4,724,027	13,645	2,056,654

In the above Tables the different countries stand in the order of the tonnage of British vessels trading with them. We shall find, on reference to them, that the greatest amount of trade, both export and import, is carried on with the British North American colonies.

The value of our foreign commerce has still to be set forth. By this we shall see not only the vast extent of the international trade carried on by this country, but the immense amount of property entrusted annually to the conveyance of the Merchant Seamen. It would, perhaps, hardly be credited that they are engaged in transporting to and from this country, every year, merchandise to the value of near upon *one hundred millions of pounds sterling.* A glance at the collective value of the exports and imports will, however, assure us of the fact.

TABLE SHOWING THE OFFICIAL AND DECLARED VALUES OF THE EXPORTS AND IMPORTS INTO GREAT BRITAIN FOR THE FOLLOWING YEARS :—

	EXPORTS				IMPORTS	
	British and Irish Produce and Manufactures from Great Britain		Foreign and Colonial Merchandise, from Great Britain		Into Great Britain	
	Official value. £	Declared val. £	Official value. £	Declared val. *£	Official value. £	Declared val. *£
1840	96,947,122	52,701,509	12,779,057	6,946,834	60,346,066	32,802,714
1841	102,263,512	50,896,556	13,765,618	6,841,370	65,873,411	32,785,200
1842	101,780,753	51,217,658	14,714,635	7,404,633	62,684,587	30,561,255
1843	99,911,012	47,012,651	13,577,000	6,388,593	63,589,080	29,921,053
1844	117,574,563	51,932,056	13,947,513	6,160,542	68,433,050	30,226,520
1845	131,338,347	58,316,315	14,387,518	6,388,439	73,547,788	32,656,311
1846	134,385,892	59,837,660	16,259,126	6,793,183	83,330,609	37,253,238
1847	132,041,651	57,545,985	16,291,204	7,099,982	73,057,696	31,839,779
1848	125,907,063	58,738,945	19,999,344	9,330,226	82,886,971	37,541,125
1849	132,617,681	52,849,445	18,360,026	7,316,122	89,253,156	35,568,181

* The rates by which the official value of the exports are estimated were fixed in 1696, so that they have long ceased to be any test of their real value, and are of use only as showing the fluctuations in the quantities exported. The real or declared value for foreign and colonial merchandise exported, as well as for the imports into Great Britain, is not given in the returns from which the above statement has been compiled. It has, however, been here calculated after the same ratio as the real or declared value of the British and Irish produce and manufactures from Great Britain bear towards their official value.

We shall find from the above table that there was a decrease in the British exports in 1842 and 1843; while in 1847 and 1848 the exports were again less than in the previous year. The foreign and colonial exports show a decrease in 1843, and again in 1849. The imports into Great Britain show a decrease in 1842 and again in 1847. The greatest amount of exports appears to be—for British and Irish produce, in 1846—for foreign and colonial merchandise, in 1848: while the imports into Great Britain were largest in 1849. The amount of increase in the last 10 years has been as follows:—

Increase in the value of British and Irish produce and manufactures from Great Britain	£147,936
Increase in the value of foreign and colonial merchandise from Great Britain	367,288
Total increase in the value of exports from Great Britain in 10 years	£517,224
Increase in the value of imports in Great Britain in 10 years	£2,765,467

Hence it will be seen that in the last ten years our exports have increased upwards of half a million, and our imports upwards of two millions and a half sterling in value.

It may then be safely asserted that the mercantile marine of the British Empire consists, in round numbers, of 34,000 vessels, of 4,000,000 tons burden, and manned by 240,000 seamen, who are annually engaged in transporting to and from this country merchandise to the value of upwards of seventy-five millions of pounds sterling.

The number and tonnage of the coasting vessels that entered and quitted the several ports of the United Kingdom in the year 1849 was as follows:—

ENTERED INWARDS.	
Vessels	133,275
Tons	11,967,473

CLEARED OUTWARDS.	
Vessels	149,160
Tons	12,915,584

I now come to that particular part of the merchant service *appertaining to the port of London.*

According to the census of 1841, the number of seamen in the metropolis was as follows:—

Merchant Seamen 7,002

Navy 1,092

8,094

This, I am informed, may be said to represent the number of seamen in London in the month of June of each year; in the spring and autumn, however, I am assured that the number of sailors in the metropolis is decreased nearly one-half.

The subjoined table will enable us to judge concerning the relative importance of the several ports of the United Kingdom. It will be seen that the port of London, for the extent of its commerce at least, ranks far above all the rest.

STATEMENT OF THE NUMBER AND TONNAGE OF VESSELS WHICH ENTERED THE UNDERMENTIONED PORTS IN THE FOLLOWING YEARS :—

Ports.	1847.			
	British.		Foreign.	
	Ships.	Tons.	Ships.	Tons.
London	6,271	1,436,986	3,132	494,791
Liverpool	2,841	953,760	1,366	541,701
Bristol	405	96,618	46	7,928
Hull	1,119	281,302	1,357	174,548
Newcastle	1,826	291,161	1,617	181,778
Plymouth	437	50,869	71	10,976
Leith	369	58,078	626	54,244
Glasgow	362	75,524	153	27,616
Greenock	310	99,557	11	3,093
Cork	452	74,456	252	45,338
Belfast	279	55,919	191	45,237
Dublin	359	67,125	134	28,321

Hence it appears that the port of London ranks the most important of all: Liverpool stands next; then comes Newcastle; after this Hull, and so on.

The number of vessels (British and Foreign), and their tonnage, which have entered the Port of London annually since 1841 are as follows:—

	Ships.	Tons.
In 1841	6,641	1,306,867
1842	6,407	1,283,921
1843	6,222	1,317,671
1844	6,885	1,361,809
1845	7,562	1,502,491
1846	7,711	1,529,177
1847	9,403	1,931,777

The increase in the number of British and Foreign ships entering the port of London has been 2,762 in seven years, and the increased amount of tonnage during that time 624,910. The total number of vessels which entered the several ports of the United Kingdom in the year 1847 was nearly 39,000, and the gross tonnage upwards of 7,000,000. Hence it appears that *one-fourth of the entire maritime commerce of this country is carried on at the port of London.*

The countries with which the foreign trade of the port of London is conducted are particularized in the table below:—

STATEMENT OF THE NUMBER AND TONNAGE OF VESSELS WHICH
ENTERED THE PORT OF LONDON WITH CARGOES FROM FOREIGN
PORTS, DISTINGUISHING THE COUNTRIES WHENCE THEY ARRIVED.

	1847.			
	British.		Foreign.	
	Ships.	Tons.	Ships.	Tons.
Russia	719	155,752	314	55,961
Sweden	11	1,103	197	49,498
Norway	3	240	164	47,462
Denmark	40	6,518	587	39,938
Prussia	231	32,066	362	70,844
German States	193	51,817	324	22,600
Netherlands	..	..	..	..
France	693	88,880	325	23,089
Portugal, Azores, and Madeira ..	350	36,095	13	1,761
Spain and Canaries	245	24,471	50	5,120
Italian States	127	16,902	45	11,239
Ionian Islands	32	4,136	..	
Moldavia and Wallachia	18	2,716	26	5,186
Turkey and Continental Greece .	136	2,294	10	2,805
Morea and Greek Islands	..	..	..	..
Egypt	106	28,652	15	3,330
Tripoli, Barbary, Tunis, Algeria, and Morocco	12	1,579	..	..
Foreign Possessions in Africa ...	4	777	2	756
„ „ Asia	33	12,122	3	1,557
China	62	28,347	..	..
America, United States of	84	31,322	180	92,248
„ Central and Southern States	188	50,223	11	2,637
Holland	588	116,159	286	21,720
Foreign West Indies	127	34,054	44	9,259
Foreign Continental Colonies in America	..	..	..	..
Belgium	223	42,467	133	20,787
Whale Fisheries	16	5,306	..	..
Total	4,241	793,698	3,091	487,797

There appears (according to the above table) to have been a larger number of ships from Russia in 1847, than from any other country. The next largest number came from France—and after that the
greatest amount of trade was done with Holland.

To this must be appended a statement of the number of vessels
arriving in the Port of London from the colonies and dependencies
of England:—

STATEMENT OF THE NUMBER AND TONNAGE OF VES-
SELS WHICH ENTERED THE PORT OF LONDON WITH
CARGOES, FROM THE COLONIES AND DEPENDEN-
CIES OF ENGLAND.

Colonies.	1847.	
	Vessels.	Tons.
Gibraltar	9	818
Malta	34	6,488
British Possessions in Africa	214	58,072
„ „ Asia	439	210,125
„ N. American Colonies	470	208,541
„ West Indies	369	111,340
Channel Islands	503	52,077
Total	2,048	647,461

By the above table it will be seen that the greatest amount of tonnage from the colonies and dependencies of England has come from British possessions in Asia and British North-American colonies, while the greater number of vessels has been from the Channel Islands.

The number of coasting vessels (including colliers and Irish traders) was, in 1847, no less than 21,926, and their tonnage 3,118,360; so that the vessels employed in the coasting trade, and entering the Port of London, are more than twice as many, and their tonnage nearly three times as great, as those in the foreign trade.

Let me now state as briefly as possible the *present state of the law respecting sailors:*—

The reckless and improvident character of sailors, and the peculiar nature of their service, coupled with a consideration of their vast importance to our national welfare, have long induced both the Legislature and Courts of Justice to treat them differently from other labourers, to dictate the form of their contracts, and to construe those contracts in a peculiar manner. So long ago as the reign of George II., an act was passed requiring that seamen's articles should be in writing, and should contain particulars of the voyage and of the amount of wages. From that time down to the reign of William IV., many other acts were passed for the further regulation of articles, and for preventing seamen from deserting, or from being abandoned abroad. During this period Lord Stowell may be said to have laid the foundation of the present law by his many admirable decisions on the subjects of wages and discipline. He first invaded the old principle, that freight is the mother of wages; he used to consider these "favourites of the law," as he termed them—the sailors—like persons of weak minds, incapable of binding themselves by stipulations which they ought not to have been asked to make. Some of the rules he laid down were found fault with by the Common-law Courts, but they have since been virtually adopted by the Legislature. In 1835 an act was passed, by which all the previous acts were repealed and consolidated, forming in fact a code for merchant seamen. The principal features were—the establishment of a registration of seamen—the regulation of articles, not only by requiring the insertion of an accurate statement of the wages, the voyage, and the scale of provisions, but by forbidding certain inequitable stipulations, and compelling the use of certain given forms, which it was supposed would render evasion impossible—the infliction of forfeiture of wages and other penalties, for desertion and misconduct—the affording means for recovering wages by summary proceedings before a justice—stringent regulations to prevent men from being abandoned abroad—provisions for compelling all ships to be provided with medicines, and large ships with surgeons—regulations for binding apprentices—and provisions for obtaining full returns of all casualties happening on the voyage. This act was repealed in 1844, by 7 and 8 Victoria, 112 (the act now in force), which re-enacts in substance the important provisions of the former act, with additional means for effecting them. It also provides for a more complete registration, by requiring all seamen to be provided with register tickets, which are numbered in succession, and which must be delivered to the captain on signing articles, and retained by him till discharge. It further requires all ships bound on long voyages to be provided with lime juice and other vegetable acids, which have proved so efficacious in the navy for preventing scurvy. These acts, it will be observed, did not touch the crimping system; and in 1845 an attempt was made to check the evil by an act (8 and 9 Vict., 116), which requires crimps to obtain licenses from the Board of Trade, and makes penal certain of their habitual mal-practices, *e. g.*, detention of the sailor's effects, and boarding ships on their arrival in port for the purpose of soliciting sailors to come to their houses. This act, however, has proved utterly ineffectual, partly from the want of machinery to enforce it, and partly from the extremely low character of the crimp. In the meantime, at Liverpool, a successful effort has been made to establish an office where sailors may hear of ships, and where captains may find crews—in which each man is registered, with the character he has borne on previous service—and where, at the commencement of the engagement, the agreement is signed, and at its termination the crew is discharged and paid off. The superintendent stands by, and is frequently able to settle misunderstandings which would otherwise cause litigation. A savings bank is connected with the office, and efforts have been made, with considerable advantage to the seamen, to induce them to deposit a part of their wages when paid, instead of squandering them in vice and dissipation.

The Mercantile Marine Bill now before the House of Commons provides an office in every seaport, in which hands may be engaged and discharged, in the same way as by the establishment of the Coalwhippers' office. The act proposes to give to the superintendent, among other things, power to recover the wages of deceased seamen, and to pay them over to their families, without the tedious and expensive process of procuring letters of administration. The bill also contains means for enforcing sanitary regulations on board. Additional means are provided for enforcing discipline. Another feature in the measure is the requiring all future masters and mates to pass examinations, and the giving powers to cashier those who are convicted of incompetence, drunkenness, or tyranny. There are, however, no express provisions for the education of officers or men.

I have thus cited the principal provisions of the bill now before Parliament. It is my object at present to inquire into the state of the merchant seamen, with the view of ascertaining, among other matters, the opinions of the men mainly interested, as to the necessity for, or the benefits likely to accrue from, the proposed measure. I shall restrict myself merely to the collecting of evidence. It will be for the public to draw their conclusions from the facts I may bring forward.

I purpose directing my attention in this and the following letters, first, to the state of the *seaman afloat*—after which I purpose following him *ashore*, and describing the impositions which are there practised upon him. The Merchant Service afloat is divisible into the *foreign* and *coasting* trade. The foreign trade, again, has many distinct branches, such as the East India and China trade—the Baltic—the Mediterranean—the Greenland—the South Sea—the United States—the British North American—the Australian—the African—and other trades. In the present letter I have space only for an exposition of the state of the seaman on board the Australian ships. Upon this subject a man who was much more than bronzed—as he was actually red in the face and neck—gave me the following statement. He had free and jovial manners, but sometimes evinced much feeling, especially when speaking of the emigrant ships. He wore three shirts—a clean one over two which were not perfectly clean—for he could not bear, he said, to show dirty linen. This happened only, however, he told me, when he was "out on the spree," for then he was in the habit of buying a clean white shirt as soon as he wanted "a change," and putting it on over his soiled one, in order to obviate the necessity of carrying his dirty linen about with him; so that by the stratification of his shirts he could always compute the duration of "the lark." He wore only a jacket, and felt inconvenience, when on the spree, in having a dirty shirt to carry about; and to obviate this he adopted the plan I have mentioned:—

"I was *boatswain of an emigrant ship* last voyage. They were Government emigrants we had on board. The ship was 380 tons according to the new mode of measurement, and 500 tons according to the old mode. She had eight able men before the mast, four apprentices, a second mate, steward, cook, first mate, and captain. In addition to these, there were eight supernumeraries. You see, sir, all the Government emigrant and convict ships are obliged to take out four men and a boy to each 100 tons. We were near upon 400 tons burden; so we were obligated to have 16 able seamen and four boys; but, as I told you before, we had only eight able seamen. To make up the deficiency, we shipped eight supernumeraries. These supernumeraries were no sailors at all—not able to go aloft—couldn't put their foot above the shearpole. They were mostly men that the Government had refused to assist to emigrate. The shipping masters had put them on blue jackets, and told them the names of ships to say they had served in, so as to get them a berth. The shipping masters will get them a register, ticket and all; and these are the men who are taken in preference to us, because they go upon nominal wages of a shilling a month. I tell you what it is, sir. I saw to-day half a dozen of these fellows taken instead of six good able-bodied seamen, who were left to walk the streets: that's the candid fact, sir. It's a shameful thing to see the way we are treated. We are not treated like men at all; and what's more, there's no dependence to be placed on us now. If a war was to break out with America, there's thousands of us would go over to the other country. We're worse than the black slaves; they are taken care of, and we are not. On board ship they can do anything with us they think proper. If in case you are a spirited man, and speaks a word against an officer that tyrannicalises over you, he will put you in irons, and stop your money—six days for one: for every day you're in irons he stops six days' pay, and may be forfeits your whole wages. There's as good men now before the mast as there is abaft of it. It ain't the same now as it used to be. Our fathers and mothers, you see, gives us all a little education, and we're now able to see and feel the wrongs that are put upon us; and if in case people doesn't do better for us than they do now, why, they'll turn pirates. The navy is just as much dissatisfied as the merchant seamen. If a war was to come with France, we might turn out against them—for we owe them a grudge for old times past. For myself, I can't abear the hair of a Frenchman's head. It would never do not to stand by the little island again the Mounseers; but, again America, I'd never fire a shot! They have got feeling for a seaman there. There's no people running after you there to rob you. The pay's a great deal better, too, and the food twice as good as in the English ships. There's no stint of anything; but in this country they do everything they can to rob a seaman. They're cutting our allowance of bread down from one pound to three-quarters, and our sugar is reduced from one pound to three-quarters as well; and they're trying to cut down our wages to 35s. a month besides. But what's it matter what they give us? They can trump up any charge they please again us, or they can tyrannicalize over us till a man's blood can't stand it, and then can stop as much as they like, and we can't say nothing again it. I was out thirteen months and a half. I went away last Christmas-eve twelvemonth, and I arrived in London the 8th of February last; and what do you think I got, sir, for the whole of my service—for risking my life, for working all hours, in all weathers—what do you think I got, sir? Why, I had £10 2s.—that's it, sir—for thirteen months and a half. I ought to have received about £32. My wages as boatswain were £2 10s. a month. I have had £4 and £3 10s. for the same duty. But the little petty owners is cutting down the wages as low as they can, till they're almost starving us and our families. The rest of the money that was due to me was stopped, because I spoke out for my rights; and five of the other hands was served in the same manner. The owners saved near upon a hundred pounds in this way; and, what's more, they were not satisfied with this. The owners (I give you my word) stopped one pound more out of the little that was coming to us, for a charitable institution as they called it. What it was I don't know. The petty owners take every advantage on us they can. They can build their new ships—one or two every year—and they gets them all out of fleecing us. I tell you what it is—such men will be the ruin of the country, sir; for the tars that kept the little island in old times is now discontented to a man. The reason why the owners stopped our pay was because we spoke out when the ship was short of hands. There was only four able men in her, and there should have been eight; so we had to do double work all of us, night and day. We complained to the captain that the ship was short-handed. But, you see, the wages for able seamen is more in foreign countries than in England; so, to keep the ship's expenses down, the captains object to take on fresh hands in foreign ports. Well, the captain promised us to get some new men at Sydney, but he went to sea short-handed as we were. So we axed him again to get fresh hands, as the ship was leaky, and we wanted our full complement of men; but he refused to do so, because the wages at the next port was nearly double the pay in London; and then we told him we wouldn't do any more work. This he called a mutiny, and our wages was stopped to near upon £20 a man. The usual rate of pay in an emigrant ship for an able seaman is £2 a month. The tonnage varies from 200 to 1,000. Ships of 200 are not safe to go as far as Sydney or New Zealand; but that the owners don't trouble their heads about, so long as they can get their ship full of emigrants. The greater number of emigrant ships are about 500 tons. To understand how many emigrants can be comfortably accommodated in a ship, I should first tell you that in the best ships the emigrants are divided—that is, the single people are separated from the married; the single men are for'ard, the married people are 'midships, and the single women aft. In a vessel of such an arrangement not more than sixty emigrants to every 100 tons can be taken out with comfort. I have known near upon 100 emigrants taken out to each 100 tons— that is to say, I have known a ship of 380 tons have as many as 380 emigrants on board. (A carpenter, who had made his two last voyages in emigrant ships, here said 'That is too often the case, I am sorry to say.') A ship of 380 tons could take conveniently about 240 or 250 emigrants." The carpenter corroborated this, and told me that it is his duty to go down between decks each day, to open the scuttles and ports, so as to ventilate the ship, and he has frequently seen a man and his wife and three or four children all huddled up and almost stifled in a double berth (only a berth for two people). The death of some child has occurred almost every day in the ship. In bad weather, when the hatches are kept on and tarpaulined over, often for two or three days at a time, the heat between the decks of an emigrant ship is as bad as the hold of a slave ship in the middle passage. The usual allowance in an emigrant ship of the best class is six foot by two foot. But "I have often seen," the carpenter said, "the poor people, in some of the worst ships, stowed away for'ard so close that you might have said they were 'in bulk.' There were thirty people in thirty feet space. I know, as a carpenter, that many of the emigrant ships are not fit to bring home a cargo; though, as the owners say, they are quite fit to take emigrants out. I have seen right through the top sides (the timbers above the copper-sheating) of many of them—the planks have warped with the heat of the sun. A man has often to carry an emigrant ship in his arms, from one port to another, for the hands are always at the pumps. It may astonish the public that so many emigrants are lost, but we ships'-carpenters are only astonished that there are so few." The boatswain here continued:—"The carpenter has told you nothing but the truth. In the worst class ships there is scarcely any separation of the sexes. A partition is certainly run up between the sleeping-berths; but as these do not reach the top, any one can make it convenient to get over, or look over, the partition into the next berth. There is scarcely a young single woman who emigrates that keeps her character on board o' ship, and after that she mostly makes her appearance on the town in Sydney. I'm speaking of those who go out unprotected; and what else can be expected, sir, among a parcel of sailors? The captains and doctors often set the example, and the mates and the sailors, of course, imitate their superior officers. There has been no chaplain on board the emigrant ships that I have been in. Some captains read prayers once on a Sunday, but many don't; and I have often known a ship go right away from London to Sydney, without divine service ever being performed. The Government emigrants, I believe, usually pay about £7 per head, and those who are not sent out by the Government pay from £18 to £20 for the passage. For this sum they are found in provisions. There is a certain scale of provisions allowed; but this is almost nominal, for the greater number of emigrant ships carry false weights, and the allowance served out is generally short, by at least a quarter." (I could hardly credit that the spirit of commercial trickery had reached even the high seas, and that shipowners had taken to false weights as a means of enabling them to undersell their brother merchants. On inquiring, however, I was assured that the practice was becoming *common*.) "Again, the quality of the food is of the worst kind. There are regular Government surveyors to overhaul the provisions of such ships; but, Lord love you! they are easily got to windward of. The captain, under the directions of the owners, puts some prime stuff among the top casks, and all the rest is old condemned stores—rotten beef and pork, that's positively green with putrefaction—and the biscuits are all weevilly; indeed they're so full of maggots, that the sailors say they're as rich as Welsh rabbits, when toasted. The poor things who emigrate have no money to lay in their own private stock of food, and so they're wholly dependent on the ship's stores; and often they run so short that they're half-starved, and will come and beg a mouthful of the sailors. They're not allowed above one-third of what the sailors have. *We* have one pound and a half of meat, and they don't get above half a pound, and that's several ounces short from false weights. They have three quarts of water served out to them every day, and that very often of the filthiest description. It's frequently rotten and stinking; but, bad as it is, it's not enough for the poor people to cook with, and make their tea and coffee morning and evening. I have seen plenty of the emigrants hard put to with thirst—they would give anything for a drop to wet their lips with. From all I have seen of the emigrant ships, I believe it's a system of robbery from beginning to end. There are gentlemen shipowners who treat their men and the passengers justly and fairly. These are mostly the owners of the largest ships; but of late years a class of petty owners has sprung up—people who were clerks of the large owners a few years back—and they take every opportunity of tricking all in their pay. These men, I say again, will be the ruin of the country, unless something is done to protect the sailors against them. They're driving the tars out of the country as fast as they can. Convicts, when taken out, are very well treated; *the owners are obliged to take care of them;* there's a captain of marines to look after them, and it's quite wonderful how differently they fare to the poor emigrants. I never knew the convicts to be badly treated on board of ship, but I've known the emigrants to be so continually. You see the emigrants are poor people, and have no one to look after them."

The Morning Chronicle, Thursday, March 7, 1850.

We have to acknowledge the receipt of 2*l.* for the general fund from Captain S. (per W. N).

———

Mrs. W. H. has forwarded us a sovereign for the poor painter whose case appears in *The Morning Chronicle* of February 14.

———

B. T. has sent 5s. for the composition doll-maker mentioned in Thursday's paper (February 28), who had one child in its coffin.

———

THE SPITALFIELDS WEAVERS.—Last night, at eight o'clock, a numerous meeting of the broad silk handloom weavers of Spitalfields, Bethnal-green, and the vicinity, was held at the Trinity Chapel, Morpeth-street, Globe-fields, for the purpose of receiving the report of the committee appointed that day week to wait on the manufacturers for an advance of wages. Mr. Hackman in the chair. It appears that the exertions of the committee have in a measure been attended with success. A deputation waited on Mr. Slimm, who agreed to raise the wages in satin from 3½d. to 5d. a yard. That house has now fifty harnesses of silk ready, for which they would be glad to have weavers. Mr. Thorpe, Mr. Graham, and Mr. Le Mare had also raised the wages on some silks; other manufacturers expressed a similar desire, and stated that it entirely depended upon the weavers themselves to obtain an increase of wages. The firm of Messrs. Bullock had raised the wages on velvets 3d. a yard, and said that they would increase the amount to 6d., if necessary. Those manufacturers only have been waited upon who have paid the lowest wages.

LABOUR AND THE POOR.

———◆———

THE METROPOLITAN DISTRICTS.

[FROM OUR SPECIAL CORRESPONDENT.]

LETTER XLI.

Concerning the probable amount of *capital* employed in the shipping of the British Empire, Mr. G. F. Young stated in his evidence before the select committee on the Navigation-laws, in 1847, that the number of ships then engaged in the trade of the empire was 32,499, having an aggregate tonnage of 3,817,112 tons. The average value of the tonnage of the empire, he said, might be fairly rated at £10, which would give the sum of £38,171,120 for the collective value. In addition to this sum, he continued, there is "the amount of capital embarked in the several trades connected with and dependent on the building and equipment of ships (including shipbuilders, shipwrights, shipping rope-makers, sailmakers, mast and block makers, and a proportion of coopers, ship-joiners, ship-sawyers, ship-painters, riggers, ship-chandlers, ship-blacksmiths, ship-coppersmiths, ship-brassworkers, and ship plumbers and glaziers). This amounts, in my judgment, to £16,083,807, which, added to the value of the ships themselves, gives a total capital of £54,254,927. The number of ships built in the course of the year is 1,525. The aggregate burden of the new vessels is 228,764 tons, and the average cost of building about £13 10s. per ton, which makes the gross outlay £3,088,314. I estimate the amount annually expended," he adds, "in the repairs and outfits of vessels employed, at £7,634,224, making the aggregate of annual expenditure for building and repairing £10,722,538." The number of seamen employed in the mercantile service he reckons at 229,276, and the amount of wages annually paid to the officers and seamen navigating the British ships, at £5,731,900. The expense of victualling this vast body he computes at £3,486,906, making an aggregate for wages and victualling of £9,218,806. The number of workmen and artisans employed in the various trades which are exclusively connected with the construction and equipment of the British ships engaged in the commerce of this country, and the proportion of those artisans and workmen who belong to trades that are mixed up with the others, Mr. Young reckons at 79,617 individuals, earning altogether £4,968,104 per annum. The amount of freight annually earned by the commercial marine of this country he believes to be about £28,628,290.

Recapitulating then, the details of the above estimate, we have the following statement in round numbers:—

Value of 32,500 ships—of nearly 4,000,000 tons burden—engaged in the mercantile marine of the British Empire, at 10*l.* per ton	£38,250,000
Amount of capital embarked in the several trades connected with and dependent on the building and equipment of ships	16,000,000
Gross amount of capital embarked, directly and indirectly, in the navigation of this country	£54,250,000
Amount annually expended in the building, repairing, and outfitting of new and old ships	£10,500,000
Cost of wages and provisions for seamen employed in navigating these ships	9,500,000
Wages paid to workmen employed in the various trades connected with ships	5,000,000
	£25,000,000
Amount annually received for freight	£28,500,000
Adding to the 25,000,000*l.* which is above given as the annual expense of outfits, wages, and victualling, 1,250,000*l.* for the cost of pilotage, lights, port charges, insurance, and depreciation, we have for the gross annual expenditure for the mercantile marine of the British Empire	26,250,000
Deducting the gross annual expenditure from the annual income for freight, this leaves for the net profit per annum	2,250,000

Hence, according to Mr. Young, the gross capital employed in the mercantile marine of this country is upwards of £54,000,000; the annual expenditure, £26,000,000 and odd; the annual receipts, £28,000,000 and odd; and the annual profit, £2,000,000 and odd.

In my last letter I pointed out that nearly one-fourth of the entire foreign commerce of the country is carried on at the port of London.

We may assume, therefore, if Mr. Young's estimate is to be trusted, that the gross capital embarked in the mercantile marine belonging to London amounts to about £13,000,000; that the gross annual cost of outfitting, repairing, victualling, and navigating the vessels to and from this port comes to £6,000,000 per annum, and that the sum annually paid for freight hither and hence amounts to £7,000,000, thus leaving a profit of £1,000,000 per annum for the owners.

The principal trades among the merchant vessels sailing from the port of London are—1. *The East India and China trade.* The vessels belonging to this trade are the finest of all the merchant vessels. They are mostly reckoned first-class vessels at Lloyd's. The burden of them is generally from 600 up to 1,000 tons. Some, however, range as low as 350 tons. A thousand-ton ship will usually rate 20 men before the mast, and her crew altogether run to 35 hands. In the Company's time the same ships took double the number of hands that they do now. The wages of able seamen in this trade are £2 per month. The larger class of vessels are discharged in the East India Docks, and the 400 tons are discharged either at the London Docks or St. Katharine's. In the East India and China trade the ships are better equipped, the stores being much superior. The consequence is there is less desertion from the East India service than any other. The wages in this trade are the lowest of any, and the men, perhaps, the best conducted. This is due to the length of the voyage, for sailors mostly prefer long to short voyages, because the ships are larger and the provisions better, so that there is more comfort in general. Hence the vessels making short voyages are obliged to pay higher wages. The East Indiamen sail at all times of the year, but most in the spring and summer months. On returning, they usually remain in dock about two months before sailing again. The usual cargo home is tea, silks, rice, sugar, coffee, and spices. 2. *The Australian trade.* The vessels belonging to this trade are not such fine vessels as the regular East Indiamen. They are not built as passenger ships, nor fitted up in the same elegant manner. They consist of two classes, viz., traders and emigrant ships. The traders are those that go only for cargo; these vary from 300 up to 600 tons burden; whereas the emigrant vessels run from 500 up to 800 tons. Some few are larger, but this is the usual run. The complement of men for the emigrant ships (as regulated by Government) is four men and a boy for every 100 tons. The number of men on board those that go for cargo is usually fifteen, including apprentices, mates, captain, and all. The rate of wages for the able seamen is £2. The Australian vessels are generally considered to be not so well provisioned as the larger ships. They sail mostly in the spring and summer. The cargo brought home is wool, copper ore, and cotton. The cargo out consists of cutlery, machinery, agricultural implements, and Manchester goods. 3. *The West India trade* is carried on by vessels of from 300 to 500 tons burden. There are but few passengers taken from the port of London; such parties go mostly from Southampton in the mail packets. The crew usually consists of from nine to fifteen hands. The wages are £2 5s. for able seamen, and the usual time of sailing is about the spring of the year, so as to be in time for the sugar crops. They generally make two voyages, and occasionally three, in the year. The cargo out consists chiefly of coals in casks; these casks being afterwards used to bring back the sugar, which constitutes the chief portion of the home cargo. Molasses, rum, and coffee are also brought by the West India vessels. 4. *The Honduras trade* is solely for mahogany. The vessels generally run large, from 600 to 800 tons, and carry a crew of twenty-six hands (including apprentices). The rate of wages is £2 10s. for able seamen. The vessels sail about August or September, and occasionally in the spring of the year. They mostly go out in ballast. 5. *The Baltic and North American trades* are similar, both in the character and tonnage of their ships (if anything, the Baltic vessels are smaller). The time of sailing and rate of wages is the same in both trades, varying from £2 10s. to £2 15s., according to the time of the year. The higher wages are given in the spring, when men are scarce. The North American ships average from 400 to 1,000 tons burden (there are some as high as 1,100 tons), and the crews from eighteen to forty hands, "all told." The Baltic vessels are 300 to 500 tons, and carry from fourteen to twenty hands, apprentices and all. The time of sailing for both descriptions of vessels is the beginning of April, and they mostly start again, in the month of September, on another voyage. They go out in ballast, and bring home timber. The Baltic ships bring corn, tallow, flax, and hemp as well. 6. *The South American traders* are generally large ships, averaging from 500 to 800 tons, and carrying from twenty to thirty men, all told. The rate of wages is £2 a month. They sail at all times of the year, taking out cargoes of iron and general merchandise, and bringing home hides, skins, tallow, horns, hoofs, bones, and guano. 7. *The Brazilian traders* bring home sugar, coffee, spices, rice, &c. They usually average from 300 to 500 tons, and are worked by fifteen to twenty hands. The wages are £2 5s. a month. 8. *The Hudson Bay traders* are a very small class; four only are known as sailing from the port of London. These are from 350 to 500 ton ships, and carry from twenty to twenty-five hands. The Hudson's Bay Company generally man their ships better than others; the pay is from £2 10s. to £3 a month—the wages being high because the work is hard, and the men being mostly picked hands. They generally leave in the spring and autumn; the cargo out is mostly stores for the settlements; the cargo home is exclusively furs. 9. *The United States vessels* are many of them passenger-ships, especially those bound to New York. The general tonnage is from 500 to 800, and the crew averages from 20 to 30 hands, all told: they sail at all times of the year, but the spring and the summer are the busy seasons. Wages are £2 5s. a month. The cargo out consists of Manchester goods and wearing apparel; and that home of cotton, corn, sugars, rice, tobacco, flour, and provisions. 10. *The Mediterranean trade* is carried on by small vessels of from 300 to 500 tons burden, and worked by 15 or 20 hands. The rate of pay is £2 5s. a month. The cargo out is mostly coals and iron; and that home consists chiefly of corn, wine, fruits (green and dried), spices, and salad oil. 11. *The Portuguese and Spanish trade* is carried on in vessels of from 200 to 400 tons, worked by from nine to fifteen hands. They carry out passengers sometimes, and general merchandise. The rate of pay is £2 5s. a month. The cargoes home are wine and fruits. 12. *The African trade* is carried on in vessels of from 150 to 300 tons, with from seven to thirteen hands. They generally take out iron, and frequently passengers, to the Gambia, Sierra Leone, and Cape Coast Castle. The cargoes back are ivory, gold-dust, palm oil, and cocoa nuts. 13. *The Cape of Good Hope and Algoa Bay ships* are of another class, but about the same tonnage, and with the same hands as the vessels in the African trade. The wages are from £2 to £2 5s. They go out with merchandise and passengers, and return with wine from the Cape. 14. *The Whale Fishery* is now carried on in the South Seas and in Greenland. The vessels are from 400 to 600 tons, with 20 to 25 hands. The men have each £5 advanced to them, but they have no regular wages; they go "on the lay;" that is, they are paid according to the fish caught and the sum realised by the oil.

The hands for all the above vessels are supplied by the shipping-masters, who are licensed. The men call at the shipping-master's office, and are sent thence to the ship for the approval of the captain. If approved, the shipping-master tells them the day and hour of signing the ship's articles. The shipping-master, before the vessel sails, must make out the articles (agreement between master and crew), and return the names of all the crew, which list is deposited at the Seamen's Register-office. He also makes out the advance notes. There are sixteen licensed shipping-masters in London.

The process observed on a foreign vessel *entering the Port of London* is this:—Off Gravesend she makes a signal—a light if after dusk—and as the Custom-house officers stationed there are always on the watch, she is immediately boarded. At Gravesend some of the dock companies have agents, who make arrangements for carrying the vessel into the docks. Lloyd's also have their agents at Gravesend to note the arrival of each vessel. The Custom-house likewise sends reports to Lloyd's. When the officer has boarded a foreign vessel she proceeds to her station in any dock, or if she is to be moored in the river, to any station assigned to her by the harbour-master, such assignment being also made off Gravesend. The harbour-master's business, however, relates almost entirely to coasting vessels, which are not taken possession of by a Custom-house officer. The payments which have to be made by foreign and coasting vessels are the light dues and the river dues, which are levied according to the tonnage of the vessel and the course she has pursued, and which branch into a variety of divisions and sub-divisions. The pilotage of the vessels up the Thames is a subject which can here only be cursorily alluded to. When the Custom-house officer boards a vessel at Gravesend, it is usual for the master to leave her, and proceed at once to London, to report the vessel at the Custom-house. This is styled *"entering inwards,"* and on the following morning the arrival of the vessel, the number of her crew, and the nature and extent of her cargo, the names of the master and the agent, and the parties to whom goods may be assigned, are printed in the daily reports of the Customs, for the information of all interested in the matter.

I shall now proceed to give the reader a description of each of the different trades above described. I had the following narrative concerning the *South American trade* from a sedate and intelligent man, who had all his "papers" with him, his watch, and was well-dressed, and with every appearance of what is called a "substantial" man. Previous to the voyage from South America, he had served on board Australian emigrant ships, and fully confirmed what was told me by others, as to the practice of giving short weight on board many of those ships, and as to the conduct of some of the captains, surgeons, and officers towards the unprotected female emigrants. I have, however, been at considerable pains to inquire into the truth of the statement given in my last letter. This I have thought it just to do, in consequence of a communication, received from a shipowner, denying the whole narrative. The result of my inquiries is, that I find the boatswain's account borne out most fully by persons of the highest respectability and the greatest experience. I have made a point of seeing one of the mates whose duty it is to serve out the provisions, both to the emigrants and crew. I am assured that the meat is often one-third short weight, and that the men are sometimes excited to acts of insubordination on purpose that a part of their wages may be stopped:—

"I have been a seaman eighteen years," he said, "and my last voyage was to Port Phillip and Callao. I served on board a barque of 642 tons on the voyage from Port Phillip. I reached that place in another ship, and there I shipped for Callao. We had twelve able seamen before the mast, two ordinary seamen, steward, cook, first and second mates, carpenter, boatswain, and master. By rights, I consider that we ought to have had two more able seamen, but for all that she was better manned than ships usually are. They do leave the port of London so short-handed, that many accidents, and great loss of life rise from it. You see, a seaman doesn't know how many hands are to be shipped until he comes to sign the articles, and it's too late to say anything again it then. So they oft enough ship cheap foreign fellows at any foreign port, and a good man has to bear everything. That sort of thing, I can tell you, and from my own knowledge, gets worse and worse. They'll often try to knock off a good man to save his wages, or, to spite him, put him to jobs that they think he'll refuse; and they put him to them just to make him refuse, and so save the owners' money, and get favour with them. We are so treated that we are all dissatisfied; we talk of it on board ship. Plenty say that if a war broke out they would not fight for such a country as this; far more say they would rather fight against this country in an American ship than against America in an English or any ship. I fought for the country at St. Jean d'Acre, under the Hon. Captain Waldegrave, and I would fight for it again, bad as it is, but there's ten to one the other way. I have had many a dispute about it on board ship, and have been many a time abused by the hour together by my shipmates for saying I was willing to fight for the country. In my last voyage from Port Phillip to Callao, and then to London, I had £3 10s. a month as able seaman. I consider that I ought to have had £4 for going round the Horn on a homeward voyage only. From London to Callao and back £3 a month would be fair. In my last voyage we had very good provisions, and a fair proportion of them. In my voyage out the provisions were very bad. We had, last voyage, neither false weight, nor any imposition of that sort, but I know that such things are common. They do so try to cheat the seamen that way, that it oft causes great disturbances. We had a good captain, but a strict man in regard of duty. He had worked his way from the 'hawse-pipes aft,' and knew every branch. He was a seaman, every inch of him. But I have met with many an officer not fit to be trusted with either life or property at sea. In my last ship there was really nothing for a reasonable man to complain of, except in the berths, which were both too small and too large, as some were meant for double berths. We shipped a sea off the Horn, and the fore-castle was drenched, and we had to sleep on wet beds three or four nights. The captain offered to give us a sail, and let us sleep on the guano that we had on board. In the small berths we were scrouged up like pigs in a stye—hardly room to move. We brought home a cargo of guano from the Chinqua Islands. We first got sufficient guano to ballast the ship, and for that we discharged our old ballast. The way the guano is put on board is this. The guano is in cliffs—we call it 'the mountain'—it runs to a certain depth, and it's all stone at the bottom. From the sea it looks like a rocky mountain; there's nothing green about it—it's the colour of stone there. They say it's the ordure of birds, but I have my doubts about that, as there could never be birds, I fancy, to make that quantity. Why, I have seen as much guano on the Chinqua Islands—they're about two degrees south of Callao, on the coast of Peru—as would take thousands of ships twenty years to bring away. There are great flocks of birds about the guano places now, chiefly small web-footed birds. Some burrow in the ground like a rabbit. Among the larger birds are pelicans, plenty of them. A flock of them has a curious appearance. I have seen hundreds of them to-gether. There is plenty of penguins, too, and plenty of seals, but the British ships are not allowed to capture them. I believe the Peruvian Government prevents it. A Peruvian man-of-war, a schooner, lies there. The guano is put on board this way: We have two 'shoots.' A shoot is made of canvas, equally square on all sides. The diggers bring the guano a quarter of a mile, to the shore. A place is prepared on the side of the guano mountain, by the sea, railed off for security with what you would call a hurdle, but it's very strong bamboo cane. There the diggers empty their bags, through an open place into the shoot which is spread below, and held by ropes. The shoot is then

lowered down from the guano mountain by the diggers, and the seamen who hold the ropes to regulate it must keep the lines a moving,
to keep the guano from choking (going foul) in the shoots. We must
regulate it by the pitch of the ship. The ship is moved alongside, and
so the shoot is emptied down the hatchways at a favourable moment.
There is a very strong smell about the guano mountain. It oft makes
people's noses bleed. The diggers on shore and trimmers in the ship
have to keep handkerchiefs round their noses, with oakum inside the
handkerchiefs. It affects the eyes, too; no trimmer can work more
than fifteen or twenty minutes at a time. The seamen are not employed in digging or trimming; they used to be in trimming in 1843.
The diggers and trimmers are labourers who live on the guano mountain (it's an island), to do that work. I believe the trimmers have two
dollars a day when at work. The diggers have so much a bag. I don't
know how much, as we weren't allowed on the island, except with the
captain's leave. They have built huts of sticks on the mountain; the
diggers have covered them with flags—that's a sort of bulrush that
grows on the coast; others are covered over with mats. There were a
few women there, but no bad women. The diggers are chiefly foreigners, but there are a very few English and Scotch. Perhaps there's 100
of them in all. They don't look sickly. Nothing grows on the guano
mountain; there is not even a sea-weed at the water's edge. Guano
is an unpleasant cargo until you get used to it on board ship. At first
the ship smelt as if she was laden with hartshorn. I have picked large
lumps of salt, like smelling salts, out of the guano." I may add that
a cargo of guano was being unladen at the West India Dock on one
of my visits there. It was hoisted out of the hold in bags, and had
altogether the smell of very strong and unsound cheese. The whole
atmosphere of the ship was cheesy. Some of the guano, which had
been spoiled by salt water, had the appearance of yellow mud or slime.

A seaman, who was recommended to me as a trusty and well-
conducted man, gave me the following statement as to the *African
trade:*—

"I have been fifteen years a seaman, and my last voyage was to
the *Gold Coast, in Africa.* I sailed in a brig of under 200 tons. We
had five able seamen, first and second mates, cook, steward, captain,
and an apprentice. I was second mate. The able seamen had £2 7s.
6d. a month, which I think not sufficient, and they had to find their
own stores besides, though they were charged a fair price on board.
Men are generally dissatisfied, and a great many say they would never

fight for such a country as this, 'specially not against America, nor stick to the country at all if they could get away. I am a married man myself, and so I suppose I must fight for the country if a war broke out. It's a great hardship on a married man that his wife cannot be allowed a portion of his wages during her husband's absence; but there's hardly an owner in London will allow monthly notes for the wives, and some that do allow them don't pay them, or pay them irregularly. I know one young married woman who had nothing for eighteen months her husband was away at sea. What's to become of such women? Half of them left that way go on the town to keep them from starving. Ours was a ship of the best sort as regards its management and accommodation—no false weights and no humbug about fines or such like, to cheat the men and please the owners; but there's a great deal of it about. Messrs. —— are good men to have to do with, and the owners in the African trade are good men generally. It's your cheap owners mostly in other trades that pluck every feather out of a seaman if they can, and they always can somehow. Provisions were good and plenty in my last ship; grog at the master's option. Very few ships now give it as an allowance. When we reached the Gold Coast we put ourselves in communication with a consignee. We took out a general cargo, and brought back ground-nuts, ivory, gold dust, and palm oil. The great thing is palm oil. The consignee trades with the natives, giving them cowries—they're shells that are the money there—cloth, beads, cotton, iron pots, and other things, in exchange for the cargo home. We very seldom went on shore on the west coast of Africa, on account of the surf. It's very few places where you can land with a boat. I have known that coast for five years, and I have been on shore. The place was green enough, but was very sickly. The natives come on board in their canoes; as they are all naked, they get through the surf in their canoes well enough, and if the canoe be capsized they swim ashore, for they are like fish in the water. They come to sell yams, or birds, or anything they have, and some of them are good hands, rather, at a bargain. No women come with them, and the seamen are not allowed to visit the women on shore. If a man be ashore a day or two he generally has the fever when he gets on board again. Masters go off the quickest, as they are most ashore. I don't think they drink. There were some fine strong fellows among the natives; some had a few words of English; all that knew any English could swear; they soon pick that up; it's like their A B C among sailors. I never was up any of the rivers. We generally leave the cargoes at different places along the west coast. There is no regular harbour on the Gold Coast, not, I believe, until you get down to the Bight of Benin. We may lie a week or ten days where we discharge most cargo, and then the men can't get ashore; plenty would if they could, but I think it's not worth the risk. We often had talk on board about African travellers, such as Mungo Park. Sailors are more intelligent than they used to be. It's a dull coast. It seems mountainous in some parts, and with valleys in others, but all looks dull and dead. Indeed, you can't see much of the coast, for you see it chiefly at the forts. The mortality there is great; the white people die the quickest. I heard a captain say that out of twenty-one clerks he had taken out there seventeen had died. It must be a very profitable trade to those on shore who can stand the climate, or they wouldn't stay there, leading such dull lives. Many seamen won't go there. We get no provisions from the shore but a pig a week (generally), or what they call a sheep, but it's neither one thing nor the other. It's not woolly, but hairy, like a goat—though it *is* a sheep. It weighs perhaps from 15 lb. to 25 lb. I once killed one that was 13 lb. The flavour is pretty good, but there is no fat about the ribs; between the ribs, indeed, there's just the skin, like a pig's bladder. We generally make a mess of a whole sheep, with the yams; what we call sea-pie. I now like yams as well as potatoes. I brought over one yam that weighed 18 lb. The great dissatisfaction of seamen generally, is the lowness of their wages. Look how the Americans are paid, and then look at this. In the African trade, and other trades, a man may be employed nine months out of the twelve, and if he average £2 2s. a month, which is a liberal reckoning, why he has £18 18s. a year, and perhaps a wife and family to keep. What's £18 18s.? I would never go to that African coast again, only I make a pound or two in birds. We buy parrots—grey parrots chiefly—of the natives, who come aboard in their canoes. We sometimes pay 6s. or 7s. in Africa for a fine bird. I have known 200 parrots on board; they made a precious noise; but half the birds die before they get to England. Some captains won't allow parrots. There's very little desertion on the African coast. Seamen won't land to desert and wait ashore there for another ship. It's more than their life is worth."

A very fine looking fellow, as red as a hot climate could make him, with bright eyes, black curly hair, and a good expression of counten-ance, next gave me the following information concerning the *West India trade:*—

"I have been at sea," he said, "nearly eleven years, and my last voyage was to the West Indies—to Kingston, Jamaica. The vessel was a barque of 240 tons. We had a crew of fourteen, being five able seamen, one ordinary seaman, two boys, cook, carpenter, steward, chief and second mates, and captain. The wages of the able seamen were £2 5s. a month. £2 5s. is now the general rate for a voyage to the West Indies, but I think it isn't sufficient; indeed I'm sure of it. I have had £2 10s. and £2 15s. for the West Indies from the Clyde. In the Scotch ports and in Liverpool it's never less than £2 10s. I reckon that London is the worst paid port in the country. I account for it, because there are so many men here, and some of them scamps enough to take anything; and then the foreigners that want to go back will go for anything. I have often sailed with foreign seamen, but never with a Jew seaman in my life. I see *them* only in the bum-boats in England. The steward had £2 10s., the cook the same, the carpenter £4, the chief mate £4, the second mate £2 15s., the ordinary seaman £1 15s. The boys were apprentices. The crew were all foreigners, or from British colonies, except myself, the ordinary seamen, the captain, and the boys. Two of the foreigners were very good seamen. They spoke very little English. We agreed very bad—not the foreigners and us— but the captain and us. When we left the Downs, we had very bad weather in the Channel, and two men were laid up sick, and sometimes three. The captain, because he couldn't get the ship worked to his liking, kept calling all hands a 'parcel of d—d soldiers.' She worked very hard with too few hands, such as the complement we had, and dreadful hard when three were laid up. The captain swore terribly. He didn't read prayers—swearing captains do though oft enough—by way of a set-off they say. Nobody can respect prayers from such people. I do from good men. I am a Scotchman. My last captain was a good seaman, though not much of a navigator. He pretty well ran the ship ashore in coming into the English Channel off the Scilly Islands. He nearly ran ashore, too, on the French coast, and with a fair wind right up the Channel. From the ignorance I have seen in officers, I am certain it is wrong to let anybody command a ship without his being examined as to his fitness. Young fellows often get the command through favour; they're relations of the owner, or something of that kind, and so they are trusted with men's lives. Our second mate was appointed by the owners, and hardly knew how to knot a yarn. At Kingston the men could go ashore every night, but no women were allowed on board. We took out a general cargo, and

brought back a cargo of log-wood, fustic, and black ebony. Me and a
darky stowed it all. The men that were slaves in Kingston are starving.
Those that were working on board our ship had only 2s. a day, and
for such work 3s. 6d. is paid in England. It is all stuff that they
won't work. They'll work hard enough if anybody will employ them.
I have seen 100 of them come down to our ship the last voyage, a few
weeks back, and beg for a crust. Me and my mates gave them half
our grub to get rid of them, and because we couldn't bear to see them
starving. I have heard hundreds of them say, and many a hundred
times—for I've been four voyages to the West Indies—that they were
far better off when they were slaves, but I never heard them say they
wished they were slaves again. There are thousands of blacks in Kingston seeking for work and can't get it. They work pretty hard when at
work, but not like an European. No man in the world works harder
than an European. There seems no trade in Jamaica now, and all the
people is ruined. In my last ship our fare was very bad. We had pork
and beef—the regular mahogany, you see—1¼ lb. of each, and ¾ lb.
of bread each—for the bread was allowanced—but ¾ lb. of bread is
too little. We had also rice and flour, but not enough. Grog was at
the captain's option. There was no splicing the mainbrace; a glass of
grog now and then, when we reefed the topsails, and sometimes not
then. I'm sure grog does a man good on board ship, especially in hard
weather. To show what things sometimes go on in merchant ships, I
will tell you this—a man daren't speak a word for his rights on board
ship, or all the officers are down upon him. The pay gets worse, and
the accommodation worse still. To show you what may go on in merchant ships, I'll tell you what I know. We were once, and lately too,
off the Chinqua Islands, round the Horn, laying for a cargo of guano,
just astern of a Bristol full-rigged ship. On a Saturday, as is a usual
thing with merchant ships, we sent there for a 'Saturday night's bottle'
to drink 'Sweethearts and Wives,' and the skipper said he'd be d—d
if he'd give it. His own men persevered in asking him for the bottle,
and he went below and came up with a brace of pistols. He fired at
one man, and the ball grazed his forehead, and took a bit off the top
of his ear; that was the first pistol fired. He was not drunk. He then
fired the other pistol, and shot a man dead through the breast. That
man took no part at all. The man that was shot never spoke after.
We heard the two shots on board our ship. There was then a cry of
'mutiny,' from all the ships in the harbour—about a dozen—a cry of
'mutiny on board the Eleanor,' and the captains sent off their officers

and crews, with arms, to make peace. Afterwards the captains went aboard and held a council of war, and two men who had threatened to take the Bristol captain's life for shooting their shipmate were chained to the mizen topsail sheets—I saw the men there myself. Our boat and another ship's boat next day took those two men to the Peruvian man-of-war schooner on the station, and what was done in the matter I never heard; but the Peruvian man-of-war and the Bristol ship came together to Callao when we were there, and there we left them. The best way, sir—aye, and the only way, too—to stop desertion, is better usage and better pay, and more to eat, and then never a man would grumble, and there'd be no bad language either—unless when allowable. You may register and register, and go nibbling on, but I tell you it's the only way. In my last ship I had no berth: there was no room in the forecastle to hang up hammocks except for four. The cook slept there every night; he couldn't be disturbed; and the rest took their turns, turn in and turn out, but I never turned in at all, because others had the turn before me. I slept all the time on a water-cask. In the West India trade I have worked 13, and 14, and 16 hours a day, though from six to six is the law of England, and there was no necessity for longer hours, only it was the captain's whim, that was all. A quick voyage was wanted, but good seamanship and good usage—and they often go together—are enough to do that without distressing the men, who are neither so well paid, or so well treated, or so well fed, as to care about the interests of the owner. What's the owner to me? He doesn't care for me, or very seldom; if he did, I'd care for him."

A ship carpenter, a fine-looking man, in plain clothes, well and even handsomely dressed, gave me the following account of *the whale fishery in the South Seas:*—

"I have returned from a South Sea voyage in a whaler. It is the custom of whalers in the South Seas to go 'on the lay.' In Greenland the men go partly by wages and partly by the lay; but I never was in Greenland. The system known as 'the lay' is this:—The seaman is entitled (as a general rule) to the 190th share of the money obtained by the sale of the oil. There are from 30 to 36 hands generally. The officers are paid according to rank. The boat-steerer (the same officer as the harpooner in the Greenland trade) has a 140th share; so has the cook; the chief mate a 40th; the carpenter (myself) a 90th; the steward a 130th; the captain a 12th. The process of catching the sperm whale is this:—They go in schools (shoals), and I have seen as many as 40 in a school. Sometimes I have seen a stray whale, and then it is generally a large one. Well, the man at the mast-head sings out, 'There she blows—a whale in sight!' If it's a school, they lower all the boats; if a stray whale, two boats are lowered. In each boat are three harpoons and two drags; the drag is to secure a whale until he can be got at, if the men are busy with another whale, and killed with the harpoon. The boat steerer, who rows first oar of the boat, drives his harpoon into a sperm whale. When struck, the whale will often seize a boat with his teeth, and upset it with his flux (tail). The sperm whale is much fiercer than the Greenland whale. No boat is lowered after sundown, because it is unsafe; the danger is great at all times. When one of a school is struck, the whole seem to know. A few spring out of the water at the moment a whale is struck. I have seen one four miles off spring out. A cow (she whale) will miss her calf (young whale) in an instant; the men drive at the calf, and so can generally make sure of the cow. A bull (he whale) generally does not show such affection, but a cow won't go far from her calf. At 'gendering' time the cow is struck first, if possible, to make sure of the bull. While the harpooning is going on, the whole school is in commotion; blood and white water is flung about along the waves, and the moment blood flows sharks appear, though one wasn't seen previously. If a man fall overboard the shark won't touch him as long as the shark has a chance to prey on the carcase of the whale. I have seen a man and a shark swim alongside one another. One of the crew must go overboard, when cutting-in the whale; that is, cutting the blubber off the carcase when the whale is brought alongside the ship. A boat steerer generally does it, and though there are thousands of sharks about, he's never injured. I have known the sharks devour the carcase of a calf as it hung all night hooked to the ship. The carcase must first be cut, or the shark can't get hold of it with his teeth; he must have one place to fix on first. A whale dies without noise, but 'flurries;' that's the death motion. In those vast solitudes in the Pacific the feeling is often overwhelming to any thinking man. I have been for four months without seeing even a sail. Nothing but the fish and the waters, and often very few of the fish. The common seamen are terribly oppressed by the long, long solitudes. The regulations on board the whalers are not what they ought to be. Provisions are not what they should be. Of beef, ¾ lb. is allowed a day, and of pork the same, on alternate days; but they are generally of bad quality. A few casks of good provisions are put forward to the surveyor's inspection, and the bad is kept in the background. Out at sea the good is kept for the cabin. The peas, flour, and bread, sometimes kept for four years—about the term of a whaling voyage—are bad, because no care is taken to preserve them. Grog is at the captain's option; it is generally allowed when the men are 'trying out;'—that is, boiling the blubber for oil. The captain on leaving England has £300, £400, or £500 worth of slops on board ship for the use of the crew. Slops are clothing from the slop-shops—any rubbish he can pick up cheap in the Minories, or anywhere. These as a favour he serves out at about 150 per cent. profit. At many of the islands we touch at in the Pacific, money is of little or no use; but if it were, it is not in a man's power to receive it, though he's been away for three years; it's against the articles. I have known £3 paid for a monkey jacket which a man could see through. I can buy a better in London for 12s. In the whaling voyage I am describing we went out for four years, and lost our captain at two years' end; he died of fever off Copang, a Dutch settlement, an island in Torres Straits. There was no person to take charge of the ship. The mate, as his duty, read the articles to the crew, and the crew were surprised to find that instead of the 160th, they were only entitled to the 180th lay. They were deceived. In most whalers the articles are not made out before the seaman is called upon to sign them. This caused dissatisfaction: one wouldn't do this, and another wouldn't do that, until finally we worked the ship, as agreed, to the first English port (Singapore), where the matter was submitted to the magistrates, and the crew offered to finish the voyage if they had a captain on whom they could depend. The mate was examined and found incompetent; and so the English consul appointed a man to bring the ship home. Previous to this we had obtained 50 tons of oil. The ship took in a cargo of gamber (dyes), and a little sugar, and came to England. I stuck to her all the time. In England I was told by the ship-owners— merchant princes, sir—that the ship had brought home little or no oil, and I was entitled to no money. I knew the contrary. I inquired, as if I were a stranger, of the wharfinger at the London Docks, where the ship was discharged, and he told me that she turned out fifty-one tons of oil worth £80 a ton; that's £4,080. I was entitled to £30, in addition to my advances. By the articles the men on the lay are not allowed to employ their own gauger, and are often cheated by the owners. In winter time the sperm oil runs very thick, and some casks are perhaps not full. I have seen at an owner's cooperage what they call 'the sperm,' the most valuable part, taken off the oil, to the extent of 150 gallons, out of a 300-gallon cask. That oil is put in the owner's tanks, and the men are deprived of it: deprived—why, they are robbed of it. Seamen never get their full allowances. The crews of English whalers are Spaniards—and coloured men, when they can get them—ignorant fellows, easily imposed upon; and nearly all the American whalers are manned by Spaniards and coloured men. All the men were dissatisfied. They didn't care one jot for their country. Fight against America if a war broke out! Not they. Would I? No. They don't impose on sailors in America. Whalers are greatly defective in one thing. After two years at sea, a man, if it were only for his health, should have a few days, or a day or two at least on shore; but that's denied him. Indeed, I see men imposed upon so, that I wonder they don't jump overboard. If a man only speak, he is 'a d——— mutinous vagabond,' and a 'd——— worthless rascal;' put in irons directly perhaps; and when a port is reached, the captain takes a ham, or cheese, or something as a present to the authorities on shore—the consul, or anybody—and so the man's prejudged before he's ashore at all. As to desertion, why it must increase, until seamen are less robbed and better cared for."

A short man, but evidently of very great strength, brawny and muscular, and with a very good frank expression of countenance, gave me the following account as to the treatment on board the *American ships:*—

"I am a *Scotchman* born, but am now *in the American service*, and on board a transit (merchant) ship trading from New York; not a liner, which runs only to one place. I have been in the English service, and was brought up in it. I have served on board one of your English ships that was not fit to go to sea, when she started for Callao. Off the Horn she leaked 350 strokes at the pump an hour. We couldn't sleep in the forecastle for the wet. Some of my shipmates were half dead before we got to Callao. We were always in danger in her, and there's no back way out at sea. The captain and his usage of us was very bad, striking men at the wheel; he once gave her up and cried like a child. She was above 800 tons. The English Consul at Callao wouldn't interfere, and told us, when we complained to him of the state of the ship, that he would do nothing for us, and, for anything he cared, we might all die in the streets. The captain had to ship three crews between Callao, the Clinches—that's the guano mountain—and the port of London. The old crew, all but two or three, were left at Callao. Well, sir, when this ship was at last got to the West India Dock she was patched up, and was then thought good enough for an emigrant ship, and was sent out to Australia with emigrants. I have been, off and on, in the American service these last 5 years. It's a far better service than the English—better wages, better meat, and better ships. No half-pounds of meat short there; eat when you're hungry, and the best of grub. What goes into an English ship's cabin goes into an American ship's forecastle. The Americans are fast getting the pick of the English navy. I have now 15 dollars a month, or £3 2s. 6d. No trouble about bonded stores or such like. You take your tobacco with you from any American port, where it costs 3d. or 4d. a pound; and tea, and coffee, and sugar, and rum are found you. The very best tobacco is 20 cents, that's 10d., in America; but that's for chewing. The six cents tobacco, or 3d. a pound, is as good as you pay 3d. an ounce for here; so there's a pound for an ounce, you see. There's a lot of the American tobacco smoked in England; plenty of it puffed away at 3d. a pound all round the Custom-house. For the same sort of service in an English merchant ship I might get £2, or £2 5s., and starving all the time, unless I chance on a good employer, but they are scarce. The sleeping berths are far better in the forecastles of the American than the English ships—more room, and better fitted up. Why, of course, the English seamen flock into the American service as fast as they can, petty officers and all. I see a lot of foreign seamen in London now. I suppose a 'Dutchman'—that's what any foreign lubberly fellow is now called—is shipped for every English seaman driven out of your fine ports. These Dutchmen will put up with anything whatsomever—kicks and hits, and all. As for want of grub, they'll starve before they'll ask for it, and the English captains know that well, and so prefer those fellows; and the English seaman may go to America, or where he will, for what they care. In every respect, both about registry and everything else, the American service is better than the English. The English service is fast coming to be only fit for Dutchmen—that's about it, sir, you may depend. There's very little else but English seamen in the American ships. Our crew is nineteen, and only four are American born; fourteen are British subjects. If a war broke out—I could answer for myself and for hundreds besides—I wouldn't fight for England against America, but for America against England. I'll not fight for a country that starves and cheats you. I'll never fight for short weights and stinting in everything, not I. I left an English ship at Quebec, which is the greatest place in British America for sailors deserting. The living is so bad that men won't put up with it. They can easily hide in Quebec, and so go overland into the States. Nothing will check desertion in the English service but better wages, better treatment, and better food. The discipline is much the same on board the American as on board the English ships. An English seaman is very little thought of in his own country, but he's well thought of in America. He's a man there."

A very stalwart, fine-looking fellow, dressed in a drab-coloured jacket, of a texture resembling fur, with long boots, under blue trowsers, turned high up the leg, gave me the following account of the same service. He had a florid look, a quantity of long brown hair, and large whiskers, with a free off-hand manner, and was, judging from his appearance, about 35:—

"*I'm an American born,*" he said—"a New York man, and now in the American service, but I have served under the English flag as well, and I have had good living under it and bad living; but bad living has it. In one of —— ——'s ships there was the horridest living I ever knew. She was from Bombay to London. The very horridest living I have known for 37 years, as man and boy. I'm 47 now—at least my mother says so. I don't dislike the English flag, and wouldn't fight against it if I could help it. I'd go into the backwoods, or take a farm, or something of that kind, rather than fight my brothers. I'm a man of peace—an Elihu Burritt man. The American-born seamen, as far as I know, have all friendly feelings to this country. When English and American sailors get drinking together, they hardly ever quarrel. What have they to quarrel about? In an American port you can get a ship in two hours, or at worst in twenty-four, so your English seamen will always run away. Rum's cheap, you see, and New York landlords give them a glass of that aqua fortis; it's rum mixed up with snuff, and decoction stuff; I don't know the chemistry of it; and so they nail the man flat, get a customer, and get him on board an American packet, after they've drained him dry; charge what they like, and make a turn out of him. The landlord keeps a slate, and he's —— free with the pencil, ain't he? A man's dry in the morning, and goes to the bar to liquor, and asks the landlord what's on the slate. 'You were drunk last night,' says the landlord, 'and had so many glasses; and so many dollars, money, I lent you.' The man *was* drunk, and can't tell what he had or what he spent. In America it's customary in a seaman's boarding-house to take a friend in to dinner with you, and his dinner's not charged to you. I was once invited by a friend to dine at a seaman's home here; but he didn't know the ways of the place. The waiter, I guess you call him, says, 'Who are you?' I told him who I came with, and he took the plate away—'you can't dine here, or any fellow might come out of the streets and dine.' If it had been in America I'd have knocked him down. It's a land of freedom in America, certainly; but there's a deal of humbug about all that. I'm just as free here. I never was insulted in the streets of London in my life. The living is so good in American boarding-houses, and so different to what English seamen have on board ship, that it's one thing to tempt them to desert. In an American boarding-house for seamen, they will have for dinner, on different days, fish, beef, mutton, boiled ham, fowls (perhaps every day), and a dessert after dinner—always a pudding or a pie, with apples and other fruit. The rum being so cheap is another reason, and not a little one. Another reason to tempt to desertion is—but I don't reckon that it influences them so much as the better meat and drink—a tumbler of rum in a decanter at the bar in New York for three-halfpence, take what you like—a tumbler full if you will, though the landlord looks at you if you fill the tumbler—none of your wine-glasses there. Another reason is, their lower wages in England. In long voyages I believe it's the cruelty, along with the bad wages and bad accommodation, that makes English seamen desert. The discipline is the same in the two services. In America the people are kinder to a seaman, I reckon. Here they seem to keep a sort of distance like; I don't understand it. In a New York boarding-house a landlord will give you two or three or more dollars the first night, because he's sure of his money; and he'll keep you three or four weeks, for the shipping-master will pay him when the man signs articles, and it's deducted from the man's wages at the finish of the voyage. An English seaman can get from Quebec to the States for a couple of dollars. In America they can buy 'a protection' for 50 cents, or two English shillings. The landlords have plenty of protections to sell. By a protection ticket an English seaman can pass as an American in any British port in North America. I see plenty of English seamen hard up here. They come down to our ship and say they've got the key of the street, and have no other place to go to, and some beg of you. Such a thing's never known in America. People don't enjoy themselves here, I think, as they do in America; they're distant, like, and haven't that feeling for a working-man that there is across the water."

The Morning Chronicle, Monday, March 11, 1850.

To the EDITOR of the MORNING CHRONICLE.

Sir—I am requested by the Rev. Charles Smith Royds to inform you that he is much indebted to you for the intelligence supplied in your columns on the 21st ult., respecting a poor man named Thomas Botley, residing at No. 6, Elliott's-place, in this parish, to whom he has sent, through me, a donation of one guinea. I have forwarded, by this day's post, poor Botley's receipt to the reverend gentleman, and can assure you that the miserably afflicted man is truly grateful for the help which, through your kind interference on his behalf, he has received from several quarters. If, Mr. Editor, the wealthy of the land would more generally imitate the Rev. Mr. Royds' example in making the parochial clergy their almoners, a vast amount of good would be realised, and the specious frauds practised by impostors detected and thwarted. I am surrounded by many thousands of wretchedly poor and miserable families and individuals; and as the amount I am able to obtain from every available source is, when compared to the poverty and destitution of my very numerous flock, but as the drop to the ocean, any assistance that the wealthy and benevolent of the community might send me would be thankfully received and faithfully applied.

I remain, sir, your obliged and obedient servant,

TIMOTHY GIBSON,

Senior Curate of St. Matthew's (the mother parish),

Bethnal-green.

St. Matthew's Rectory, March 8.

LABOUR AND THE POOR.

---◆---

THE METROPOLITAN DISTRICTS.

[FROM OUR SPECIAL CORRESPONDENT.]

LETTER XLII.

I continue the statements of the seamen belonging to the different trading vessels sailing from the Port of London.

A tall, well-looking man, exceedingly bronzed, with an appearance of high health, and evidently possessed of great bodily strength, gave me the following account of an *East Indian voyage*, just completed:—

"I have been at sea twenty-two years, and am now 34. From that age to 40 a seaman is considered in his prime. I have been at sea all these twenty-two years, merely excepting the times the ship was in port. I never was cast away in my life, but having a good character [to prove this, he showed me different papers] I have been generally fortunate in getting good ships and good masters. Good masters can always command the very best men. I have always found it so, and so their ships are always safest. Tyrannical and ignorant masters have often enough to put up with such men as they can get. We naturally avoid such ships if we know the character of the masters." [By masters, he meant the captains of the vessels.] "My last voyage was to Aden, and from there to Colombo in Ceylon, and Cochin on the Malabar coast. The vessel was 400 tons, and carried a crew of seventeen— the master, mate, second mate, carpenter, steward, cook, seven able seamen, two ordinary seamen, and two apprentices. An able seaman is a man capable of doing every part of the duty required on board ship; an ordinary seaman can only do part of it. My wages, as an able seaman, were £2 a month; the ordinary seamen had, one 30s., and the other 25s.; the cook had £2 7s. 6d.; the steward £2 10s.; the second mate £3; the carpenter £4 10s.; and the chief mate £4 10s. The captain had, I believe, £12 a month, and two per cent. on the cargo. We took out coal and government stores to Aden, leaving that place in ballast. At the other two ports we took in cocoa-nut oil, coir rope, and junk (short pieces), bees' wax, coffee, and cinnamon. My opinion is, that £2 a month is not a sufficient payment for an able seaman, considering the nature of his work, and that he must be sail-maker and everything on board a ship. Then look at the hardships we endure on board ship— I have been kept up forty-eight hours, all hands on deck, without a minute's rest, and with hardly time for meals. Certainly there was great danger then, but we had a good captain. Masters never show any allowance for a man having been up all night on account of the weather; he must do his work all the same. I am quite satisfied, from the talk I have had with seamen situated like myself, that it is our general opinion that the wages ought to be higher; but if we tried to get better there was always some one, and good seamen too, ready to jump into the place, and take even less, especially when times are bad. In my last ship the provisions were by no means good. The biscuit, flour, beef, and pork, were all the remains from the stores of her former voyage from Ceylon. The peas and barley only were fresh at starting on the voyage. The biscuit was full of weevils (a small black insect), and we had to bake it in the oven before we could eat it. It eat better then; the baking made it crisp instead of tough, as it came out of the barrels, and killed the weevils—but we had to eat the dead bodies of the things that didn't crawl out. We made great complaints about it, but were told there was no help for it; we must eat through the bad to get to the good. There was no help unless we kicked up a row, and that wouldn't do at all. The pork and beef were both very bad, as rancid as could be. A piece of pork weighing 5 lbs. used to lose about 2 lbs. in boiling. We complained, and the master weighed it himself on deck; but he told us there was no help for it, he eat the same himself. We had three half pints of pretty good tea each, night and morning. Sugar was scarce, only ¾ lb. to each man a week. At each meal we have as much bread as we like to eat, unless the ship be on short provisions. Grog was given out at the captain's option, sometimes one glass a day, sometimes two, three, or four, according to the day's work, as well as a glass every Saturday night to drink 'Sweethearts and wives,' and another glass after dinner on Sundays. On Sundays—I ought to have told you—we had two fresh meals: on going out a pig was killed, for one, and the other was bouilli soup, from preserved beef in tins; and in coming back a pig was killed every Saturday, and, little or big, the crew had half of it on Sunday. No one can call me a drunken man, but I think grog encourages a man to do his work well—just what is fit to revive him when he flags. Too much is worse than none. In my last ship we had two forecastles, one above (the gallant forecastle), and one below (the lower). I was in the lower forecastle, which was pretty good and middling for room, though in some ships it's very bad. My berth was 6 feet by 3. I am 5 feet 10¾ in. in height. I have slept in a berth only two feet wide, so that I could hardly get into it, and, when in, couldn't slew round or anything. The gallant forecastle was very leaky, the water coming in continually in rainy weather, and wetting all the men's beds. The carpenter couldn't stop it, the ship was so slightly built, though she was only four years old. She was built at Leith. The master was a good officer, without being too severe; but the mate was a domineering, ignorant fellow; and, indeed, sir, these ignorant fellows are always the worst; he used to run tattling to the captain and make mischief fore and aft. We had two or three rows in her, and all through him. I consider there is a decided improvement in merchant ships of late. Lime juice and vinegar is a great improvement in southern-going ships. It is a very common fault in all the ships I know, to have no place to keep the bread in. It's kept in bags, and they are put anywhere—anywhere down below. No care at all is taken of it, and the damp gets to it and causes maggots and weevils. The last voyage, when we eat through the old bread, two cwts. of the new was found to be so mouldy that it had to be heaved overboard. The bags often come up so rotten with damp that they fall to pieces, and the bread falls out. I think if the bread were kept in barrels, as the beef and pork is, or in tins, it would be much better and healthier. I don't know how they manage the bread on board a man of war—I never was on board one; but they'll take care of it there you may depend. In the East India ports that I have visited lately, the native women are not allowed to come on board so freely as they were, but the men have more liberty to go on shore. I think there is not so much swearing and cursing on board ship as there used to be. If the officers swear, they always make men swear. We had prayers on board my last ship in fine weather, but I wouldn't go—for we had our choice to go or stay—because it was a mockery. The captain began swearing the moment he'd done praying. I think masters should not be permitted to take out bread, or other stores, that had remained from former voyages, and were bad in consequence. They might be sold for pig-meat, and the biscuit is often fit for nothing else. My last captain was a good navigator, or we might have been lost, as the mate couldn't be depended upon for navigation. I think, too, that six pints of water a day, our present allowance, is too little—it ought to be a gallon. The water is generally good now, being all filtered, at the principal ports at any rate, before it is shipped. As to advance notes, I think they had better be done away with, and have the plan they have in the States (United States). There, when a seaman gets a ship he goes to a shipping-office and receives the advance money agreed upon from the master of the shipping-office, without any note whatsomever. The man you lodge with, to whom the advance-money is paid, is security for you to the shipping-office, in case you run away. He will then have to make it good. The master of the ship repays the shipping-office master. That's a simpler plan than ours."

I shall now contrast the above statement with one that I had from a seaman in the employ of Mr. Green, the eminent shipowner. High as the man speaks in praise of his master, I am happy to have it in my power to state, that all I have heard fully bears out this most honourable eulogium. I shall, however, when treating of the sailor ashore, be in a better position to speak upon this subject. At present I can only record the statements made to me by others. The man said:—

"I have been to sea about four or five and thirty years, I expect. I was apprenticed in the West India trade, in 1814 or 1815. I remained in the West India trade for ten or twelve years. Then I went to Sydney for three or four years. After that I was sailing in small craft from St. Thomas's to different ports in South America and to different islands in the West Indies, till 1840. Since that time I have been sailing out of London to the East Indies in Mr. Green's employ. When I first joined Mr. Green, in 1840, his Home, for the sailors in his employ, was not open, but on my return from Calcutta it was. Before that time I had been in the habit of living in the Home in Well-street. This was opened about 1832 or '33, I can't recollect exactly which. I know I shipped out of it in 1840 to join Mr. Green's company. I had £2 a month on first joining Mr. Green's ship. In other ships I had £2 5s.; but I had heard that Mr. Green gave better employ and better usage, at £2 a month than others at £2 5s., and so I thought I'd be one of his men. I had heard of Mr. Green being one of the best masters out of the port of London, and I felt anxious to join him. I knew I should lose 5s. a month by so doing, but what I lost one way I was convinced I should gain in another, and I found such to be the fact. Of all owners I have ever shipped with I have found Mr. Green to be the best. Why, sir, in the first place, when a man comes back there is a place for him to go—a home, sir. I call it a real home, sir; and there is no other shipowner that I know of that cares so much for his men. I am a single man. I have been ten years in Mr. Green's service, and I can conscientiously state that a better master to his men I never knew." (I endeavoured to impress upon the man that, if he had anything private to communicate, his name could never transpire, nor would he be in any way injured, and he again assured me that Mr. Green was a gentleman who had invariably shown a disposition to benefit his men, and that the men had the same feeling towards their master as he had towards them; they would do all they could to serve him.) "My last voyage was made in the Northumberland, from London to Madras, and from Madras to Calcutta. She was about 800 tons. Mr. Green has one ship over 1,400 tons, and that is the largest he has in the East India trade. There are larger ships, and they run perhaps 50 tons more. In the 800-ton ship that I went out in last voyage we had 33 men and boys in the forecastle, and four officers abaft, and about eight middies. Besides these, there were carpenter, boatswain, sailmaker, ship's cook and baker, captain's cook, steward, and cuddy servants. We had about five or six passengers. It was in the winter time. Had it been in the summer we should have had double or treble that number on board. We took out soldiers as well, about 150. I should say we had six soldier officers on board. We had only about five or six soldiers' wives with us. We had full weight of provisions, always good, and plenty. We had sufficient of good water—well filtered and sweet. We had salt beef and plums and flour one day, and pork and peas the next—as much as we could eat. We had plenty of room on board Mr. Green's ship, and plenty of air. The midshipmen's berth had a port-hole and scuttle, and was a very large and airy cabin; so, indeed, were all the berths. We touched nowhere on our outward-bound voyage till we got to Madras. We had no tomfoolery at the line; no hailing of Neptune over night, and shaving of the greenhorns in the day time. No ships lie at Diamond Harbour now. We went up to Calcutta. We lay just below Fort William. Every Sunday and every night the men were allowed to go on shore, upon the condition that they came on board in the morning. I didn't know that any man deserted—it would be matter of dishonesty on a man's part to leave a master who treats his men so well as Mr. Green. A man loses more than he gains. No women were permitted to come on board—that is not allowed now; they used to do so, but we have improved much in these few years. When I came home I had Mr. Green's Home to go to. Had I belonged to any other owner I should have been uncared for. I came home ill—

ill with the liver complaint and with ulcers in the stomach—and I was received into his sailors' home, as if I had been a person worthy of being looked after. Had I belonged to any other owner I should have been left a prey to the land-sharks of London. I think that if all owners were like Mr. Green there would be fewer men to leave the merchant service of this country. What the merchant seamen generally require is to be well treated, and then they would be sure to be good men. Mr. Green has a school for the children of sailors. It will hold more than 300 I have heard, and I know the sailors love him for his regard to their little ones, and so indeed does all Poplar. I have been in ships that are as badly found and the men as little cared for as those of Mr. Green's are well provisioned and the men truly regarded; and I can conscientiously say that if all owners were like Mr. Green, our merchant service would be the envy of the world. The masters lay the blame upon the men, but from what I have seen I can declare that it is not the men's fault, but the captains or the owners, as to how the men behave themselves. I never knew any act of insubordination to occur on board of Mr. Green's ship, and I attribute this solely to the good treatment of the men. What man can speak again a master like that? There is a good home and a good bed always to go to, and I only wish such masters were more general, and then the country would be safer I can tell you."

The Baltic and North American trades are somewhat similar. I subjoin, however, an account of the condition and earnings of the seamen belonging to each:—

A man of very quiet, sedate demeanour, with the thoughtful look common to men who have often to watch and observe, gave me the following statement as to the treatment of seamen on board the ships belonging to the Baltic trade:—

"I have been at sea thirty-two years. I began when I was ten years old. My last voyage was to Memel, as mate. She was a brig of upwards of two hundred tons, with a crew of seven—captain, mate, cook, one able seaman, and three apprentices: one of the apprentices was nearly out of his time. My pay as mate was £4 10s.; the cook had £3 5s.; and the able seaman £3 2s. 6d. The payment in the Baltic timber trade is better, but the voyages are less frequent than in other trades. As to the fare, the articles we sign in the Baltic trade are to this effect: We are to be found a sufficiency of beef, pork, bread, rice, flour, and peas; and no waste. The articles express it. As a rule, I think—though there may be many exceptions—the provisions are abundant and good. There

are often complaints, however, and besides there is this grievance—
bonded stores, such as coffee, sugar, tea, and tobacco especially, are
at the disposal of the captain, who acts as purser, and often as a very
hard purser, too. A seaman is robbed on all sides. I believe that by law
a seaman can demand a bill of fare from the captain; but to do so is to
give offence, and lead the life of a dog on board. So, you see, a seaman
(I tell you from experience) must buy all he wants of the captain. The
captain generally charges a very high profit. The seamen know the
captain breaks the law, but what can the poor fellows do? They daren't
complain, and don't know how to set about it if they would. You see,
if they make a public complaint against a captain, it's known, and the
other captains—for *they* all stick together—won't then employ such a
man. They consider a complaint a crime. I have paid as high as 1s. a
pound for raw coffee, out of bond, and had to burn it myself. I have
paid 4½d. a pound for sugar, when the fair price was 3½d. I have paid
2s. 3d. a pound for tobacco—it was good tobacco, certainly. Soap has
to be found by the men. I never knew any of them go aboard without
soap. The men, as far as I have seen, are generally well treated in the
Baltic trade, but underpaid, and consequently generally dissatisfied,
particularly when they think of how men are paid in the American
ships. If a war broke out with the United States, in my firm opinion,
the sailors on board the British merchant ship, wouldn't fight again
America. What have they to fight for? An English seaman feels he
hasn't his just rights: give him them and he'll fight like a bull dog for
the island. That's my opinion, and I feel it; and it's the opinion of
plenty that I know. It is this and such like things that make us care
nothing for the country. Why should we? Now, what have we to care
for? We are slaves on salt water, and the captain is a god. 'Britons
never shall be slaves' is all stuff now—regular stuff, sir. I'm disgusted
to hear it. Why, a Russian is happier in his slavery and his ignorance
than is an Englishman with any feelings, if he's poor. Now, here's
another grievance seamen have. It is very common for a master to
leave London short-handed, and even to boast of it. I have heard of it,
though they know they're breaking the law. But a man has no remedy.
After a voyage, a word again a good man from a bad captain is ruin
to him, for the man can't get another ship. Some institution like the
coal-whippers' office, just by us here, would be a very good thing for
us. As to the men now masters, I know very many utterly unfit to
have charge of a vessel. They could never tell where they were. Men's
lives as well as property are at stake. These ignorant fellows too are

always the worst to the men. Any fellow is reckoned, by some petty owners, good enough to knock seamen about, and curse them until his tongue's tired. I think, as well as I can judge, that there's not so much vice among the sailors as there used to be, and marrying in this port and in that—that sort of carrying on is chiefly by boys, now. The timbers we took in at Memel in my last voyage were floated alongside on immense rafts; some of them came hundreds of miles down the rivers. There are vast forests there, and they'll last for centuries to come. The first I saw I thought was more like a black cloud than anything else. The timber (the rough timber) is cut in windmills built for the purpose, and the deals cut and squared in them. I have seen scores of windmills on the Russian coast and in the Gulf of Finland. Some of the windmills, I have seen keep twenty sawyers going—not men, but a frame of machinery called a sawyer, as it does the work of one. There they go, up and down—up and down. I have seldom been in merchant ships where there were prayers read by the captain. I have met with them, and with plenty of hypocrisy. Swearing after praying is common. Fines and forfeitures, as punishments on board ship, are no good: they can be so abused, you see, when a captain wants to spite a man. Confinement on board ship is a rest for an idle fellow that shirks work, and nothing else. It is impossible to reduce the number of deserters while you pay men so badly, and let them be so plucked."

A man, who had been a seaman for eleven years, gave me the following account as to the *Quebec trade:*—

"My last voyages were to Quebec and the River de Loup, in the port of Quebec. I last sailed in a barque of about 400 tons. We went out in ballast, and brought back deals. We had 17 in crew—7 able seamen, 2 ordinaries (one fell overboard from the maintop-sailyard, and was drowned), cook, carpenter, steward, first and second mates, captain, and two apprentices. I had £2 10s. a month. It's not enough, as no sailors see more hardships than those that go to North America. It ought not to be less than £3. The provisions were good and plentiful, but the accommodation, in the forecastle, was very bad and very leaky. I had to heave my bed overboard when we returned, as it wasn't worth bringing on shore; it was rotten from the wet. I have heard many men say they would never fight for England; but I would fight for England—that is, if I saw occasion—to be sure I would. The seamen put the deals on board through the port-holes. They are brought down to the ship in lighters, which they call 'bateaux.' The deals are cut ready in mills up the country, but I never saw one. In the River de Loup they slide the deals down a shoot (a sort of spout), into the river; the shore is high. French Canadians—they're not very active—pick them out of the river, put them on their bateaux, and take them to a pier-head, where they pile them ready for the loading of the ship. The forests there look very black. Along the Gulf of St. Lawrence they have a cold, miserable look—the wind's always blowing, and you don't see a sign of life about the forest (we were close in shore too) except a few birds. The noise of the wind among the trees there is very outlandish. Desertions are very common in Quebec; the reason is, that men can hide there better than in smaller places, and so get away to the States, perhaps, and have far better pay, and far better food. But some seamen are never satisfied. Plenty go to British North America on purpose to desert. I never ran away from a ship in my life. But men are sure to desert until you give them better wages and better living; and a glass of grog comes very handy at sea. I like a glass of grog at sea now and then myself; but I don't care for liquor on shore. The captain drank very hard aboard, and was mad from it. He was so mad that we ran back 700 miles, to bring the ship to England. Within twenty-four hours of Plymouth, he came to his senses, and persuaded us to take the ship back to North America. He was eleven days below, ill. When he did come on deck, he looked very fierce about the eyes. He drank hard in America, and was unshipped when we got to England. Men's lives weren't safe with him, but the mate was a good seaman. When we left England we were bound for Quebec; if it hadn't been for the captain's drunken management, in the gales of wind, we should have made Portugal in forty-eight hours. We kept standing away to the southward by his orders. It was a mercy we got home at all. Off Dungeness the captain was that mad after liquor, that he gave £1 for a gallon of spirit to a pilot cutter. There was three and a half gallons of brandy on board when we left America. The captain drank it nearly all himself, and there was no liquor on board for nine days before we got to Dungeness. The steward told me the captain would drink vitriol, to keep his spirits up, when there was no brandy left. I was sorry for the captain, for he wasn't a tyrant, with all his drinking."

A north-country seaman gave me the following statement as to the *Brazilian* trade:—

"I have been nine years and a half at sea, and have returned from a voyage to Bahia and Brazil. We brought home a cargo of sugar. I sailed in a full-rigged ship of about 380 tons. Our crew was 23 in all—12 able seamen, 4 apprentices, 3 mates, cook, steward, carpenter, and captain. She was the best-manned ship, and there was the best usage of any in my experience. I have been in ships that were so short of hands that our safety really depended on good luck and good weather. In the voyage to Bahia I had £2 5s. a month as able seaman. I consider that not a fair payment. Reasonably, it ought to be £3 or £2 15s. at the least; and then seamen like myself—I have heard it debated often—would not grumble nor leave the country. Desertion is owing only, in my opinion, to bad wages and bad usage. It's not that the seamen prefer the American service, to the English, but you see we prefer good wages to bad, and good food to bad, and who wouldn't? I have heard many seamen say they wouldn't like to fight again this country—but they would never fight *for it*, especially again America. I have heard men say they would like to fight again it for the Americans. I myself wouldn't fight for the country unless the condition of merchant seamen was improved; I have so many friends in the service that I wouldn't. Arguments as to sides in fighting, if a war broke out, are very common on board ship. I have heard scores, many scores, say they would leave the country the very first chance, they were so badly used. The provisions in my voyage to Brazil were very bad; the captain said so himself, and blamed the agent—honestly, I do believe, for the captain was a good man. He was a good seaman, but I have sailed with officers quite ignorant of navigation. One captain that I sailed with believed he was on the north-west coast of Ireland when he was off the Lizards, on the Cornish coast. The bread on the voyage I'm telling you of was good, but the beef and pork was very bad. Cheap American beef and pork is sent to Ireland, and repacked there as good Irish provisions. We had fair weight, but that was small advantage, as the meat was not fit to eat; it looked like a bit of mahogany rolled in coal dust when taken out of the coppers. In very few ships are more than fourteen ounces given to the pound. I was on shore at Bahia. It is not a very large town. If an English seaman be found there without a pass from the captain, he is put on board a Brazilian man-of-war, and made to serve there for two years. Men desert when they have a chance, they're thought so little of on board an English ship."

To show the opinion of a *chief mate* as to the men in the merchant service, I give the account of a very intelligent man, whose last voyage was *in the Mediterranean:*—

"I have been at sea for 30 years—from 15 to 45 years of age—and my last voyage was up the Mediterranean to Constantinople, and then up the Black Sea, and into the Sea of Azof to Kertch. She was a brig of 240 tons, with a crew of twelve—captain, chief mate (myself), eight able seamen, and two apprentices. Within my own knowledge I can vouch for a far better state of things now existing on board ship. Little, however, has been done for the better accommodation of the men. There is still shocking crowding in the forecastles; and the deck over the forecastle is often so leaky that in rainy weather the men may really sleep in the rain—go down wet, and come up wetter, oft enough. I have seen them—aye and often—come smoking like a steam apparatus, up from the forecastle. Talk of sanitary regulations, sir—have them afloat as well as ashore. The men are constantly suffering from cold, and frequently from ague, as I have seen. In respect to cleanliness, there is decidedly a great improvement; and even that might be increased by making the men air their bedding when the weather permits, which they seldom do now. Perhaps the bed-clothes in the berths are not changed once in a whole voyage, or the bed aired. The want of something for the purposes of a water-closet is also a very great defect in our merchant ships at present. There *is* something of the kind. The head-rail is used for such purposes; but when it blows very hard and heavy, men cannot go to the head-rail—many men have been lost by going there in stormy weather. The officers have conveniences, and the men could easily have the same. In my last voyage the able seamen had £2 a month each. My opinion, as an officer, is that it ought not to be less than £2 5s. for any long voyage—men deserve it. The officers had the usual rate. We discharged our cargo, bale goods and manufactured iron, at Constantinople. The men were allowed to go ashore on Sundays. No women are admitted on board, on any pretence, in any of the Mediterranean ports. To have examinations of the officers in merchant ships, as to their nautical knowledge and their sobriety, and certificates after passing examinations, will, in my opinion, be a very great improvement. Many a bright vessel has been lost through the ignorance or drunkenness of her commander. When a master is ignorant, his crew soon find it out, and all take advantage of it; there is no good discipline; while in case of peril, the men have no confidence in their master, and the danger is greatly increased. In one of my voyages, through not having a chronometer on board chiefly, we made Scilly two days before we expected even to see land. If it had not been fine summer weather we must have gone bump on shore among the wreckers. Every vessel, as a regulation, ought to have a chronometer on board, and the master ought fully to understand its use. Fines on board ship would, in some respect, be proper. Confinement does no good; it's ridiculous, for one man in a fault is confined and idle, and another, in consequence, is overworked, for no fault of his. As to wages, I think that, in justice to the seaman, wages ought to commence from the time of signing the articles; as it is, a seaman has often to wait eight or ten days before his vessel sails, and, as his wages only reckon from the sailing of the vessel, he is compelled to be eight or ten days idle, and unless a very steady man, soon gets through all his means. Why not have the men on board? It would save their lodging, and save them all sorts of temptations, and it would be no loss to masters or owners, for they have to pay riggers and labourers as it is. A better way of keeping the log, so as to answer regularity and accuracy, is very desirable. I have seen a log where the mate put down the vessel as steering N., and the wind in the other column as N. by W., as if the vessel lay within a point of the wind, while she was not within 5½! There can be no doubt that there ought to be some readier means of recovering wages due to seamen's representatives. I mean seamen who have died on the voyage. I think it would be better, as regards wages generally, that there should be an uniform rate of wages, as in the United States. It would be found a great improvement in this country. In some ports here £2 is given for the East Indies; in Liverpool it is £2 5s. Men would know what to expect with an uniform rate—indeed, they could reckon it with certainty. In the United States there is an uniform rate, the men being engaged at shipping offices. An able seaman has $15 a month for Europe, and $12 a month for the East Indies and China. No wonder so many Englishmen are in the American service—the pay is better, the provisions are better, and the accommodations are better. Now, a better and more uniform rate of wages in English ships would prevent many men deserting at New York, and other cities in the States, where they are tempted naturally by the better state of things among the Americans. Do what anybody will, sir, the only true way to check desertion is to pay the men better, and to accommodate them better. That goes to the root of the matter."

A seaman gave me the following statement as to the Portuguese trade:—

"My last voyage was to Oporto and back. I went out in a brig of 180 tons. We had eight in crew—three able seamen (one being cook and seaman), one ordinary, two apprentices, captain, and mate. I think that she was at least one short-handed. In my experience ships generally go out short-handed, worse than my last voyage. I had £2 10s. a month as able seaman. I do not consider it sufficient; but wages are very low in London now. We were not allowanced in provisions; they were of as good quality as ever I had on board a ship, and I have been a seaman for sixteen years. I have very often known short weight and bad provisions given; far oftener short and bad, than good and full weight. The accommodation was good in my last ship. I think £2 15s. at the least should be the wages in the Portuguese trade. In short voyages a seaman is not so fully employed; indeed you may put him down as about four months in the year unemployed. We have to pay our shilling a month, too, apiece to the Seamen's Fund, which seems never to come back to us. I don't know where it goes to. My last captain was a good seaman; but I know many captains who are not by any means fit to be trusted with men's lives. I have known the command taken from a captain, he was so drunken. When seamen meet now-a-days, they talk over their grievances, and I have heard very many say they would never fight for such a country. I fought in China for this country, and think I might fight again, possibly—I can't tell. What makes men desert is bad usage, and bad provisions, and bad wages. Altogether the Royal Navy now, though an able seaman in it has only 34s. a month, is far better than the merchant service. Indeed the merchant service gets worse and worse. I'm afraid that wages will fall still lower, and then nobody can tell the consequences."

I had a statement from a middle-aged and, as I was assured on the best authority, a very trusty man, concerning the *Hudson's Bay Ships*. He stated as follows:—

"My last voyage was in the *Hudson's Bay Company's service*. I have been 24 years at sea in various services. I have been out as boatswain, mate, and able seaman. In the Hudson's Bay Company's service there is really nothing to complain of. I have been in that service for, say 20 years. Before that I was in the employ of good shipowners. When men complain, they generally have not been kindly treated, or have been underpaid. Underpaid men are never good men—never good seamen. My last voyage, as I have said, was in the Hudson Bay Company's service in the fur trade. In my last voyage I was boatswain, and I was formerly able seaman. Last time I went to Mouse River for furs. The half-breeds—the descendants of an Englishman and an Indian woman—are the principal people that the company deals with. The men who bring the skins to the factories are Indians, and they have a strong sense of religion. They do nothing on a Sunday. I don't understand much about their religious feelings on a Sunday, but they're very clean and won't work then. They are copper-coloured, and with long hair hanging loose about the neck, all black. They had a good expression—that they had. If I met one of them I should feel confident he would conduct me safe wherever I wanted to go. Some of them were fine-looking fellows. The old men are pensioned (as you would say) by the Hudson's Bay Company. I don't know at how much. Money is nothing there; but these natives have provisions served out to them to keep them. They really love the company. I'm certain of it; they would go through fire and water for it; they would give their lives for it—certainly they would. When I first went to the Mouse River I felt no great sense of novelty, I can tell you. The country was flat—plains, you see—what may be called the bush. Our principal trade was in beaver skins. The beaver is shot as well as trapped; it is a very ingenious creature, and is trapped and shot as it builds its house in the marshes, or by the brook or river's side. There's not such a demand for beavers as there was, as far as I know; there's slop hats instead of beaver hats. Beaver is really good eating. The skins go to the company, and the flesh is eaten. It's very like beef, and fat beef too—tasty, uncommon. I have tasted it in the Indians' huts; it's generally roasted before a wood fire. Its flesh never comes to the factories to be served out to the people; the Indians take care of that. They carry quantities of wild geese and ducks to the factories. It's all barter. The barter is regulated by the price of the beaver skins. Powder and shot was for a long time exchanged for beaver skins, and is indeed still; so is bread, flour, tobacco, tea, and sugar; the Indians there like tea four or five times a day. The Hudson's Bay Company's ships are well manned and the crews well treated. I know as much from my own experience, and can bring plenty of men to prove it, as well as myself; and if other shipowners acted as the company does, there wouldn't be that grumbling, and that reasonable grumbling, that there now is. Before I went to Hudson's Bay, I was in the Greenland whale fishery, and the ice I met with in that fishery wasn't to compare with what I saw in Hudson's Straits (which leads into Hudson's Bay), and in Hudson's Bay itself. I have been fifty days in Hudson's Bay, and the ship has only made twelve miles one way or other in those fifty days, as she was bound up in the ice, and couldn't move for a fortnight together. In Hudson's Straits we saw—for they were counted—35 icebergs in an evening, when we were outward bound; there are more counted homeward bound. The first I saw was above 200 feet high; the ship's masthead might be 100 feet. I have sometimes seen them topple over; the top parts are melted by the sun, and run down as they thaw in channels, and so the iceberg capsizes. The first I saw was like the Tower of London moving on the water, only the real Tower here was a fool to it in size. I have seen icebergs a tremendous size, and looking as if one church steeple was piled upon another. A high iceberg looks as if it carries clouds on its top; and in going along in a dark night it makes a clear atmosphere about it. A mile, or a mile and a half off, it shows itself like a white mountain of light. The great care is to avoid icebergs; for small pieces of ice we don't care if we run again them. I have known an iceberg 200 fathoms (1,200 feet) under the water, and the computation is that it is one-third above the water. In the sunlight you can see an iceberg twenty miles off glittering, just the same as you see windows lighted up here by the sun. An able seaman's wages are £3 3s. a month in the Hudson's Bay service. I consider that fair pay. If the seamen in other trades were paid in the same proportion there would be no grumbling and no dissatisfaction."

The above, with those before given, constitute the principal classes of sailing vessels trading with foreign countries from the Port of London. It now only remains for me to give an account of the condition of the seamen on board the steamers and the coasting vessels. For the present I shall conclude with an exposition of the number of steamers belonging to the British Empire, and also the rate of increase, year by year, since their first introduction:—

TABLE SHOWING THE NUMBER AND TONNAGE OF STEAM-
VESSELS BUILT AND REGISTERED IN THE UNITED KING-
DOM AND THE BRITISH COLONIES, AND THEIR PROGRESS
IN EACH YEAR FROM THE TIME OF THEIR FIRST INTRO-
DUCTION.

Years.	Steam-vessels belonging to the British Empire.		Steam-vessels built and registered in the United Kingdom and the British Colonies.	
	Vessels.	Tons.	Vessels.	Tons.
1814	2	456	6	672
1815	10	1,633	10	1,394
1816	15	2,612	9	1,238
1817	19	3,950	9	2,054
1818	27	6,441	9	2,538
1819	32	6,657	4	342
1820	43	7,243	9	771
1821	69	10,534	23	3,266
1822	96	13,125	28	2,634
1823	111	14,153	20	2,521
1824	126	15,739	17	2,234
1825	168	20,287	29	4,192
1826	248	28,958	76	9,042
1827	275	32,490	30	3,784
1828	293	32,032	31	2,285
1829	304	32,283	16	1,751
1830	315	33,444	19	2,226
1831	347	37,445	36	4,436
1832	380	41,669	38	4,090
1833	415	45,017	36	3,945
1834	462	50,735	39	5,756
1835	538	60,520	88	11,281
1836	600	67,969	69	9,700
1837	668	78,288	82	12,147
1838	722	82,716	87	9,837
1839	770	86,731	65	6,522
1840	824	95,807	78	10,757
1841	856	104,845	54	12,391
1842	906	118,930	67	14,931
1843	928	118,962	53	6,739
1844	988	125,675	73	6,930
1845	1,012	131,202	73	11,950
1846	1,070	144,784	88	17,172
1847	1,154	156,557	115	17,333
1848	1,253	168,078	128	16,476

The following table will enable the reader to contrast our steam
power with that of other countries:—

TABLE SHOWING THE NUMBER AND TONNAGE OF THE STEAM-
VESSELS FOR CONVEYING PASSENGERS AND GOODS BELONGING TO
OTHER COUNTRIES.

Countries.	Ports.	Number of Steam Vessels.	Their Aggregate Tonnage.	Aggregate power of Steam Engines.
Russia	St. Petersburg, Riga, Odessa	65	—	6,982
Sweden	Stockholm, Gottenburg, Carlserona, and Ystad	61	15,203	3,275
Norway	Christiana	10	2,312	643
Denmark ...	Copenhagen, Elsinore	15	1,568	1,068
Prussia	Dantzig	2	96	56
Mecklenburg	Rostock	2	200	52
Hanse Towns	Lubec	4	2,054	560
„	Hamburg	8	1,986	860
„	Bremen	7	1,100	342
Hanover ...	Embden	1	35	25
Netherlands .	Amsterdam	7	1,460	616
„	Rotterdam	31	12,200	3,750
Belgium	Antwerp, Ostend, &c.	3	3,464	1,030
France	Calais, Havre, Granville, St. Malo, Cherbourg, Brest, Nantes, Charente, Bordeaux, Bayonne, Marseilles, Corsica	119	not given in every case.	9,027
Spain	Corunna, Cadiz, Barcelona	13	3,621	1,450
Portugal	Lisbon, Oporto	10	2,167	815
Sardinia	Genoa, Cagliari	12	4,240	1,265
Tuscany	Leghorn	4	1,356	530
Two Sicilies .	Naples, Palermo ...	5	2,135	910
Austria	Trieste and Venice ..	16	5,957	1,620
Turkey	Constantinople	14	4,315	1,864
„	Alexandria	8	not stated.	644
Barbary States	Tunis	1	90	18
United States of America	Portland, New York, Lakes Champlain, &c., Philadelphia, Baltimore, Norfolk, Charleston, Savannah, Mobile, and New Orleans	261	not stated.	not stated.
Texas	Galveston	2	130	55
Mexico	Vera Cruz	5	2,690	645
Venezuela ..	Caracas	1	122	35
Chili	Valparaiso	2	1,369	360
Brazil	Rio Janeiro, Bahia ..	30	not stated.	1,833
Peru	Lima	2	1,400	360

It is not unlikely that the returns from which the above abstract has been made may omit some vessels of this kind in their enumeration, but these omissions cannot be to any great extent; and it thus appears that the progress made by this country in the adoption of this new and great invention is fully equal to everything hitherto accomplished by all other countries in the aggregate.

The steam-vessels belonging to the different ports of the United Kingdom are thus proportioned:—

TABLE SHOWING THE NUMBER AND TONNAGE OF THE STEAM-VESSELS REGISTERED AT THE FOLLOWING PORTS ON THE 1ST DAY OF JANUARY, 1849.

Tons.	London.		Liverpool.		Glasgow.		Dublin.		Other Ports.		Total.	
	Vessels.	Tons.	Vessels.	Tons.	Vessels.	Tons.	Vessels.	Tons.	Vessels.	Tons.	Vessels.	Tons.
Not exceeding 100	119	7,943	18	1,468	10	735	3	220	379	21,521	529	31,887
From 100 to 250	70	11,579	43	6,342	46	7,299	11	2,267	102	16,252	272	43,739
„ 250 to 400	54	15,938	8	2,683	9	2,919	13	4,106	52	16,225	136	41,871
„ 400 to 600	25	12,451	4	1,961	3	1,547	9	4,475	30	15,024	71	35,458
„ 600 to 1000	18	14,054	2	1,265	4	3,279	11	7,494	32	21,483	67	47,575
1000 and upwards	23	36,913	1	1,300	9	13,592	...	...	2	3,036	35	54,841
Total	309	98,878	76	15,019	81	29,371	47	18,562	597	93,541	1,110	255,371

It appears then from the above that more than one-fourth of the entire number, and one-third of the aggregate tonnage, of the steam-vessels belonging to the United Kingdom appertain to the Port of London.

———————

The Morning Chronicle, Thursday, March 14, 1850.

NEEDLEWOMEN DESIRING EMPLOYMENT.

———◆———

In consequence of the disclosures which have been made, in the Letters of our Metropolitan Correspondent on "Labour and the Poor," respecting the condition of the needlewomen of London, we have been constantly applied to, by persons wishing to give occasional employment in family needlework, for the names and addresses of sempstresses who are desirous of obtaining work. We have much regretted our inability to afford the requisite information to any great extent; nor can we now undertake fully to supply the want which is so often complained of in regard to this subject. But we are anxious to meet, to some extent, the existing deficiency; and we have therefore undertaken to receive, and from time to time to publish in our columns, the names and addresses of such needlewomen as may be solicitous of obtaining casual employment from private families. A complete list of all the names thus furnished to us will be kept in our Publishing Office, and it will be always open to the inspection of those seeking for such information. It is but right, however, to add, that we cannot undertake to guarantee the qualifications or character of applicants for needlework; and that our object is merely to make the public acquainted with the names and addresses of those who desire employment. The following is the list of names which has been handed to us:—

M. A. Foley, 19, Little Wild-street, Drury-lane.
E. Eveson, 47, Cartwright-street, Tower-hill.
E. Hickson, 21, Stanhope-street, Clare-market.
J. Hutton, 9, Cross-court, Duke's-court, Drury-lane.
M. Jolly, 2, Globe-place, Globe-road, Mile-end.
A. Murray, 6, Great Wild-street, Drury-lane.
M. Harwood, 65, Park-street, Poplar.
M. Wilson, 2, Burley-court, Smart's-buildings, Holborn.
E. Smith, 24, White Horse-yard, Drury-lane.
H. Brown, 22, Red Lion-street, Wapping.
M. A. Lyon, 17, Peter-street, Cow-cross.
J. Redfurn, 6, Cock-court, Poppin's-court, Fleet-street.
M. A. Cuthbert, 22, Pear Tree-court, Clerkenwell-close.
E. Williams, 3, Cross-court, Duke's-court, Drury-lane.

THE SPITALFIELDS WEAVERS.

———◆———

To the EDITOR of the MORNING CHRONICLE.

Sir—The broad silk weavers of Spitalfields request of you to insert the following statement in your paper, and by doing so you will confer a benefit on a body of persons whose real condition—in spite of the prosperous trade they enjoy at present—is truly miserable; good trade with them being a privilege to work sixteen hours a day for a bare subsistence. We are subjected to every kind of physical, social, and moral evil. We are badly housed, badly fed, and badly educated; and what, if anything, is still worse, we are made to feel our degraded state by the harsh treatment we receive from many of our employers, especially when they are desirous of lowering our wages. But we are glad to say there are some who are willing to act justly, who wish to be on friendly terms with their workpeople, and think the best way to be so is to pay them the highest wages possible, and by their exemplary conduct hold forth an inducement to others to do likewise. Some of those gentlemen's names appeared in *The Morning Chronicle* of last week; but as the deputation appointed had not time to wait on the whole of their employers, the names of Messrs. Sanderson and Reed did not appear. The weavers therefore consider it a duty they owe to those gentlemen and themselves to give publicity to their upright conduct, hoping it will be the means of procuring an advance of wages throughout the trade.

Messrs. Sanderson and Reed have advanced four pence per yard on their vestings, or fifteen per cent., which will add sixpence a day to the wages of the weaver; and they are willing to raise the price of all the goods they manufacture, provided other manufacturers will do the same.

Signed on behalf of the committee,

G. HACKMAN, President.
JAMES ARCHER, Secretary.

March 13.

The Editor of *The Morning Chronicle* is requested to divide the amount of letter-stamps enclosed (15s.) between the poor maker of mouse-traps, assisted by his dutiful daughter (the man suffering from incurable disease in the thigh) and the manufacturer of dolls'-heads, whose child was lying in its coffin (dead of hooping cough) when visited by the Metropolitan Commissioner of *The Morning Chronicle*.

The Morning Chronicle, Monday, March 18, 1850.

To the EDITOR of the MORNING CHRONICLE.

Sir—I send 10*l.* to your relief fund, to be applied as your kind and able reporters, who best know the cases, by the assistance given them, judge best. I must, however, express a hope that the two middle-aged needlewomen mentioned in your supplement of January 11, Letter XI., who maintained a four years' struggle against starvation with such enduring honesty and perseverance, will have met with more than temporary succour, and I should be glad to aid those rather who have kept a good course amidst the manifold temptations of their misery than those who have failed to do so, though many of these are not much less to be pitied. Some of the unnoticed cases you have detailed (and how many more must be privately known to your reporters) have equally deserved relief with those which have so justly, and many of them so largely, attracted public sympathy. Your inquiries will probably soon cease, but should your charitable work be continued through the pressure time of another winter, many I think will rejoice to aid, and I trust do so more largely, a good work in which they have the security from such accurate investigation that their benevolence will not be misapplied. Your painfully interesting disclosures can hardly fail to bring about some amendment in the condition of the labouring classes.

I am, sir, your obedient servant,

March 14.   C. F.

The Editor of *The Morning Chronicle* is requested to have the kindness to distribute the enclosed sovereign (P. O.) as follows:—5s. to the Shoebinder who lived with the Painter; 5s. to the Painter himself; 5s. to the Shoemaker who wished to emigrate; and 5s. to the Toymaker who had lost his child in the hooping-cough.

CHRISTIANUS.

LABOUR AND THE POOR.

—◆—

THE METROPOLITAN DISTRICTS.

[FROM OUR SPECIAL CORRESPONDENT.]

THE RAGGED SCHOOLS OF LONDON.

LETTER XLIII.

I am obliged to defer, for a few days, the continuation of my letters upon the Merchant Seamen belonging to the port of London, in order to allow time for the making up of certain official returns which are necessary for the comprehensive exposition of the subject. Meanwhile, I purpose devoting a few letters to the consideration of the means and institutions existing in the metropolis for the Education of the Poor.

In my letters upon the London Vagrants I entered at some length into the cause of juvenile crime. I had no theory to advocate—I came to the subject determined to investigate patiently, and to generalize cautiously. It is with the same determination I now return to the matter.

There are of course two modes of combating all crime—the one *preventive* and the other *corrective*. The preventive mode acts only by punishment—that is, by seeking to deter the criminal from the exercise of his vicious propensities through appealing to his fears. This mode of procedure therefore can at the best give us only a negative result. It may prevent the criminal appetite or desire from being put into action, but it cannot possibly implant one virtuous desire in its stead. It is the implanting of this virtuous desire which constitutes the corrective method of dealing with crime. This seeks to arrive at a positive result by cultivating some good feeling, rather than endeavouring to eradicate some bad one. Hence, to destroy idleness, it sets to work to create a habit of industry—to put an end to theft, it tries to call forth a feeling of honour. Law seeks to make good citizens, principally by punishment or the prevention of vice. Education strives to gain the same end by correction, or the cultivation of virtue.

I purpose in this and the letters immediately following, to consider how far the correction of crime has been as yet, and may be, effected by education; and with this object I shall devote some three or four to the Ragged Schools of the metropolis. I shall, in the first place, endeavour to test their efficacy by the returns of the number of juvenile offenders since their establishment. This, I am aware, is putting them to a severe test; but if we find that the young criminals have been decreasing rapidly in number from the year 1845 (the first year in which the Ragged Schools were brought into extensive operation in the metropolis), then we may readily assume that they are among our most noble and valuable institutions. If, however, the official reports show that, notwithstanding the rapid and great increase of these establishments, the juvenile offenders have in no way declined in numbers, then we may safely conclude, on the other hand, that, as at present conducted, they are of little or no service.

Let us see what the Government returns say upon this subject. First as regards the criminals, adult as well as juvenile, of England and Wales, the following table, calculated up to the latest returns, will show us the rate of increase year by year since 1839.

CRIMINALS OF ENGLAND AND WALES.
TABLE SHOWING THE NUMBER OF CRIMINALS, THE ESTIMATED POPULATION, AND THE PROPORTIONS OF CRIMINALS TO THE POPULATION.

Years.	Total Number of Persons Committed.	Estimated Population in each year.	Number of Population to One Prisoner.
1839	24,443	15,492,867	One in 633
1840	27,187	15,698,044	„ 569
1841	27,760	15,906,741	„ 573
1842	31,309	16,118,589	„ 514
1843	29,591	16,333,659	„ 551
1844	26,542	16,551,713	„ 623
1845	24,303	16,772,678	„ 690
1846	25,107	16,996,593	„ 676
1847	28,833	17,055,660	„ 591
1848	30,349	17,214,727	„ 567

Here we perceive that the total number of offenders has increased no less than 5,906 in ten years, and that while in 1839 only 1 in 633 of the population of England and Wales were criminals, in 1848 the ratio had risen to 1 in 567.

Let me, however, now proceed to show how many of the criminals in the numbers above given, are under the age of 20 years. This will enable us to discriminate between the juvenile and adult offenders, and so to perceive whether the young criminals have increased throughout the country in a like ratio:—

JUVENILE OFFENDERS FOR ENGLAND AND WALES.

TABLE SHOWING THE AGES OF PERSONS COMMITTED IN ENGLAND AND WALES FOR THE LAST SEVEN YEARS.

Committed.	Total Number of Offenders of all Ages.	Under 15 Years of Age.	Above 15 and under 20.	Total under 20.
In the year 1842 ...	31,309	1,672	6,884	8,556
„ 1843 ...	29,591	1,670	6,725	8,395
„ 1844 ...	26,542	1,596	6,190	7,786
„ 1845 ...	24,303	1,549	5,850	7,399
„ 1846 ...	25,107	1,640	6,136	7,776
„ 1847 ...	28,883	1,767	6,967	7,734
„ 1848 ...	30,349	1,087	7,232	8,319

Hence we see that from 1842 to 1848, the number of offenders under 20 years of age has declined 235, and the number under 15 years nearly 600. The following table, however, will give us more clear information as to the rate of decrease among the juvenile offenders throughout the country by showing us the ratio that they bore to the total population at the different years:—

JUVENILE OFFENDERS FOR ENGLAND AND WALES.

TABLE SHOWING THE NUMBER OF CRIMINALS UNDER 20 YEARS OF AGE, AND THEIR PROPORTION TO THE WHOLE OF THE JUVENILE POPULATION IN ENGLAND AND WALES, FROM 1848 TO 1848 INCLUSIVE.

	Criminals under 20 years.	Computed Population in each year under 20 years.	No. of Juvenile Population to one Juvenile Criminal.
1842....	8,556	7,378,829	One in every ... 862
1843....	8,395	7,451,877	„ ... 887
1844....	7,786	7,524,934	„ ... 966
1845....	7,399	7,597,991	„ ...1,026
1846....	7,776	7,671,048	„ ... 986
1847....	7,734	7,744,105	„ ...1,001
1848....	8,319	7,817,162	„ ... 939

By the above, then, it is evident that there has been a gradual and steady decrease in the proportion of our juvenile offenders since 1842. In that year 1 in every 862 persons under 20 years of age were criminals. In 1848 the ratio had fallen to 1 in every 939. We may, then, safely assert that while the total number of criminals in England and Wales has been rapidly increasing, the number of our juvenile delinquents has been materially on the decline.

I shall now lay before the reader the criminal returns for the metropolis, so that he may see whether the same result has taken place:—

METROPOLITAN OFFENDERS OF ALL AGES.

Years.	Total taken into Custody.	Estimated Population of the Metropolis.	Number of Population to one taken into Custody.
1839....	65,965	1,836,204	one in 27
1840....	70,717	1,854,940	„ 26
1841....	68,961	1,873,676	„ 27
1842....	65,704	1,892,412	„ 28
1843....	62,477	1,911,148	„ 30
1844....	62,522	1,929,884	„ 30
1845....	59,123	1,948,620	„ 32
1846....	62,834	1,967,356	„ 31
1847....	62,181	1,986,092	„ 31
1848....	64,480	2,004,828	„ 31

Upon an average for the last ten years, I find that only about 7 per cent. of those who are taken into custody are committed for trial. The reader, therefore, must be warned against confounding the numbers given in these criminal tables for the metropolis with those above given for England and Wales; the numbers in the one being the total of those taken into custody, and the other the total of those committed for trial. I have been obliged to follow this conflicting mode of calculation, owing to the criminal returns of the metropolis furnishing no means of arriving at either the age or degree of instruction of those committed for trial. The reader therefore must, in seeking to compare the state of crime in the metropolis with that in England and Wales, allow for this defect.

According to the above table the total number of persons, of all ages, taken into custody in the metropolis has decreased 1,485 in ten years, while the population has increased 168,604—or in other words, while only one in 27 individuals was taken up for some breach of the law in 1839, only one in 31 was arrested in 1848.

The juvenile criminals of the metropolis have, strange to say, not-withstanding the rapid increase of the Ragged Schools throughout London, increased at an alarming rate:—

CRIMINAL RETURNS OF THE METROPOLIS.

Taken into custody.	Total all ages.	Under 10 years of age.	Ten years and under fifteen.	Fifteen and under twenty.	Total under twenty.	Proportion of the total number of offenders to those under twenty years.
In 1839 ...	65,965	159	2,697	10,731	13,587	1 to 4
1840 ...	70,717	148	2,202	11,681	14,031	„ 5
1841 ...	68,961	196	2,584	14,645	17,425	„ 3
1842 ...	65,704	146	2,591	14,250	16,987	„ 3
1843 ...	62,477	131	2,459	13,726	16,316	„ 3
1844 ...	62,522	273	3,639	12,688	13,600	„ 4
1845 ...	59,123	359	3,506	11,622	15,128	„ 3
1846 ...	62,834	310	3,310	11,932	15,552	„ 4
1847 ...	62,181	362	3,682	11,654	15,698	„ 3
1848 ...	64,480	384	4,239	12,294	16,917	„ 3

In 1839, the number of metropolitan offenders under 20 years was 13,587. In 1844 it was the same. In 1848 it had increased to 16,917. Since 1845, the increase has been no less than 1,789. The number of juvenile offenders under 10 years of age and those under 15, will be found to have increased at a similar fearful rate. In 1839, it will be seen by the above, only 1 youth in 53 was taken into custody; in 1848 the ratio had risen to 1 in 47. In 1845 the proportion was 1 in 51, and since that date it has gradually increased to 1 in 47.

The following table will show the proportion of the criminals under 20 to the population of the metropolis under the same age:—

METROPOLITAN JUVENILE OFFENDERS.

Years.	Number of persons under 20 years taken into custody.	Estimated population under 20 years.	Number of population under 20 years to one taken into custody.
1839	13,587	733,487	one in 53
1840	14,031	740,971	„ 52
1841	17,425	748,455	„ 42
1842	16,987	755,939	„ 44
1843	16,316	763,423	„ 46
1844	13,600	770,907	„ 56
1845	15,128	778,391	„ 51
1846	15,552	785,875	„ 50
1847	15,698	793,359	„ 50
1848	16,917	800,843	„ 47

Let me now show the rate of increase among the Ragged Schools of the metropolis since the first establishment of the union in 1844. Previously, no sufficient returns were kept to supply proper data for statistics:—

	Schools.	Teachers.	Children.	Amount collected.
First year (1845) ..	20	200	2,000	£61
Second year (1846)	26	250	2,600	£320

The three following reports, for 1847-8-9, respectively, give further details, distinguishing the voluntary and paid teachers, &c.:—

SUMMARY.	Schools.	Vol. Teachers.	Paid Teachers.	Scholars.
Eastern Division ...	5	44	4	653
Central and Northern	15	87	19	1,202
Western	14	153	20	1,741
Southern	10	115	12	1,180
	44	400	54	4,776

SUMMARY.	Schools.	Attendance of Scholars.			Attendance of Teachers.		Room to Accommodate.
		Sunday.	Weekday.	Evening.	Voluntary.	Paid.	
Eastern Division	8	1,311	550	505	146	11	1,300
Cent. & Nor. Div.	21	1,656	865	895	197	20	1,955
Western Division	20	1,686	1,935	1,308	308	38	3,310
Southern Division	13	1,190	130	792	171	11	2,000
Total	62	5,843	3,480	3,500	822	80	8,565

SUMMARY.	Schools.	Attendance of Scholars.			Attendance of Teachers.		Room to Accommo-date.
		Sun-day.	Week-day.	Even-ing.	Volun-tary.	Paid.	
Eastern Division	15	1,865	735	981	210	20	2,045
Cent. & Nor. Div.	24	2,479	1,463	1,388	223	39	3,235
Western Division	20	2,065	1,684	1,140	259	43	3,090
Southern Division	23	1,721	413	1,315	237	22	3,340
Total	82	8,130	4,295	4,824	929	124	11,710

Hence it would appear that the number of Ragged Schools in London has increased from 20 in 1845 to 62 in 1848; the teachers from 200 to 882; and the scholars from 2,000 to 12,823, in the same period. In 1849 the number of schools was 82, the scholars 17,249, and the teachers 1,053. And yet, notwithstanding all this vast educational machinery, the increase of the juvenile criminals of London has not abated one jot.

Such, then, are the bare facts of the case. In my next letter I will endeavour to point out the cause, by showing the relation that ignorance really bears to crime. For the present, I shall content myself with the following brief history of the Ragged Schools in general:—

The Ragged School Union was formed in April, 1844, and its first annual report appeared in June, 1845. Prior to this concentration, as it may be called, of Ragged School institutions, for purposes of manage-ment, efforts, successful and unsuccessful, had been voluntarily made by benevolent and humble persons in some of the poorest localities in the metropolis to impart some portion of knowledge—were it but the ability to read or repeat the Lord's Prayer, or to write their own names—to outcast children, to the deserted or runaway inmates of low lodging-houses, or to those whose only shelter is the streets or the filthy and furnitureless room of depraved parents. The difficulties overcome by the earliest promoters of Ragged Schools were of no ordinary character. The windows of the schools were broken by the urchins, who regarded it as "a lark" to insult a teacher; their entry into the school was as uproarious as they could make it; the lamps were extinguished; filth and stones were flung about amidst noise and rib-aldry; the boys on some occasions would neither listen to the teachers, nor to one another; they would neither sit down nor retire from the apartment, but kept up a hubbub that alarmed the neighbourhood, and made landlords very unwilling to encourage Ragged Schools on

or near their property. The services of the police were not seldom required. Perseverance and kindness of demeanour, however, subdued
even the vagrant insolence and boldness of these outcast lads, and
they gradually subsided into some degree of order and attentiveness.
A "row" in a Ragged School is now, I believe, a thing of very rare
occurrence.

The title "Ragged School"—and there are schools for both sexes—
sufficiently denotes the character of the institution. It is open to all,
and gratuitously; there is no restriction as to hours; no introduction
is needed. The children can come and go as their inclinations prompt
attendance, or as their necessities compel absence, that they may earn,
or beg, or steal a scanty meal. To go straight from a theft or from
a prison to a Ragged School is not unfrequent; while a "hanging-
match," or a Lord Mayor's-day, or any business that causes a large
concourse of people, deprives the Ragged School teachers of the great
majority of their pupils.

"The teachers," says Lord Ashley, in an able and interesting article in the "Quarterly Review" for December, 1846, "seek to reclaim
a wild and lawless race, unaccustomed, from their earliest years, to
the slightest moral influence, or even restraint, and bring them back
to notions of civilization and domestic life. Their first difficulty lies
in the roving habits of many of these infants of nature, who often-
times quit their residences, if residences they have, and migrate in
flocks to other districts of the great city. Those, again, who, while
in town, are more stationary in their nightly resorts, indulge, nevertheless, in long absences from London, and roam for weeks together
over the neighbouring counties. The fine months of summer are fatal
to learning; the chills and rains of winter drive them to the schools for
warmth and shelter. But such broken studies and imperfect discipline
leave on such vagrants few traces of progress in which the teacher can
find his consolation. Authority he cannot exercise; the children may
be coaxed, but they cannot be coerced; fines it is absurd to think of;
beating would not be efficacious, nor indeed safe; expulsion is no punishment. They must come when they like, or they will not come at all,
for we offer neither food nor clothing, nor immediate temporal advantage of any kind; their hopes and their fears are alike unawakened,
and wanton tastes find nothing to counteract them. A procession or
a new show throws confusion into every 'gymnasium,' and shears the
master, in the twinkling of an eye, of half his listeners. It was our
lot, a few weeks ago, to visit one of these Ragged Schools at eight

o'clock in the evening; we found it comparatively deserted; but the mystery was soon solved by the announcement that, it being Lord Mayor's-day, many had determined to avail themselves of so glorious an opportunity for pleasure or for profit.

"The habits, too, of their daily life, the associations they necessarily form, are all alike in the way of the teacher: the lessons of the evening are reversed by the practice of the following day—passed, too probably, amidst the lowest scenes of vice and revelry. If kept at home, they are witnesses of all that is most vile in language and conduct; if sent abroad, it is to beg on prepared falsehoods—or cheat methodically in their small trades—or steal for immediate consumption or for sale at the receiving shop. Hence the difficulty of infusing into these wanderers a sense of shame, and delicate notions of *meum* and *tuum*. Having nothing of their own, they are under no terrors of the law of retaliation; being destitute of common necessaries, they cannot recognize the exclusive possession of superfluities; and so, less with a desire to infringe another man's rights than to assert what they consider to be their own, they help themselves to everything that comes in their way. They make little or no secret of their successful operations, cloaking them only with euphonious terms; they 'find' everything—they 'take' nothing; no matter the bulk or quality of the article, it was 'found'—sometimes nearly a side of bacon—just at the convenient time and place; and many are the loud and bitter complaints that the 'dealer in marine stores' is utterly dishonest, and has given for the thing but half the price that could be got in the market.

"Nor does punishment humble them more effectually than crime; they see in it less of the justice of the law than of the skill of the policeman."

The Ragged School, then, presents a peculiar class, and the title is peculiarly appropriate. "We entertain no fanatical passion for the name," says Lord Ashley, "though we could quote many instances in which some of the most degraded of the race have been invited by the belief that the place and the service were not too grand for their misery." Of the mode of their education—industrial training, both of boys and girls, forming part of it in some schools—I shall speak, from personal observation, in my subsequent letters.

The readers of my letters on the "Vagrants and Juvenile Thieves of London," will not be unprepared to conjecture the character of the boys who originally resorted, and who continue to resort, to the

Ragged Schools. As a confirmatory and unexceptionable evidence on the subject, I again quote Lord Ashley's article:—

"It is a curious race of human beings that these philanthropists have taken in hand. Every one who walks the streets of the metropolis must daily observe several members of the tribe—bold, and pert, and dirty as London sparrows, but pale, feeble, and sadly inferior to them in plumpness of outline. Their business, or pretended business, seems to vary with the locality. At the West-end they deal in lucifer-matches, audaciously beg, or tell a touching tale of woe. Pass on to the central parts of the town—to Holborn or the Strand, and the regions adjacent to them—and you will there find the numbers very greatly increased: a few are pursuing the avocations above-mentioned of their more Corinthian fellows; many are spanning the gutters with their legs, and dabbling with earnestness in the latest accumulation of nastiness; while others, in squalid and half-naked groups, squat at the entrances of the narrow, fœtid courts and alleys that lie concealed behind the deceptive frontages of our larger thoroughfares. Whitechapel and Spitalfields teem with them like an ant's-nest; but it is in Lambeth and in Westminster that we find the most flagrant traces of their swarming activity. There the foul and dismal passages are thronged with children of both sexes, and of every age from three to thirteen. Though wan and haggard, they are singularly vivacious, and engaged in every sort of occupation but that which would be beneficial to themselves and creditable to the neighbourhood. Their appearance is wild; the matted hair, the disgusting filth that renders necessary a closer inspection before the flesh can be discerned between the rags which hang about it, and the barbarian freedom from all superintendence and restraint, fill the mind of a novice in these things with perplexity and dismay. Visit these regions in the summer, and you are overwhelmed by the exhalations; visit them in the winter, and you are shocked by the spectacle of hundreds shivering in apparel that would be scanty in the tropics; many are all but naked; those that are clothed are grotesque; the trowsers, where they have them, seldom pass the knee; the tailed coats very frequently trail below the heels. In this guise they run about the streets, and line the banks of the river at low water, seeking coals, sticks, corks—for nothing comes amiss as treasure-trove: screams of delight burst occasionally from the crowds, and leave the passer-by, if he be in a contemplative mood, to wonder and to rejoice that moral and physical degradations have not yet broken every spring of their youthful energies. * * * * The children that survive noxious influences and awful neglect are thrown, as soon as they can crawl, to scramble in the gutter, and leave their parents to amusement or business; as they advance in years they discover that they must, in general, find their own food or go without it. At an age when the children of the wealthy would still be in leading strings, they are off, singly or in parties, to beg, borrow, steal, and exercise all the cunning that want and a love of evil can stir up in a reckless race. They are driven to these courses, in many instances, by their parents; in more by their stepmothers; in most by necessity and general example. The passion for shows and the lowest drama is nearly universal; 'Panem et Circenses'—food and the penny theatres—these are their paradise, and their chief temptation to crime. They receive no education, religious or secular; they are subjected to no restraint of any sort; never do they hear the word of advice, or the accent of kindness; the notions that exist in the minds of ordinary persons have no place in theirs; having nothing exclusively of their own, they seem to think such, in fact, the true position of society; and, helping themselves without scruple to the goods of others, they can never recognise, when convicted before a magistrate, the justice of a sentence which punishes them for having done little more than was indispensable to their existence.

"Well, then, we discover that they are beings like ourselves; that they have long subsisted within a walk of our own dwellings; that they have increased, and are increasing in numbers with the extension of this overgrown metropolis; and that they recede, if to recede be possible, in physical and moral condition, as the capital itself advances towards the pinnacle of magnificence and refinement. Will no one roll away the reproach? We have an Established Church, abundant in able and pious men, and she boasts herself to be the church of the people. We have a great body of wealthy and intelligent dissenters, who declaim, by day and by night, on the efficacious virtues of the voluntary principle. We have a generous aristocracy and plethoric capitalists, and a Government pledged to social improvements. Who will come forward? Why not all?"

Since their first foundation Ragged Schools have continued to increase rapidly, and since 1845 reports have yearly appeared. In the first report (1845) I find the following statement:—"No less than forty-five of the children who attended one Ragged School are now transported, the school not affording them any permanent protection against vicious influences." In the second annual report there is this statement:—"Some of the schools formerly reported have been so much improved as to come no longer under the denomination or character of Ragged Schools." By what means this change was wrought the report does not explain. The third report describes the exertions of the committee of the Ragged Schools Union, reiterates (in accordance with the preceding reports) that 100,000 poor children in the metropolis are growing up in ignorance and vagrancy, and details the plans and discipline of the committee. "In addition to frequent inspection," it is stated, "two delegates are summoned once a quarter from every school to meet the committee, and report how matters go on; and this meeting is becoming more useful and interesting each succeeding quarter. At the last quarterly meeting forty delegates attended." The fourth report insists, that "while we are spending a great amount in supporting or punishing the *man*, we do little to improve and elevate the *boy*," and cites one among other difficulties experienced by the promoters of Ragged Schools: "One great hindrance to success has been the difficulty of getting employment for boys after they became steady and anxious to earn their own living; many lads have continued to attend the schools destitute of food as well as proper clothing, in the hope that some situation could be procured for them by their teachers or their friends. In many instances employment *has* been found both for boys and girls, but hundreds are still unprovided for." The fifth (and latest) report (May last) mentions that the children of Roman Catholics came in large numbers to the Ragged Schools, and did not object to reading the Bible.

The following were the amounts of donations and subscriptions received for the years ending May, 1847-8-9, respectively. The balances in hand show the proportion of the expenditure to the receipts:—

Balance last audit	£179	9	11
Donations	564	17	11
Annual subscriptions	72	2	6
Cash for sale of Bibles to children, at 6d. each.	7	16	6
	£824	6	10

Balance last Audit	£461	18	11
Donations	520	5	0
Collection at Third Annual Meeting	43	13	2
Collection at Trinity Chapel after Sermon preached by the Rev. H. H. Beamish ..	42	13	6
Annual Subscriptions	89	13	6
Cash for sale of Bibles to children at 6d. each and Hymn-books	16	0	0
	£1,174	4	1

Balance last Audit	£444	10	10
Donations	3,168	14	6
Subscriptions	338	0	0
Collection at Annual Meeting, 1848	76	10	8
Collecting Cards, Boxes, &c.	49	16	1
Sale of Bibles, Hymn Books, Anthems, Reward Books, and Magazines	65	4	7
	£4,142	16	8

Ragged Schools have been established in the following places:—

EASTERN DIVISION.—Foster-street, Bishopsgate; Dolphin-court, Spitalfields; Vine-court, Spitalfields; Thrawl-street, Spitalfields; King-street, Spitalfields; Spicer-street, Spitalfields; Goldsmiths'-row, Hackney-road; Twig-folly, Bethnal-green; King Edward-street, Mile-end; North-street, Whitechapel-road; Cumberland-place, Whitechapel-road; Lomas-buildings, Stepney; Cotton-street, Poplar; Bere-street, Ratcliff; Darby-street, Rosemary-lane.

CENTRAL AND NORTHERN DIVISION.—Field-lane, West Smithfield; Plumtree-court, Shoe-lane; Golden-lane, St. Luke's; Turk's Head-yard, Clerkenwell; Lamb and Flag-court, Clerkenwell-green; Vine-street, Liquorpond-street; Fox-court, Gray's-inn-lane; Yeates-court, Clare-market; Brewers'-court, Great Wild-street; King-street, Drury-lane; Neales-yard, Seven-dials; Streatham-street, St. Giles; Irish Free School, St. Giles's; Phillip's-gardens, New-road; Little Camden-street, Camden-town; Agar-town, St. Pancras-road; Compton-place, Judd-street; Coram-place, Little Coram-street; Britannia-street, King's-cross; Elder-walk, Islington; Brand-street, Holloway; Phillip-street, Kingsland-road; Providence-row, Kingsland; Stoke Newington.

WESTERN DIVISION.—Westminster Juvenile Refuge and School of Industry, 56, Old Pye-street; New Pye-street, Westminster; Pear-street, Westminster; Broadway, Westminster; New Tothill-street, Westminster; Exeter-buildings, Chelsea; Camera-street, Chelsea; Temperance Hall, Hammersmith; Richmond-street, Lisson-grove; George-street, Lisson-grove; Paddington Wharfs; Huntsworth-mews, Dorset-square; Brook-street, New-road; Union-mews, Wells-street; Grotto-passage, Marylebone; Grotto-place, Marylebone; Hindes'-mews, Marylebone-lane; Edwards-mews, Portman-square; Gray's-yard, James-street; Hopkins-street, Golden-square.

SOUTHERN DIVISION.—Lambeth; Little East-street, Lambeth; Jurston-street, Lambeth; Grove-lane, New-cut; Windmill-street, New-cut; Waterloo-road; Broadwall, Blackfriars; Chapel-place, Great Suffolk-street; John-street, Mint; Mitre-court, Mint-street; Henry-street, Kent-street; Vine-yard, Tooley-street; Jacob-street, Dockhead; Deptford, Duncan-yard; Greenwich, East; Greenwich, West; Blackheath, Queen-street; Peckham, High-street; Camberwell, Nelson-street; Clapham, White's-square; Clapham, Union-street; Walworth, Crown-square; Newington, Francis-street.

In a speech in the House of Commons in July last, in submitting a motion that means should be annually provided for the emigration of a certain number of Ragged School pupils, Lord Ashley gave the results of his inquiry into the condition of outcast children. "He and others," he said, "perambulated the metropolis. They dived into its recesses. The House would be surprised to hear what was the condition in which they found those young people. Most of them were living in the dry arches of houses not finished, inaccessible except by an aperture only large enough to admit the body of a man. When a lantern was thrust in, six or eight, ten or twelve people, might be found lying together. Of those whom they found thus lodged they invited a great number to come the following day, and then an examination was instituted. The number examined was 33. Their ages varied from 12 to 18, and some were younger; 24 had no parents; six had one; three had stepmothers; 20 had no shirts; 9 no shoes; 12 had been once in prison; 3 twice; 3 four times; 1 eight times; and 1 (only 14 years old) twelve times. The physical condition of these children was exceedingly horrible; they were a prey to vermin; they were troubled with itch; they were begrimed with dirt; not a few were suffering from sickness; and two or three days afterwards two died from disease and the effects of starvation. He had privately examined eight or ten. He was anxious to obtain from them the truth. He examined them separately, taking them into a room alone. He said, 'I am going to ask you a variety of questions, to which I trust you will give me true answers, and I, on my part, will undertake to answer any question you may put to me.' They thought that a fair bargain. He put to several of them the question, 'How often have you slept in a bed during the last three years?' One said, perhaps twelve times; another, three times; another could not remember that he had ever done so. He asked them how they passed the night in winter. They said, 'We lie eight or ten together, to keep ourselves warm.' He entered on the subject of their employments and modes of living. They fairly confessed they had no means of subsistence but begging and stealing."

I need not dilate upon the fact of the far superior charity (in proportion to their means) not seldom extended by the industrious poor to their utterly destitute friends and neighbours, compared with that of even the most benevolent of the wealthy classes—nor need I speak of the greater labour they will undergo in aid of the helpless and the destitute; and I may fairly surmise therefore that among poor people there have been individual and desultory efforts, now forgotten, to extend some schooling to the ignorant children around them. The case of John Pounds, however, has not been forgotten, and he—with Mr. Walker, of Westminster, and a few others—is classed among the founders of the Ragged Schools. I give a brief and popular biography of John Pounds:—

"John Pounds, the cripple and the cobbler, yet at the same time one of nature's true nobility, was born in Portsmouth in 1766. His father was a sawyer, employed in the royal dockyard. At fifteen, young Pounds met with an accident, which disabled him for life. During the greater part of his benevolent career he lived in a small weather-boarded tenement in St. Mary's-street, Portsmouth, where he might be seen every day, seated on his stool, mending shoes in the midst of his busy little school. One of his amusements was that of rearing singing birds, jays, and parrots, which he so perfectly domesticated that they lived harmoniously with his cats and guinea-pigs. Often, it is said, might a canary-bird be seen perched upon one shoulder and a cat upon the other. During the latter part of his life, however, when his scholars became so numerous, he was able to keep fewer of these domestic creatures. Poor as he was, and entirely dependent upon the hard labour of his hands, he nevertheless adopted a little crippled nephew, whom he educated, and cared for with truly paternal love, and, in the end, established comfortably in life. It was out of this connection that his attempts and success in the work of education arose. He thought in the first instance that the boy would learn better with a companion. He obtained one, the son of a wretchedly poor mother; then another and another was added; and he found so much pleasure in his employment, and was the means thereby of effecting so much good, that in the end the number of his scholars amounted to forty, including about a dozen little girls.

John Pounds, the Philanthropic Cobbler, and Founder of Ragged Schools

"His humble workshop was about six feet by eighteen, in the midst of which he would sit engaged in that labour by which he won his bread, and attending at the same time to the studies of the little crowd around him. So efficient was John Pound's mode of education, to say nothing about its being perfectly gratuitous, that the candidates were always numerous; he, however, invariably gave the preference to the worst as well as poorest children—to the 'little blackguards,' as he called them. He has been known to follow such to the Town Quay and offer them the bribe of a roasted potato if they would come to his school. His influence on these degraded children was extraordinary.

"As a teacher, his manners were pleasant and facetious. Many hundred persons, now living usefully and creditably in life, owe the whole formation of their character to him. He gave them 'book-learning,' and taught them also to cook their own victuals and mend their shoes. He was not only frequently their doctor and nurse, but their play-fellow: no wonder was it, therefore, that when, on New Year's Day, 1839, he suddenly died, at the age of seventy-two, the children wept, and even fainted, on hearing of their loss, and for a long time were overwhelmed with sorrow and consternation. They, indeed, had lost a friend and a benefactor. Such was the noble founder of the first Ragged School."

LABOUR AND THE POOR.

THE METROPOLITAN DISTRICTS.

[FROM OUR SPECIAL CORRESPONDENT.]

LETTER XLIV.

In my last Letter I proved by tables, made up from the Government reports, that the number of offenders under 20 years of age taken into custody by the Metropolitan Police, since 1839, has increased from 13,587 to 16,917 per annum—or, in other words, from 1 in every 53, to 1 in every 47 of the juvenile population of London; and this, notwithstanding the great exertions that have been made, and the large sums of money that have been subscribed of late years, with a view to reforming the class. Let me, however, for the sake of greater perspicuity, place the increase of the Metropolitan Juvenile Offenders side by side with that of the London Ragged Schools, since the first establishment of their Union, in 1844, so that the reader may compare the one with the other:—

	Increase of Ragged Schools since 1844.				Increase of Juvenile Offenders since 1844.	
Year.	Schools.	Teachers.	Children.	Amount Collected.	Number of Juvenile Offenders taken into custody.	Number of population under 20 to 1 Juvenile Offender.
1844	20	200	2,000	£61 0 0	13,600	One in 56
1845	26	250	2,600	320 0 0	15,128	„ 51
1846	44	454	4,776	824 6 10	15,552	„ 50
1847	62	902	12,823	1,174 4 1	15,698	„ 50
1848	82	1,053	17,249	4,142 16 8	16,917	„ 47

Hence it appears that the increase in the number of Ragged Schools throughout the metropolis since 1844 has been 62; of Ragged School teachers, 853; of Ragged School pupils, 15,249; and of Ragged School funds, upwards of £4,000. And yet, in spite of all this vast educational machinery, the number of offenders under 20 years of age has increased in the same period to no less than 3,317—or very nearly one for each guinea that had been subscribed in the hope of diminishing juvenile depravity.

This stubborn array of facts and figures admits of no scepticism. The increase of the Schools is calculated from the annual reports of the Union—that of the juvenile offenders from the reports of the Government. Either we must assert that the criminal returns are "cooked," or else, admitting their credibility, we must confess that the Ragged Schools are not as efficient as their benevolent founders and patrons believe. As a further assurance of the fact, however—for it is a subject upon which I am most anxious not to err—I have calculated the ratio of the annual increase or decrease for a series of years before and after the establishment of the Ragged School Union. Subjoined is the result:—

TABLE, SHOWING THE INCREASE OR DECREASE PER CENT. OF THE METROPOLITAN JUVENILE OFFENDERS TAKEN INTO CUSTODY FOR EACH YEAR, BEFORE AND AFTER THE INSTITUTION OF THE LONDON RAGGED SCHOOL UNION.

BEFORE THE INSTITUTION OF THE RAGGED SCHOOL UNION.

Years.	Increase per cent.	Decrease per cent.
1839-40	3·2	—
1840-41	24·4	—
1841-42	—	2·5
1842-43	—	3·9
1843-44	—	16·6

AFTER THE INSTITUTION OF THE RAGGED SCHOOL UNION.

Years.	Increase per cent.	Decrease per cent.
1844-45	11·2	—
1845-46	2·8	—
1846-47	·9	—
1847-48	7·7	—

Here it will be seen that for the three years immediately preceding the establishment of the Union there was a rapid and extensive decrease in the juvenile depravity of the metropolis; whereas, during the four years that succeeded the incorporation of the schools, the number of offenders under twenty years of age increased almost as rapidly and extensively as it had previously declined. The next step was to ascertain whether this increase of juvenile offenders had prevailed generally throughout the country, or whether it had been confined principally to the metropolis. With the view of arriving at an accurate conclusion upon this point, I estimated the average of the centesimal proportion of the criminals of different ages during ten years in London and the country; and the result is given below:—

TABLE SHOWING THE AVERAGE PER CENTAGE OF THE EXCESS AND DEFICIENCY OF THE OFFENDERS OF DIFFERENT AGES IN THE METROPOLIS, OVER AND UNDER THOSE OF ENGLAND AND WALES.

The per centage here given is the average of ten years, from 1839 to 1848.

	England and Wales.	Metropolis.	Excess.	Deficiency.
Under 15 years	5·8	7·6	1·8	—
15 and under 20 „	23·6	28·7	5·1	—
20 „ 25 „	24·2	24·1	—	·1
25 „ 30 „	15·0	13·1	—	1·9
30 „ 40 „	16·0	14·2	—	1·8
40 „ 50 „	8·0	7·6	—	·4
50 „ 60 „	3·6	3·2	—	·4
60 and upwards ...	1·8	1·5	—	·3
Age not ascertained	2·0	—	—	—
	100·0	100·0		

The above table gives us the following results:—

Average per centage of offenders *under* 20 years in the metropolis, from 1839 to 1848 .... 36·3
Average per centage of offenders *under* 20 years in England and Wales, from 1839 to 1848 .... 29·4

Excess of offenders *under* 20 years in the metropolis 6·9

Average per centage of offenders *above* 20 years in England and Wales, from 1839 to 1848 .... 70·6
Average per centage of offenders *above* 20 years in the metropolis, from 1839 to 1848 .... 63·7

Deficiency of offenders *above* 20 years in the metropolis .... 6·9

It may therefore be asserted, that there are in the metropolis (in round numbers) seven per cent. *more* of offenders *under* twenty years, and the same proportion *less* of offenders *above* twenty years, than in England and Wales.

Let us look at the facts, then, in whatever light we may, it appears that the London Ragged Schools have not been attended with that amount of benefit which it was generally hoped would follow their establishment. But so vast a machinery, it will be said, cannot have been entirely powerless. A thousand teachers acting upon seventeen thousand scholars of the lowest and most depraved propensities and habits must have produced *some* effect. Assuredly they must; and operating on a mass of beings, concerning whose age and condition we have an accurate yearly register, we certainly ought to be able to discover an expression of the influence of the Ragged Schools somewhere in the criminal records of the country. Let us then, still confining ourselves rigidly to facts, endeavour to find whether the criminals of the metropolis are gradually becoming better educated through such means; for it is evident that since the Ragged Schools do not tend to decrease the number of offenders, at least they must be the means of improving the education of the class. The following table will prove to us that such is really the case:—

EDUCATION OF CRIMINALS (METROPOLIS).

TABLE SHOWING THE DEGREES OF INSTRUCTION OF THOSE TAKEN INTO CUSTODY, OF ALL AGES, FROM 1839 TO 1848.

Year.	Neither read nor write.	Read and write imperfectly.	Read and write well.	Superior instruction.	Total.
1839	29,418	29,864	5,853	830	65,965
1840	23,938	37,551	8,121	1,107	70,717
1841	23,331	42,128	3,009	493	68,961
1842	19,850	38,829	6,464	561	65,704
1843	16,918	39,067	5,823	669	62,477
1844	24,856	33,372	3,797	497	62,522
1845	15,263	39,659	3,615	586	59,123
1846	22,223	35,470	4,632	509	62,834
1847	22,075	35,228	4,413	465	62,181
1848	22,968	36,229	4,186	1,097	64,480

Here it will be seen that in 1844, the number of offenders in the metropolis who could neither read nor write was 24,856—in 1848 it had decreased to 22,968; whereas the number of those who read and write imperfectly had risen in the same space of time from 33,372 to 36,229. But we shall find the result still more forcibly expressed in the centesimal proportions of the degrees of education existing among the criminal offenders.

EDUCATION OF CRIMINALS (METROPOLIS).

TABLE SHOWING THE CENTESIMAL PROPORTION OF THE
EDUCATION OF OFFENDERS OF ALL AGES WHO WERE
TAKEN INTO CUSTODY FROM 1839 TO 1848 INCLUSIVE.

Years.	Neither read nor write.	Read and write imperfectly.	Read and write well.	Superior Instruction.
1839	44·6	45·3	8·9	1·2
1840	33·8	53·1	11·5	1·6
1841	33·9	61·1	4·3	·7
1842	30·2	59·1	9·8	·9
1843	27·1	62·5	9·3	1·1
1844	39·8	53·3	6·1	·8
1845	25·8	67·1	6·1	1·0
1846	35·4	56·4	7·4	·8
1847	35·5	56·6	7·1	·8
1848	35·6	56·2	6·5	1·7

Here, then, we find that in the last ten years the proportion of
those offenders who can neither read nor write has fallen from 44 to
35 per cent., while those who can read and write imperfectly has risen
from 45 to 56 per cent.—or, in other words, the uneducated class of
criminals has declined precisely to the same extent—11 per cent.—
as the imperfectly educated class has increased. It seems, then, that
notwithstanding the vast increase of our scholastic machinery of late
years, we are not *reforming* but merely educating our criminals. We
are teaching reading and writing to thousands of the most depraved
class of society in the hope of lessening our criminals; but still the
number increases, year by year, at an overwhelming rate. Not one
the less appears in our gaols. The whole and sole difference is, that
whereas, a few years back, the offender was registered among the utterly ignorant, now he takes rank among the imperfectly educated
class. The returns for England and Wales show precisely the same
result, though not to so great an extent. In 1839 the proportion of
criminals who could neither read nor write was 33½ per cent.; in 1848
the per centage had decreased to 32. In the same period the proportion who could read and write imperfectly had risen from 53½ per
cent. to 56½. Can it then be truly said that ignorance is the cause of
crime—or, *vice versâ*, that a knowledge of reading and writing is the
great panacea for all moral evil? That such is the creed of the day I am
well aware; but I fear it is one of the many fallacies which arise from
hasty generalization. Let us look calmly and dispassionately at this
part of the subject—let us discard all preconceived notions from our

minds, and see whether those counties that are the most uneducated are necessarily the most criminal. Here is a table, first, as to the relative state of crime in the different counties of England and Wales. The counties, it will be seen, are divided into two classes—those which are above the average in crime being placed in order on one side, and those which are below the average on the other.

RELATIVE STATE OF CRIME IN THE DIFFERENT COUNTIES
OF ENGLAND AND WALES IN 1846.

Counties which are above the Average in Crime.	Number of Offenders committed.	Number of Persons to one Offender.	Counties which are below the Average in Crime.	Number of Offenders committed.	Number of Persons to one Offender.
Middlesex	4,641	339	Berkshire	250	676
Worcestershire ...	535	475	Hertfordshire	243	679
Northamptonshire	270	463	Suffolk	471	702
Gloucestershire ..	884	512	Kent	815	706
Warwickshire ...	799	527	Oxfordshire	228	744
Cheshire	767	541	Herefordshire ...	158	756
Lancashire	3,072	569	Huntingdonshire .	81	762
Buckinghamshire	283	578	Devonshire	721	776
Norfolk	720	601	Westmoreland ...	74	801
Essex	602	601	Dorsetshire	225	816
Hampshire	608	613	Rutlandshire	26	860
Bedfordshire	185	623	Lincolnshire	419	908
Wiltshire	436	623	Nottinghamshire .	286	917
Cambridgeshire ..	276	625	Derbyshire	277	1,031
Staffordshire	851	629	Yorkshire	1,560	1,071
Leicestershire ...	358	633	Shropshire	227	1,106
Surrey	958	638	Cumberland	147	1,271
Monmouthshire .	217	650	Cornwall	280	1,279
Somersetshire ...	701	653	Durham	249	1,367
Sussex	468	672	South Wales	350	1,545
			Northumberland .	169	1,555
			North Wales	220	1,891

Number of Offenders　Number of Population
Committed.　　　to one Offender.

Average for England and Wales .... } 25,107 676

By the above, it will be seen that Middlesex is the most, and North Wales the least criminal, part of the country; the proportion in the former being 1 offender in every 339 individuals, and in the latter 1 in 1,891. Now, on consulting the returns as to the ignorance of the different districts, it will be found that many, and indeed the majority, of the places which are above the average in crime are likewise above the average in education. Thus Middlesex, which is the most highly criminal, will be found to be the least ignorant and North Wales, which is the least criminal, will be discovered to be, on the other hand, far from eminent for the education of its people—as witness the following table, framed from the returns of the Registrar-General:—

RELATIVE STATE OF IGNORANCE IN THE DIFFERENT COUNTIES OF ENGLAND AND WALES IN 1846.

Counties which are above the Average in Ignorance.	Number of Persons who signed the Marriage Register with Marks.	Number of Persons to One uneducated.	Counties which are below the Average in Ignorance.	Number of Persons who signed the Marriage Register with Marks.	Number of Persons to One uneducated.
Worcestershire ...	4,192	58	Norfolk	2,964	146
Monmouthshire .	1,982	71	Berkshire	1,137	148
Lancashire	20,709	84	Cornwall	2,407	148
Northamptonshire	1,467	85	Hertfordshire ...	1,102	149
South Wales	5,565	97	Buckinghamshire	1,074	152
Bedfordshire	1,124	102	Shropshire	1,544	162
Staffordshire	4,920	108	Wiltshire	1,642	165
Cheshire	2,608	120	Essex	2,163	167
Cambridgeshire ..	1,398	123	Gloucestershire ..	2,698	167
North Wales	3,219	129	Hampshire	2,185	170
Lincolnshire	2,166	129	Devonshire	3,224	173
Huntingdonshire .	466	131	Somersetshire ...	2,632	173
Yorkshire	12,688	131	Westmoreland ...	321	184
Suffolk	2,389	138	Derbyshire	1,544	185
Warwickshire ...	2,958	142	Oxfordshire	880	192
Leicestershire ...	1,579	143	Kent	2,855	201
Nottinghamshire .	1,834	143	Dorsetshire	905	203
Durham	2,378	143	Sussex	1,534	205
			Herefordshire ...	576	207
			Northumberland .	1,244	211
			Rutlandshire	99	225
			Middlesex	6,163	239
			Cumberland	647	288
			Surrey	1,441	424

	Number of Persons who signed the Marriage Register with Marks.	Number of Persons to One uneducated.
Average for England and Wales ..	.. 117,633	 144

The above table, compared with the one immediately preceding it, gives us the following results:—

COUNTIES HIGHLY CRIMINAL AND HIGHLY EDUCATED.

Counties.	Proportion above the average in Crime.		Proportion above the average in Education.
Middlesex	337	......	95
Gloucestershire .	164	......	23
Buckinghamshire	98	......	8
Norfolk	75	......	2
Essex	75	......	23
Hampshire	63	......	26
Wiltshire	53	......	21
Surrey	36	......	280
Somerset	23	......	29
Sussex	4	......	61

COUNTIES SLIGHTLY CRIMINAL AND SLIGHTLY EDUCATED.

Counties.	Proportion below the average in Crime.		Proportion below the average in Education.
North Wales ...	1,215	......	15
South Wales ...	869	......	47
Durham	691	......	1
Yorkshire	395	......	13
Nottinghamshire	241	......	1
Lincolnshire ...	232	......	15
Huntingdonshire	86	......	3
Suffolk	26	......	6

That the crime of the country has another origin than mere ignorance, is patent to all who will read patiently and philosophically the criminal facts and records of the country. Hence institutions like the Ragged Schools, which seek to reform our juvenile offenders merely by instructing them, cannot be attended with the desired results. It becomes, however, very questionable whether the association of so many youths of the most vicious propensities may not have a tendency very different from that which the benevolent founders of the establishments originally contemplated. I have been at considerable pains in collecting the evidence of the most experienced persons upon this point. And I now append the result of my inquiries.

A superintendent of police who had lately retired, and who had "served" principally, for many years, in the Westminster district, gave me the following account:—

"I have known this district for upwards of twenty years, and re-member the Ragged Schools starting. Nothing worse under the sun could exist than Westminster when I first knew it in 1829. A compet-ent authority convinced me that it was worse than St. Giles's, when St. Giles's was at its worst. And when St. Giles's was rookeried out afterwards, Westminster got worse, although I reckoned it worst long before—as bad as could be. But hundreds came from St. Giles's. They must go somewhere. The low lodging-houses here were crammed from cellar to garret. I can't describe the places in decent language. Crimes went on there that are not fit to be mentioned—nothing could be compared to the crime but the dirt. Male and female lay promis-cuously. Such places are the great facilities of crime; they give *such* facilities. The lodging-houses are the policeman's great hindrance. He needn't look for criminals there—they're hidden. The lodging-house beats Scotland-yard. There is a large class, too, of 'general deal-ers' who buy anything brought to them; the key of his mother's door, stolen by a child next door to the general dealer—he buys that for a halfpenny, and says, 'There's a clever boy.' I have seen decent chil-dren in those places, and went and expostulated with the man, who laughed at me, as the law was then on his side. At the time when New Oxford-street was building, the streets in Westminster swarmed with vicious boys and girls, driven from their St. Giles's haunts, and added to the Westminster vice. I knew one ——, living near the police-station, who regularly lived on his three daughters' prostitution; he and his wife did. The girls durstn't go home empty handed. There are lots of such in Westminster, I can tell you. Such men may have been bad mechanics, or lazy fellows, who would do anything rather than work. The general dealers, who buy door-keys or anything, are what you may call loose traders; the trading class that won't work is far the worst. They take to buying and selling, and sit idle, with their hands in their pockets. A shocking class, sir; they ought all to be re-gistered. A working man is a king to such fellows. They carry on in a cellar, or anywhere, and boast that they are respectable tradesmen, and pay their rents regularly—many of them do. All lodging-houses should be licensed like beer-shops; no doubt at all about it. They are brothels some; some thieves' houses; all bad, where *anybody* can be ad-mitted. Many that keep lodging-houses are general dealers too, such as I've told you of, and so they pull both ways. Most children, not bred thieves by their parents, begin stealing at home, and go to the general dealer; they may hear of him from boys in the street who look out for decent children. When the Ragged Schools were started, the streets did seem to me rather thinned. But they want supervision. If bad poor children meet together, and go away together, they are sure to go to some mischief or some robbery. Without complete super-vision, Ragged Schools are of no good effect—nothing adequate to the good meant. The intent is good, merciful, and kind; and I believe they have done good. I believe that I could have given instances of their having done good, but I can't recollect one now, with any par-ticulars. No doubt there is a great risk run at these Ragged Schools; bad boys, in a cluster, will always corrupt good boys. Worse still with girls. A decent girl *must* be corrupted among bad girls. Bad women and bad girls corrupt more of their own sex than men do; that's quite obvious." [I may here remark that it is my intention, before long, to devote a series of letters to the question of juvenile and general prostitution—a question of the greatest moment.] "I never knew a girl, a scholar in a Ragged School, in the streets afterwards; but they're young when they're at the school, and would grow out of my know-ledge. Many houses have been pulled down in Westminster, and that has swept away many a curse of a house—to carry a curse somewhere else, perhaps—and has made the streets less crammed with vicious boys and girls; besides that they go to the Ragged Schools, many of them, and are then out of sight. The beer-shops are a great evil. The streets are better now; but they are too bad still. At one time, before the police began, a man could hardly go into the Almonry, or some of the streets off Orchard-street, without being robbed, or perhaps stripped; aye, even in the day-light. A man could hardly get through with a good hat, or a woman with a decent bonnet. If either was tipsy, it was all up with them. A complaint about it was laughed at, and a man was told he had no business there. At night the people there went prowling all over. I can't charge my memory with any particular boy or girl at the Ragged Schools going wrong afterwards, but no doubt there are such. My opinion altogether is this: with a proper supervision, and a prudential training, Ragged Schools do good; without it, they are dangerous. The nation loses far more in stolen property than would provide honest means of living for all the young thieves of London. There's far more property stolen than you hear of. Some won't prosecute; some compromise. I'll tell you how to help Ragged Schools better than money. Register general deal-ers: the young thief begins there. Just look at Orchard-street, and license the low lodging-houses, with the police to inspect them, or else our Ragged Schools haven't much chance. The clergymen may labour, and the Rector of St. John's is indefatigable in doing good, but general dealers and low lodging-houses are too much for them. Children mixed up together must turn out either thieves or prostitutes, whether they've been at a Ragged School or not; they have no other chance; they can't meet and mix one with another, anywhere, without supervision, but the bad will corrupt the good. I've known numbers of thieves, grown-up fellows, go out in the morning, smoking at the corners of the courts or at some doors here in Westminster, and they talk of their doings, and what they will do—and children going to a Ragged School, perhaps, to hear something good, will stop and listen to these fellows, and know they live well, and can drink and be idle—and so they may go to the Ragged School to say to others what a fine life a thief's was. Mere reading and writing is a harm to a vicious child. It makes him steal more boldly, because with more judgment, for he sees prices marked. Without moral training it's a harm. The smartest thieves I have met with, and those having the longest run, could all read and write, and some could defend themselves at trial without a lawyer, just by having studied the newspapers. The nation is paying the penalty now for so long neglecting the care of the youth of London."

An experienced gentleman, to whom I was referred as a person who could give me information as to the influence of the Ragged Schools on the criminal juvenile population of Westminster, was of opinion that they tended to increase the evil which benevolent persons, through the agency of such schools, sought to check. The congregating of so many boys, he considered, must be full of harm, as it was known that vicious boys were of the number, and they were sure to make acquaintanceship with poor boys who were not corrupted, and the consequence was an increase of thievery. As far as his observation went, these schools had done harm, and were doing it, as one schoolmaster, however good, could not check the propensities of boys inured to thieving to corrupt other boys. He told me of the school having been robbed by the boys (as was believed), but that it was not brought before the public. Another gentleman, whose peculiar calling gave him an equal opportunity for judging of the effects of the Ragged Schools, expressed an unhesitating opinion that they were bad schools—for a small proportion of bold, vicious boys would corrupt the better-disposed boys far more readily than the schoolmaster could inculcate principles of honesty into them. The young thieves in a Ragged School knew, he said, very well how to appeal to the spirit of daring and emulation in honest poor boys whom they met in the school and talked with afterwards. Many young thieves, my informant said, went to the Ragged School just for what might be described as "a lounge," and to see if they could in any way form a connection with boys unknown to the police there.

In the course of my inquiries I heard that several boys who had been in the Ragged Schools, had subsequently been in prison, and that some were there now. I therefore called upon Lieut. Tracy, the governor of the Tothill-fields prison, to inquire into this subject. He expressed an opinion—cursorily given he said—that Ragged Schools were not adapted to the reformation of the juvenile criminals of London who resorted there; inasmuch as the great evil to be guarded against, to arrest the progress of criminality, was the *congregating* of criminals. Evil always resulted, and must result, from that; and criminal offenders met in Ragged Schools, and congregated afterwards. He summoned one of his principal officers who was familiar with the habits and character of juvenile offenders, and the latter expressed an opinion—unequivocally—that the boys in prison from Ragged Schools were generally worse than boys who had not been so educated. He had known above a dozen boys in that prison who had been in Ragged Schools within a recent period. He attributed great evil to vicious boys associating together, under any circumstances, at the Ragged Schools, or elsewhere. The schoolmistress of the prison stated that the girls who had been in Ragged Schools, and afterwards in prison, were neither better nor worse than other girls in prison. Through the courtesy of Lieut. Tracy, I am enabled to give two statements from children then in prison. The first was an intelligent-looking boy (who had an impediment in his speech), and declared his anxiety to speak nothing but the truth—the governor and officer being convinced that his statement might be relied on. He said:—

"I am 12, and have been three times in prison, once for stealing cigars, once for a piece of calico, and once for some pigs' feet. I have been twice whipped. I was twelve months at the Exeter-buildings Ragged School, Knightsbridge. I learned reading, writing, and Church of England there. I was brought up there to the Church of England. I know I was, because I went to church with the schoolmaster. I know it was a church. A church is bigger than a chapel, and has a steeple. I learned sums, too, and the commandments, and the catechism. I can't read well." [He was tried on an act of Parliament as to his ability to read. It began "whereas the laws now existing." "Whereas" he could not make out anyhow, and "the laws now" he called "the lays no." He was unable to read any word of two syllables.] "At the Ragged School, there were forty or fifty boys. We went at nine, left at twelve, and went back at two. Between twelve and two I was out with the other boys, and we often made up parties to go a thieving. We thieved all sorts of things. We taught one another thieving. We liked to teach very young boys best; they're pluckiest, and the police don't know them at first. I knew good boys at the Ragged School—good when they went there—and we taught them to thieve. If we could get a good boy at the Ragged School we taught him to thieve, for he's safe some time from the police, and we share with him. At the Ragged School I was taught that I must keep my hands from picking and stealing, but I thought it fun to steal. The schoolmaster didn't know I ever stole. God is a spirit in heaven, and is everywhere. If I do wrong I shall go and be burnt in fire. It frightens me to think of it sometimes. I was first taught and tempted to steal by a boy I met at the Ragged School. He said 'Come along, and I'll show you how to get money.' I stole some cigars, and the other boy, a little boy, kept watch. I was nailed the first time. I shouldn't have been a thief but for the Ragged Schools, I'm sure I shouldn't."

The other boy, a healthy-looking child, said:—

"I am ten, and have been twice in prison, and once whipped. I was in prison for 'a fork' and 'some lead.' I sold them in rag-shops. I was three months in Pye-street Ragged School, Westminster. I was a month at the St. Margaret's National School (Westminster). At the Ragged School I learned reading, writing, tailoring, shoemaking, and cleaning the place. [He then read a verse in the Bible imperfectly, and by spelling the words, but quite as well as could be expected.] There were forty or fifty boys at the Ragged School; half of them were thieves, and we used to go thieving in gangs of six. When we were away from school we went thieving. We taught any new boy how to thieve, making parties to do it. We would teach any good boy to thieve. I know four or five good boys at the Ragged Schools taught to thieve by me and others. We got them to join us, as we got afraid ourselves, and the police don't so soon 'spect new boys. Thieving is wrong. Some boys where I lived taught me to thieve. They did not go to a Ragged School, that I know of."

From a poor woman whom I visited in a garret in Westminster, I had the following statement. Her children were intelligent, and had a look of quickness without cunning, rarely seen in uneducated people. The boy I found in bed, I concluded from sickness, but the cause appears in the narrative:—

"My little girl," said the mother, "goes now to the Ragged School, and is a good scholar, and a very good girl, and never misses school. This is her. I consider the Ragged School here," said the mother, "has done great good. My children have had a good education. They can read and write well, and God knows how they would have learned *that* but for the school here." The boy said:—"I met three bad boys in my reading and tailoring class at the Ragged School, and they often tempted me to go thieving with them; beginning with knocking down apple-stalls and scrambling for the fruit. That's the way they often begin. I always remembered what my father and mother said, and refused. These boys used to try and persuade me when we were sitting in school to go and steal after school hours at night. They wouldn't say much about it, or the master might have noticed it in school. I know some boys, who were good before, and met with bad boys at the Ragged School, who tempted the good lads to go thieving. I know four, or perhaps five such. Many of the boys in the Ragged School had been in prison. I have heard them speak of it. Some said they were sorry to have been thieves, and were tired of it, and wished to do better." The mother here interposed, and said that she and her husband never allowed their children to be in the streets, or mix with others after school hours, or she wouldn't answer for the consequences. "I remember," the boy resumed, "the Ragged School being twice robbed. Once the thieves got in at the first-floor window, from the top of a small house by it, and they stole all the money in the poor-box. It was most likely some that knew the place. They were never found out that I know of. The second time all the lead was stripped off the roof of the Ragged School, and the houses by it. That was never found out. I was well treated at the school, and encouraged to be honest and to learn. The boys often ran away. I am now in want of a place—any honest employment; but I'm here in bed because I haven't clothes to get up in. I can't go out at all. I'm forced to stay in bed, and stay day and night, except when I get up sometimes to read the Bible. On Sunday evening I manage to go to the Broadway Ragged School, but can only do that after dark, and there I get a book to read at home." The mother showed me the child's trousers and shirt, which were mere rags, his shoes hardly held together. "My husband is a costermonger," she said, "but has no money to carry on with, for he was ill six or seven months, off and on, with rheumatism. Thank God, he's better now; but we've been obliged to part with everything but what you see. I have pawned all, but all the tickets are gone now. I lost my last blanket that way last month. My husband, last week, earned just 4s. on cauliflowers. Mr. ——, a neighbour, lent him the money to trade with." "I think, sir," said the boy, "that if the bad boys weren't allowed to mix with the good, it would be far better for the school—there's such bad characters there—one-half of them." I may add that the room was very bare of furniture—a large bed—in which the boy, a lad of thirteen, was lying—being the principal thing there. The room was quite clean, which was the more remarkable, as these poor persons were living in a wretched neighbourhood of filth and wet, with slip-shod half-dressed women standing at some of the doors in the courts and alleys, while boys were fighting and shoeless girls with matted hair were pelting each other with any missile, mud or anything that came to hand, and that with evident enjoyment. My visit was unexpected. The boy I have spoken of seemed proud of his little library, and showed me a book which he said had been given to him by Lord Ashley. He did not repine or murmur; he seemed to think the tedium of his life in bed was his lot as a poor boy. The father's trade was manifest, for in a sort of second small chamber or recess, were a few cauliflowers, and the leaves of fresh vegetables trimmed off to give them a marketable appearance. The door between this room and that occupied by the family was off its hinges, and the paint which had once roughly covered it had peeled off from age. The mother gave me the names of persons who she said were respectable tradesmen, who would vouch for the truth of all she had stated. She had another son, she said, who was sixteen, and who supported himself by selling flowers, but instead of being able to help his parents could hardly keep himself.

From a good-looking and well-spoken girl I had the following statement. I called to see her father, who was absent, and the girl gave me the information I required:—

"I learned all I know," she said, "(and I can read any chapter in the Bible), at the Ragged School close by here. But for it I mightn't have known how to read or write. I hope it's a good place but I'm sure I don't know, I've met such bad girls there. I've known them bring songs and notes that they'd written at night, to give to the boys when they met them out of school. I don't know what sort the songs were, or what was in the notes. I never saw either, as it was a secret among them. The schoolmistress knew nothing about it. I don't think I ever heard the girls say anything bad in school; but often when I've left at night I've seen the girls waiting for the boys, or the boys for the girls as happened. I don't know how many, but a knot of them, and they used to go away together. I don't know where they went, whether thieving or what; but if I've been behind the other girls a minute or so in leaving school, I've had to go through a little knot of them, and might stop a minute or two perhaps, and I've heard them swear and curse, and use bad words, such as no modest girl ever would use. I've never done anything a modest girl mightn't, though I've been tempted [she blushed]. Nine at night is such a late hour to stay at school, that the scholars get tired and long for a change. There's too much of it. I always went straight home, and the bad girls never troubled or teased me. If I hadn't gone straight home I should have been beaten by my father. My brother went to the same Ragged School, and I'm afraid it did him harm. He has ran away every now and then, and has always come back ragged and poorly—far worse than when he left home. I don't know what made him run away, unless he was tempted to do it by boys he met at the Ragged School; but I can't speak as to that. I don't know whether he went thieving or not. He never says anything about it when he comes back, let him be punished anyhow. He is a worse boy now than when he went to the school first. I don't know if he has any young girl he runs away with when he's absent. He's about fifteen or more, perhaps. I don't know exactly how old we are. The boys and girls I've seen go away together after we left the Ragged Schools were too young to be honest sweethearts and to think of marrying. If they would only listen to the schoolmistress they would know what it was to do wrong; but some of them don't, for in going home of a night I've heard them boast of having been wicked with men and boys; but I can't tell you more about that—I can't, indeed. My brother is playing in the street there—shall I call him in?" I requested her to do so; but on being desired to come in the youth disappeared. "My father," the girl continued, "is a tinman, but he seldom has work; my mother sweeps a crossing, and has the cleaning of two and sometimes three gentlemen's houses. My father and mother are kind to me. When I'm not washing or cleaning here, as you've found me now, I go out a hawking, chiefly with tins. We are often badly off—often wanting a meal. I can't say how much we earn in a week. I've told you nothing at all, indeed, sir, but what I know, or have seen, or heard myself."

I was favoured with the names of some masters to whom boys had been apprenticed from the Westminster Ragged School (the premium being generally £5), and from three of these parties, all bootmakers—small masters apparently—I received the following information. One master spoke highly of the honesty, quickness, and obedience of his apprentice, of whom, indeed, except in "requiring the curb" (as it was worded to me), he had no complaint to make; he was a better behaved boy, indeed, than his master's former apprentice, not from a Ragged School. The boy told me that he had been eighteen months at the Ragged School, and remembered the school having been robbed, but it was never found out, he said, by whom. He had known four or five boys, who were good when first sent to the school, led away to be thieves by their vicious schoolfellows. In leaving school at night he had sometimes seen the boys waiting for the girls, and the girls for the boys, and they went away together. He kept apart, he said, from the young thieves, and they never troubled him. A second master spoke well of his apprentice, who was tidy in his habits, honest, and sufficiently intelligent. The chief fault that he attributed to the boy was a great repugnance to go to church and school on the Sunday mornings and afternoons. On one occasion, when the master supposed that his apprentice was at a Sunday afternoon school, he found him with some other boys busy at pitch and toss. His master, however, had the best hopes of the boy's doing well. The boy told me that he had been about two years at the Ragged School, and was searched, as was every other boy, the last time the school was robbed. He said the thieves were never discovered; but he supposed it was somebody who knew the premises. He had known honest boys led away by young thieves whom they had met at the Ragged School; he knew half-a-dozen at least who were so led away to thievish courses. He had a father living, to whom he used to go straight home from school, or he could not tell what might have happened to him. He had been asked by the bad lads to go along with them, but he wouldn't listen to it—he wouldn't go either with them or the girls. He (as well as the other boy I have here mentioned) spoke of their having been well and kindly treated at the Ragged School, as did others whom I saw. A third master, a Frenchman, spoke well of his apprentice from the Ragged School, who had been with him 18 months, and was a very "willing" boy. The boy was not in the place when I called, so that I could not make inquiries of him, as in the other cases.

A chandler in the neighbourhood of a Westminster Ragged School said he had noticed no great change any way in the neighbourhood while he had been there, which was only a year or so. He did not think the boys improved, as far as he could judge, by going to the Ragged School.

The Morning Chronicle, Wednesday, March 27, 1850.

To THE EDITOR OF THE MORNING CHRONICLE.

SIR—I should feel much obliged to you if you would transmit the accompanying cheque for 12*l.* to your Metropolitan Correspondent, for him to lay out as he thinks will do most good, reserving 5*l.* to be given to the "Refuge," a description of which was given in a letter that appeared in *The Morning Chronicle* some short time back.

I remain your obedient servant,

Trinity College, March 23.   C. B. M.

A. B. has forwarded a sovereign, requesting us to hand the sum of 15s. to the poor boy who had no clothes, and 5s. to the girl who hawked tins, mentioned in *The Morning Chronicle* of the 25th inst.

A. J. encloses 10s. worth of postage stamps to buy clothing for the poor boy mentioned in *The Morning Chronicle* of March 25, who was obliged to remain in bed for want of clothes.

We have to acknowledge the receipt of 5s. from L. S., which shall be duly applied.

The Morning Chronicle, Wednesday, March 27, 1850.

RAGGED SCHOOLS.

◆

To THE EDITOR OF THE MORNING CHRONICLE.

SIR—The letter from your Metropolitan Correspondent, in your paper of yesterday, contains some very serious reflections on the value and efficacy of Ragged Schools.

Nothing but the long and deep interest I have felt in the success of these efforts to alleviate a mighty evil would have induced me to request a place in your columns for two or three observations.

The objectors to Ragged Schools demand much more from them than ever was demanded by their advocates. We have never regarded them but as palliatives of a terrible and pressing mischief—as experiments to try what can be done—as efforts to manifest our sympathy rather than our power. We say that the good they have effected cannot be stated in tables and figures. It consists more in the prevention of what would otherwise have been enormous, than in the positive and palpable advancement of good over evil. We appeal to every one with the slightest knowledge of London to state what would have been the present condition of the metropolis had not these efforts been called in operation.

The scheme, besides, of Ragged Schools is incomplete without an accompanying scheme of emigration. Wherever this has been effected, our success has far surpassed our hopes; and hundreds, now in her Majesty's colonies, testify, by their condition and conduct, that however low and miserable in their former lives, they are far from irreclaimable.

That many should be obdurate, that many should return to their former courses, and disappoint the hopes of their best friends, is incidental to all schools; and is almost inevitably the lot of our ragged establishments. The children come for daily instruction from scenes of vice, filth, and destitution nearly unparalleled, and return to them every evening. They are beset by every temptation that appetite, want of employment, and necessity can suggest; and distress and suffering threaten every moment of their existence. Many fall away, no doubt; but this only confirms what I have ever ventured to assert, that so long as our population is permitted to continue in its present state—in its courts, alleys, and overcrowded dwellings, as rife with disgusting immorality as with disease—all effort at education is nearly vain: the work of months is undone in an hour.

It is a consolation, however, to those who have laboured, that not a few have been saved from sin and wretchedness; and they feel the rescue of but one to be so blessed a result that they will neither shrink from the toil, nor quail under any discouragement.

I am, sir,

Your very obedient servant,

March 26, 1850.   ASHLEY.

LABOUR AND THE POOR.

———◆———

THE METROPOLITAN DISTRICTS.

[FROM OUR SPECIAL CORRESPONDENT.]

Letter XLV.

It seems almost incredible that the Reports of an institution which, like the London Ragged School Union, professedly attempts to deal with the "destitute and depraved" children of the metropolis, should give us no means of testing, year by year, the efficacy of their several establishments. One would naturally expect to find an annual record kept of the number of London criminals under 20 years of age—and the utility of the schools proved by the decrease of the juvenile offenders being shown to be in proportion to the extension of the means taken for their reformation. Or—if the facts recorded in the Criminal Returns of the Metropolitan Police did not admit of this being done—one would imagine that *some* notice would be taken of the continued increase of the youthful offenders, and an attempt made to account for it. The five Annual Reports which have as yet been printed, contain, however, no information upon the subject of the amount of juvenile crime in the different districts of London. It is true we are told, quite cursorily, in a note (1st Report, p. 18)—that "no less than 45 of the children who attended *one* Ragged School are now transported." In the second Report, page 29, we are further informed that 27 of the boys attending the Jurston-street School had been in prison; while in the fourth Report, page 10, it is stated again in a footnote, that 16 of the lads attending the Old Pye-street School were "known thieves." The sole allusion that I have been able to detect as to the omission of all statistical facts upon this most important and essential point, is at page 9 of the same Report. "It is clearly proved," says the annual statement for 1848, "that in addition to the good done (by the Ragged Schools) to the children and parents as individuals, the public are benefited by improved neighbourhoods and diminution of crime." (The Metropolitan Returns of that year exhibited an alarming increase of offenders.) "It is difficult in a place like London to show this—the operations being so extended and the population so vast, though even here the police *invariably* give their testimony in favour of Ragged Schools." (The reader is referred to the statements of no less than four of the most experienced police officers given in this letter.)

In the hope of obtaining some more satisfactory and particular account from the secretary of the London Ragged School Union concerning the working and influence of these institutions, I addressed the following letter to that gentleman:—

"*Morning Chronicle* office, March 27, 1850.

"Sir—I am particularly anxious to know whether the 'Ragged School Union' keeps any account of the number of 'Ragged Scholars' who have been taken into custody or imprisoned, as well as those who have been transported for felony, in the course of each year.

"In the first annual report there is a statement—and that in a footnote, by the way, as if the information was of minor importance—that as many as forty-five of the boys attending one Ragged School had been transported. In the succeeding reports I have not as yet been able to detect any returns of a similar nature.

"Will you, therefore, oblige me by stating whether you receive any such returns annually, or whether any statistics of this character are kept by the masters of the different Schools throughout London? If you have any such returns, or can put me in the way of procuring them from other parties, I shall be most happy to print them, as I consider them most essential for exhibiting the influence of the Schools, and do not wish to assert positively that no facts are given in connection with this point, in the annual reports of the union, until I have heard from you upon the matter.

"Have you also any returns concerning the number of juvenile offenders in the metropolis, year by year, since the institution of the Ragged Schools?

"If, moreover, you have any evidence as to the beneficial tendency of the education received at these institutions, I shall be most happy to make use of it, for I can assure you my object is simply to come at the truth upon this most important question.

"I am, sir, your obedient servant,

"THE METROPOLITAN CORRESPONDENT OF THE MORNING CHRONICLE."

The answer returned was, that the Society kept no such records as I desired to be furnished with, nor was any evidence as to the beneficial effects of the institution proffered.

Through the courtesy of the Commissioners of Police, I have obtained a return of the number of the juvenile and adult offenders apprehended in the B, or Westminster division for a series of years. The commissioners have, moreover, in the most kind and considerate manner, given instructions to the superintendents of the other divisions throughout the metropolis to prepare similar returns for me, so that I may be able to test the influence of the London Ragged Schools upon the different districts. Of this most valuable information I purpose availing myself when I come to treat of the habits, haunts, and character of the London Criminals in general—adult as well as juvenile, which I purpose doing at the earliest opportunity—and when, through the kindness of Inspector Walker, of the statistical department of the police, to whose intelligence and experience I already stand indebted for many similar favours, I shall be enabled to avail myself of many most valuable and novel facts in connection with the Crime of the Metropolis.

It is but right I should add, that the evidence given in my last letter as to the pernicious influence of the schools upon the boys of better character, was not obtained from lads who had been discharged from the school. Indeed, it is now publicly acknowledged by the teachers of the Ragged Schools that the statements given are substantially correct. With the exception of the two scholars seen in Tothill-fields Prison, the children and the parents may be said to have belonged to the superior class. With a view to assure myself of this fact, I caused inquiries to be made into their characters, and find them most satisfactory. The statements of the apprentices given in my last letter were obtained from youths whose address I procured—specially for the occasion—from the secretary of the Union, so that I might not do the society any injustice by using unauthentic sources of information.

Actuated by the same motive, I applied to the Commissioners of Police for permission to avail myself of the experience of their different officers as to the influence of the Ragged Schools in the districts with which they were familiar. Mr. Commissioner Mayne, after stating that he considered Ragged Schools to be most praiseworthy in their intention, added, on consideration, that it certainly *might* be possible that the congregation of some hundred boys of vicious propensities and depraved habits would have an effect never contemplated by the founders of these institutions. It was very desirable, he said, that the best evidence should be collected as to the tendency of the association of so many ill-disposed lads, and he readily granted me permission to consult the most experienced police officers, that the truth might be arrived at as to the working of the schools in question. Among these officers I met with a high degree of intelligence, and great quickness of observation on general matters, as well as concerning questions of police. From an officer who had had many years' experience in the B or Westminster division, I had the following statement, in the truthfulness of which his superintendent fully concurred. Other officers also expressed a similar opinion, always temperately and guardedly stated:—

"The particular effects of Ragged Schools I have no precise means of describing. Certainly the returns show a decrease of juvenile offenders in the Westminster district; but it must be recollected that hundreds of houses in what may be called the criminal quarters have been pulled down, and this, I am convinced, is the cause of the decrease in juvenile offenders here. In the Almonry alone, some thirty houses have been taken down, having, perhaps, an average population of ten to each house, all of the lowest class, and with children who would probably have frequented the Ragged School, and would have been, with equal probability, in the list of juvenile offenders here. In the New-way, fourteen houses have been pulled down— eight-roomed houses, formerly inhabited by noblemen and gentlemen, old fashioned mansions. Some houses of a similar class are still existing in other streets, such as Lord Dacre's, in Dacre-street, and that of Admiral Kempenfeldt, in Orchard-street, who went down in the Royal George at Spithead. These New-way houses were occupied by the lowest class; a few of the rooms, however, were inhabited by working men; but the other rooms were occupied by prostitutes and thieves. Westminster was the nursery for Newgate for a long time. Each house might average a score of inmates; all are now gone to other quarters. These houses were like rabbit warrens, from cellar to attic. Duck-lane is swept away almost entirely. The population there was of the worst sort—the lowest of the low. The most respectable class were the costermongers, which isn't saying very much. They were six-roomed houses—perhaps twelve inmates to a house, and perhaps thirty-five houses in all. It was the noted place for 'Charley Eastrup's' bear-baiting, for the famous 'dog Billy,' and for dog-fighting, boxing, and all the blackguard amusements that thieves are fond of. They were all quite at home there on the Sunday mornings, dog fighting and such like. About half of Strutton-ground has been removed too; perhaps twenty-four houses, eight-roomed houses, have been pulled down there. The population was chiefly of the labouring class, and I think of the better description; the average number of inmates being—say twelve to each house. From the top of Duck-lane to the King's Head public-house in Orchard-street (where Mr. Bellchambers was on the night of his murder), all the houses have been removed. These had also been gentlemen's houses; but before they were pulled down the kitchen had most likely a costermonger and his family for tenants; of such class were the inmates chiefly, with a sprinkling of prostitutes, and numbers of children were there, and not of the most honest class. The poor have large families. If a drunken man is brought to the police-station, in Rochester-row, the place is soon surrounded with children. About a dozen of such houses have been removed from the top of Duck-lane—eight-roomed houses, with an average perhaps of a family in each room—say twenty-four in a house. Many houses in Peter-street have been pulled down as well, for the new church, the foundation-stone of which was laid by Lord Robert Grosvenor. Eighteen houses may have been there removed—six and four roomed—containing, it may be, a family to each room. Perhaps 150 houses have been removed altogether, with from 1,500 to 2,000 of the worst class of population, and where they have gone to we cannot tell. I have no hesitation in saying that the decrease in criminal offenders in the Westminster district is owing to this rooting out of the population as I have described. All these houses have been removed within these two years for the contemplated improvements. We cannot state positively whether we have had boys in custody from the Ragged School, as the question, 'Do you go to a Ragged School?' is not asked of any juvenile charged at a police-office. Where criminals are congregated together vice always flourishes, even at the foot of the gallows. Our experience teaches us that it is very dangerous to bring together any number of vicious persons. The Ragged Schools, no doubt, are most praiseworthy in intent; the founders and promoters of them have the good of the criminal children really at heart. I think it injudicious, however, to plant Ragged Schools in the most vicious neighbourhoods, because, when children leave the school, they are in the very heart of the haunts of thieves. I have seen young thieves waiting about the door of the Ragged School in ——; I don't know for what purpose."

I subjoin the Criminal Returns for the Westminster district, with an estimate of the number of the population to one offender. On reference to the tables, previously given, it will be found that the same plan has been invariably adopted, so that a due allowance might be made for the increase of population:—

METROPOLITAN POLICE (B DIVISION).
TABLE SHOWING THE NUMBER OF PERSONS TAKEN INTO CUSTODY FROM 1839 TO 1848 INCLUSIVE, FOR THE B DIVISION.

Year.	Populat-tion.	Number of Offenders under 20.	Number of Offenders above 20.	Total Number of Offenders.	Number of Population to One Offender.
1839	83,917	1,079	2,531	3,610	One in 23
1840	85,370	1,140	3,334	4,474	19
1841	86,823	1,151	3,676	4,827	17
1842	88,276	1,149	3,160	4,309	20
1843	89,729	1,141	2,797	3,938	22
1844	91,182	1,115	2,830	3,945	23
1845	92,635	1,105	2,727	3,832	24
1846	94,088	1,217	3,086	4,303	21
1847	95,541	1,060	2,759	3,819	25
1848	96,994	873	2,134	3,007	32

By referring to the above Table it will be seen that the centesimal increase or decrease for the ten years on the total number of offenders has been as follows:—

(B DIVISION.)

	Increase on the total number of offenders.	Decrease on the total number of offenders.	Increase of offenders under 20.	Decrease of offenders under 20.	Increase of offenders 20 and upwards.	Decrease of offenders 20 and upwards.
From						
1839-40 ...	23·93	...	1·69	...	22·24	—
1840-41 ...	7·89	...	·25	...	7·64	—
1841-42 ...	...	10·73	...	·04	...	10·69
1842-43 ...	...	8·60	...	·18	...	8·42
1843-44 ...	·17	...	...	·66	·83	—
1844-45 ...	...	2·86	...	·25	...	2·61
1845-46 ...	12·29	...	2·92	...	9·37	—
1846-47 ...	...	11·24	...	3·64	...	7·60
1847-48 ...	...	21·26	...	4·90	...	16·36

It appears, then, by the fourth and sixth columns of the above table, that in the year 1847 there was a decrease of a little more than 7½ per cent. of the adult offenders, and 3½ per cent. of the juveniles, while in the following year the decrease was more than 16 per cent. on the offenders above 20 years, and nearly 5 per cent. on those under 20. Hence the older criminals in Westminster have decreased in the last two years of the returns within a fraction of 24 per cent., whereas the younger ones have diminished only a little more than 8½ per cent. in the same time.

An experienced officer, who attended at a Ragged School in Lambeth, gave me the result of his observation on the subject. The superintendent of the district, to whom I had been directed by the Commissioners, referred me to two officers as best qualified to give me information. I subjoin the statement of the first I saw:—

"At the —— street Ragged School (Lambeth), none live in the house, but the attendance in the winter averages about 400 boys and girls every Sunday evening. The gentlemen who manage the Ragged School do everything they can to instruct and encourage the children in well-doing; they make them presents of Testaments and Bibles" (I find by the Reports that they are sold), "and give them occasional tea parties. In fact, everything is done to improve them in the school. The patience of the teachers is surprising. The boys and girls are separated in school; there are more boys than girls—perhaps 300 boys to 100 girls. The girls are better behaved than the boys; they are the children of very poor people in the neighbourhood, such as the daughters of people selling fruit in the street, and such like. Some few years ago I had some inquiries to make on the subject, and found several children of street-beggars there. I have not recognized a girl in this part on the town whom I knew at the school. Most of those that have grown into women since I knew them at the school sell things in the streets; they are very audacious, but I can't say that they are prostitutes. I have, however, seen bigger boys, not of the school, but street vagabonds whom I knew to be of bad character, waiting about the school until it broke up, and then go away with the bigger girls. These girls when in the street are indecent in their language, and immodest in their behaviour; quite different from what they appear in the school. The boys, as I have said, are worse than the girls. When gathered in the street, previously to being let into the school, their conduct is very bad. Some of them smoke short pipes which they pocket when let into school. While waiting on the Sunday evening, they sing, and caper, and some stand on their heads and clap their feet together, and fight frequently and swear, and make all manner of noises. As soon as they get into school they pull long faces. I have often heard them, when hymns were sung, sing something along with it quite different to a hymn. I have seen them too, when a gentleman has been addressing them on religious topics, wink one to another, and put their tongues in their cheeks. The school has been opened perhaps nine years. The police have been obliged to be in attendance since within three months of the opening, and I often turn a dozen boys out of the school in a night for misbehaviour. These boys, in my opinion, have different objects in going to the Ragged School. Some few go really with the intention of learning. The great proportion go for warmth, or a change, or for shelter, or for a lark. I know it from their behaviour, for I can tell the boys who wish to learn from the others, by their conduct to the teacher. The worst class of boys always laugh and make faces at the teacher the moment his back is turned, and sometimes even before his face. I have seen many boys at the school whom I have known in custody for felony, and others whom I have seen in prison. On leaving school their behaviour is very disorderly; you can hear them half a mile off; they never seem to have benefited by the excellent things they may have heard; in fact, for bad and obscene language, cursing, swearing, and noise of every kind, they are worse in coming out than going in. When school is over they throw off all restraint. I can only judge by their conduct, and from that it does not appear to me that they pay the least attention to the good and religious advice given to them by their excellent teachers. I have often known the Rev. Mr. —— visit the school, and take great pains to impress upon the children the evil of their ways, but from their conduct after his lessons, after they get outside the door, and from their filthy and bad language, I fear no good effect has been produced. The boys generally go to the school in small parties, who know each other—four, five, or six; and if one won't go in the others won't; and when they leave, they go away together. After that they are beyond my observation. In the school I think the boys do behave rather better than they once did, but no better in the street. There is as much street gambling as ever. The boys are very bad in this neighbourhood. The boy-thieves are generally intelligent in all their wicked ways; clever, artful, and deceitful to the last degree; they would impose upon any one; they are capable of making people believe they are quite good innocent boys, and laugh at them just after. I've seen some of the most hardened shed tears, and protest they had never done anything wrong; and so naturally that it would impose upon any person unacquainted with their deep tricks."

The other officer gave me the following statement:—

The Lambeth "Ragged School"—(Boys)

"I attend one of the Lambeth Ragged Schools to keep order, and have been there for eighteen months, since the school was opened. After being two Sundays opened, it was found necessary to call a policeman in. There might be 150 scholars—100 boys, the rest girls—when I first went. It was summer time. In winter there may be 300 boys and 100 girls—there is not room for more girls. Cold and wet weather sends them to the Ragged School in winter. I know this from the fact that on a fine night in winter there are not near so many scholars as when the weather is wet or very cold. I have often heard them say they went for warmth and shelter. I see the boys assembling for school—their behaviour is very bad. They are always larking, but they are not so bad as they were; when I first went they pelted me away with bricks. Many of the boys at the school are mud-larks, and persons picking up their living along shore. At first when I attended the school, they let off crackers and threw detonating balls at the teachers, and then laughed at it. They 'took sights' at the teacher, and made all manner of games of him. They would burst out into nigger songs at school, and would sing vulgar songs instead of the hymns. They are better now. One reason may be that several master-potters attend to teach in the school, and they are the great employers of boys in the neighbourhood, and boys are quieter, in hopes of a job at the potteries. I have frequently seen boys, while a teacher was giving religious instruction, put their tongues in their cheek, one to another. The girls on going to school are decent in their behaviour compared to the boys. Some are better dressed than when they went, as they have got places through the kindness of the teachers. The girls leave school a quarter of an hour sooner than the boys, but some will wait about for the boys. If I ask them what they are waiting for, they will often answer, for their brothers, which I know is not the case, both by their conduct, and by girls having declared boys of different families to be their brothers on different nights. I have known boys, not going to the school, come down just before school is over and wait for the girls, and the girls walk away with them. When the boys leave they hollow, cat-call, swear, and make a great disturbance. Their language is most obscene. They appear as if their lessons had not the slightest effect upon them, except upon a few of the better disposed. I know the boys that are better disposed by their appearance, and by their bringing their bibles with them. I have heard the worst lads, when they have been waiting, try to contaminate the better—wanting them to go along with them when school is over. I interfere when I hear them, and caution the better lads. I don't know of any good boy who has been tempted to do wrong by the worst class going to the school, as I am only there just for the occasion. I don't see any improvement in the neighbourhood in going or returning on a Sunday evening. There is as much gambling, cursing, swearing, and mixing together of boys and girls as ever. A great many know how to impose upon their teachers—they pull long faces, and laugh when the teacher's back is turned, about how they've 'gammoned' him, as they call it. The teachers take great pains, and show great patience, kindness, and forbearance. They certainly ought to succeed better than they do. It seems to me, from what I observe of the boys' behaviour after leaving the school, that very little good follows."

The Ragged School to which I principally directed my attention is situated in one of the worst quarters of Westminster. The street— in which it is the best and cleanest house—and all the circumjacent streets, with their many courts and alleys, and what are well described as "blind passages"—is mainly occupied by the destitute and the criminal. Low lodging-houses abound. "Lodgings for Travellers," at "3d." (and sometimes 2d.) "a night," are the predominating signs. The shattered and ill-patched windows of very many houses—where sheets of brown paper occupy the place of glass—and the open and unpainted doors, allow even a cursory observer to notice much filth

The Lambeth "Ragged School"—(Girls)

and laziness in the rooms within. In some houses each room has its family, and sometimes almost every upper window has its yellow patched or ragged linen hanging out to dry on something like a small bowsprit rigged out of the window. Young thieves, with greasy side-curls, and unoccupied costermongers are lounging at the corners of the streets—some few smoking—some tossing in the open road, with an eager crowd of lads gathered round them—some gambling at pitch and toss, in a dirty corner or bye place—others leaning against a post or a wall, seemingly as much asleep as awake—and all appearing to strive to while away the time as best they can. Empty costermongers' carts stand by the edge of the kerb-stone, and capless women, with fuzzy hair, eyes bloodshot with drink or want of sleep, and with dirty shawls over their shoulders, either loll out of the windows or sit on the door step. An oppressive odour seems always to pervade the atmosphere—and cocks and hens scratch at the heaps of filth in the street. The people look generally unhealthy. Here and there, as you emerge from the low and filthy streets, there rises in startling contrast, some towering gin-palace, the squalor of its noisy customers being again in full contrast with its glittering decorations and glare of light. The house that now forms the Ragged School (I learn from Mr. Walker's account) was once a public-house, in which thieving, or rather one of its branches, that of pocket-picking, was taught as a science, a pair of trowsers supplying the means of tuition. A master-thief illustrated and explained the adroitest modes of picking pockets to perhaps half a hundred keen pupils. A mock Old Bailey trial frequently followed, and the lads who evinced most skill either in practising on the trowsers (which were hung from the ceiling), or in defending themselves from any Old Bailey charge, were encouraged with drink and skittles. Very near to this spot stood another public-house—a resort of Dick Turpin and of others whose names modern literature has made more familiar to that criminal neighbourhood, and far more popular than did tradition or any other previous cause. Turpin's resort is now an Institute for Working Men.

The number of boys employed in tailoring, when I visited the school, at the time of industrial training, was 26. Of these 3 were four-teen years old, 1 was thirteen, 8 were twelve, 6 were eleven, 2 were ten, 4 were nine, 1 was eight, 1 was six. There were also 22 boys engaged in shoemaking, whose ages were in the same proportion as those who were tailoring. All these boys, as far as I ascertained, expressed their sense of the kindness with which they were treated, and of the pains taken to do them good. Of these boys, I learned from their own ad-missions, that six had been (collectively) thirteen times in prison. As they detailed their experience in prison, the other boys, who declared that they had never been in prison, laughed and grinned admiringly. One boy said to a gentleman who accompanied me, "Master, what do you think that boy was in prison for?" "I can't tell," was the an-swer. "He stole a pig," whispered the urchin, laughing and smiling approvingly as he whispered.

The Master Tailor, who was the only officer in attendance when I called, did not know, he said, of any boy having been transported; nor could he at first remember any boy having been imprisoned from that school. At last he suddenly recollected that two boys were in prison at that time from the Ragged School (the two I had seen at Tothill-fields); even this fact, however, he could not remember, until

reminded of it by my inquiry whether Ragged Schools were not intended, if possible, to bring about the reformation of thieves. Neither
did he know of any boys of the Ragged School who had been in prison
within the last twelve months, but the school-boys present (one especially) numbered up eight very rapidly. When a boy disappears, he
added, the Ragged School managers do not inquire after him, as they
have not time to go to the police-office. They keep no records of the
imprisonment of their scholars.

The Master Tailor had been there about three years. He had belonged to a society in connexion with the honourable trade about ten
years ago. Within three years ten boys had been apprenticed to tailors. A premium of £10 used to be given—now it is £5. Small masters
generally get the apprentices. The articles made by the boys, I was
informed, were given to the scholars as rewards for good conduct. I
found out afterwards, by inquiry among the boys, that a small price
was charged for them. I was furnished with an account of the number of shoes, jackets, &c., made by the boys in the course of last year,
and upon investigation I found that "forty-eight boys in school had
received nineteen jackets, thirty-four pairs of trowsers, and twenty-
eight pairs of shoes;" four of the lads, however, were without shoes,
and five wore women's or girls' boots, and often odd boots.

A boy in school told me he had known the school boys go thieving
after school hours. Another lad knew boys, but not school boys, go
thieving in small gangs. Another boy remembered the school being
robbed; the police came, but no charge was made. He had heard
that the thieves about the street corners had got hold of some of the
boys. A policeman searched the boys. Four of the boys I saw in the
school had fathers only living (one of whom was in prison); eleven
had only mothers (but two of the fathers of these children were not
dead, for one was transported and one was in a workhouse); and one
had neither father nor mother living. The others had both parents
alive.

In order that I might have the best and most trustworthy information as to the quality of the work and the probable consequences of
the instruction of the boys of a Ragged School (with industrial training superadded to the usual reading, writing, and arithmetic), I took
with me two well-informed, experienced, and unprejudiced men—a
tailor and a shoemaker—on whose judgment and fairness, from my
inquiries among the trade, and from my recent investigations, I knew

I could rely. I give their statements—the first being that of the tailor. He said:—

"I have noticed the work of the Ragged School boys, whom I have seen making or repairing their clothes, and I have formed the following opinion. The boys have attained just that degree of proficiency in their tailoring which would make them available for the slopworker or the sweater—more particularly for the slopworker, as the work of the sweater must be of a better character. They are proficient enough to do their work regularly, but not well; the sewing is thin but regular; by thin, I mean too small a number of stitches in a given space; but the stitches, as I have said, are regular and in good form. Indeed the work of some of the poor little fellows rather surprised me, as it is not very easy to sew fustian and cord, such as their jackets and trowsers are made of. I consider that the teacher of the children has exercised due pains and skill. I think that boys so circumstanced, whatever may be the immediate advantage, are likely ultimately to prove a very serious injury to the working men in my trade—I mean, of course, the honourable trade. It is not possible that these boys can remain long in their present state, so that some other place must be found for them, or they must resort to thieving. I see no alternative for the poor fellows. If, indeed, they are apprenticed, it will most likely be to small masters, or sweaters, for sweaters are often small masters—that is, they are able to do a small quantity of work on their own account, underselling the very masters who employ them. They may not be so apprenticed now, but this is what it must come to. To small masters or sweaters the premium is generally the grand object; they care nothing what becomes of the boy, as our police reports too frequently prove. The boy, if not thus apprenticed, may possibly resort to the slop-market, and there he can never rise into the means of earning a fair remuneration, for his abilities are not sufficient to elevate him. He may, and *will*, drag better workmen down to his level, but he cannot rise; and so he may marry—as reckless people will—and his children may be reared in a poverty that will tempt them to crime far more promptly than any institute (however well intended) can check them. I see no other career for such a boy, and no other likely result. If he is to be sent abroad, where is the use of teaching him the trade of a tailor? Let him go to any of the colonies, he will find that the slop-seller—maintained by such labour as schools like these create—is there before him. There is not a market they do not supply. One of these poor lads, when he has had two or three years' instruction (according to his quickness) at a school such as that we have visited to-day, is able to earn a trifle from a slop-worker, and he grows up a slop-workman, and adds to the poverty, and perhaps the crime, of the country, as a consequence of the very system adopted to make him a good member of society. It is impossible he can become a first-rate workman, unless he be altogether an exception to the general rule; and so he adds to the already overstocked, little-skilled, or unskilled labour-market, which is producing such sad consequences to the superior artisans, and to the best masters in England. I have very carefully watched this matter in all its bearings for more than sixteen years—Government contracts, police clothing, prison and workhouse labour, philanthropic and industrial schools; and this last and worst phase of all—Ragged Schools. The conclusion forced upon me is, that there is no hope for bettering the condition of any trade in which these things exist, or upon which they are brought to bear, whilst such practices are persevered in. Such practises produce starvation wages, on which men cannot live. Some parish authorities are so convinced of this that workhouse labour has been abandoned. I am afraid that many excellent persons who encourage such institutions as the Ragged Schools look only at the surface. Ragged School tailors must ultimately lower tailors' wages, and so increase the very evil they are intended to destroy."

The Shoemaker's statement I now give, which is as follows:—

"I found, on counting heads, while at the school, that twenty-one boys were at work there; but I was told by several of these boys that there were others who were not at present in the shop. The number absent were some nine or ten. Mr. ——, the master, was not there at the time, so I had no means of testing the variety of ability displayed. One, the eldest of the number, had a rather more conspicuous seat than the rest; his age was sixteen, and he had the name given to him of monitor, by way of distinction. Here I may state that the boys were somewhat grotesquely grouped in three separate classes. The first, or youngest class, were six in number, and were seated round a low square table, garnished with a few much-worn knives, a pair of very narrow-nibbed pincers, and an edged tin plate, covered with small bits of rounded wax. This, the initiative, class were generally employed in what is called 'stabbing' bits of leather, this being a mere exercise of the awl. The scrap of leather is held in the instrument called the 'clams,' which are two long bowed staves, the mouth or upper part tightly nipping whatever substance may be placed between them, and thus enabling the operator to have complete command over whatever material he may be engaged upon. None of these boys had any knowledge of, or had received any instruction in the sort of work named '*blind* stabbing'—a very beautiful and most essential process—indeed, one which cannot be done without when the boy is intended to be the 'boot-closer;' and a process, too, which only can be effectually learned in early life, when the sense of touch is most delicate, and the fingers the most expert. The second class were the cobblers; and these I found numbered seven, and they appeared to take much more delight in making the hammer sound, in beating the leather on the 'lapstone,' than in putting in stitches. Some were sewing patches on the upper leathers, or drawing together rents; but the greater part, as I have said, kept striking away on the stone; while two or three were nailing pieces on the heels, which, as I observed, they found to be very weak, in consequence of the severe battering which the bit of bull-hide had received. The third class—with the 'monitor,' in the absence of the 'master baker,' presiding in a somewhat dignified manner over his fellow-boys of younger years and less size—were the 'new' shoemakers. The 'monitor' himself had just finished the sewing round or the 'stitching' of a shoe which would fit a lad of about fourteen years of age. He said that his own age was sixteen, and that he had been at the shoemaking for upwards of a year; that he could sew a shoe round, of the sort I have mentioned, in an hour, which is about half the time a man would take to accomplish a similar piece of inferior work, although the perfect 'stitching' of a light boot or shoe will often require from two to three hours. Two other of these boys of the third class gave me likewise their work to examine; this, although very coarse in quality, as might be expected, seemed to be drawn together firmly—the workers, as I perceived, appearing always to make the best use of the 'hand-leather,' in accordance, no doubt, with their instructions. As this, though a means, is however no security for solidity, it often happens that the mere fact of the shoemaker *labouring* at his work is only doing so in vain; for if there is not the proper foundation laid in the getting up of a shoe, as of a house, in the nice and close fitting and adjustment of the materials beforehand, no mere thickness of thread or strength of pull will avail in securing a truly serviceable article. The generality of these boys had very bad shoes, and the rest no shoes at all. On inquiring how this happened, the information was given that the right to have shoes came by purchase; ninepence per pair being the price charged to every boy or girl to whom shoes are given. 'And these trowsers,' said one of the little shoemakers, 'cost me also ninepence;' while another told me that he also paid the same sum for his jacket." "And if you have not this money," I asked, "you neither get shoes, nor trowsers, nor jackets?" "No," was the general and immediate reply. "My mother," one said, "is to give me the ninepence on Saturday, and then I shall have these shoes to go out in on Sunday." And the poor boy had here, indeed, a great blessing in prospect, for he was actually barefoot. "Do you want an apprentice, sir," now inquired the "monitor," perceiving that I was examining somewhat closely the pair of shoes which had just been handed to me, and imagining, as I suppose, that I was in quest of a boy, from the manner of my inspection. I gave him to understand that I was not seeking an apprentice, but only came there for general information. The work which I examined, though very inferior indeed, was still, considering all things, as well got up as might be expected, the boys being employed only at short intervals; the early part of the day, from nine in the morning till the hour of dinner, being set apart for schooling purposes; and the afternoon, from two till five, for learning shoemaking, five days in the week. Boys so taught, however, are never to be supposed capable of earning a livelihood through the extent of their capacity, but can only be made so far useful as to become the apprentice of the slop home-worker, or garret-master—a class of people who are always on the look-out for cheap labour and an "apprentice fee;" the latter to enable them to buy "stuff," or the material for their low-priced goods. With such people the helpless position of the apprentice allows every chance of their compelling the greatest possible amount of exertion from the lads.

The following intelligence, though not given to me as derived from any official source, is the opinion of two gentlemen who are observant of public and local affairs, and who have certainly every means of coming to a correct and dispassionate conclusion. "It was painful," both agreed in saying, "to give an unfavourable opinion of an institution founded with such excellent and benevolent motives, and conducted with so much painstaking and Christian feeling. But the boys imposed upon the supporters and teachers of the Ragged School, just in proportion to those gentlemen's benevolence, for those artful lads pretended to be reformed characters, fond of their Bibles and of public worship, while they were as depraved as others." "The Ragged Schools" (they both agreed again) "were in reality nurseries for criminals—houses of call for thieves; and three out of every five boys who swelled the lists of our juvenile criminals were taught roguery at a Ragged School, or had taught it there to others." My informants stated, moreover, that it was the most dangerous experiment ever attempted in hopes of doing good, to bring some hundred boys together—a majority of them being vicious—as nothing but ill could result, for that one scabbed sheep would not more surely infect a flock, than a few daring, artful young thieves would corrupt other children who were honest but suffering from poverty, and often, perhaps, from hunger. The young thieves knew well how to show the poor boys they met at such places that the easiest mode to obtain any enjoyments was by theft. "What need you care for other people," they would say to honest lads, "they don't care for you." It is right to add, that these gentlemen advocated no theory whatever; they were strictly practical men, with, I repeat, excellent means of forming a sound opinion. My informants asserted, moreover, that they were convinced that for every one child that might derive benefit from a Ragged School two were corrupted. Indeed, all the really practical men with whom I have conversed on the subject of Ragged Schools, expressed not less admiration of the benevolence of the founders and maintainers of such schools, than wonder at the short sightedness that had led good men to be the means of so much evil.

In conclusion, it is my duty to add that, after patiently investigating the operation of the London Ragged Schools, I cannot but arrive at the conclusion that, however well intended such institutions may be, they are, and must be, from the mere fact of bringing so many boys of vicious propensities together, productive of far more injury than benefit to the community. If some boys are rescued—and that such is repeatedly the case is cheerfully and fully conceded—many are lost through them, as is now admitted by the teachers themselves; and such, indeed, is the opinion of all the practical and experienced men I have seen upon the subject. In a word, they may be thieves' houses of refuge, but they are likewise thieves' houses of call.

[In presenting to the public the results of our Correspondent's investigations into the operation of the benevolent institutions above treated of, we are anxious not only to express our warm admiration of the philanthropic zeal and earnestness of their founders and supporters, but also to indicate what we conceive to be the true cause of their imperfect success. The Ragged School system, regarded as a scheme for rescuing destitute and neglected children from brutish ignorance and from the influence of depraved parents and associates, is undoubtedly a first step in the right direction—it is the beginning of the greatest of all social reforms. The evils which experience has shown to be incidental to its workings are to be attributed not to the principle of the system itself—nor, we fully believe, to any avoidable error on the part of its promoters—but to the external conditions by which its operation is controlled and limited. An educational organization designed for the purposes contemplated by Ragged Schools obviously requires, in order to render it effectual, larger powers, ampler pecuniary resources, the means of *incessant* supervision over the pupils, and a more comprehensive field of action, than private benevolence can command. The discipline of such an institution ought to be upheld and enforced by some public authority—its lessons ought to be preparatory to schools of a higher grade, admission to which should be a privilege awarded to good conduct—its industrial training ought to be of a nature to qualify the pupils for a life of self-supporting labour in the colonies—and the whole scheme should be connected with a plan of systematic emigration, which would secure honest employment in other lands for those who cannot find it here. It is obviously not the fault of the founders and managers of our Ragged Schools that their existing means and resources preclude them from giving a wider development to their generous project, and that, in too many cases, they merely send back to the streets, with sharpened faculties and increased powers of mischief, those whom they took from the streets. In a word, the great flaw of the system lies, properly speaking, not in what it does, but in what it necessarily and unavoidably leaves undone.]

The Morning Chronicle, Friday, March 29, 1850.

We have to acknowledge the receipt of 10s. from "T. S." for the poor modeller.

The Morning Chronicle, Monday, April 1, 1850.

L. has enclosed 10s. for the woman named in the Supplement of January 8, whose husband was paralyzed, and who gained but one shilling in the week by needlework, and bowed in cheerful and meek submission to the will of God.

S. X. encloses 10s., to be applied to the poor boy confined to bed for the want of clothes; but if sufficient has been sent for him, requests it may be applied to any other case of distress.

C. G. has handed to us 10s. for the poor woman who lived in a garret in Westminster, to procure clothing for her boy, who remained in bed for want of clothes, mentioned in Letter 44, of the 25th March.

LABOUR AND THE POOR.

---◆---

THE METROPOLITAN DISTRICTS.

[FROM OUR SPECIAL CORRESPONDENT.]

THE COASTING TRADE.

LETTER XLVI.

I now return to the consideration of the condition of the Merchant Seamen of the Port of London. The present Letter I shall devote to an exposition of the state of the men engaged in the Coasting Trade. First, however, let me repeat as briefly as possible the results arrived at in my previous Letters as to the Mercantile Marine employed in the Foreign Trade.

The present number of British seamen is about 270,000, of whom 200,000 belong to the mercantile marine, and 25,000 to the navy—the remainder being in foreign service. The total number of vessels belonging to the merchant service of the British empire was in 1848 no less than 33,672, having an aggregate tonnage of 4,052,160, and carrying collectively 230,069 men. The average rate of increase in the merchant vessels for the last ten years has been 600 per annum, while the annual increase of burden amounts, within a fraction, to 100,000 tons. By this means employment is found for 5,000 fresh hands every year. The British empire possesses one-third more vessels than France; while the aggregate tonnage of the British ships is upwards of four times as great as the French, and one-third more than the collective burden of the American vessels. Some idea of the extent of the foreign trade carried on by this country may be formed from the number of British and foreign vessels that annually enter the several ports of the United Kingdom. Those in the year 1848 amounted to nearly 35,000 vessels (13,000 of which were foreign), having a gross burden of 6½ million tons, and giving employment to nearly 350,000 men. The total value of the exports and imports effected by such means amounts to upwards of seventy-five millions sterling per annum. According to the estimate of Mr. G. F. Young, the ships engaged in the mercantile marine are worth £38,000,000. The sum annually expended in building, repairing, and outfitting new and old ships amounts to £10,500,000—and the cost of the wages and provisions for the seamen engaged in navigating the merchant vessels to £9,500,000; while the amount annually received for freight by the shipowners is said to come to £28,500,000. The foreign trade, in connection with the port of London, is very nearly one-fourth of the entire maritime commerce of the United Kingdom. The number of vessels that entered the port of London in 1847 was upwards of 9,000, and the gross tonnage nearly 2,000,000; the rate of increase being about half a million tons and 2,500 vessels in five years, or 100,000 tons and 500 vessels per annum. The principal foreign trades among the merchant vessels sailing from the port of London are—the East India and China, the Australian, the West India, the Honduras, the Baltic and Russian, the North American, the South American, the United States, the Brazilian, the Hudson's Bay, the African, the Cape of Good Hope, the South Sea and Greenland, the Mediterranean, and the Portuguese and Spanish.

Descriptions of the condition and earnings of the men serving on board the vessels trading to the above-named places, from the port of London, have already been given. At the conclusion of my forty-second Letter I began an account of the steam vessels belonging to the British empire, and I then showed, by official returns, that whereas in 1814 our entire steam maritime power consisted of two vessels of 456 tons joint burden, so rapidly had it increased since that period, that in 1849 the number was 1,110—their gross tonnage 255,371—and their united force equal to 92,862 horse power. In connection with these returns, I gave a table showing the steam maritime power of other countries, and proving that the progress made by this country, in the application of steam to the purposes of navigation, is equal to what has been accomplished by all other countries in the aggregate—America (which has the largest steam marine next to ourselves) possessing only 261 steam vessels—and France, which comes next, but 119. To give the reader a more definite idea of the steam maritime power of this country, I have drawn up the following:—

STEAM-VESSELS BELONGING TO THE BRITISH EMPIRE.

TABLE SHOWING THE NUMBER, AGGREGATE DIMENSIONS, AND TONNAGE OF THE REGISTERED STEAM-VESSELS OF THE UNITED KINGDOM, ON THE 1ST DAY OF JANUARY, 1849.

Number of Vessels.	Aggregate Length.	Aggregate Breadth.	Aggregate Gross Tonnage.	Aggregate No. of Horse Power.
1,110	125,283ft. 4in.	19,748ft. 8in.	255,371	92,862

The above table shows the aggregate length of the steam-vessels belonging to the British empire, in feet. It may be added, that they are collectively of such dimensions that, by placing them stem to stern one after the other, they would reach to a distance of 23½ miles, or form one continuous line across the Channel from Dover to Calais; while, by placing them abreast or alongside each other, they would occupy a space of upwards of 3½ miles wide.

The 1,100 steamers of 255,000 tons burden in the aggregate, belonging to the different ports of the United Kingdom, were shown in Letter XLII. to be thus distributed:—London had (in round numbers) 300 vessels of 99,000 tons gross burden; Liverpool, 75 vessels of 15,000 tons burden collectively; Glasgow, 80 vessels, whose united burden was 30,000 tons; Dublin, 50 vessels of 19,000 tons in the aggregate—while the minor ports had altogether 600 vessels of 90,000 tons; so that more than one-fourth of the entire number, and one-third of the aggregate tonnage, of the steam vessels belonging to the United Kingdom, appertain to the port of London.

In the present Letter, I purpose completing my account of the condition of the merchant seamen afloat, by giving the statements of men employed in steam vessels and the coasting trade. Before doing so, however, it may be as well to subjoin a synopsis of the foreign trade of the United Kingdom, as carried on by steamers:—

FOREIGN TRADE OF THE UNITED KINGDOM (STEAM-VESSELS).

AN ACCOUNT OF THE NUMBER AND TONNAGE OF STEAM-VESSELS EMPLOYED IN THE FOREIGN TRADE (INCLUDING THEIR REPEATED VOYAGES) WHICH ENTERED THE PORTS OF THE UNITED KINGDOM AND CLEARED FROM THE SAME EACH YEAR, FROM 1822 TO 1848; SEPARATING FOREIGN FROM BRITISH VESSELS.

Years.	INWARDS.				OUTWARDS.			
	British.		Foreign.		British.		Foreign.	
	Vessels.	Tons.	Vessels.	Tons.	Vessels.	Tons.	Vessels.	Tons.
1822	159	14,497	10	520	111	12,388	—	—
1823	129	8,942	7	364	108	9,027	7	364
1824	139	10,893	6	312	208	15,796	8	416
1825	186	16,155	11	652	256	19,685	13	756
1826	334	32,631	38	2,256	268	27,206	31	1,742
1827	443	50,285	74	4,558	439	47,322	43	2,566
1828	482	52,679	58	3,406	472	51,887	31	1,802
1829	497	51,754	3	405	428	47,480	22	1,486
1830	560	62,613	42	7,781	475	54,372	53	10,274
1831	537	65,946	85	11,345	563	67,930	57	12,046
1832	537	71,493	74	7,000	564	73,898	71	12,636
1833	681	98,224	51	3,708	704	102,039	45	6,604
1834	988	146,720	12	3,164	896	137,607	57	12,018
1835	1,015	170,151	18	5,058	1,146	189,305	77	13,826
1836	1,122	195,722	50	10,948	1,225	202,499	188	23,514
1837	1,123	217,640	60	12,508	1,278	234,919	207	26,338
1838	1,983	286,264	441	54,401	2,004	289,977	466	63,009
1839	2,293	356,595	511	70,773	2,296	351,361	479	69,560
1840	2,057	321,651	476	61,626	2,173	341,397	494	66,881
1841	2,182	360,675	478	55,832	2,219	362,825	499	59,872
1842	2,397	389,977	492	69,426	2,428	399,879	517	76,301
1843	2,663	438,347	533	77,225	2,684	448,383	548	82,538
1844	3,124	507,549	558	85,917	3,063	491,115	569	85,176
1845	3,126	539,389	491	68,393	3,117	536,563	488	67,115
1846	3,093	576,306	616	92,555	2,985	558,302	621	92,053
1847	3,535	681,982	721	115,442	3,215	623,552	725	115,566
1848	3,377	693,344	722	110,935	3,162	646,807	714	126,294

This account does not include vessels arriving and departing in ballast, or with passengers only—they not being required to enter the Custom-house. Steam-vessels were not employed in foreign trade earlier than 1822, except for carrying passengers.

We find, by referring to the preceding table, that there has been a gradual increase, both in the number and the tonnage of our steam-vessels since their first introduction. Their increase, since they were first employed in the conveyance of goods in 1822, has been—In vessels, inwards, 3,930—outwards, 3,761; in tonnage, inwards, 789,262—outwards, 763,710.

After this, in due order, comes the steam foreign trade of the port of London, as compared with that of the other ports of the United Kingdom, of which the following table will give us a sufficiently accurate idea:—

FOREIGN TRADE OF THE UNITED KINGDOM—(STEAM VESSELS).

TABLE SHOWING THE NUMBER AND TONNAGE OF STEAM VESSELS THAT ENTERED AND CLEARED FROM AND TO FOREIGN PORTS, AT EACH OF THE PORTS OF THE UNITED KINGDOM, DISTINGUISHING BRITISH FROM FOREIGN VESSELS, IN THE YEAR 1848.

PORTS.	INWARDS.				OUTWARDS.			
	British.		Foreign.		British.		Foreign.	
	Vessels.	Tonnage.	Vessels.	Tonnage.	Vessels.	Tonnage.	Vessels.	Tonnage.
London	1,080	247,457	115	30,836	834	185,290	89	24,566
Dover	692	82,899	512	64,679	691	81,875	516	64,252
Folkestone	654	88,392	—	—	653	88,280	—	—
Hartlepool	1	259	—	—	7	1,813	—	—
Hull	191	68,224	73	18,172	222	79,695	86	20,773
Liverpool	72	43,079	1	960	68	43,033	1	960
Newcastle	11	2,849	3	873	10	2,590	4	1,164
Plymouth	1	155	—	—	3	465	—	—
Poole	2	350	—	—	2	350	—	—
Shoreham	37	5,680	18	15,415	37	5,680	18	14,579
Southampton	209	69,481	—	—	196	62,371	—	—
Yarmouth	38	7,248	—	—	23	4,623	—	—
Leith	60	11,879	—	—	58	11,623	—	—
	3,048	627,952	722	130,935	2,804	567,688	714	126,294
Channel Islands	53	7,387	9	510	51	7,206	9	513

I now give the statements of two long-experienced men on board *steamers belonging to the foreign trade of the Port of London*—one in the engine-room, the other on deck as a general seaman. The fire-man was very well-informed, and produced his papers, when necessary, to vouch for the truth of what he stated. His appearance was not that of a strong man, and his narrative accounts for it:—

"I have been 20 years fireman in steam-vessels," he said, "and have acted as engineer. When I first knew steam-vessels the boilers were larger than they are made now, as the cargo was less an object then than the conveyance of passengers. As to the berths, and the accommodation generally, it's worse now than it was 20 years ago. They care nothing where we are crammed—in any hole. If you complain, there's plenty of men out of employ will jump at it. I have been employed in steamers in all parts of the Mediterranean (in Government and merchant service), from Gibraltar to Odessa; in the West Indies; on the French, Belgian, and Dutch coasts; to Hamburg, too; also the Baltic, and to Spain and Portugal. I was in Don Pedro's expedition, and didn't make so badly out of it either—I served in the Royal Tar, Captain McDougal (Admiral Sartorius commanded the squadron)—and in the coasting trade of England, Scotland, Ireland, and the Channel Islands. Twenty years ago I served in a steamer which plied between London and Boulogne. I had 30s. a week, finding my own provisions. Now, if I were in the same trade, with twenty years' experience at my back, I should have 24s., instead of 30s. The engineer twenty years ago had £3 a week in that trade, finding his own provisions; now he has from 38s. to 44s.; the last is the very highest. My last voyage was to Marseilles, and I had then at the rate of 20s. a week, as fireman, for taking the vessel out, but provisions were found to us. The first engineer had, I believe, £20 a month, and the second £16. I greatly prefer finding my own provisions (but that can only be done in short voyages)—for those found us by the masters are often very bad and very salt, and eating that stuff with constant fire and steam about one is terribly trying. In a hot climate we work at 190 degrees at least, in the engine-room of a steamer. Now look at this; in all this heat I have had to chop my meat; it was like a salt board, and with proper tools I could have carved and cut it into 'baccy boxes; that I'm sure I could. My health of course suffered from this. There is another grievance—no merchant steamer, that ever I knew or heard of, carried lime-juice; and that's the very thing wanted by men in my capacity; it's better than all the grog in the world. I don't know why the law don't make merchant steamers carry lime-juice. Grog, you see, revives one only for the time, but lime-juice cools you without inflaming you. I have told you the berths are not what they were on board steamers. The iron boats are the worst for accommodation. The iron is always wet and cold, and the cold is always in the berths, and into them such as me have to go from the heat of the engine-room. A man to stand it should have the constitution of a negro by day, and an Esquimaux by night, especially in bad weather. The water keeps always working its way between the iron plates of the vessel, and so into the forecastle. I have been drenched so in bad weather that it has brought on four weeks' rheumatics. In our berths there is (as a general rule) no ventilation, except by the very hatch that you come into the place by. A lamp is generally there night and day, however, or there would be no light. I can't complain of having been so much cramped for sleeping-room in steamers; the berths are mostly 6ft. 2in. by 2ft. Some of the engine-men, in some steamers, have to sleep in the engine-room, and there we cannot sleep from the heat, and from the damp caused by the steam. There are mostly swarms of bugs too, helping the heat and the damp to keep one awake. I hardly knew what bugs were, in comparison, on shore, but their head-quarters are in the engine-rooms of steamers (I don't say of all steamers). There is another thing I must tell you of. When new machinery is put into a steam-boat, the engineer of the factory puts his own man on board the steamer as engineer, to manage the machinery, which the makers generally warrant for twelve months. The captain of the vessel has nothing to do with the appointment of the men in the engine-room (except in the Oriental and Peninsular Company), and the engineer selects his own men. The engineer from the factory, ten to one, has never been to sea before, and is very often sea-sick when we get out to sea—not able to take care of himself, let alone of a pair of engines. And the other men selected by the engineer are no more seamen than he is, and they are sea-sick too, and laid up, and the vessel may take her chance. I have known the seamen sent down from the deck to do the work of the engineer's people below. A bad system prevails as regards boys. An engineer, or a captain, will employ boys in the place of men, who must stand idle while boys are underselling them, and the boy is registered as a fireman, and the registrar can't help it if the captain applies. The way the work on board a steamer is carried on by us in the engine-room is this:—The engineer has the charge of the engines, and is to attend to the commands of the captain and the pilot, as to 'stop her,' and any such order; he is looked upon as the responsible man. The business of a fireman, or stoker, is to keep up the supply of steam, by regulating the water pumped into the boilers, and by keeping the fires up to the required height. A great deal of responsibility as to the safety of a ship depends upon the fireman. In voyages of more than twenty-four hours' duration, there are two engineers generally, and firemen according to the length of the voyage and the power of the boat. I have worked in a West India boat with twenty-eight firemen, seven coal-trimmers, and five engineers. The engineers relieve each other every four hours; only the head engineer in a West India boat keeps no regular watch, and the others may relieve each other oftener if they choose; the firemen keep their regular four hours the same. The work is very exhausting. We must have something to drink, and ought really to have lime-juice, for it gives an appetite. In the Gravesend and Richmond boats there is no relief; one engineer and one stoker does the work; but they are not considered in our class at all. In the above-bridge boats there is generally nothing but a parcel of boys, had cheap. The stokers are not at all satisfied. I have served on board an American steamer, and know what good reason we have to be dissatisfied. None of us, I believe, if a war broke out, would fight against America. In the American steamer I was in we were all Englishmen, captain and all, but three. We were 136, or near that, in crew. I wish I was in the American service again. Better pay, and better provisions, and better accommodation. They know how to behave to a man, in America, and I would never have left them but for family matters. As to the quantity of coal consumed in steamers, I can only give it, as near as I can, according to horse-power. A vessel of 300-horse-power will, on the average, burn 120 bushels of coal an hour. Steamers may average that consumption at sea eight months in every year—120 bushels an hour, day and night." (Considering, then, the horse-power of the whole of the steam-vessels of the United Kingdom to be estimated at 92,862, we shall find that they will consume 216,628,473 bushels, or 6,017,456 chaldrons of coals per annum.) "I have known great carelessness on board of steamers," continued the fireman, "and wonder that there are not more accidents and explosions. There is often great carelessness from drunkenness by the engine-men—ten minutes' neglect might blow a vessel out of the water. I have often known short weights given in steamers. The way we are provisioned, both the seamen and the engine-men, in some long voyages, is this: the provador (steward) of the steam-vessel has perhaps to provision thirty or forty passengers, and what's left out of the cabin dinner is sold by him to the crew at 9s. a week generally, we paying him that for our board out of our wages. The steward hands over what's spared out of the cabin dinner to the cook, who serves it out to the crew. If there's not enough, we ask the cook for more; and he will say 'I have none to give,' and so there's a sort of a row; and as of course we pay for full provisions, and come short oft enough (a general thing, indeed), it's the same as cheating us by giving short weight. If you complain you are called 'mutinous.' The provador has the greater profit that short-feeding way, and can pay a larger sum to the owners for his situation, for he buys his place. I have known a provador pay £300 for his place for the summer season. In the Mediterranean trade the fireman has £3 a month, and salt, *very* salt, provisions found him. On board a man of war a fireman has £2 6s. a month, with lime-juice after forty-eight hours at sea. In an American merchant seaman there's lime-juice always at your command, as well as sugar. I had at the rate of from 36s. to 40s. a week, on board the Yankees, and capital provisions found. A good engineer will have, I believe, from £18 to £20 a month in the Yankee steamers, and is treated like a gentleman there. In the Dutch and Belgian trades, and in all short foreign voyages, the fireman has 24s. a week, and the engineer 44s., all finding their own provisions. The same in English and Scotch coasting, except that one company gives firemen only from 15s. to 20s. a week, but allows them beer. In the Irish trade 20s. a week is paid a fireman, and 44s. or 46s. an engineer. Can you tell me, sir, why it is that we stokers have to pay 1s. a month to the Merchant Seamen's Fund, and have never had any benefit from it? I never heard of a stoker ever getting anything from it. A fireman cannot be admitted into the Sailors' Home, either, in Wells-street—and why not, for we are more liable to accidents than seamen?"

A Seaman on board a steamer gave me the following account:—

"I have been 17 years employed in steam navigation, as mate and master. I was 15 years master, and two years mate, in steamers in connection with the Continental trade. I had £160 a year as master, and £91 a year as mate. I was all the time upon Continental stations— at Hamburg, Rotterdam, Antwerp, Ostend, Calais, and Boulogne. I have been in, I may say, ten different steam-vessels—quite that. Their tonnage was from 200 to 300 tons, exclusive of the engine-room. I never was in a steam-vessel under 150 tons. A steamer of 300 tons will carry twenty-two hands, with the exception of stewards. There will be eight able seamen, two apprentices, two engineers, six stokers, two mates, boatswain, and master or captain. A steamer of 150 tons will carry only six able seamen, two apprentices, two engineers, four stokers or firemen, two mates, and the master—in all seventeen hands. The steamers in the Continental trade are well manned, and have good men. The wages of the able seamen are £1 per week, of the firemen 24s.; the first engineer gets £2 4s., and the second £1 15s. per week, the first mate has £1 15s., the second £1 6s., and the captain has generally £2 13s. a week, or £140 a year. The apprentices are bound for five years, and have about £120 for the whole of their servitude. The foreign and continental steam trade with this country is now very considerable. There is the West India steam trade. The steamers belonging to that run from Southampton, and are a very fine class of vessels. Then there's the Peninsular Company's vessels running from the same port to the Mediterranean. The Oriental steam vessels also run from the same port, and are very fine vessels. The American steamers run from Liverpool, and are the largest steamers running. They usually carry about 120 hands. The wages are nearly the same as those I have mentioned. Besides these steamers, there are vessels running from the port of London to Hamburg, Rotterdam, Antwerp, Ostend, Boulogne, and Calais. This we call the Continental steam trade. Then there are steamers in connection with the coasting trade. These run from London to Yarmouth, Ipswich, Hull, Newcastle, Leith, Edinburgh, Cork, and Dublin. The steamers running to the Channel Islands used to run only from Southampton, but recently vessels have been put on from London to those parts. All these steamers I have spoken of take both passengers and cargo. They are generally built for passengers, but take a good deal of cargo. The Margate, Ramsgate, Herne Bay, Southend, Sheerness and Chatham, Gravesend, and Greenwich steamers, are especially for passengers. Besides these there are the steamers above bridge—but those we consider to belong quite to a different class. Any vessel running to a place this side of Yantlet Creek, near Sheerness, comes under the Watermen's Act, and a master like me is not privileged to take command of such a boat. I have been to sea altogether thirty-six years. I served my time in the fishing trade. When I first went to the steam service there were not half the number of steamers that there are now. I don't remember the first steamer out of the port of London, but I recollect very well coming up the Pool, in a fog, in 1814, in a fishing smack, and hearing the noise of the first steam-vessel I ever saw. We were all of us plaguy frightened on board. The noise of the steam blowing off, and the beat of the paddles, produced a very terrible effect in the darkness. The first steamer I saw after the one that I heard, I thought a very comical affair, and for years after that I used to swear I'd never go to sea in one. Now I think they are the safest and best vessels of all. The accommodation for the seamen on board steamers is very small and very bad. Every usable part of the vessel is sacrificed for passengers and for cargo. I have often represented to the managing director of the steam company that I belong to, that the men had not fit places to live and sleep in. The answer was that they would see that it was remedied, but no alteration ever took place. In the men's berths there is little or no ventilation, and scarcely any room. The men always find themselves in provisions in the Continental trade, and they are glad to do so. I think the men have nothing to complain of, with the exception of their accommodation. The wages are fair, and the treatment good. I was in one vessel nine years, and several of the hands had been longer than I had; so I leave you to judge we are not very discontented in the steam service. The men are not allowed any grog. I think the owners of the steam vessels should be compelled to give better accommodation to the seamen—the men should be thought of *a little*. I think a drop of weak grog is necessary for the firemen when coming off the fires in the violent perspirations that they do. I fancy nothing could supply the place of weak grog to such men—it's the same as medicine to such men; and any other drink I should think would be dangerous."

This completes my account of the condition of the men engaged in sailing and steam vessels in connection with the foreign trade.

The *Coasting Trade* may be classified in the following manner. The most important of all is *the coal trade*. The coal ships from the northern ports, Sunderland, Newcastle, the Shields's, Stockton, &c., carry from five to twenty-four keels of coals, a keel being twenty-one tons. The tonnage of the colliers is from 80 to 300; they usually carry from four to fourteen hands, but the seamen complain that they very frequently go out very short-handed. The coasting trade from the Scotch ports to London is carried on in vessels of from 100 to 190 tons—schooners generally—they carry from seven to ten hands. There are hardly any smacks now. The schooners take general cargoes. The majority are from the east coast. The Irish coasting trade is carried on in vessels of from 97 tons to 190 tons—schooners and brigantines carrying from five to nine hands. They bring corn, butter, bacon, cattle and pigs. The Welsh coasting trade is carried on in vessels of from 25 to 300 tons, manned by from four to eleven hands. They bring coals, lead, iron, tin, slates, and some timber (such as white oak for the navy). Between London and the English ports, as Hull, Liverpool, Portsmouth, &c., small vessels—generally schooners (called billy-boys on the east coast), ply continually with general cargoes. They call at several ports frequently. A vessel, for instance, bound from London to Bristol, may touch at Portsmouth, Plymouth, Falmouth, before reaching Bristol. The regular traders, however, such as those to Ipswich, Scarborough, Hartlepool, Boston, &c., ply merely from those places to London and back, direct. Others take intermediate voyages, taking up cargoes in one place if not obtained in others.

The following table exhibits the importance of the coasting trade of the United Kingdom:—

COASTING TRADE OF THE UNITED KINGDOM (STEAM AND SAILING VESSELS).

STATEMENT OF THE NUMBER AND TONNAGE OF VESSELS WHICH ENTERED INWARDS AND CLEARED OUTWARDS, WITH CARGOES, AT THE SEVERAL PORTS OF THE UNITED KINGDOM, DURING THE UNDERMENTIONED YEARS, COMPARED WITH THE ENTRIES AND CLEARANCES OF EACH YEAR, DISTINGUISHING THE VESSELS EMPLOYED IN THE INTERCOURSE BETWEEN GREAT BRITAIN AND IRELAND FROM OTHER COASTERS.

Years.	Employed in the Intercourse between Great Britain and Ireland.				Other Coasting Vessels.				Total.			
	Entered Inwards.		Cleared Outwards.		Entered Inwards.		Cleared Outwards.		Entered Inwards.		Cleared Outwards.	
	Vessels.	Tons.	Vessels.	Tons.	Vessels.	Tons.	Vessels.	Tons.	Vessels.	Tons.	Vessels.	Tons.
1840	9,423	1,150,395	17,369	1,677,264	123,876	9,615,661	128,758	9,740,727	133,299	10,766,056	146,127	11,417,991
1841	10,005	1,200,457	16,520	1,628,358	120,397	9,676,293	127,357	10,121,794	130,402	10,876,750	143,877	11,750,152
1842	9,060	1,148,907	17,453	1,682,828	118,780	9,636,543	123,557	9,619,829	127,840	10,785,450	141,010	11,302,657
1843	10,104	1,255,901	16,760	1,670,574	121,357	9,566,275	124,937	9,650,564	131,461	10,822,176	141,697	11,321,138
1844	10,147	1,349,273	16,948	1,817,756	123,751	9,615,434	128,294	9,877,105	133,898	10,964,707	145,242	11,694,861
1845	11,481	1,511,023	19,785	2,111,481	133,427	10,974,831	138,669	11,002,623	144,908	12,485,854	158,454	13,114,104
1846	9,133	1,416,130	19,624	2,211,696	131,983	10,569,279	137,051	10,769,760	141,116	11,985,409	156,675	12,981,456
1847	8,085	1,296,610	17,935	2,047,387	134,440	10,923,186	140,987	11,218,238	142,525	12,219,796	158,922	13,265,625
1848	9,109	1,470,309	18,941	2,153,054	131,332	11,053,563	136,804	11,162,295	140,441	12,523,872	155,745	13,315,349
1849	8,607	1,478,059	18,000	2,159,954	124,668	10,489,414	131,166	10,755,630	133,275	11,967,473	149,166	12,915,584

By referring to the above return, we shall find that there has been a slight decrease since 1840 in the total number of vessels entered inwards; but at the same time there has been a considerable increase in the amount of their tonnage. With regard to the vessels entered outwards, there has been an increase both in number and burden.

Of the steam vessels trading to different parts of the coast of Great Britain and Ireland, from the several ports of the United Kingdom, the following will give us a concise account:—

COASTING TRADE OF THE PORTS OF THE UNITED KINGDOM (STEAM-VESSELS).

TABLE SHOWING THE NUMBER AND TONNAGE OF STEAM-VESSELS THAT ENTERED AND CLEARED COASTWISE AT EACH OF THE PRINCIPAL PORTS OF GREAT BRITAIN AND IRELAND, ISLE OF MAN, AND CHANNEL ISLANDS (INCLUDING THEIR REPEATED VOYAGES) FOR THE YEARS 1847 AND 1848.

PORTS.	1847.				1848.			
	Inwards.		Outwards.		Inwards.		Outwards.	
	Vessels.	Tonnage.	Vessels.	Tonnage.	Vessels.	Tonnage.	Vessels.	Tonnage.
London	1,099	329,685	1,100	329,603	1,023	315,444	1,027	316,624
Bristol	1,221	159,459	1,424	157,976	1,257	161,619	1,417	157,556
Hull	779	120,242	784	119,520	785	113,386	788	112,995
Liverpool	2,841	821,782	2,979	807,181	2,953	868,561	3,074	828,665
Newcastle	375	55,394	375	55,394	445	76,638	429	73,925
Plymouth	361	124,555	438	137,338	415	135,649	509	149,986
Preston	618	122,435	735	140,453	613	120,373	622	123,504
Swansea	413	46,085	478	51,082	562	57,838	594	61,827
Glasgow	817	232,347	929	235,872	856	252,104	937	261,703
Leith	538	159,862	538	160,674	811	192,911	799	191,154
Belfast	917	240,061	915	239,221	898	252,704	896	251,627
Cork	293	112,367	293	114,330	280	112,529	286	116,593
Dublin	947	253,139	961	255,379	881	236,389	895	239,129
Other Ports	6,337	1,175,488	5,548	1,082,679	6,021	1,189,831	2,491	1,013,065
Total	17,556	3,952,901	17,497	3,886,702	17,800	4,085,976	14,754	3,998,373

Of the number of sailing vessels in connection with the same trade, and proceeding from the different ports, the subjoined table will enable us to compare not only the traffic of 1847 with that of 1848, but that of the different ports of the kingdom with each other:—

COASTING TRADE OF THE PORTS OF THE UNITED KINGDOM (SAILING VESSELS).

TABLE SHOWING THE NUMBER AND TONNAGE OF SAILING VESSELS THAT ENTERED AND CLEARED COASTWISE AT EACH OF THE PRINCIPAL PORTS OF GREAT BRITAIN AND IRELAND, ISLE OF MAN, AND CHANNEL ISLANDS (INCLUDING THEIR REPEATED VOYAGES), FOR THE YEARS 1847 AND 1848.

Ports.	1847 Inwards Vessels	1847 Inwards Tonnage	1847 Outwards Vessels	1847 Outwards Tonnage	1848 Inwards Vessels	1848 Inwards Tonnage	1848 Outwards Vessels	1848 Outwards Tonnage
London	20,827	2,788,675	10,605	722,721	21,561	2,927,128	9,932	694,143
Bristol	5,064	231,470	2,518	146,880	5,417	258,450	2,638	164,459
Cardiff	1,122	43,225	5,475	339,380	838	24,293	6,195	390,671
Chester	1,075	54,279	2,344	103,325	830	39,166	2,400	105,781
Gloucester	2,043	90,651	3,127	119,526	1,427	69,932	5,056	115,871
Goole	2,704	145,743	3,040	153,845	3,006	159,649	2,982	149,974
Liverpool	5,041	366,944	7,055	460,293	5,708	442,125	6,234	415,687
Llanelly	1,354	51,315	2,430	140,047	1,582	64,061	3,045	177,940
Newcastle	3,212	251,450	15,671	1,887,932	2,225	174,186	12,951	1,606,899
Newport	1,558	72,665	7,691	422,721	1,411	72,318	6,842	380,721
Plymouth	3,084	195,440	1,409	75,520	3,153	209,923	1,312	73,602
Rochester	2,277	167,959	1,327	47,670	2,366	175,518	1,509	56,557
Sunderland	1,096	88,699	9,907	1,309,970	1,273	102,016	10,170	1,364,046
Swansea	3,651	217,882	6,463	374,238	3,702	225,514	6,151	366,549
Whitehaven	854	35,910	3,521	253,272	858	35,551	3,438	254,491
Yarmouth	3,320	226,069	1,158	69,496	2,915	206,040	1,233	76,102
Dundee	2,231	160,230	1,057	71,824	2,096	154,975	842	61,786
Glasgow	2,193	149,069	4,102	255,475	2,005	145,484	3,950	238,719
Leith	2,317	142,125	1,256	85,074	1,774	111,153	1,122	79,341
Belfast	3,641	225,163	1,099	56,684	3,766	240,175	889	50,382
Cork	2,023	147,896	1,875	108,051	2,603	212,874	1,752	110,665
Dublin	4,388	362,174	1,798	140,451	4,796	423,156	2,003	198,671
Other ports	69,037	4,141,668	54,814	4,282,524	68,845	4,220,655	65,799	4,723,024
Total	144,112	10,356,701	149,652	10,746,419	143,157	10,696,342	148,445	10,856,061

The foregoing tables show us that London has four times the number of sail-impelled coasting vessels, and ten times the amount of tonnage, over and above any other port in the kingdom; while, of steam-impelled coasting vessels, it has but a little more than a third the number belonging to Liverpool. The coasting trade of the port of London is exhibited, however, more particularly below:—

COASTING TRADE OF THE PORT OF LONDON (COLLIERS AND OTHER COASTERS).

TABLE SHOWING THE NUMBER OF COLLIERS AND OTHER COASTING VESSELS THAT ENTERED THE PORT OF LONDON IN EACH OF THE FOLLOWING YEARS.

Years.	Coasting Trade.				Fishing Vessels.	
	Colliers.		Other Coasters.			
	Vessels.	Tonnage.	Vessels.	Tonnage.	Vessels.	Tonnage.
1800*	—	—	—	—	2,125	
1810*	—	—	—	—	3,033	
1820	5,921	No record.	11,096	No record.	4,949	
1830	6,944	1,413,243	12,113	1,023,458	4,851	
1835	7,980	1,617,530	12,491	1,147,452	4,483	
1836	8,035	1,650,177	12,730	1,160,701	—	No record kept of the tonnage of vessels entering the port with fish.
1837	8,725	1,799,874	12,597	1,111,862	—	
1838	9,089	1,804,558	12,503	1,103,618	—	
1839	9,112	1,787,009	12,000	1,041,692	—	
1840	8,970	1,768,301	12,649	1,082,512	—	
1841	10,099	1,942,958	12,627	1,087,755	—	
1842	9,739	1,885,299	12,228	1,044,268	—	
1843	9,684	1,815,806	12,616	1,085,465	—	
1844	9,816	1,783,683	12,922	1,106,713	—	

* The accounts for these years were destroyed in the fire at the Custom-house in 1814.

Fishing vessels are not required to enter and clear at the Custom-house; and there are no returns furnished of them since 1835.

The above table is made up from the Custom-house returns. But by referring to the returns of the Chamber of London, we find that the quantity of coals brought into that port is much greater than stated in this table. In 1844 the Custom-house returns give 1,783,683 tons, whilst the returns from the Chamber of London show in the same year 2,507,709 tons. In 1845, 2,695 ships were employed in carrying 11,987 cargoes, containing 3,403,320 tons; and during the year 1848, there were 2,717 ships, making 12,267 voyages, and containing 3,418,340 tons of coal.

I shall now proceed to give instances of the condition of the men on board the vessels employed in each of these different kinds of coasting trade—beginning with the "*Colliers*":—

A man, as clean as if he had never seen coal-dust, gave me the following intelligence:—

"I have been nearly twenty years at sea, and was brought up in the coal trade. I'm a native of Sunderland. I have been in the coal trade all the time, except three voyages to North America. Since I knew the service there have been many changes in it. When I first went to sea the coals were put on board in the Wear out of keels; they're a sort of lighters. You've heard of 'Weel may the keel row'—that's it. The coal was shovelled out of the keels at that time through the port-holes into the hold—or rather out of the keel on to a stage, and so into the hold—just as they put in ballast now. In Sunderland, now-a-days, the coal is mainly lifted out of the keels in tubs; a keel contains 21 tons, or eight tubs. A steam-engine, fixed on shore, on the Wear, lifts a tub out of the keel, heaving it up like a crane, and the bottom is let go, by being unclasped, and so the coals are shot into the hold. Twenty years ago I was bound apprentice for seven years. I can't read or write. I was never taught navigation, and don't understand it now. I had £45 apprentice wages for the seven years, with 8s. a week for board when the ship was at home, and 12s. a year for washing money. I found my own clothes. Those are the payments to apprentices in the coal trade still. I think all seamen ought to be taught navigation. I have a brother now master of a London ship in the coal trade, who knows no more of reading, writing, arithmetic, or navigation than I do. When I was first at sea, an able seaman had £3 a voyage from Sunderland to London in summer, and £4 to £4 10s. in winter. Twelve voyages in a year is an average, though more are made sometimes. Take the average wages, twenty years ago, at £3 15s. a voyage, and calculate that, you'll find it comes to £45 a year. Now the wages of an able seaman are (from Sunderland to London) £3 a voyage in summer, and £3 7s. 6d. to £4 in winter, but £4 very seldom. Reckon twelve voyages a year at £3 5s. a voyage, and it comes to only £39. We generally have the best of provisions in colliers—always fresh meat—boiled beef mainly. We are not allowanced. There is no grog; only small beer. In a gale of wind the captain *may* give us perhaps a glass of grog. We are often very short-handed in crew—more often than not—and then certainly it *is* slavery. We pay to the Merchant Seamen's Fund 1s. a month, but I never met a man who knew what became of it. To be sure I have known widows at Sunderland have 2s. a month, but that's only when their husbands had paid twenty years to the fund. The seamen in colliers don't complain of their treatment nor of their food—they can't reasonably; but they do complain of bad wages. I can't say whether they would fight for the country or not in a war. Education would be good for seamen; I wish I had education, and I might be a captain. I have been mate often enough. Drunkenness is not common among the seamen in colliers. It's a very hard trade. Off Yarmouth is about the worst place between the North and London; there are so many sands. We have often had to heave the coal overboard to lighten the ship."

Another person, a very smart and intelligent man, in the same trade, gave me the following further information:—

"The coal trade has made excellent seamen. It was called a nursery for the navy, and it bears that character still—the men in colliers are so numerous, and they must know every branch. The boys are continually heaving the lead, which is a most important part of seamanship, and doing handreefing and steering besides, in all coasting. In a dark night, in the narrow channels, they have little beyond the lead to trust to. A seaman brought up in the coasting trade is the best man at a push; though he may not be so good at dandy work in the rigging, such as grafting, splicing, and knotting. The apprentices are always at sea, and receive no education through the care of the masters or owners, while in the coasting coal trade. In a foreign voyage with coals, from the north country ports, the boys are taught navigation, and reading and writing, if they look for it, not without. But boys and captains in the coal trade are generally ignorant. One half are captains one voyage, cooks the next, then mates—then before the mast—and then, may be, round to be captains again. They are no navigators, but capital coasters; blind as they are as regards education, they know every set of the tides and channels from Newcastle to London. If they lose sight of land, they are regularly at sea, as the saying goes, and always steer west. That's sure to bring them in sight of land, and then they know where they are in a minute. Or else they hail any ship they meet, and ask where the land bears. They never ask about latitude or longitude; that's no use to them. Boys are more used in manning coal vessels than ever, if you can call it *manning*. It's done for cheapness. A boy may have £20 or £24 for four years. I had £34 when apprentice, but that's sixteen years ago. I know a collier manned entirely with 'prentice boys—captain, mate, cook, and all—every one of them—boys; the oldest apprentice is the captain. When the heavy North American ships lay up at home for the winter, the owners take the boys out of them, and put them on board colliers from the north to London. The cost of all hands on a voyage in a collier of eight keels may be £29 or £30. When boys only are employed, the saving to the owner will be above £20 the voyage, at the very least. Boys' labour is fast displacing men's. That's one reason there are so many idle seamen about. The way in which the colliers are disposed when they reach the port of London, is this:—The master goes ashore at Gravesend to the harbour-office with his papers. The office instructs him where to lie; whether to go to the Pool or not. I have known colliers three and four weeks in the river before their turn came for the Pool. Only a certain number of vessels are admitted into the Pool at one time; and while out of the Pool they can't unload or sell the cargo. Why that's allowed, I don't understand. It's nothing but a monopoly to keep up the price for the rich merchants. At the north-country ports, too, there is the 'limitation of the wend'—I think they call it. Each ship there must wait for its turn; that's the general practice. That's another way to lessen the supply for the London market—all to serve the owners and merchants, I can tell you. Look what happens. Freights go down, in consequence of the supply being limited, because so many vessels are lying idle; and our wages go down with freights; so the men are thrown adrift. Now, suppose there was no limit to the supply of London, why, coal would soon be half the price that it is, and then there would be double and treble the quantity consumed. Compare a public-house fire in Newcastle with one in London; why, they burn four tons there to one here. I can't tell how people put up with dear coals. Without the limit there would be twice and thrice the quantity of coals to bring, and twice or thrice as much employment for seamen and for ships, and then up would go freights and wages. There would be also a great increase in the coal trade for foreign ports. There wants a little stir about it."

Concerning the *Scotch Coasting Trade*, I obtained the following statement:—

"I belong to the Scotch coasting trade. I served my time in the coal trade. I know navigation and have been mate eight years in the foreign and coasting trade. The Scotch vessel I belonged to was 163 tons burden. We had eight men on board. The able seamen had £2 10s.—the cook had 2s. 6d. extra—the mate got £3 10s., and the captain about £6—I don't know exactly. I am a single man, but for my part I don't know how the married men do with their money. I was mate in the Scotch trade. We came from Leith. The vessel was a schooner. There are no smacks now. We carried passengers when we could get them, but seldom enough we could get them—what with the steamers and the rail, there are very few left for the schooners. In the days of the smacks, the passengers were plentiful. I have been in sailing vessels with as many as thirty passengers, and twenty of those cabin ones. The vessels of the present day are quite as fine, and even faster than the smacks. They are of the 'clipper build,' and can sail thirteen knots an hour. I have seen them beat the steamers. The Scotch coasters have always been the best and fastest of all. A Scotch coasting vessel is, and as long as I can recollect ever has been, the crack thing of the day. The passage from London to Leith is reckoned at three days—over that time it's reckoned long. I have known it made in thirty-six hours. The distance from port to port is 416 miles, and that makes the rate of sailing to have been 11½ knots an hour all the way. The Scotch clippers, as they are called, were first built by Mr. Hall, of Aberdeen. He built one upon trial out of the wreck of an old vessel, and, immediately she was found to answer, the build was generally adopted throughout Scotland, and now they are getting very common in the English ports. The bows are as sharp as a wedge; they have a flatter bottom, or 'floor,' as we call it, and their length is greater than the usual kind of sailing vessels. They are not only fast, but safe, and now they are building iron 'clippers' upon the same model. The accommodation for the men is pretty fair. The berths are airy and dry, and better than they were in the smacks. The provisions are liberal and good—always fresh meat, just the same as in the coal trade; and the same hard work—or even harder, for in the coal trade the men have not to stow and unstow the cargo, but in the Scotch trade we have to do both. In coasting vessels, with the exception of those in the coal trade, it is usual for the men to load and unload the ship, but in the foreign trade labourers are employed either at the wharfs or the docks, as the case may be. The masters in the Scotch trade are generally better educated than those in the coal trade. They almost all are acquainted with navigation. The crews and the masters mostly stick together; so much so that it's difficult to get a berth on board a Scotch clipper. The clippers carry a general cargo. They bring a good deal of whisky, ale, paper, gunpowder, and pig-iron. They take back porter, leather, sugar, and anything else they can get hold of. The wages of the men have remained the same for the last sixteen years. The coal trade fluctuates in summer and winter, on account of the number of vessels lying idle at the other end. It's that what brings the wages down in that trade; but in the Scotch coasting trade the wages are the same all the year round. The men on board the clippers are not allowed grog nor beer, except in London. They are never teetotallers, and seldom drunkards: they are generally contented with their wages and employment. In case of war, I think they would fight for the country to a man. The men in coasting vessels are generally married."

A strong, sturdy man gave me the following account of the *Irish coasting trade:*—

"I have been a seaman nearly sixteen years, and was last in the Irish coasting trade, in a Cork schooner. She is 133 tons register, carrying five hands, all told; we ought to have had two more. As able seaman, I had £2 5s. a month; it's not enough. I make £27 a year in a regular-going Irish coaster, and am kept the greater part of the time. The provisions are not very good in the Irish vessels. They are too salt generally—poor lean stuff, the beef especially; the best of the pork is sold for the Queen's ships. You see the captains of the Irish coasters victual the ships themselves, with so much a month from the owners (I believe 20d. a day for each hand), and the captain generally gives bad meat, to make a profit out of the bargain. I have often known men complain, and even leave the ship in Newport (Monmouthshire) on account of the bad provisions, but that was before the register tickets came up. If we do so now, we may be put into prison, or have to pay 10s. Us poor fellows are compelled to put up with everything. There's no grog in the Irish coasters that I have been in for five years, but plenty of good water. The bread is very dark, and often weevilly. No wonder sailors are all dissatisfied. I shouldn't like to fight against this country while my father and mother are living, but I wouldn't fight against America if I could help it. I have been four years in the American service, and was treated there, in wages, food, usage, and accommodation, as a seaman should be treated. In the Irish coasters the berths and accommodation are not so very bad; we don't complain of that. The masters who come to London from the Irish ports are generally fair seamen; but those who go along coasting on the Irish coasts, or go to Wales, are often very ignorant, and their ignorance loses many a ship. Never a chronometer on board any of them— just a quadrant, an almanac, and an epitome. All that ought to be remedied."

I had the following statement concerning the *Welsh Coasters* from a Welshman. He was strong built, and very brown, and spoke with great deliberation:—

"I have been 16 or 17 years at sea, and was at first a good while in the coasting trade; then I had a turn at foreign, and then a turn with the Americans, as we all like to have, and now for some time I have been coasting again. I am a native of Aberystwith, in Wales. Did my master teach me navigation, do you say, when I first went to sea? He did not, sir, for he didn't know it himself. The coasting trade is the most difficult of any. Suppose now you had a ship coming from China or the East Indies, when the master reaches the Irish or English Channel, he's not half so good a seaman as we are, because he doesn't know how to make allowances for his tides. I knew the master of a foreign ship, meaning to make Holyhead, go bump on a reef of rocks near Cardigan Bay. When I first went to sea, the wages for an able seaman from Aberystwith, to London and back, was £2 10s. a month. Now it's £2 5s. generally, but some give as low as £2. I do not consider £2 5s. at all fair pay for an able seaman. We come to London from Aberystwith, and our cargo is generally lead ore, or, if that be not got, ballast with empty casks returned, or such like. In London we may stay six or seven weeks to take in cargo, having our wages go on as if we were at sea, and living on board. It comes expensive staying long in port. There's one's bits of enjoyment on shore. I'm noways backwards in going to the play; it's a precious sight better than a public-house. Indeed, it does a man good. I have seen T. P. Cooke, and think he's a regular good 'un; just what a sailor was, not as what he is. We don't hitch our trowsers so much now, nor shiver our timbers, nor 'd—n our eyes and gallant eyebrows' as we used to do. The sailor's hornpipe is much the same as in T. P. Cooke's day. But we don't fling about money and grog as he does on the stage, because we haven't it to fling. From Aberystwith to London a man may make three voyages in a year, on an average (I have lain in London, at Pickle Herring-wharf, nearly three months), so we receive £27 a year. It ought to be £3 a month, for we work night and day. Why can't England pay like America? For a man to keep himself respectable, it will cost him for clothes and for washing when he's in port, £12 a year; and so that leaves £15 to keep a wife and family on, if a man has them, reckoning nothing for a drop of beer, or a shilling to help a friend. If a man spends only 2d. a day in drink, reckon the year through—and that's very moderate—it's £3 0s. 8d. out of his £15. In the American service I had fifteen dollars a month—that's better than £3—and better food, and better accommodation. The usage is much the same, good and bad as it happens. If a war broke out between America and this country, I'd never fight against America—I never would. I would fight against any other flag for this country. We are losing our best seamen out of this country. I have met a gunner's mate, who had deserted from a Queen's ship, and is now a gunner in an American ship, and a gentleman too. Seamen are taught in England for the American service like. I have been in other parts of the coasting trade, and generally had £2 5s. a month. In coasters, generally, our provisions are pretty good, and we are not allowanced in meat, bread, or water. Some allow 1 lb. of butter and 1 lb. of sugar a week, and some don't. I have met with the greatest ignorance of seamanship that could be shown in masters of coasting vessels, though not often. I have met with it, too, in the foreign trade. I have known great risk of our lives from the drunkenness of officers. One captain (who was intoxicated, and so was the second mate) brought a gun on deck to shoot me because I was laughing with a shipmate, but the gun was taken from him and hid. After that he never left his cabin to look after the ship, as long as the grog lasted (and his officers were not qualified for their business). It was a good thing for us when his grog was out, as he came out then a good man, and took the ship home. Coasters are middling as to hands, generally; some are very light-handed, and none carry too many. One hand for every twenty tons (except a very small vessel) is the custom. The berths are not the best generally; some are very wet; some have a bit of fire in the forecastle—chiefly in colliers. Seamen, coasting and foreign, are not treated as they ought to be. In a foreign-going ship, if a captain uses a man badly, and is afraid of a complaint, he buys him over with grog."

The Morning Chronicle, Wednesday, April 3, 1850.

We have to acknowledge the receipt of one sovereign for the doll's dress maker from "R. H. C."

———

"T. S." has forwarded us 5s. 6d. for the poor Modeller.

———

The Morning Chronicle, Thursday, April 4, 1850.

THE BALLAST HEAVERS.

———◆———

To the EDITOR of the MORNING CHRONICLE.

Sir—I beg leave most respectfully to solicit a small portion of your space for the purpose of directing your attention, and that of your benevolent readers, to the distressed situation of a most meritorious and industrious class of men, whose case will be submitted to Parliament immediately on its re-assembling.

I shall not on the present occasion attempt to depict the sufferings of the men known by the name of Ballast-Heavers—that has already been done by your Metropolitan Special Correspondent in a style and manner which reflect upon him the highest credit; the fearful picture portrayed by him of the misery and suffering endured by those much-oppressed men must be too fresh in the recollection of your readers to render any repetition at present necessary. I will, however, as an eye-witness of the sufferings of the men, take the present opportunity of stating, that there has been no exaggeration about the matter, that their distress is daily increasing, and that unless some timely remedy is applied to the evils arising from their present destructive system of employment, this once fine athletic race of men will be completely sacrificed, and be compelled to seek refuge in the parish workhouse.

My object at present, sir, is to direct the attention of your benevolent readers, who have so generously come forward to render their aid towards relieving individual cases of suffering and distress which have been brought before their notice, to the efforts which are now being made to relieve these men from the worse than Egyptian bondage under which they have so long suffered—efforts which, if backed by anything like a fair amount of sympathy and support, cannot fail of being attended with the happiest and most beneficial results.

As a first step towards the accomplishment of this most desirable object, a small working committee, with extremely limited resources at their command, have prepared two petitions to be presented to Parliament—the one from the ballast-heavers themselves, the other from the inhabitants of the Tower Hamlets, signed by nearly the whole of the clergy of this large maritime district. I think, sir, the fact of so large a number of the clergy signing the petition is one of the strongest proofs that can be adduced of the evil and pernicious effects of the present system. These petitions will be followed by a most respectful and numerously signed memorial, praying the Government to bring in a bill for the abolition of the present complicated and compulsory-drinking system of employment, and to establish in the place thereof a public office, similar to that from which the coal-whippers of the port of London are employed.

Knowing, sir, that there is a strong disposition on your part, and an anxious desire on the part of many of your benevolent readers, to remedy the evils your Correspondents are every day bringing to light, provided those evils are within the scope of remedy, I am emboldened thus imperfectly to submit the case of the ballast-heavers to your notice, in the earnest hope that they may be induced to render some pecuniary aid to enable the committee to bring their labours to a speedy and successful conclusion.

I remain, sir, your obedient servant,

HENRY BARTHORP,

Secretary to the Ballast-heavers' Association,

3, John-street, White Horse-lane, Stepney.

P.S.—I would state, for the information of your readers who may not be conversant with the subject, that the ballast-heavers are employed under a most complicated and compulsory-drinking system, which, upon the lowest calculation, absorbs the one-half of their earnings. This, in addition to the severe competition to which they are exposed, has left them in a most pitiable condition. The ramifications of the system are so wide-spread and so extensive, that nothing short of a legislative enactment can relieve them.

RAGGED SCHOOLS.

———◆———

To the EDITOR of the MORNING CHRONICLE.

Sir—My attention has just been called to your Special Correspondent's Letter of March 29, and as there is therein some extended remarks on the Ragged Schools with which I am connected, I trust you will allow in your next number the insertion of these few lines. My object in writing is simply to express the hope, that the numerous supporters of our schools who may have read the letter alluded to will, before withdrawing their valuable assistance, do what it is evident your Special Correspondent has *not done*, make a personal inspection of the schools. Had he adopted this course, or waited on any member of our committee, we should have felt great pleasure in referring him to very many, both boys and girls, who, though once in the very lowest depths of ignorance and vice, subsisting either by begging, imposture, or theft, have, through the agency of these schools, risen to the dignity of responsible and intelligent creatures, occupy honourable positions in life, honestly working with their own hands. Such facts would, sir, I think, have somewhat modified the extraordinary conclusion at which your correspondent arrives, namely, that "Ragged Schools are productive of far more injury than benefit to the community." That this, indeed, should be the result of all that patient investigation which he assures us he has given to this subject must be a matter of the greatest surprise to all who are intimately acquainted with the working and results of such institutions.

While, sir, there is a great deal in the extract relative to the Lambeth Schools for which there is not the slightest foundation, there is at the same time much that is undoubtedly true; and while the knowledge that such things are so, clearly proves the necessity which exists for Ragged Schools, so I trust it will stimulate all who are engaged in this work to more increased and active exertions.

I am, sir, very respectfully yours,

FREDERIC DOULTON,

Hon. Sec. of Lambeth Ragged Schools.

High-street, Lambeth, April 1.

——————

[Mr. Doulton is perfectly right in saying that the Lambeth schools were *not* visited by me. I was informed that the subjects taught and the mode of teaching at those institutions differed in no way from the others; and, with all deference to the honorary secretary, it was not considered necessary to waste time (in so large an inquiry as that in which I am engaged) by going over precisely the same educational routine as that with which I had already made myself familiar. A note, printed in my letter of March 29, was sent to Mr. Gent (the secretary of the Ragged School Union), in which I requested that gentleman to furnish me with any evidence he might possess beyond what I had printed as to the beneficial influence of Ragged Schools in general, adding that I should be most happy to lay the same before the public. Mr. Gent, however, favoured me with no answer to this part of my letter, and I therefore concluded that the Ragged School Union could give no other instances of the good effects of their schools—over and above those with which they had already supplied me—such as the characters of the apprentices, and the letters of the emigrants sent out by them. If, therefore, the schools conducted by Mr. Doulton form any special exception to the generality of Ragged Schools, and a wrong has accordingly been done to the teachers in connection with them, I can only say that Mr. Gent and not myself is the party to be blamed for the omission. I have not the least doubt that the conductors of the Lambeth Ragged Schools can adduce many instances of their beneficial results, similar to those I have given in my letters; but it should be remembered by Mr. Doulton and others, that these individual instances of good are *not* and *never* have been denied by me. What I have asserted is—*not* that Ragged Schools do *no good at all*, but that, by the association of hundreds of boys of the most depraved propensities, they do and must necessarily produce "*more injury than benefit* to the community." Of the benefits resulting from such institutions, I have given both examples and testimonials. But I have also, I believe for the first time, pointed out the evil effects attending them, and elicited facts of which the annual reports of the Ragged School Union have made no mention, and concerning which the Ragged School teachers have never thought fit to inquire, or furnished any statements whatever to the society. Under such circumstances, of course it would have been idle for me to have sought for evidence from the teachers themselves, as to the danger of congregating so many young thieves together. I therefore availed myself of the best sources of information upon this point *exterior to* the Ragged

Schools. The result is before the public; and all that I have now to say upon the matter is, that the statements printed respecting the evil tendency of Ragged Schools in general are either true or false. Let their falsity be proved, and no man will be more ready than myself to acknowledge my error in the most public manner possible; but while such statements are allowed to be based on fact (and every letter from every Ragged School teacher that they have called forth admits them to be so—and even Mr. Doulton himself confesses that "*much*" of what I have printed "is undoubtedly true"), it appears to me that gentlemen who have the good of the class they seek to reform really at heart, should, instead of finding fault with me, feel grateful for having had such facts made known to them and others, for the first time. Ragged School teachers who have paid any attention to the influence of association—especially upon boys at an age when the character is being formed—must be well aware that, however some few of the children of the very poor may withstand the temptation of obtaining property by the easy and rapid process of theft, still the majority at least cannot but fall a prey to such influences, when made to encompass a greater extent than usual. The assertion of one master, with tastes, thoughts, and feelings utterly at variance with those of his scholars, and talking of tastes, beauties, and virtues, to lads who are wholly deficient both in moral sense and moral faculties, cannot possibly be supposed to outweigh the associations of some fifty or a hundred boys, of congenial thoughtlessness of temperament and depravity of principle. Even if the vagrant dispositions and the lax discipline of their homes would not make ready converts of such scholars to a life of adventurous dishonesty, assuredly the temptation of their extreme poverty and destitution must tend to bring about such a result. Without complete and incessant supervision of the whole of the boys by the teacher, and the separation of the better disposed from the more vicious class, Ragged Schools appear to me to be rather a retrograde than an advance movement towards the reformation of our juvenile offenders. Not only are a large body of young thieves brought into close connection and intercourse at such places, but, after having been instructed for a few hours, they are all turned loose together into the streets, with none to watch over them but the police, and there left to contaminate one another.—YOUR METROPOLITAN CORRESPONDENT.]

The Morning Chronicle, Monday, April 8, 1850.

CASE OF THE BALLAST-HEAVERS.

—◆—

To the EDITOR of the MORNING CHRONICLE.

Sir—I beg to present to you an order for 1*l.* in aid of the efforts now being made on behalf of the ballast-heavers.

HUMANITAS.

LABOUR AND THE POOR.

—◆—

THE METROPOLITAN DISTRICTS.

[FROM OUR SPECIAL CORRESPONDENT.]

Letter XLVII.

In several preceding Letters I have given ample particulars concerning the number, condition, pay, and provisions of the Merchant *Seamen Afloat*. I have described the state of the men in the different classes of vessels—both sail and steam-impelled—belonging to the foreign and coasting trades appertaining to the port of London. It now remains for me, in order to complete the picture, to set forth the treatment and habits of the Merchant *Seamen Ashore*.

In the present Letter I purpose giving an account of the better class of "Homes," or boarding-houses, provided for the reception of the sailor on his arrival in the port of London. After which I shall proceed to deal with the crimps, or the worse class of boarding-masters, and to lay bare the manifold iniquities practised in the metropolis upon the thoughtless and unsuspecting seaman.

First of all, however, let me endeavour to give the reader a picture of the port of London itself.

In the hope of obtaining a bird's-eye view of the port, I went up to the Golden Gallery that is immediately below the ball of St. Paul's. It was noon, and an exquisitely bright and clear spring day; but the view was smudgy and smeared with smoke. And yet the haze which hung like a curtain of shadow before and over everything, increased rather than diminished the giant sublimity of the city that lay stretched out beneath. It was utterly unlike London as seen every day below, in all its bricken and hard-featured reality; it was rather the phantasm— the spectral illusion, as it were, of the great metropolis—such as one might see it in a dream, with here and there stately churches and palatial hospitals, shimmering like white marble, their windows glittering in the sunshine like plates of burnished gold—while the rest of the scene was all hazy and indefinite. Even the outlines of the neighbouring streets, steeples, and towers were blurred in misty indistinctness.

Clumps of buildings and snatches of parks loomed through the clouds like dim islands rising out of the sea of smoke. It was impossible to tell where the sky ended and the city began; and as you peered into the thick haze you could, after a time, make out the dusky figures of tall factory chimneys plumed with black smoke; while spires and turrets seemed to hang midway between you and the earth, as if poised in the thick grey air. In the distance the faint hills, with the sun shining upon them, appeared like some far-off shore, or a mirage seen in the sky—indeed, the whole scene was more like the view of some imaginary and romantic Cloudland, than that of the most matter-of-fact and prosaic city in the world. As you peeped down into the thoroughfares you could see streams of busy little men, like ants, continually hurrying along in opposite directions; while, what with carts, cabs, and omnibuses, the earth seemed all alive with tiny creeping things, as when one looks into the grass on a summer's day. As you listened you caught the roar of the restless human tide of enterprise and competition at work below; and as you turned to contemplate the river at your back, you saw the sunlight shining upon the grey water beneath you like a sheet of golden tissue, while far away in the distance it sparkled again as the stream went twisting through the monster town. Beyond London-bridge nothing was visible; a thick veil of haze and fog hung before the shipping, so that not one solitary mast was to be seen marking the far-famed port of London. And yet one would hardly have had it otherwise! To behold the metropolis without its smoke—with its thousand steeples standing out against the clear blue sky, sharp and definite in their outlines—is to see London as it is *not*—without its native element. But as the vast city lay there beneath me, half hid in mist and with only glimpses of its greatness visible, it had a much more sublime and ideal effect from the very inability to grasp the whole of its literal reality.

From St. Paul's I made my way to the Custom-house, where, by the courtesy of the authorities, I was allowed to view the port of London from the roof of the "Long Room." A noble sight it was! The river before me bristled with a thousand masts, and the city behind me with a thousand steeples. On the opposite side of the shore, chimneys as tall and straight as the masts in front of them, poured forth their clouds of black smoke, while over the tops of the warehouses might be seen the trail of white steam from the railway engine cutting through the roofs. The sun shone bright upon the river, and as its broken beams played upon the surface, it fluttered and sparkled like a swarm of fire-flies. Down "the silent highway" barges tide-borne floated sideways, with their long thin idle oars projecting from their sides, like fins. Others went along with their windlass clicking, as they raised the mast and sail that they had lowered to pass under the bridge. Then would come a raft of timber, towed by a small boat, and the boatman leaning far back in it as he laboured at the sculls; and presently a rapid river steamer, stuck all over with passengers, would flit past, and you would catch a whiff of music from on board as it hurried by. The large square blocks of warehouses on the opposite shore were almost hidden in their shadow, which came slanting down far out into the river, covering as with a dark veil the sloops, schooners, and bilanders lying in the dusk beside them. Further down the river stood a clump of Irish vessels, with the light peeping through the tangled rigging, and their masts thick together as their native pine trees, some with their sails hanging loose and flaccid, and others with them looped in rude festoons to the yards. Beside them lay barges filled with barrels of beer and sacks of flour; and a few yards beyond was a huge foreign steamer, with its short, thick, black funnel, and blue paddle-boxes. Then came hoys laden with straw and coasting goods, so deep in the water that, as the steamers dashed by, you could see the white spray beat against the tarpaulings that covered their heaped-up cargoes. Next to these, black-looking colliers, and Russian brigs from Memel and Petersburg, lay in a dense mass together. Behind them stood the old "suffrance wharfs" with their peaked roofs, and unwieldy cranes; while far at the back might be seen one solitary tree. Further down by the river side was a huge old-fashioned brewery, with its jet of white steam shooting through the roof; and in the haze of the extreme distance the steeple of St. Mary's, Rotherhithe, loomed, grey, dim, and spectral-like. Then, as you turned again to look at the bridge, you caught glimpses of barges in the light seen through the arches below, and the tops of carts, omnibuses, and high loaded waggons moving to and fro above. Looking down towards the wharfs next the bridge, you could see the cranes projecting from "Nicholson's," with bales of goods hanging from them and dangling in the air. Alongside here lay a schooner and a brig, both from Spain, and laden with fruit, and, as you cast your eye below, you beheld men with cases of oranges on their backs, bending beneath their load as they passed from the ship across the dumb lighter to the wharf. In front of the schooner were lug-boats and empty lighters, standing high above the water, as they waited to be laden. Next to this was

Billingsgate, with the white bellies of the fish just visible in the market beneath, and streams of men passing backwards and forwards to the river-side. Immediately beneath me was the gravelled walk of the Custom-house Quay, where children strolled with their nursemaids, and hatless and yellow-legged blue-coat boys, and youths fresh from school, had come either to look at the shipping, or to skip and play among the barges. Here boats went by with men standing up in the stern and working a scull behind, like a fish's tail. Some yards off, were Dutch eel boats, of polished oak, with round bluff bows and unwieldy green-tipped rudders. Then came a tier of huge steamers with gilt sterns and mahogany wheels, and their bright brass binnacles glittering in the sun; at the foremost head of one, the blue-peter was flying as a summons to the hands ashore to come on board previously to starting, while the clouds of smoke that poured from the thick red funnel told that the fires were ready lighted. Behind these lay the Old Persius—the receiving ship of the Navy—with her top-masts down, her tall black sides towering high out of the water, and her white ventilators hanging above the hatchways. After her came other clumps of foreign vessels, coasters, and colliers—schooners, brigs, and sloops—with their yards aslant, and their sails looped up. Beside the wharf in front of these lay lug-boats and sloops, filled with square cases of wine, while bales of hemp, barrels of porter, and crates of hardware, swung from the cranes, and were lowered into the boats or lifted out of the sloops and "foreign brigs" below. Further on you could just make out the Tower-wharf, with its gravelled walk and the red-coated and high-capped sentry pacing to and fro. Beyond this again you saw the huge, massive warehouses of St. Katharine's Docks, with their big signet letters on their sides, their many prison-like windows, and their cranes to every floor. At the back stood the square old Tower, with its four turrets, and its grey, buttressed walls peering over the waterside. As I stood looking down upon the river the hundred clocks of the churches around me—with the golden figures on their black dials twinkling in the sunshine—chimed the hour of two in a hundred different tones, while, solemnly above all, boomed forth the monster bell of St. Paul's, filling the air for minutes afterwards with a deep, melodious moan; and scarcely had it died away before there rose from the river the sharp tinkle of "four bells" from the multitude of ships and steamers below. Indeed, there was an exquisite charm in the different sounds that smote the ear from the busy port of London. Now you would hear the tinkling of the distant purl-man's bell, as in his boat he flitted in and out among the several tiers of colliers. Then would come the rattle of some chain suddenly let go; after this, the chorus of many seamen heaving at the ropes; while, high above all, would be heard the hoarse voice of some one from the shore, bawling through his hands to his mate aboard the craft in the river. Anon, you would catch the clicking of the capstan palls, as they hove some neighbour-ing anchor, and, mingled with all this, would be heard the rumbling of the waggons and carts in the streets behind, and the panting and quick pulsation of the steamers on the river in front of you. Look or listen which way you would, the many sights and sounds that filled the eye and ear told each its different tale of busy trade and boundless capital. In the many bright-coloured flags that fluttered over the port, you read how all corners of the earth had been ransacked, each for its peculiar produce. The massive warehouses at the water-side looked like the storehouses of the wealth of the world, while, in the tall mast-like chimneys, with their black flags of smoke streaming from them, you saw how all around were at work, fashioning the far-fetched pro-duce into new fabrics. As you beheld the white clouds of the railway engine scudding above the roofs opposite, and heard the clatter of the carts and waggons behind, and looked down the endless vista of masts that crowded each side of the river, you could not help feeling how every power known to man was used to bring and diffuse the riches of every part of the world over this little island.

The officers upon whom principally devolves the care of regulat-ing the shipping, and all matters connected with it, in the Port of London, are the harbour-masters. Of these there are four. The first has a salary of £500 a year; the second, £400; the third, £350; and the fourth, £300. It appears that in 1836 the harbour service cost the corporation of London £6,363; and I find it incidentally mentioned by Sir John Hall, in the evidence he gave before a select parliamentary committee, appointed to inquire into the state of the Port of London, in the same year, that the corporation derived annually £50,000 from their tolls upon coals, corn, fish, seeds, vegetables, fruits, roots, and indeed all measurable goods conveyed, water-borne, on the Thames to be sold in the London markets. The harbour dues consist of a halfpenny or three farthings per ton on every vessel trading coastwise between the port of London and any part of the United Kingdom, as well as on every vessel entering inwards or clearing outwards from or to a foreign port. Three farthings per ton is the charge on every ves-sel from or to France (between Ushant and Spain), Portugal, Spain (within the Mediterranean), the Azores, Madeira, and Canary Isles, all ports in the Mediterranean, North and South America, the West Indies, Africa, East India, China, or any other place to the south of 25 degrees of north latitude. For all other destinations the "due" is a halfpenny per ton. For the sake of greater perspicuity, however, I subjoin the following table of receipts and expenditure in connection with the harbour service of the port of London:—

TABLE SHOWING THE AMOUNT OF DUES UPON SHIPS WHICH ENTERED THE PORT OF LONDON IN EACH OF THE YEARS 1836 TO 1844, BOTH INCLUSIVE; ALSO, AN ACCOUNT OF THE EXPENDITURE DURING THE SAME PERIOD.

RECEIPTS.

Years.	Harbour Dues.			Other Receipts.			Total.		
	£	s.	d.	£	s.	d.	£	s.	d.
1836	11,751	5	0	...			11,751	5	0
1837	11,349	8	0	797	7	4	12,146	15	4
1838	10,732	8	8	391	6	0	11,123	14	8
1839	12,000	1	4	492	1	7	12,492	1	11
1840	12,362	7	4	511	17	8	12,874	5	0
1841	12,402	19	5	570	12	8	12,973	12	1
1842	12,465	7	3	716	17	8	13,182	4	11
1843	12,196	5	6	1,188	15	10	13,385	1	4
1844	12,208	12	5	999	6	2	13,207	18	7

EXPENDITURE.

Years.	Salaries to Harbour Masters and other Officers.			Expenses for Moorings, &c.			Wages, &c., for Harbour Service.			Other Expenses for Harbour Service.			Law Expenses, Stationery, &c.			Total.		
	£	s.	d.	£	s.	d.	£	s.	d.	£	s.	d.	£	s.	d.	£	s.	d.
1836	2,399	16	6	1,569	17	6	1,705	6	11	410	3	10	278	4	5	6,363	9	2
1837	2,399	16	6	2,625	13	7	1,595	14	9	458	1	4	582	4	0	7,661	10	2
1838	2,452	6	6	3,830	11	5	1,847	8	7	924	1	6	161	3	0	9,215	11	0
1839	2,601	1	6	5,181	0	8	4,142	9	4	1,000	13	4	456	16	6	13,382	1	4
1840	2,755	19	2	2,453	18	2	2,387	17	9	723	12	3½	215	17	10	8,542	5	2½
1841	2,847	16	6	2,385	1	2½	2,919	1	0	345	15	6	376	3	10	8,873	18	0½
1842	2,832	10	6	2,170	17	6	2,476	11	9	412	9	2	248	0	1	8,141	9	0
1843	2,883	16	6	2,225	3	5	2,674	5	10	409	8	6	118	3	8	8,310	17	11
1844	2,916	16	2	3,227	9	5	3,902	6	10	377	1	10	200	3	2	10,623	17	5

The corporation of London are the conservators of the river Thames, and the Lord Mayor is the chief magistrate of the Thames as well as of the city of London. The corporation, under the charter of Henry VI., claims the right to the banks and soil of the Thames—subject, however, to the power of the corporation of the Trinity House to dredge for ballast below bridge. The Lord Mayor, however, according to the opinion of some of the witnesses before the parliamentary committee, is the servant, rather than the director, of the harbour-master; and the reason assigned is, that the harbour-master is a practical man acquainted with the management of the Thames, which the Lord Mayor is not. To assist in the proper conservancy and regulation of the Thames a "navigation committee" is annually appointed, consisting of 46 members—16 aldermen and 30 common councilmen; the common councilmen not being selected because they are considered the fittest men, as having some knowledge of the duties undertaken, but merely according to a system of rotation, by right of seniority in office. The appointment is for four years, and a commoner on the committee cannot be re-appointed to the performance of the same functions so long as a junior member of his ward has not been upon the committee; so that it very rarely happens that a four years' experience can be made available for the behoof of new and inexperienced committeemen. One-fourth of the committee goes out every year, the like number of new members being appointed. When the select parliamentary committee was sitting, the chairman of the navigation committee was "an importer and dealer in spruce." The chairman in the previous year was, according to the evidence of Mr. E. Tickner, "a very strong-minded and practically clever" retail baker; and his predecessor was an upholsterer. "Almost every application," Mr. Tickner has stated, "is treated *ad referendum*, and referred to the sub-committee, which is appointed also by rotation, every month. The committee meets once a week, and determines on applications for jetties, driving of piles, and other matters connected with the use to which individuals or companies wish to apply the banks of the river." The "fines," or quit-rents for permission to cut through the banks of the Thames, or to erect buildings or works, drive piles, &c., amounted, in 1836, to £1,216; in 1844 to £1,657. The duties of the harbour-masters are "to superintend and direct the entering, mooring, unmooring, moving, and removing," of all vessels in the port of London, and "to have the sole and active control of the executive part of the harbour service." Also to inspect the state of the mooring chains, &c., to take soundings, and to report to the navigation committee any alterations that may have taken place in the navigation of the port of London. "I have also," says Capt. J. Fisher, the principal harbour-master, "to attend all orders from the Right Hon. the Lord Mayor, the Hon. the Elder Brethren of the Trinity House, and to appear, at Guildhall or elsewhere, upon the Worshipful Thames Navigation and Port of London Committee, when duly summoned."

In the Acts of Parliament regulating the *Port of London*, more especially as regards the functions of the harbour-master and the management and disposal of colliers, the port is represented as extending from London-bridge to Bugsby's-hole, below Blackwall. But the 1st and 2d Vict., c.101 (dated November 14, 1838)—an Act consequent upon the parliamentary inquiry in 1836—extends, or recognises, the power of the harbour-master (in the by-laws for regulating vessels laden with coals in the Port of London, established by authority of the Act cited) to below Gravesend. The extent of the harbour-master's jurisdiction down the river is popularly known as from London-creek to Yantlet-creek—a point indicated, in day-light, by a flag hoisted near a place known as the "Stone," and at night by two lights, the upper one green and the lower red, "Vessels laden or in part laden,"— says Mr. Rowland, the principal harbour-master, in a very useful little book on the subject,—"with coals for the London market, are required to send their boat on shore at Gravesend to Wates' landing-place, situated at the extreme end of Gravesend eastward, and proceed to the 'collier-office,' at the back of Wates's Hotel, and deliver their 'certificates of cargo' and 'Custom-house papers,' which are forwarded to the factors each day at eight in the morning and four in the afternoon. By this arrangement the papers are delivered with despatch and certainty, and the expense of forwarding them by a person from the ship is avoided." The harbour-master at Gravesend assigns to each collier the section to be occupied until the vessel's rotation for proceeding to the pool for the purpose of discharging her coal. These collier sections are:—No. 1. From *Blackwall Point* to the Ferry-house on the south side of the river. No. 2. *Gallcons*, on the south side of the river. No. 3. *Gallcons*, on the north side of the river. No. 4. *Half-way Reach*, on the south side of the river. No. 5. *Long Reach*, from below *Dartford Creek* to *Lamb Wharf*, on the south side of the river. No. 6. From the causeway at *Greenhithe* to the lower Chalk Wharf in *St. Clements*, on the south side of the river. (This section is only used when not required for the use of her Majesty's ships.) No. 7. From below the Beacon, or *Broadness Point* to the upper side of *Northfleet Creek*, on the south side of the river. When these sections are full, colliers are detained eastwards of the Medway Canal entrance, below Gravesend. Colliers ordered to or transferred from the lower sections of the river to Nos. 1, 2, and 3, have their orders for the pools delivered to them from the Harbour Master's-office, at Greenwich, in rotation, and by a list furnished each market day from the Coal Meters'-office. In the pools, as I have before stated, the colliers are disposed in tiers; the maximum number which may be thus disposed is as follows:—

	Vessels.
Lower pool	147
Hanover-hole	14
Church-hole Tier	14
Moorings above Church-hole	27
Tower tiers (for traders)	15
Tiers between London-bridge and Cherry-garden (colliers for trans-shipment and traders)	10
Wapping Dock, King James's, and New Crane	8
	235
When the pools are full, and vessels require despatch, colliers are accommodated at Limehouse-hole Tier	8
	243

When a collier is leaky or damaged, the harbour-master at once assigns her a berth for the discharge of the cargo, or to lay up for repairs, as the exigencies of the case may require. If also a collier be bound to a dock or wharf, on the usual report at Gravesend she is ordered to proceed there straightway, without further delay, by the regulations of the port.

All the coasters and steamers are bound for some wharf, dock, or regular station in the river, and with these the harbour-master has nothing to do, beyond seeing that they observe the rules for the navigation of the river, and are properly moored in their places, if—as in the case of the Guernsey, Jersey, some Dutch, and other vessels—their regular moorings are in the river.

The chief regulations to be enforced by the harbour-master as to the navigation of the Thames are, that there shall be a clear water passage in the middle of the river 300 feet across; that the ferries and inshore passages shall be kept clear; that the dock entrances and public landing places be kept clear, no vessel being allowed to anchor or moor within 200 yards of the entrances to the East India, West India, or London Docks, within 150 yards of the West India South Dock, within 100 yards of the St. Katharine's, Commercial, East Country, and Grand Surrey Canal Docks, or within seventy-five yards of the piers in the river and the entrance to the Regent's Canal. The by-law enacting that there shall be a clear water passage of 300 feet is one which is not, and it appears cannot, be enforced. One difficulty, independently of the crowded state of the river, is this: Should a collier, for instance, be so moored in its tier as to obstruct the navigation, the harbour-master must by law give the master of the collier twelve hours' notice, when he is required to remove the obstruction, and for those twelve hours—comprising, perhaps, the whole term required for the most important navigation of the Thames—the collier can be kept in its berth unmolested.

The subjoined table will give the reader a comprehensive view of the river and shipping from London-bridge to Limehouse-reach on the north, and the Surrey-canal on the south side of the river Thames:—

A LIST OF TIERS AND FERRIES, DESCRIBING THE NUMBER OF VESSELS AT EACH TIER, ALSO THE WIDTH OF THE NAVIGABLE CHANNEL, FROM LONDON-BRIDGE TO THE UPPER PART OF LIMEHOUSE-REACH ON THE NORTH SIDE, AND FROM LONDON-BRIDGE TO THE SURREY CANAL ON THE SOUTH SIDE OF THE RIVER THAMES.—MARCH, 1846.

North Side.

North Side. Tiers and Ferries.	Number of Ships.	Navigable Channel.	Waterway at low water across, as per feet.
Custom House Upper Stairs			
Eel Chain	6	10	630
Yarmouth Chain	6	10	
Steamboat Tier	4	11	
Custom House Lower Stairs			
Dublin Chain	6	15	
Tower Stairs			593
Steamboat Tier	3	12	
King's Moorings ...... }The Persius and			
King's Stairs, Tower }Episcopal ship ...			
Tower Upper Tier	6	15	
Tower Middle Tier	5	13	
Tower Lower Tier	5	12	
Iron Gate Tier	6	12	
Iron Gate Stairs			700
Steamboat Upper Tiers	4	13	
Steamboat Lower Tiers	4	12	
St. Katharine's Dock Entrance			
Alderman's Upper Tier	6	13	690
Alderman's Stairs			
Alderman's Middle Tier	7	14	
Alderman's Lower Tier	7	15	
Hermitage Stairs	7	12	
Hermitage Stairs			645

South Side.

Waterway across at low water.	Navigable Channel.	Number of Ships.	South Side. Tiers and Ferries.
	11	6	Battle Bridge.
			Battle Bridge Stairs.
	13	5	Pickle Herring Upper Tier.
	12	5	Ditto Middle do.
	12	5	Ditto Lower do.
			Pickle Herring Stairs.
	14	7	Merritt's (private) Swing Tier.
	12	7	Limekiln Chain.
	13	7	Lighter Road Small Coasters.
	11		Ditto ditto.
			Horselydown Old Stairs.
	13	8	Garland's Chain.
	15	7	Old Rose Tier.
	12	7	Horselydown Upper Tier.
			George's Stairs.
	13	6	Horselydown Middle Tier.
			Horselydown New Stairs.
	13	7	Horselydown Lower Tier.
			Mill Stairs.

North Side.

Tiers and Ferries.	Number of Ships.	Navigable Channel.	Waterway at low water across, as per feet.
Hermitage, Middle	7	14	…
Hermitage, Lower	7	14	…
Union Tier, Upper	7	15	…
Union Stairs	6	16	655
Union, Lower	…	…	…
Wapping Entrance, London Docks	…	…	…
Wapping Old Stairs	…	…	677
Shadwell Entrance, London Docks	…	…	…
Bell Wharf, Upper Tier	20	15	…
Bell Wharf Stairs	…	…	845
Bell Wharf Lower Tier	20	13	…
Stone Stairs	18	17	730
Stone Stairs Tier	16	15	…
Ratcliff Cross, Upper	…	…	…
Ratcliff Cross Stairs	…	…	680
Ratcliff Cross, Lower	14	15	…
Regent's Canal	…	…	656
Dowson Dock	…	…	590
Duke Shore Causeway	…	…	566
Limehouse Hole Stairs	…	…	688
Limehouse Hole Tier	7	15	…
West India Dock Entrance	…	…	695
Canal Upper Tier	8	15	740
City Canal	…	…	854
Tier below the Canal	9	14	…
Second Tier ditto	10	14	800

South Side.

Tiers and Ferries.	Number of Ships.	Navigable Channel.	Waterway across at low water.
Mill Stairs Tier.	6	14	…
Bishop's Chain.	6	15	…
East Lane, Upper, Sm. Vessels.	2	14	…
East Lane Stairs.	…	…	…
East Lane, Lower.	2	16	…
Fountain Dock.	2	20	…
Fountain Stairs.	…	…	…
Cherry Garden, Upper Tier.	6	19	…
Ditto Middle.	6	18	…
Cherry Garden Stairs.	…	…	631
Cherry Garden, Lower Tier.	6	18	…
Rotherhithe Upper Tier.	7	17	…
Rotherhithe Stairs.	…	…	597
Rotherhithe Lower Tier.	7	15	…
King Stairs.	…	…	595
King Stairs Tier.	7	15	…
Princes Stairs Tier.	8	16	…
Princes Stairs.	…	…	607
Elephant Stairs.	…	…	…
Trinity Tier.	7	15	…
Church Hole.	8	14	…
Church Stairs.	…	…	670
Hanover Hole Tier.	18	16	…
Hanover Hole Stairs.	…	…	770
Mill Hole Upper Tier.	18	17	…
Ditto Lower Tier.	18	16	…
Surrey Canal.	…	…	…

Among the institutions of late years affecting the condition of seamen, one of the most prominent is the establishment of the *Sailors' Home*—or, as it is familiarly called by the seamen, "the Home"—in Well-street, near the London Docks. The building is erected on the site of the Brunswick Theatre, the iron roof of which fell in a very short time after its completion, in February, 1828. The destruction of the theatre excited public attention as to the best use that might be made of the site. Many friends of the seamen exerted themselves energetically (the late Captain Elliott, whose bust is now an ornament of the Sailors' Home, being one of the most indefatigable) to establish "a depôt for unemployed seamen;" and in August, 1828, a sufficient sum was raised to purchase the lease of the ground of the theatre. On the 1st of May, 1835, the present building was externally completed, and opened for the reception of 100 seamen. It is now capable of accommodating upwards of 300.

The Sailors' Home, Well-street, London Docks

At the time the Home was founded, the sailor was the prey of the "*crimp*" (as the fraudulent and extortionate boarding-master was generally called), of the slop-seller, and of a host of harpies, who enriched themselves on the systematized ruin and degradation of the thoughtless and improvident mariner. The intent of the Home was to prevent or check these abominable practices, and to give to the sailors a healthful boarding and lodging house, with other advantages to which I shall allude.

On entering the Home from Well-street, you step into a well-lighted and very spacious hall, supported by plain iron pillars. Seated on the oaken forms beside the fires at each end of the hall are some twenty or thirty seamen, newly "rigged out," some in their sleek and glossy blue clothes and clean straw hats, and others in bright red or dark-blue flannel shirts—all smoking and chatting together. Some stand apart in small groups, conversing upon matters of business; while others, in couples, pace half across the hall, backwards and forwards, as if still upon the deck. A few yards from the door is seen, perhaps, the last new comer, fresh from a long voyage, with his hammock rolled up like a mummy, and his ample sea-chest lying beside him on the whitened stones. On one side of the hall hang framed lists of "Ships to Sail," "Cancelled Mariners' Register Tickets," "Qualifications for Masters and Mates," cards of "Navigation Taught," placards of tailors "Recommended by the Sailors' Home"—on the opposite side the windows look into the skittle ground, where some half-dozen seamen are busy at the game. As I entered the hall, a sailor was swearing and gesticulating as only drunken men in a passion do, with his friends gathered round about him, and endeavouring to pacify him. The secretary, who accompanied me, placed his hand on the man's shoulder, and said kindly to him, "My good fellow, when I saw you this morning you were all I could wish you to be. Now do quiet yourself, there's a good man, and, above all, don't drink any more, I beg of you." The man answered the secretary respectfully enough, but retired towards the fire muttering that he would have his revenge if he got six months for it.

The dining-hall, or saloon, in which the men take their meals, is over the entrance-hall, and is of the same ample dimensions. Down the middle were ranged several long tables, two of which, at the time of my visit, were ready covered with white table-cloths, and set out with some fifty cups and saucers. At each end of the tables stood large piles of thick bread and butter, and in the centre plates of fresh-looking watercresses. Along one side of the saloon stood tables of a similar kind, covered with green baize, and strewn with books and periodicals in brown paper covers, chiefly of a religious, and partly of a nautical character. Here some sit reading, others writing. Against the wall above each of these tables is a small book-shelf, one of which contains a copy of the Scriptures in almost every known language. "Not long since," I was told by the secretary, "a New Zealander might be seen sitting by the fire there, reading the New Testament in his native tongue."

Above the saloon is the museum, containing models of ships, Malay proas, Madras catamarans, maps, charts, and foreign curiosities. Next to this is the school-room, with slates, scribbled over with sums and problems, and the tables littered with lunar observations, "epitomes," and Mariners' Assistants. Here an evening school is conducted, at which instruction in navigation is afforded gratuitously to as many as will avail themselves of the opportunity. Lectures on navigation, or on other matters connected with the seaman's calling, are also given.

The dormitories, some of which are at each end of the entrancehall, and some at the two extremities of the saloon, consist of a series of handsome oak cabins, with a passage down the middle. Of these there are in each dormitory two tiers on either side, placed one above the other. The topmost tier, round which there runs a continuous balcony, is reached by a small ladder, in the centre of the dormitory, and similar to that by which the captain of a steam-boat mounts the platform between the paddle-boxes. The doors, and what may be called the windows, are made after the fashion of Venetian blinds, so that by the mere pull of a string light or air may be excluded or admitted, at the pleasure of the occupant. The ventilation is admirable. You feel, as you walk along the passages, by the soft and regular current of air, that the place is as well ventilated as science can effect it. Each inmate has a cabin to himself; it is furnished by the institution with a wooden, or, in those of a later erection, an iron bedstead, and in the berth is stowed the seaman's chest. In the apprentice ward cards exhorting the inmates to prayers, beginning "My dear young friends," and signed with the chaplain's name, are nailed against the walls. On the windows at the end of the other dormitories lie tracts in brown paper covers, with some sailors' names inscribed on them outside; and all over the institution hang small cards, in all languages, beseeching the men to put their trust in God. The institution contains eight dormitories, making up altogether 300 beds. These dormitories are called by different names, and have many of them been built by different parties since the opening of the institution. The mercantile interest in the city of London supplied the means for two dormitories, when increasing applicants showed the need of increased accommodation. Another was erected by means of contributions from Edinburgh—less through the liberality of merchants or shipowners, I was informed, than that of benevolent persons unconnected with the trade; and the last dormitory was erected at the cost of the late

Queen Dowager, who expended upon it £420 5s. 9d. This dormitory is styled "The Royal Adelaide;" the others are called "The City of London," "The City of Edinburgh," or are distinguished by names familiar to seamen, such as, "Madras," and "Canton." One is occupied by the "lads"—another by the "apprentices." The cleanliness which distinguishes the cabins in a man-of-war marks all those of the Sailors' Home, but with *that* the resemblance to a man-of-war ceases. In the Home I observed no man-of-war, or even merchantman, sort of discipline—there was no "aye, aye, sir," no "salute" to a superior. The officers of the institution, including Captain G. Pierce, R.N., the secretary, and indeed manager (for whose ready courtesy, in placing at my disposal every source of information, I am bound to express my obligations), are addressed by the sailors familiarly and as friends.

The Sailors' Home is not only used as a pay-office where several shipowners now pay off their crews, but it also fulfils the functions of a savings bank to the seamen. The pay-office is that used by the clerks of the institution, and stands on one side of the passage leading to the entrance-hall, while the bank for the deposit of the men's pay is on the other. On entering the pay-office I found a young gentleman seated at a small table with a canvass bag full of sovereigns by his elbow, and a wooden bowl in front of him awaiting the coming of the sailors for their wages; while in the bank, on the opposite side of the passage, I found two seamen. One—a good-humoured and even merry-looking, but very deaf man—had resorted to the establishment on his return after eight voyages, and declared he knew no better place; while the other, who was there for the second time, expressed a similar opinion. The last-mentioned seaman deposited 14 sovereigns with the cashier, saying that he would keep 10s. to spend; but finding that he had more change left, he said, "Well, it's Saturday night, so I'll just keep all the silver for my pocket."

Every inmate is urged to make the institution his banker; the money so deposited is placed in the savings' bank, but is paid over at once to a seaman (with the savings' bank rate of interest) on the depositor's demand at the Home; and so he is saved any trouble, delay, or hindrance, through any mere informality, that might pester him at the savings bank, and make him unwilling to use it a second time. I cannot better show the effects of this branch of the arrangements of the Sailors' Home than by an extract from last year's report.

"The directors have the pleasing satisfaction of being enabled to state, that out of 25,960*l.* of the sailors' private money which has passed

through the cashier's hands during the last year, 5,485*l.* *has been for-*
warded by the officers of the institution, in order to reach the men in safety
when they arrived at their homes, or else to their relatives and friends in
different parts of the country, to help them in the hour of need. In the savings bank 2,540*l.* is now invested, belonging to 235 depositors; and
a pleasing instance of the pecuniary benefit arising to the men may
here be mentioned. One of our oldest boarders, on first entering the
institution, was induced to place a portion of his wages, received after
a long Indian voyage, in the savings bank. This he has increased on
every subsequent visit, until the amount reached 185*l.*, after which no
further investment could be made; 200*l.* was therefore purchased for
him in the 3¼ per Cents., and he has still something left in the savings
bank. To his credit it may be stated that this sailor never came to the
institution *without sending some assistance to his sisters in Ireland.*"

The day-book of the institution, which was shown to me, exhibits
the deposit of the seaman's wages in sums varying from £5 to £20;
this is afterwards drawn out by the men for daily expenses, in sums
generally of 5s. The depositor can pay or receive his money at any time
on any day, Sunday excepted, between 9 and 5. A deposit, however,
will not be refused after five—and very properly not; for in the evening
the seaman with money in his pocket is most beset with temptations.
For boarding, lodging, and a fair allowance of washing, each man
pays 2s. a day, or 14s. a week; the lads pay 12s. a week for the same
fare, and the apprentices 10s. 6d., washing for both included. Four
meals a day are provided. For breakfast there is bread and butter and
coffee, with fish by way of a relish, and always water-cresses, or some
vegetable, as an anti-scorbutic. For dinner good roast or boiled joints
are provided, and as much as any one chooses to eat. With tea, bread
and butter and green vegetables are given; and for supper, meat, bread,
and vegetables again. The doors are closed invariably at eleven at
night. Prayers are read by the chaplain every week-day, morning and
evening, which all are invited to join in; and on Sundays, the inmates
attend public worship in the Seamen's Church, close by. A printed
card, which the Rev. C. B. Gribble, the chaplain, causes to be placed
in the hands of the apprentices, thus concludes:—"I entreat you, my
dear young friends, to use the means for improvement which are now
within your reach. Do not laugh at them; do not neglect them. By
using them rightly you will be useful, honoured, and blessed; and in
godliness, temperance, and purity, you will find peace, happiness, and
honour.—Your faithful friend and pastor, C. B. GRIBBLE."

The number of men who have been, for longer or shorter periods, inmates of the Home, since its commencement, are—In 1836, 528; in 1837, 1,002; in 1838, 1,263; in 1839, 1,329; in 1840, 2,183; in 1841, 2,822; in 1842, 3,833; in 1843, 3,846; in 1844, 3,370; in 1845, 3,917; in 1846, 3,766; in 1847, 4,567; in 1848, 4,932; and in 1849, 4,633—making a total of 41,992 sailors received into the house since May, 1835, up to the 30th April, 1849; of whom 11,191, or nearly one-fourth, have been men who have resorted to the institution more than once.

The following is the account of the receipts and expenditure from April 30, 1848, to April 28, 1849:—

RECEIPTS.

To balance at last audit				£671	5	1
Annual subscriptions				425	13	6
Donations:	Her Majesty Queen					
	Adelaide	£420	5	9		
	Special appeal	432	0	0		
	Usual donations...	274	0	0—1,126	5	9
Advance notes				29	13	8
Collection at public meeting				9	14	1
Sale of old stores and seamen's effects				13	13	5
Sailors' board money				5,052	4	3
Dividends on stock				78	16	3
Legacies				324	9	6
Teignmouth Association				3	10	0
Durham	ditto			11	5	0
Totness	ditto			3	5	0
Norwich	ditto			5	12	0
Newcastle	ditto			9	15	0
Sheffield	ditto			6	0	0
Guernsey	ditto			12	0	8
Torquay	ditto			18	0	0
Bath	ditto			30	11	6
Edinburgh	ditto			2	15	0
Derby	ditto			1	10	0
Cheltenham	ditto			15	8	6
York	ditto			23	15	6
Clifton	ditto (2 years)			9	0	0
Plymouth	ditto			8	15	0
				£7,892	18	8

EXPENDITURE.

By advertising	£6	2	6
Cleaning, sand, scouring blankets, rugs, &c.	59	6	2
Completion of building	615	8	7
Coals	80	13	6
Collector's poundage	21	6	7
Expenses incurred boarding ships	25	12	1
Furniture and bedding	215	15	8
Gas	72	5	6
Hire of rooms for public meeting	7	2	6
Insurance	29	5	0
Losses upon advances to seamen	16	1	6
Linen	32	15	6
Lectures, library, museum, and school expenses	57	4	0
Printing	46	12	6
Petty expenses	12	16	5
Provisions	3,404	6	7
Postages	21	5	10
Porterage and parcels	1	1	5
Quarterly salaries to secretary, chaplain, accountant, cashier, and examiner of accounts	590	0	0
Repairs of building, painting, &c.	121	2	11
Rent of back-yard and offices	71	15	0
Rates and taxes	66	2	7
Stationery	45	12	10
Soap, candles, and oilman's account	31	14	8
Scripture Reader	22	0	4
Travelling expenses	0	9	10
Washing sailor's clothes	185	8	6
Washing house-linen	69	19	8
Weekly wages to suprintendent, schoolmaster, two agents, messenger, storekeeper, cook, doorkeeper, night watchman, steward, cook's and steward's mates, porter, and six waiters	581	3	9
Purchase of 850*l.* Reduced Three-and-a-Quarter per Cent. Annuities	738	16	3
Balance at Messrs. Williams, Deacon, and Co.'s	643	10	6
	£7,892	18	8

By the above it will be seen that £5,000 and odd were paid by the seamen for board at the Sailors' Home, and nearly £2,000 contributed towards the support of the institution by charitable persons, either in the shape of "donations," "subscriptions," "legacies," or "collections" in 1849. By these and other means, £7,892 was obtained in the course of last year. Of this nearly £3,500 was paid for provisions, £150 went for lighting and firing, £350 for washing clothes, linen, and cleaning, £250 for furniture, bedding and linen, £800 for completing buildings and doing repairs; while the salaries of the officers in connection with the institution, amounted to upwards of—£1,200!! That an institution like the Sailors' Home, of which the lease of the ground and cost of the building were originally paid for by voluntary subscriptions, and which has consequently only £70 to pay for "rent of back yard and offices," and about the same amount for rates and taxes every year; that such an institution with upwards of 4,500 boarders in the course of the year, paying each 14s. a week, should not be self-supporting—but require still to be maintained by charity to the extent of nearly £2,000 per annum—appears at first sight almost inexplicable. But when we find that, what with secretary, chaplain, scripture reader, accountant, cashier, examiner of accounts, superintendent, schoolmaster, two agents, messenger, storekeeper, cook, doorkeeper, night watchman, steward's cooks and steward's mates, porter, and six waiters—the salaries amount to upwards of £1,200 per annum, it is easy to understand that an Establishment so conducted must always be obliged to resort to alms in order to "make both ends" in any way "meet." The Sailors' Home is most assuredly an excellent institution, and one that doubtless, even at present, is attended with manifold benefits to the seaman; but it requires many alterations before it can be said to carry out fully the intention of its benevolent founders. Of these I shall speak more particularly in my next letter.

A middle-aged man, of very sedate appearance, and residing in the Home, gave me the following statement:—

"This is my fourth visit to the Sailors' Home in the course of nine years. I consider it an excellent institution for seamen. We have good strong grub, but we don't look for so many hares and things as at some boarding-masters'. At breakfast, at eight o'clock, we have always corned beef, salt fish, bread and butter, and coffee. For dinner, at one to-day, we had bouilli soup, roast and corned beef, meat-pie, and vegetables, with a pint of beer a man. That's the usual style of our dinners here. We have hot dinners on Sundays. For tea, at six, bread and butter and tea, with water-cresses. For supper, at nine, bread and cheese, with a pint of table ale. At half-past ten another pint of table ale is served out to each man, and then we can smoke till eleven, and go to bed. We can smoke as we please all day in the hall. They close the doors at eleven, and never open them on any account. We have prayers regularly every morning and evening. I generally attend, but we are not compelled; Roman Catholics go to their own places. The savings-bank at the Home is a very good place, for it makes a man more careful. I received £33, and put it in the bank. I draw it out as I want it, by 5s. and 10s. I've known rogues of boarding-masters who would have made me drunk, and have left me without money next morning. I knew a man who found himself the next day after a voyage, without a penny, and the boarding-master, when he told him he was robbed, said he was 'slewed' the night before, and came home without a penny. He was a shipmate of mine, and I saw him home to his boarding-house, and I'm sure he had the money about him then. He and I believed the boarding-master had robbed him when dead-drunk—that's five years ago. He made no stir about it; he had no evidence. The boarding-master kept him a few days without any charge, and then he got a ship. If a man's sober and steady, he can keep himself happier and cleaner here than in a boarding-house. Here we have all cabins to ourselves; in many boarding-houses, but not those of the best sort, we sleep two in a bed. Our friends can come and see us here, but not any female friends; though a man's mother or sister may sit down and talk half an hour to them—not by themselves privately, but in the hall, or upstairs in the dining-room. I think the steadiest-going seamen will always speak well of the Sailors' Home—I've found it so. If we have no money to stay longer, we must go, and can be admitted, if we are destitute, into the asylum below; but that's reckoned bad; it lowers a good man. I should be very badly off before I went there—very hard-up indeed. I could stay here a week or ten days after my money was out; but if I leave then—and leave I must—without getting a ship, I must leave my chest of clothes until I can get money to take them out. I don't know how long they keep the chest for any man leaving in debt. No grog is allowed in the Home, and men are better without it. We all agree very well here. After staying out all night, a man can go back next morning as usual."

I shall complete the present description of the better kind of Homes for Seamen with an account of a seamen's boarding-house (of the best class), for such it was described to me on excellent authority. The house was of the description known as a "gentleman's house;" it stood at the top of a street, not a thoroughfare, and behind it was a spacious garden, with out-houses where the more cumbersome luggage of the lodgers was stowed, and a very clean piggery. The garden walls were well covered with vines, and there were broad gravel walks, on which the seamen sauntered and smoked their pipes. At the end of the garden was an arbour, in which a sailor's old sea chest did duty as the seat. In an open recess built out from the kitchen window, the top of which was on a level with the ground of the garden, hung six hares, four ducks, a joint of beef, a shoulder of mutton, and a ham—tolerable specimens of the seamen's fare. I was told that the boarding-master was enabled to afford what may be accounted sumptuous dinners—considering that 14s. per week, the same amount as is paid at the "Home," is the charge for board, lodging, and a fair proportion of washing—by going himself to the same markets, and making his purchases on the same terms, as a wholesale dealer in game or poultry. On my visit some lodgers had just arrived from sea, and were refreshing themselves at a well-furnished tea-table. Four meals a day are supplied to the boarders, meat being given at three of them, whilst the supply of green vegetables, such as watercresses, is abundant at breakfast and tea. The inmates are single men, or those whose wives, home, or friends, are in other ports. The grand staple of the furniture of the house I speak of was shells. They were in every room, as if the owner of the house were studying the conchology of the East. They had been presented to him as little tokens of respect or remembrance by his guests. Some nautilus shells were specimens of exquisite beauty, while other shells were remarkable for their size, or for the delicacy, richness and iridescence of their colours. Mixed with the shells were masses of coral in different forms. In one of the best rooms, where the lodgers could resort to write their letters, or where they could see any visitors, the grate was filled with a large mass of coral and shells, and curiosities of all kinds covered the mantelpiece and side-tables. With these, too, were mixed the teeth of the whale, on some of which were carved, or scratched, drawings relative to a seaman's life. The house I am describing could accommodate thirty boarders, for whose use eight sleeping apartments were provided, a separate bed being allotted to each man.

In addition to the above I visited several other boarding-houses—all of the better class—being directed by a competent person. I did so that I might satisfy myself that the first house I saw was not an exception to the rule; nor was it. The other houses more or less presented the same characteristics; shells, and other sea curiosities, were the chief ornaments, with live parrots and cockatoos, some of them noisy enough. In two houses I saw two pleasant-looking old women (housekeepers), who were described to me as great favourites with the seamen. Some of the houses were beautifully clean, none could be called dirty; but, in point of ventilation, none could be compared to the Sailors' Home.

I will now give the statement of the *Boarding-house Master* himself, merely observing that I was referred to him by gentlemen of the greatest experience, as a fair sample of the better class, and as a person upon whose word every reliance might be placed:—

"I have had seven years' experience in keeping a boarding-house for sailors. I charge 14s. a week for board and lodging, supplying four meals a day, with meat or poultry at three meals. When the hare season is in I cook upon an average 20 hares a week, my boarders being in number about 30. Sometimes they tire of hares. When on shore, seamen are, however, generally fondest of hares, or rabbits, or poultry, and such things as they seldom get at sea, but I always provide roast and boiled joints as well. I find also to each man a pint of beer at his dinner and supper. The following, as my books here show you, is a statement of the numbers who have been in my house for three-and-a-quarter years past:—

> The number of men from January 1, 1847, up to December 31, 1847 402
> January 1, 1848, up to December 31, 1848 487
> January 1, 1849, up to December 31, 1849 594
> January 1, 1850, up to April 1, 1850 109

"I have most men at home in May, June, and July:—

> Last May at one time . . . . 47 men.
> June ditto . . . . 52 men.
> July ditto . . . . 39 men.

"I may be said, in some sense, to act as banker to my lodgers, so far as this:—When any boarder comes from sea he will place his money in my hands for safe keeping, and will draw it out in small sums as he requires it. I keep it in a book this way." [He showed me the book, which was kept with perfect system and regularity, some of the boarders testifying to the accuracy of the accounts.] "I never advance a man a farthing when he's drunk—not one farthing. Every morning I call over to each man a statement of his account, and if the boarder be not able to read and write, I call upon his shipmates to look at the book, and explain and satisfy him that it *is* right. The book always lies on a table for anybody's inspection. I mostly see my old customers, voyage after voyage, and they often bring their shipmates with them. My lodgers are of the better sort, and are well-conducted men, all things considered; by that I mean, that if a small tradesman or mechanic were suddenly to find himself in possession of £10 or £20, or more pounds, after having known many hardships, he would be more likely to commit greater excesses and offences than a sailor does. The sailor is, as a rule, a manly fellow, and I never knew any one of my lodgers strike a woman, unless aggravated by women of the town when drinking. These things, however, come very little under my observation, unless when sent for to help any of my lodgers out of a scrape; for in my house no disorder or bad language is allowed. Men who do not behave themselves must go. The board at houses like mine I consider to be better than at any other place, as we consult the men's tastes more than they can do at places carried on strictly by rule. The charge is the same as at the Home. I would very gladly undertake to carry on the Sailors' Home, and pay servants' wages and *rent* into the bargain (which they do not, the building having been raised by subscription), and every other expense, and make a handsome thing of it too, without any charitable donations or subscriptions, or any-thing of that kind. As to the destitute men, who are now sent from the Home to the Seamen's Asylum, I should deal with them as I do with the men in my house who get through their money before they leave. I keep them until they can get a ship. I have lost very little in-deed (and that chiefly by death) by men neglecting to pay me on their return from a voyage for what I let them have on credit. I have had post-office orders for such payments from all parts of the kingdom. If a man has left in my debt, and his first voyage afterwards is a bad one, I wait till the next, and almost always get paid. When men come to my house straight from the ship I advance them 5s. a piece, or if it's a steady man or an old customer 10s. They pay me when the ship is paid off. As to advance notes, I cash them for my regular customers without any charge. To those who are not regular customers I charge 5 per cent., but if the advance note is in payment of what they owe me I charge them no per centage, and may advance them something beyond the payment of the note. If the men be not all in my house at eleven—and sometimes they are not if they have gone to Astley's, for instance, or any place of amusement—I keep open till two in the morning; but I will open my doors at any time rather than subject any lodger to lose his clothes, as he most likely will if he be locked out all night. I have known men who have been out all night 'skinned' as it is called; that is, they have lost everything, shirt and all. Perhaps a woman of the town will come or send to me—every day may be it happens—and will bring a pawnbroker's ticket for a seaman's clothes pledged by her, the man having been drunk sometimes. The woman demands so much money for the duplicate of the clothes; if the duplicate be for 10s. she will ask 3s. or 4s. more than the 10s. If I threaten to take her before a magistrate, as perhaps the clothes have been pledged unknown to the man, she may give up the ticket, but not if it be only for 5s., as a magistrate then won't interfere. I have known the men—plenty of them—lose their clothes in the middle of the day. The Home closing at eleven has subjected many men to lose their clothes to my knowledge. I have known men locked out of the Sailors' Home come to their shipmates at my house for a night's shelter. If they have no money left, they may either walk the streets all night, or try and get a lodging with a friend, or go home with some girl who is tolerably certain to rob them of their clothes, and this while they have plenty of money in the Home. As to clothes, my lodgers employ any tailor they please, and I pay any strange tailor's bill if instructed so to do. Seamen will very well bear talking to when I tell them what fools they are to throw away their money as they often do, without any reasonable enjoyment for it. I have known great bearded men cry like children when I have reasoned with them as to their extravagance and tomfooleries; but they can't bear any threat of exposure, or anything like compulsion."

Of Mr. Greene's Home I shall speak in my next letter.

LABOUR AND THE POOR.

—◆—

THE METROPOLITAN DISTRICTS.

[FROM OUR SPECIAL CORRESPONDENT.]

OF SAILORS' HOMES AND BOARDING-HOUSES.

LETTER XLVIII.

In my last Letter I gave an account of some of the better class of lodging-houses for seamen. I described the peculiar character of the institution known as the Sailors' Home, in Well-street, London Docks, as well as the establishments kept by the more respectable boarding-masters. In my present communication I purpose completing my picture of the better class of seamen's lodging-houses, with a short sketch of "GREEN'S HOME" in the East India-road.

This institution is somewhat similar in its arrangements and regulations to the Home in Well-street. It differs from that establishment, however, in being a private rather than a public institution, it having been built by Mr. Green, the shipowner, solely for the accommodation of his own men, and being contributed to by him every year to a considerable amount with the same view. The Home in Well-street is maintained by subscriptions from charitable individuals to the extent of very nearly £2,000 per annum. "Green's Home," however, receives eleemosynary aid from no one but the benevolent founder himself; and I have been assured, that, though the institution is not self-supporting, by at least from three to five hundred pounds a year, still the gentleman whose name it bears does not hesitate to make up the deficiency out of his own pocket, rather than allow his men on their return to this country to fall a prey to the crimps that infest the neighbourhood of the Docks.

After the many scenes of overwhelming misery that it has been my lot to contemplate within the last few months, it is impossible to convey to the readers of these letters the sense of delight experienced on visiting an abode like the institution in the East India-road. For nearly six months I have witnessed the most heartless indifference on the part of employers to the welfare of those whom they employed—and heard the most bitter invectives poured forth by the workpeople against those for whom they worked. The misery, the heartlessness, and the bitterness which it had become my duty to witness and listen to, day after day, made my task a most melancholy one. It was, however, this very circumstance that gave a tenfold pleasure to my visit to Mr. Green's Home. The cleanliness and pleasantness of the place were so diametrically different from what I had lately been accustomed to—the men spoke so lovingly of their master— and the master betrayed everywhere such kindness and consideration for his men—that, after half a year spent among sweaters, slopsellers, chamber-masters, lumpers, ballast-contractors, and a host of others who live and fatten on the physical and moral degradation of those whom they employ, the comfort, happiness, and air of sympathy that pervaded the whole building had indeed a most cheering effect. On a settle before the fire in the entrance-hall (which, though smaller, is something like the hall of the Home in Well-street) were ranged some dozen sailors smoking. All of these were old servants. Only one had been but a single year in Mr. Green's employ. Two had been eight years—two others six years—one had made nine voyages in Mr. Green's ships—another five—and another four. The others had been from two to three years in the service of Mr. Green. As I interrogated the men, one said, "I never was in any other employ out of England since I have been to sea. I was always treated kindly by Mr. Green, and am satisfied I never could meet with a better master. I always heard he had a good name, and am sure I can give him one."

On one side of the hall stood a large model of one of Mr. Green's "crack ships," the OWEN GLENDOWER. I was contemplating the symmetry of the hull, when an old sailor, with a freckled, weather-beaten face, and whiskers of the colour and texture of "coir" rope, came up to me. "Ah! that's a fine ship, sir," said he; "I was captain of the maintop in her one voyage. She's one of the finest vessels I ever sailed in, and I've been nearly forty year at sea. Ain't she a pictur' now, sir?" The man then digressed from the ship to his master. "Ah, sir! his treatment to us will become proverbial by-and-by. He has fitted up this place for us, and we pay less here than we should have to do anywhere else. We have better treatment and better victuals too than we could get at any other place. I have been six years in his employ. I have served more than a dozen masters in my time, and never knew any one like Mr. Green for his regard for his men. Here we are; we have always got a home over our heads, and can get a ship when we like. If we don't like one we can stop for another. I never knew or heard of a man being turned out of here, like he is at the Home in Well-street, because he had outrun his money. If he has a good char-acter on board his ship he is never turned out of this place, let his arrears be what they may. The superintendent takes care of our pay. We have got a library, and can get a book and sit down and read. We have most of the new publications, and the daily papers, and *Cham-bers' Journal.* We in general prefer 'Chambers' to any other—it's so amusing. I don't see anything that Mr. Green omits for our gratific-ation. The victuals is of the best, and the pay only 12s. (The Sailors' Home charges 14s.) And we have ten pieces a week washed gratis."

After this I crossed to the other side of the hall, and stopped op-posite a bill, which announced that "No Smoking or Lucifers were allowed upstairs."

"We're not allowed to smoke upstairs in the dormitories, you see, sir," said another sailor, who observed what I was reading. "No, no; that would never do. The rules are very good in this house, and very considerate for the men. Eleven o'clock is the hour for coming in, but we're let in after that—indeed at any hour. There's a watchman sitting up for us all night, rather than we should be locked out. But eleven is a good enough hour for any decent man to be in. I have turned in regular at nine o'clock every night since I have been home. At eleven the lights are put out. I can make myself more comfortable, reading here by a good fire, than knocking about the streets. It's *really* a home—not like the other place. If I was to be here three months, they'd never say—What, you are not looking for a ship!—any more than they would the first day I came into the place. We're just as well treated the last day as the first. We can get ships without going out of doors. If all owners treated their men as well as Mr. Green, the men would be as good as we are. If men are badly treated, why, in course, they're bad, for bad treatment makes bad men."

On the walls of the hall were bills, stating the "scale of victual-ling for ships in the employ of Messrs. Green, for a mess of five men, per week at sea." One of these bills, I was informed, was gen-erally pasted or nailed to the mast of Mr. Green's vessels before the men were shipped. In another part of the hall hung a notice, that "the ship Seringapatam pays on Thursday next." Over the mantel-piece were cards and bills of ships to sail, while all around hung pic-tures of East India ships, such as "the Roxburgh Castle and Sir E. Paget, off Dover;" "the Delafield, Simon Taylor, and Repulse"—all three built in the Blackwall yard, I was told. In the centre stood a new kind of French bagatelle board, played with marbles, at which a young apprentice was amusing himself, while two other "youngsters" were seated at a table strewn with books, and deep in a game of draughts. The following rules "respecting conduct" I copied from a bill headed "Sailors' Home," East India-road, opened on the 1st June, 1841—Regulations:—

> "All swearing and improper language, so unbecoming the character of a man, and so dishonouring to God, must be entirely avoided in this place.
> "Drunkenness, that disgraceful vice, which sinks a man to a level below the very beasts that perish, and which is so contrary to order and decency, the men must judge of themselves, cannot in any measure be permitted here.
> "All quarrelling and abusive language one to another, must be guarded against; and a respectful manner towards those who superintend the institution will be expected of every man."

The Museum—which was likewise the pay-office—was stocked, or rather crammed, with an infinity of curiosities from the Indies, the South Sea, and China. There were flying foxes in glass cases, Bengalee shoes of Nabobs, snouts of saw-fish, penguins' skins, immense horns from the Cape, ostriches' eggs, stuffed kangaroos, Madras Masulah boats, models of Bengalee policemen, Chinese idols, tiger skins, albatrosses, shells, bottles of centipedes and scorpions preserved in spirits, Chinese umbrellas, engraved teeth of the whale, wigs of South Sea chiefs made of the hair of their victims, flying-fish, Chinese compasses and tom-toms, Caffre war bugles, and a little world of knick-knackeries, each linked with a thousand curious associations, that carried the mind half over the globe as you walked round the room.

The dormitories at Green's Home are built after the model of those at Well-street. The number of men received into the institution for the last four years has been as follows:—

1846	....	392	men
1847	....	383	„
1848	....	406	„
1849	....	487	„

The officers and servants of the institution consist of one superintendent and assistant, with five attendants, consisting of cook, waiters, and house servants. The amount paid in salaries I could not obtain at the institution, but I learnt from other quarters that it was scarcely a tithe of the £1,200 annually expended upon the officers and attendants of the Sailors' Home, and yet I could distinguish no difference in point of cleanliness, order, and conduct at the two places; so that no little credit appeared to be due to the superintendent who, with so small a staff of officials, could maintain so much comfort, tidiness, and regularity. Though the institution was not self-supporting, still I was informed that if it was filled in winter as it is in summer, even the 12s. per week paid by each sailor (the Home in Well-street charges 14s.) would be sufficient to defray all outgoings, such as rates, taxes, wages, lighting, firing, provisions, &c., with the exception of rent. The building originally cost £15,000, so that there is no rent to pay.

In connexion with the Home, Mr. Green has built a chapel for the accommodation of his men, and not many yards removed from it are the schools, at which he educates 1,500 children, and clothes a considerable portion of them—indeed all around the place there appears to be an atmosphere of benevolence and sound practical Christianity. Of Mr. Green's schools I shall have occasion to speak at a future period.

I must now pass from the better to the worse class of lodging-houses for seamen. But, first, I must speak of certain malpractices at the Sailors' Home in Well-street, which appear to me to detract greatly from the intended excellence of that institution. I am convinced that the managers of the Home are not cognisant of the conduct of certain parties in connection with that establishment, nor of the evil effect of some of the regulations concerning the men, and that the facts have but to be made public for what is really wrong in the management to be immediately rectified.

It will be remembered that in my last letter I drew attention to the fact that, though the Sailors' Home was doing the largest business of any boarding-house in London, still it required no less than £2,000 to be collected in charitable subscriptions and donations before it made both ends meet. The cause of this is evidently the immense amount annually expended in salaries and wages, which come to no less than £1,200 per annum—a sum that totally precludes all hope of the institution, under such a system, ever being self-supporting. This, indeed, is the main defect of the Home, for unless its expenditure can be kept within its legitimate income, it is evident that the establishment cannot last long.

The Sailors' Home, however, has many other defects. The fore-most of these is the system of touting for custom, carried on by the runners of the tailors in connection with the establishment. Of this touting I had the following account from a man who spoke from personal knowledge:—

"There are three tailors—or outfitters generally, for they supply shoes, hats, shirts, &c., as well as clothes—who reside in the neigh-bourhood of the Sailors' Home; and the conductors of the Home do not willingly allow any other tailors to enter the establishment, and would demur to paying a bill, out of a seaman's cash in their hands, to any other tailor. These three outfitters employ at least 11 regular runners or touters, at 30s. a week each, or £16 10s. altogether; besides that, some of the principals and their families tout also. I have seen as many as 14 runners on board an East Indiaman, all trying for the custom of the sailors. Sometimes we board the ship at Gravesend—sometimes lower than Gravesend, well down to the Nore—and some-times at Blackwall. If we get aboard a Quebec or West Indiaman, or any two or three months' ship, we mustn't waste time there, as the crews of such ships have no great sum of money to receive, but we must hurry off to a Calcutta ship, if there be one. When on board, the runner inquires as to the money the men have to receive, generally asking the mates and apprentices such questions as, 'Has So-and-so been the whole voyage?' 'Will his pay be stopped, or any of it?' And, when the answer is satisfactory, the runner goes to work. When the ship reaches the dock we go on shore with a seaman that we have stuck to like wax, telling him that there's no place like the Sailors' Home. 'No robbery there,' we say; 'no! there men are taken care of, and the best of victuals.' We go touting as for the Home, but it's for our em-ployers' interests. If the ship come up on a night's tide, too late for the Home, as is often the case, we get the men who are bound for the Home a night's lodging, paying the cost of it; or if they are inclined to go on the spree, then we plant them on some woman or other that we know, pay the expenses, and then look them up in the morning to convey them to the Home. On our way we generally have a glass with them. I can say that there are runners connected in this way with the Sailors' Home, who are drunk five days out of six. These runners for the Home are generally dissipated people, and drink hard. Our first object is to get a seaman to one of the Sailors' Home tailors. We are employed by the tailors and not by the Home, but the Home people know—they *must* know—how we are employed by the tailors to get men to the Home, for we are all introduced by our employers to the superintendent there. I have seen eight tailors' runners (all belonging to the three firms) plying in the Home at once, to the great annoyance of the men, whom I've heard say, 'D— you, I won't be bothered. I'll go where I like.' A runner's is a miserable life—we're looked upon as anything but respectable when we get aboard a ship; but aboard you must, as it's all in the way of business for employers. A seaman just landed of course wants a little money. He can't get any at the Home if he arrives after six in the evening, though he's charged for a day's boarding—so he gets all he wants of the tailors. This used to be charged as cash, and is still charged as cash, if advanced by the tailor after six at night; but if a man be regularly installed in the Home, and want a pound or two, or £3, to buy any useful thing at a good shop, he's asked by the cashier at the Home what he wants the money for. They won't advance money unless they are satisfied that the money's worth will be in the man's possession when he returns to the Home. But if a seaman wants a sovereign for any purpose of his own that he don't wish there to be any prying into, he goes to the tailor, and says, 'I want a pound for this, or for that;' and the tailor says, 'Well, I can't let you have money, you know it's against the rules, but I can, as you're so pressing, let you have what you want and charge it as a garment, and put it down with a per centage.' So said, so done. I have known a seaman, when the tailor or his man took in his bill to the cashier at the Home, say 'I've never had those trowsers'—and I have been behind the man myself, and have whispered, 'the money, you know' (I can't say that the superintendent heard me), and the man answered, 'Oh, yes, I remember, now.' The tailor's bill was then paid; but it wouldn't be paid unless the sailor had money in the bank to meet a fortnight's board. The three tailors with their profits and extent of business can afford to run risks and give credit; knowing their position with the Home, they must do it; but they can charge accordingly. I once had 25s. a week, and 5 per cent. commission, from an outfitter, for touting, and have under that agreement received from £2 10s. to £3 a week. My commission has been often 35s. on £35 custom, carried by me in one week from Sailors' Home men to the tailor who employed me. I have known £120 worth of clothes supplied in one week by one man to different men at the Home, nearly half being profit. Take £3 as an average price for a 'round suit' (cloth jacket, waistcoat, and trowsers) for this I reckon that 38s. at most would be the prime cost, but the outfitters try for cent. per cent. I believe that they pay for making a jacket from 4s. to 4s. 6d.; trowsers (two shops pay more than others), 2s. 6d. to 3s.; waistcoat, 2s. The cloth is not to be complained of. Some round suits of the better sorts are charged £4. Sometimes one of these tailors has from sixty to seventy sailors to clothe in a week, but for three or four weeks he may have nothing, or next to nothing, to do. I should say that three out of four sailors want suits when they land after a longish voyage. After a long voyage, a man in the Seamen's Home is allowed to draw £1 before he is paid his wages; after short voyages, he has a smaller sum, in proportion. If he has been a long voyage he is sure to want more than £1 before he gets paid off, as, perhaps, he has £25 or £30 to receive; and he runs to the tailor to get an extra advance, and pays for it as I have told you, and that seems to me one reason why the Home is of more benefit to the tailor than the sailor. Many a seaman has been sucked uncommonly dry by persons connected with the Home. Some of the officers of the Home have watches to sell them, and then they may buy them back of their customer, if he happens to want money afterwards—as is a common case—at half-price. An officer too will sell clothes that he's bought cheap of some former lodger who was out of funds, to any new comer wanting them. A respectable boarding-master feels bound, for the sake of his character, to keep his lodger until he gets a ship; but that is not the case at the Home. There, after a man's money in the office or bank is run out, they sometimes give him a week's grace, but not until they are certain, from the waiter who has care of the dormitory where the man is lodged, that he has a chest and clothes sufficient to pay for a week's board. In case the man don't get shipped in the course of the week, his clothes are taken from his cabin and put into the store room, and then the poor fellow is refused a meal's victuals and turned into the street. The officials say it's the rule, and must be enforced. Then the man must get to any place he can, and when he gets a ship he of course must pay the person who was kind enough to take him in and supply him with board; after that he may not have enough to pay the Home out of his advance; he goes to sea, and is away perhaps eighteen months or two years, and when he returns and inquires at the Home what has become of his chest and clothes, he is informed they were sold. I'm told that's against the law, but the sailor don't know there is any redress. Such a case as I have described is of common occurrence at the Home: seventy or eighty forfeited chests and clothes are sold every second year." [According to the last year's account the sale of seamen's effects and old stores amounted to £13 13s.] "Then the officers of the establishment are not allowed, by the rules, to have any perquisites. But I will tell you how it's managed. When men come to the Home they are entered on the books, and then the waiter, who knows his business very well, has perhaps a nice watch to sell, which he 'bought cheap of a man before he went to sea.' This of course yields a good profit. It's the same with any other article; or the waiter may recommend a tailor, for which he gets a commission. Then comes the doorkeeper, and he gets plenty of pickings. The doorkeeper, of course, knows his customers, and would like to drink their healths; they'll ask him to have a glass with them; but the doorkeeper can't stir out, and would rather have the money; the sailors of course can't think of giving a respectable-looking man 2d. for a drop of beer, so they give him 6d. or 1s., and as much as 2s. sometimes. The seamen, when they require money, get cheques from the superintendent on the cashier, but if the office is closed the doorkeeper lends money on them at very good interest. I have known when the clerks have been in the office they have been denied, just for this lending of money and getting of interest. I don't suppose that the committee knows anything about these things. The chief officers of the Home are licensed shipping agents. When the Home is quite full—say 300 in it—not more than half that number will sit down to dinner, as sailors won't be tied to hours ashore, when they've money of their own; and that must leave a good profit. If the lodgers come in after meal-times they can get something to eat in the kitchen, that is if they don't mind the steward's black looks. Men are so sucked, as I have told you from my own knowledge, by runners, and tailors, and the servants of the Home, that I'm satisfied £20 in a sailor's pocket will go further at a boarding-master's than at the Home. The tailors expect their runners to look sharp after the seamen that they've had as customers, and get them ships before all their money is done, or they may be troublesome to the tailors when they want money or such like. The tailors' runners will follow a ship from Blackwall to the London or St. Katharine Docks, coming up by the railway, though I'm told that going on board ship and touting that way is contrary to Act of Parliament. The tailors' runners do all the touting for the Home, which now has only one agent of its own for that purpose, but *he's* not seen at work more than one tide in a week perhaps. The Home professes to cash advance notes at 5 per cent. This is the way it's done: if a sailor wants his advance note cashing, an officer of the Home perhaps will say, 'Well, what do you want the money for?' and the man may answer, 'Why, for clothes, I want 30s.' Then says the officer, 'Here, ——, send for so-and-so, and let him supply 30s. worth of clothes.' The Home won't give money if it can be avoided, in such cases; and as the tailor sends in the clothes, why he, and not the Home, runs the risk if the man shirk his engagement."

As a proof of the money supplied by the tailors to the seamen at the Home, the three following accounts were given to me. It will be seen that £1 15s. is charged for cash lent in the first, £1 13s. 6d. in the second, and £4 17s. in the third:—

RECOMMENDED BY THE DIRECTORS OF THE SAILORS' HOME.

Ship—Mary Ballantyne. Dec. 30, 1848.

W—— W—— :—Bought of M. P——, tailor, &c., Well-street, London Docks, opposite the Sailors' Home.

	£	s.	d.
Pilot coat	£2	0	0
Two flannels	0	8	0
Silk hat	0	6	0
Fancy trowsers	1	2	0
Cash—10s., 5s., 5s., 10s., 5s.	1	15	0
	£5	11	0

Captains and mates supplied.—Sea chests, beds, and bedding. Settled—M. P—— and Co.

RECOMMENDED BY THE DIRECTORS OF THE SAILORS' HOME.

Ship—Mary Ballantyne. Dec. 30, 1848.

J—— C—— :—Bought of M. P——, tailor, &c., Well-street, London Docks, opposite the Sailors' Home.

	£	s.	d.
Fine suit	£3	5	0
Cash—5s., 5s., 11s. 6d., 5s., 5s., 2s.	1	13	6
	£4	18	6

Captains and mates supplied.—Sea chests, beds, and bedding. Settled—M. P——.

RECOMMENDED BY THE DIRECTORS OF THE SAILORS' HOME.

Ship—Mary Ballantyne. Dec. 30, 1848.

J—— D—— :—Bought of M. P——, tailor, &c., Well-street, London Docks, opposite the Sailors' Home.

	£	s.	d.
Fine suit	£3	10	0
Two striped shirts	0	5	0
Cash—5s., 7s. 6d., 45s., 7s. 6d., 12s. 6d., 5s., 1s., 10s., 3s. 6d.	4	17	0
	£8	12	0

Captains and mates supplied.—Sea chests, beds, and bedding.

I now give a statement made to me concerning a regulation of the Home:—

"I came home in the ship Mary Imrie, of Liverpool, and came from Liverpool to the Sailors' Home in Wells-street. I stopt there and paid one week's board, and 6s. for my things coming up. They kept me three days over the week, and then turned me in the streets without a piece of food to put in my mouth, and kept my clothes for the amount of the three days' board, being 6s., and 1s. for steward. They told me to go to the straw-house (the Asylum for Destitute Sailors). I said I understood that there was a shipping-master at the Home to get us ships. And —— said 'No, we have no ships, and you must go.' I was turned out on Saturday morning, and was obliged to sell my clothes off my back to buy some food with, until Monday. I fell in with one of my shipmates on Monday morning, the name of S—— G——; and he spoke to ——, and asked him if he would give his poor shipmate some food, as he was turned out of the Sailors' Home without a farthing, and he was a stranger in London. And so I got kept until I found a ship." This man had certificates to show that he was a well-conducted man.

A young man, but with eight years' experience at sea, gave me the following account:—

"I was ordinary seaman on board the Liberty, of Seaham, a collier, bound for Hamburg, with eleven keels, and on last Wednesday, March 18, she was wrecked about fifty miles from Cuxhaven. There was a very strong gale and thick weather, and her anchor parted; she went ashore, and was not long before she was knocked to pieces; no lives were lost, but we didn't save a thread, nothing but what we had on. The Consul at Cuxhaven kept us three days, and then sent us to London in a steamer, which we reached on Good Friday morning. At Cuxhaven the Consul gave me these trowsers, and this shirt—all the clothes I have. At London I got my register ticket without trouble, and was advised to try the Sailors' Home as a place for shipwrecked men. I asked to be admitted as a shipwrecked man, and to be kept there until I could get a ship; but I was refused admission, and told that I might go to the asylum, a straw-yard, close by. I didn't like to go there, because a decent man feels degraded in such a place—all the good men I have talked to are of the same opinion. It's like going to a workhouse, turning into the straw-yard, and we would as lief starve."

The subjoined statement was given to me, as to a regulation of the Sailors' Home in case of the sickness of a lodger:—

"I was discharged from my last ship with a good character, as an able seaman, and went direct to the Sailors' Home. I had £9 pay when

I went there. I was there six or seven weeks, and paid £2 in advance for my board and lodging. I met with an accident to my hand, about three days after I was on shore. I was told that the surgeon of the Sailors' Home would attend to me free, but I was charged 12s. by him for lancing my hand, for two bottles of medicine (which I never took), and for two pills. I stopped there about a week after this, when, having no money, Mr. —— took me into the secretary's office, when they told me that I was getting into debt, and that while my hand was bad I had better go into the Straw-house (Asylum), as they could not get me a ship while my hand was bad. I refused to comply, and was obliged to leave, and was taken into the boarding-house of Mr. ——."

Another seaman not then in the house, but who had been on a former occasion, gave me further information. He spoke in very high terms of the order, cleanliness, and comfort of the Sailors' Home.

"If," said he, "the Sailors' Home would stick up for a sailor's rights when there is a dispute about wages, or the likes of that, it would be the best place in England; for you see, a lot of gentlemen, such as manage there, if they would undertake it, could make up any dispute oft enough, without any bother at a police-office, and masters wouldn't be so ready to try it on to lower men's wages by fines, stoppages, and such likes, if they knew there was such a place as the Home to stand by a seaman when he had right on his side. As it is, the Home won't trouble itself that way, and men having wages in dispute, if it's ever so much, needn't go there; indeed they wouldn't be admitted. The Home's best for steady men, for it won't exactly interfere to get a man out of a scrape if he's robbed by women or the likes, though money may be got through people connected with the Home to get you out of a scrape. I should have gone to the Home oftener, but unless we has a tidy bit of money it don't answer, for there's no credit there when your money's run through, but on your clothes. At a boarding-master's, though, you can go on credit, and yet *they* make it answer. But then it's the regular rule at the Home, and so men know what's to come, and haven't a right to complain if they have to quit and look out for another place. That's a reason why men after short voyages, when they haven't much money to take, needn't go to the Home—that's my case. As I tell you, the Home's best for steady men, that can keep a-head with the bank there; and indeed them kind of steady men are middling safe anywhere, but safest at the Home, I think. If a man be ill at the Sailors' Home, he must pay for the doctor himself. There's a doctor's name in the list of officers, or whatever you may call them, connected with the Home, but a seaman lodging there must pay him for attendance. I believe any seaman can employ his own doctor if he pleases."

At a meeting of boarding-masters—sixteen being present, and all being described to me on good authority as among the better class—the following opinions were expressed:—

The rules of the Home, they said, allowed no man to remain in it when his funds were exhausted; he was then, in fact, turned out—his clothes, in all probability, being detained at the Home for sums ranging from 6s. to 24s., as he might have been trusted, according to the value of his effects. If the man thus compelled to leave the Home were at all a decent man, he shrank from the Asylum, but would draw up to any old shipmate at a boarding-master's, and ask for admission. The shipmates would expect him to be admitted; and the boarding-master, to keep up his character as a good man to a seaman, must take him in, penniless as he was; then he must keep him till a ship was got; advance money to get his clothes from the Home, perhaps, and run every risk of loss, while the Home avoided any risk whatever. The boarding-master, notwithstanding, would charge no more for board and lodging than the Home, though he had to pay rates, taxes, rent, servants' wages, and all, out of his profits. The Home had funds from subscriptions to pay the greater part of such expenses—while, as in the case of rent, it had scarcely any at all to pay, the building having been paid for by charitable donations. Every boarding-master present cited cases of the above kind from his own experience, some having incurred losses, and some still holding I O U's which might never be met. Some boarding-masters had kept men turned out of the Home for four and five weeks before a ship could be got; as, once taken in, the better class never turn a man out, unless for roguery or misconduct. The boarding-masters, I was assured, did not sell men's effects left in their custody for money due; one master had in his possession valuable clothes which he had kept for nine years, whereas the Home sold the men's effects periodically. Moreover, I was told that a seaman would sometimes land, and complain of injustice done to him by his captain in attempting to deduct so much from his wages under this or that pretence. The Home would not give admission to sailors so circumstanced unless they had a trifle of money with them, and when that was exhausted, they would have to leave the Home. In case of their not being admitted, or being turned out, the boarding-master, for the reasons stated before, must take the men in. Then, too, he must get a solicitor to conduct the man's case (if necessary, as it often is), and keep the man until a magistrate adjudicates. The boarding-master, indeed, must run every risk, while the Home avoided any risk at all, though it was popularly believed that the Sailors' Home was an institution to befriend seamen. This it could hardly be, it was urged, if it did nothing to help them to their rights. Some solicitors who take cases at the Thames Police-office go on the principle of "No cure, no pay," but that's only in clear cases, or such as the solicitor believes to be clear. As a rule—it was stated as an established fact—the Home will not support any men who are waiting for an adjudication of their claims, and will not do anything adverse to shipowners. Shipowners are a main support of the Home, so the conductors of the Home will not interfere, whatever unfair attempt may be made to mulct a man in penalties, and so save the amount payable in wages to benefit the shipowner. I heard at this meeting, however, of one exception to this rule. There was a case before the magistrate as to the claims of some men after a voyage from Callao, and two of these men, who refused to take what was offered, as it was a very great reduction upon what was due to them, and preferred appealing to a court of justice, were in the Home, and would have been turned out, had not a solicitor, who was employed by the boarding-masters that the other part of the crew had gone to lodge with, represented to the Home authorities that the magistrate would be sure to decide in favour of the seamen. But for the representation of the boarding-master's solicitor the men must have been turned out.

The boarding-masters present made several statements, all fully corroborative of the narrative I have given, as to the procedures of the tailors or outfitters connected with the Home, and the runners employed by the tailors.

The following opinion was given unanimously as to the 53d clause of the proposed Mercantile Marine Bill, all the boarding-masters present representing the other provisions of the Bill as, in their opinion, likely to benefit the seamen. This 53d clause provides that so much of the General Merchant Seamen's Act and of the Seamen's Protection Act as relates to the detention of chests, tools, moneys, documents, or other property or effects of seamen by keepers of public-houses or lodging-houses, or other persons claiming money from them for board or lodging shall be repealed, and that no person shall detain any effects belonging to a seaman, so as to prevent or delay his going to sea, *on any pretence whatever*. Another provision of the clause, as at present understood, is this, that a boarding-master (or any one lodging a sailor), even if the sailor had money in the boarding-master's hands, could only deduct what was justly due for board and lodging, even if the man had clothes or other effects supplied to him through the agency of the boarding-master, and for which very clothes the boarding-master had made himself liable. This clause, all concurred in representing as a premium for dishonesty, and as if for the offences of some—who kept brothels rather than boarding-houses, it was said—all respectable boarding-masters were to be exposed to such a reproach. It was represented also that such a clause would cause great distrust between seamen and those with whom they lodged, as rogueish fellows might scheme together how best to "do" a boarding-master. A boarding-master said:—"If a man came from sea, he might (under the proposed clause) deposit his clothes and effects with any one, and say, 'I shan't want them until pay-day;' the legal time of pay-day is seven days after the arrival in port; but men are sometimes paid sooner. He may have ordered through the boarding-master, or any other party, a suit of clothes (say £3 value), and they may have been supplied, and the bill delivered to the seaman, who locks them in his chest, on which they become the seaman's legal property, while the boarding-master has made himself responsible for the payment. The seaman may then absent himself from the party holding his chest and clothes until he is ready to go to sea. Then he can go and demand his property, the suit of clothes he never paid for included; and if the party holding his effects refuse to deliver them up, he will be summoned before a magistrate; and the magistrate will be compelled, by law, to fine the party holding the seaman's effects (though the fine may be reduced to 1s.); and not only that, but the party so summoned must pay over again the £3, the value of the clothes, and the adjudged value of any other effects, to the seaman so summoning, and must give up the effects as well; this is actually a premium for dishonesty to any fellow who might go a short voyage—say to Hamburg—for the very purpose of this fraud." A memorial presented to the Board of Trade by the boarding-masters, and protesting against the above clause of the proposed bill, expresses on the part of those signing it, their "perfect readiness and willingness strictly to observe and submit to any rules or regulations which your honourable board (the Board of Trade) may be pleased hereafter to adopt for the future guidance of ourselves in our business connection with seamen on shore."

As to advance notes, the following opinion was unanimously expressed. That men could not possibly (as a general rule) go to sea without an advance of money; for necessaries of various descriptions were wanted, even by the steadiest men, who rarely provided for a voyage until the point of sailing. An honest man, too, will not like to go away in debt to parties who have befriended him. The present system of advance notes was represented as very bad. The difficulty of recovery from the agents of the vessels is so great (the agents upon whom the notes are given not being at all responsible for the payment), that the seaman holding such advance note, must consequently pay a very heavy discount, as much as 50 per cent. having been given, so that even the note held by a good seaman on a respectable party can hardly, in some instances, be cashed at all. Mr. Green, Mr. Wigram, Mr. Smith, Mr. Dunbar, and other owners, have advance notes made payable to themselves, and there is no difficulty in getting the amount; but petty, grinding owners, it was stated, generally give orders on agents. The outport owners, however, who may be very honourable men, are also compelled to do the same, on account of having no residence near the port. The clause in the proposed bill, however, protecting both owners and seamen—giving a remedy to a seaman against an agent in the county court—all agreed was equitable, and an improvement in every way on the present system.

It was also stated that at a public vestry meeting, well attended, of the parishioners of St. Paul, Shadwell, a resolution was agreed to (with only one dissentient), condemnatory of the 53d clause, and a deputation was appointed to wait upon the Board of Trade on the subject.

In my next letter I shall give an account of the "Crimps," or low boarding-masters.

The Morning Chronicle, Monday, April 22, 1850.

RAGGED SCHOOLS.

———◆———

To the EDITOR of the MORNING CHRONICLE.

Sir—I shall feel greatly obliged if, in the columns of *The Morning Chronicle*, you can favour me with an early insertion of the accompanying reply, to the statements of your Correspondent respecting Ragged Schools.

You will perceive that our opinions upon the subject differ very widely, and hence some of us must be in error. If I am the erring party, I shall be glad to see my opinions disproved and my statements corrected. But, as the matter now stands, convinced as I am that my views are correct, I feel that in justice to the Society, the children of the poor, and also *The Morning Chronicle*, I ought to place them before the public, however imperfectly expressed.

As it is likely to be the only instance when the insertion of any such statement will be required on behalf of the Society, I trust you will be kind enough to give it publicity through the same medium as those of your Correspondent.

I am, sir, your obedient servant,

ALEXANDER ANDERSON.

Ragged School Union, 15, Exeter Hall, April 16, 1850.

———

To the EDITOR of the MORNING CHRONICLE.

Sir—As the statements of your Special Correspondent respecting the London Ragged Schools, may tend in some measure, to mislead those who are not practically conversant with the subject, I beg to reply, through the medium of your paper, to some of his assertions. I had not intended to do this until very lately, which may account for the time that has elapsed since the letters of your Correspondent appeared. As those statements extend over nearly fourteen columns of your paper, I may therefore be excused for occupying a greater portion of your space than I otherwise would have done. My remarks shall be chiefly confined to a few of the more prominent points on which he rests his conclusions. In doing so I wish to be influenced by a strict regard for truth, and not by any undue respect I may have for the institutions in question. In your leading article on the subject, on the 1st inst., you say to the promoters and superintendents of Ragged

Schools, "persevere." In reply to this, we say "No," we cannot persevere, if the statements of your Correspondent are true. We are not the mere slaves of a maudlin sentimentality. We have neither time, nor money, nor energies to expend in efforts worse than useless. We love too much our homes, our country, and our God, to waste the contributions of our Christian brethren in the propagation of criminality and vice, and the degradation of the children of our honest poor. Hence we say, if Ragged Schools are what your Correspondent has represented them to be, for the sake of our beloved country, and all that is dear to us as men and citizens, let him have the credit of their speedy annihilation. But he will have to show a more practical acquaintance with the subject, and adduce facts of a more satisfactory nature, before he gains the unenviable honour.

The first error into which he seems to have fallen is respecting the object for which the schools were established. They were not *expressly* intended for the reformation of juvenile offenders, and hence, with several columns of statistical tables, he tests their merits by a wrong standard. They were established, as the name implies, for the education of children "who are too poor, too filthy, and too ragged to be admitted into ordinary schools;" and although a portion of the criminal class have attended them, in a majority of cases they are the exception, not the rule. This may be distinctly understood from the printed documents of the society with which your Correspondent was furnished. In our labours we embrace a much wider sphere than he has assigned us, unless he can prove that all ragged children belong to the criminal class. Of that class, however, we can point to many cases of decided reformation, and to many others who, but for the schools, would have been added to the lists of criminals. Hence frequent allusion is made to that feature of the subject; but in most of the schools the criminal class forms a small minority. Our object is to prevent as well as to cure. Hence he may be able to understand why it is, that we do not test the utility of the schools by the increase or decrease of our prison population, or spend our time and limited means in furnishing the public with "information upon the subject of the amount of juvenile crime in the different districts of London." But if their efficiency is to be tested by such a criterion, let it be done honourably and fairly. Let due account be taken of those circumstances that materially affect the increase or decrease of crime, and over which such institutions can have no control. Your Correspondent has not done this, nor even alluded to them, although he must have been fully aware of the importance of doing so. It is evident, from his own tables, that the number of juvenile offenders, in different years, is very much affected by causes of which he takes no notice. He does not tell us, for instance, why it is that in 1841 there was an increase of 3,800 over that of 1839, nor what caused the remarkable decrease in 1844 of 2,700 below that of 1843.

Ragged Schools may feed the hungry, clothe the naked, and reform the vicious, but they cannot prevent a railway panic, an Irish famine, or a French revolution; nor should they be made responsible for the conduct of children who may be instigated, or driven into a course of crime by such misfortunes. May not the "alarming increase" of juvenile offenders in 1848 be more reasonably attributed to the above and other such causes, than to the operations of Ragged Schools? It is necessary to remind him that in 1848 the streets of the metropolis were swarming with destitute Irish, driven by famine from their own country; that from January 1st to 31st of that year the number of Irish applicants to the Mendicity Society, who had been less than twelve months in London, was no fewer than 18,589, and that the number of vagrants committed to the Houses of Correction at Coldbath-fields and Westminster was 1,200 more than in 1847? Is no account to be taken of the severe privations to which very many of the working population were exposed, by the commercial panic in 1847 and 1848, to the effects of which, if I am not mistaken, your Correspondent refers in his previous articles? Is the "ever-memorable 10th of April," and the riotous meetings which occurred for several weeks before and after it, to be entirely exonerated from having any connection with this "alarming increase;" when, according to the accounts of *The Morning Chronicle*, "Scotland-yard grew pale," and the metropolis had to be guarded by "three hundred thousand men, including a formidable vanguard of regular troops?"

The same authority states that "the new recruits were, for the most part, young lads, filthy and ragged in their appearance," and that in others "the insurgent patriots were dirty boys, with a sprinkling of professional thieves," and that "prigging was carried on throughout on the very largest scale that circumstances permitted." On another occasion, I find that "scenes of the most indescribable blackguardism were enacted by those wretched boys, who evidently represented the lowest scum of the metropolis, and hoped to reap a rich harvest in picking pockets," and that in addition to this a "band of blackguard boys, amounting to several hundreds, and not having a full-grown man amongst them," paraded the streets until midnight, smashing in windows, and stealing where they could, and that next day "the principal station-houses of the West-end were filled with prisoners." May not these transactions have had more to do with the "alarming increase" of juvenile offenders in 1848 than the "guineas" subscribed to the Ragged School Union?

There is another important point in connection with the increase of committals in 1848 to which your Correspondent makes no reference. I allude to the Larceny Act, which came into operation in August, 1847, giving to magistrates the power of committing to prison, for very short periods, children under fourteen years of age, without the intervention of a jury. Of the effects of this act, Mr. Sergeant Adams, in his charge to the grand jury in 1849, says:—"It is a singular fact that the increase of committals of boys not exceeding fourteen has been more rapid in the City than the county at large; the number in the first six months of the second year of the operation of the act, committed by the City magistrates, amounting to within twenty-one of the whole number of committals in the twelve months preceding the enactment." He further adds that, "since the passing of this act persons have appeared as prosecutors against children who would otherwise have let the offence pass unpunished," and that "but for this act the committals would have continued slightly to decrease, as they have been decreasing for four or five years." He also states that he believes "the Larceny Act has been a dead letter in the agricultural districts."

Is it fair, I ask, to submit an institution so recently established to such an ordeal as your Correspondent has done, and make unqualified statements calculated to damage it in public estimation, while he leaves entirely out of view such circumstances as those to which I have alluded? If it does not appear like "making out a case," it less resembles an impartial inquiry.

But this is not all, "for the sake of greater perspicuity" he places the increase of juvenile offenders side by side with that of the Ragged Schools, since the formation of their Union in 1844. By "this stubborn array of facts and figures, which admits of no scepticism," he shows that "the number of offenders under 20 years of age has increased in the same period to no less than 3,317, or very nearly one for each guinea that had been subscribed in the hope of diminishing juvenile depravity."

We are also informed "that for the three years immediately preceding the establishment of the Union there was a rapid and extensive decrease in the juvenile depravity of the metropolis."

In his subsequent statements I find that very much of this "rapid increase" he ascribes to the injurious effects of Ragged Schools.

But is it really so—that the number of juvenile offenders has increased 3,300 during the five years the Ragged Schools have been established? Of this I am yet sceptical, however stubborn he may consider the statements he has adduced. By his own figures I discover a very considerable decrease during that period. I arrive at this conclusion by the same process which in another case he has himself adopted. I take the number of juvenile offenders for the five years succeeding the establishment of Ragged Schools, and place them side by side with that of the five years preceding. The following is the result:—

METROPOLITAN JUVENILE OFFENDERS.

Taken into Custody.	Number of persons under twenty years taken into custody during the five years preceding the establishment of the Ragged School Union in 1844.	Taken into Custody.	Number of persons under twenty years taken into custody during five years since the establishment of the Ragged School Union in 1844.
In 1839 ...	13,587	In 1844 ...	13,600
1840 ...	14,031	1845 ...	15,128
1841 ...	17,425	1846 ...	15,552
1842 ...	16,987	1847 ...	15,698
1843 ...	16,316	1848 ...	16,917
Total ...	78,346	Total ...	76,895
Average ...	15,669	Average ...	15,379

Thus it appears that, regardless of the increase of the population, the *average* number of juvenile offenders during the latter period is less than the former by 290. Surely this does not look like an alarming increase. The difference will appear still greater when the increase of the population is taken into account:—

PROPORTION OF CRIMINALS UNDER TWENTY YEARS TO THE
POPULATION OF THE METROPOLIS UNDER THE SAME AGE.

Years.	Number of persons under twenty years to one taken into custody from the years 1839 to 1843 inclusive.	Years.	Number of persons under twenty years to one taken into custody from the years 1844 to 1848 inclusive.
1839	One in 53	1844	One in 56
1840	„ 52	1845	„ 51
1841	„ 42	1846	„ 50
1842	„ 44	1847	„ 50
1843	„ 46	1848	„ 47
Average ...	One in 47	Average ...	One in 50

By the above the matter will be seen in its true character; so far as it can be seen from the returns of the last ten years. During the five years that preceded the establishment of Ragged Schools, the total number of juvenile offenders committed in the metropolis was 78,346, giving an average for each of those years of 15,669. Whereas, during the five years that succeeded the establishment of the schools, the total number of committals was 76,895, giving an average for each year of 15,379; thus showing an average decrease of 290. If we attend to the proportion of juvenile offenders to the estimated increase of the population, the case will appear still more evident. It will be seen by the above tables that during the five years preceding the Ragged Schools, there was, on an average, one youth taken into custody in every 47; and during the five years succeeding the commencement of the schools, there has only been one youth committed in every 50. Is this the "overwhelming rate," at which "the number of juvenile offenders has been increasing year by year?" That the above is a more accurate view of the case than that given by your Correspondent, I leave the public to judge. It is difficult to understand why a gentleman so accustomed to statistical information as he seems to be, should have led the public into so palpable an error—yourself and "John Bull" among the rest.

In the year 1841, the number of juvenile offenders taken into custody was 17,425, being an increase over the preceding year of no less than 3,394. This unusually high number he takes as the basis of his calculations, and thereby shows a gradual decrease, until 1844. Here an unusually low number occurs, less than that of 1841 by 3,825; and, taking this very low number as a new basis, he shows, as might be expected, a gradual increase during the next four years, but certainly not an increase, as the above tables show, over the average number of juvenile offenders. And yet he tells us most coolly that "this array of facts and figures admits of no scepticism!" We are further told, that "notwithstanding the vast increase of scholastic machinery of late years, we are not reforming, but merely educating, our criminals." Not one the less appears in gaols. Can he inform us how many more would have appeared in our gaols had it not been for this increase of educational measures? The increase is evidently not keeping pace with the increase of the population.

If it is "the creed of the day, that a knowledge of reading and writing is the great panacea for all moral evil," we certainly were not aware of it until he told us. It is not the creed of the Christians of England, and never was the creed of the promoters of Ragged Schools. We have no faith in the mere knowledge of reading and writing as a cure for moral evil; although we believe that even more than that amount of knowledge ought to be imparted to every English child—but we *have* faith in the power of moral training and religious influence. We have strong faith in "the Gospel of the Grace of God," through which our country has risen to its present dignity, and without which we believe the wretched masses of our population can never be elevated. This, I fear, is one of the chief points on which your Correspondent has misunderstood us, for he is most careful in stating that we merely teach the children to read and write. Perhaps it forms "a path into which the eagle's eye hath not yet soared."

The second part of your Correspondent's statement goes to show that by "bringing so many boys of vicious propensities together," the schools are productive of "far more injury than benefit to the community." On this subject he says:—"I have been at considerable pains in collecting the evidence of the most experienced persons upon this point."

Now, sir, I wish not to impute unworthy motives to that gentleman, nor would I question for a moment the accuracy of his statements, unless I could bring proof to the contrary. But if, when inquiring into the value of the evidence he has collected, I meet with contradictory statements from some of the very parties to whom he refers—questionable of his prudence or their truthfulness—the fault lies with others, not with me. One would have supposed that "the most experienced persons" for furnishing the information he desired would have been parties actively connected with the schools—those who, by years of self-sacrifice, unremunerated, had taught the children, visited them in their homes, watched them in the streets, and thus by actual experience had become acquainted with their habits and conduct; or if they were not sufficient, the gentlemen who form the local committees of the schools (whose names and addresses are published with every one of their reports), would have been the next best authority to whom he could have applied. They are generally men of business, intelligence, and respectability, who are not likely to give their time, energies, and money for the support of institutions of which they know nothing. Many of them have property in the very localities of the schools, which, if "nurseries for criminals," would doubtless make them among the first sufferers. It ought to be known that, with the view of placing him in communication with some of those very parties, Lord Ashley supplied him with some fifteen or twenty letters of introduction; but as, by his own account, he availed himself of sources of information "exterior" to the Ragged Schools, a considerable number of those letters have, doubtless, not been delivered. This scarcely appears like an unwillingness, on the part of those connected with the society, to furnish him with information.

But we are told that because those parties do not send returns to the society of the number of the children belonging to the schools "who have been taken into custody or imprisoned," "it would have been idle for him to have sought for evidence from them as to the danger of congregating so many young thieves together." He seems to have forgotten that he only applied to the society for such returns on the 27th of March, and a very questionable part of his evidence appeared on the 25th. Perhaps they were not the most likely persons to furnish the *kind* of information he required. But who are the individuals who have investigated the subject so closely, and on whose testimony the public may more safely rely? Why, they are four policemen, five poor boys, two of whom are young thieves in prison, one girl, and three "experienced gentlemen," of whom we know nothing. Where those gentlemen obtained their experience "exterior" to Ragged Schools, we cannot tell; and as I am prepared to meet their assertions with an unqualified contradiction—unless I am bound to prove a negative, it remains for your Correspondent to give some satisfactory proof of the value of their testimony. Two of those gentlemen are reported to have agreed in saying that "the Ragged Schools are in reality nurseries for criminals—houses of call for thieves; and three out of every five boys who swelled the lists of our juvenile criminals were taught roguery at a Ragged School, or had taught it there to others."

Now, sir, before any gentleman could be warranted in publishing such a statement respecting any benevolent institution, he ought to be prepared, at least, with some amount of proof in support of it. If such proofs do exist, they may be obtained; and until he or those gentlemen can refer to one prison in London, or throughout the whole of England, where three out of every five of its juvenile prisoners have been "taught roguery at a Ragged School, or taught it there to others," I must pronounce such a statement to be both uncharitable and untrue, and unworthy of the responsible position which your Correspondent occupies.

The evidence given by the first policeman is certainly not such as could lead your Correspondent to the conclusion at which he has arrived. He can give no instance of a child having been led astray at a Ragged School. He "never knew a girl, a scholar in a Ragged School, in the streets afterwards," and he "can't charge his memory with any particular boy or girl at the Ragged School going wrong afterwards." But, evidently in answer to questions started, he admits the possibility of good children being corrupted by bad ones—which no friend of Ragged Schools would ever deny. Another policeman states, at the outset, that "of the particular effects of Ragged Schools he has no means of describing." Did this sentence creep in unconsciously? Be this as it may, your Correspondent and he are both wrong in saying that the decrease in the number of juvenile offenders in Westminster in 1847 and 1848 is owing to the removal of the buildings. The only houses taken down in 1848 were those of the Almonry, and New-court, Duck-lane, which, with very few exceptions, if any, were brothels, and therefore did not contain any families, as most of the rooms were hired by girls. Those occupied by families, and which alone could contain children, were removed in 1849: this a majority of the inhabitants of Westminster can prove. Such removals could therefore have no bearing upon the decrease of juvenile offenders in 1847 and 1848. The population increased in 1848 at its usual ratio, if your Correspondent's tables are correct. Unless, therefore, he can devise some other means of accounting for this decrease, we must be left to the conclusion that after all it is owing chiefly to the "vast educational machinery" which was brought into operation about that period, to the supplanting of the thieves' training school, to the present Juvenile Refuge, which has been so fiercely assailed, and to the establishment of other schools in the neighbourhood, at which there is an attendance of 600 children.

Not one instance is given by the policemen of the injurious effects of the schools. They only state, what every one knows, that the children are rough and unruly, and often make a noise in the streets. All is mere theory, excepting what is stated by the children who attended the schools. Something more definite is obtained from them, but the similarity of their experience is not a little striking, especially on one point of the evidence. A similar sentence appears almost in every statement, which goes to show that they had known four or five good boys led astray by their vicious school-fellows. From inquiries I have made respecting those children, I am forced to the conclusion that no gentleman wishing to obtain correct information would have put questions to those boys in the manner your Correspondent has done. I refer particularly to the two apprentices. The first questions put are respecting a robbery which occurred at the school about eighteen months ago. They are next told that many of the scholars are turning out bad; some of them are in prison and had been whipped, and that others are leading good boys astray. Thus their minds were prepared for a number of "leading questions" about the associating of good and bad boys together, and by the vague answer of yes or no, they are represented as saying things which they never intended.

In proof of this I give the following statement of one of the apprentices, taken in short-hand at the time, read over to him afterwards, and affirmed by him to be correct:—"The gentleman first asked me about the robbery at the school, and said he had reason to believe that we were suspected from evidence; to which I said I knew nothing about who took it. He then asked me what was taken? I said, I believed it was lead off the roof one night, but did not think that any one of our boys took it. He said he heard that the boys and girls were waiting at night after they came out of school to go thieving. I said I saw the girls of the night school only waiting about after school, but did not know they went out thieving. He asked me where I went at night, and whether the boys enticed me to go thieving? I said I went home to my father after school, but they would entice me to thieve if I kept their company: by this I meant the thieves in the neighbourhood, not the school-boys. He said good boys had been led away, and asked if I knew one of the name of Tucker. I said I knew Tucker, but said nothing about how he turned out. I did not say he had been a good boy, and bad boys had made him worse. He said he had been round at the prisons to hear accounts of us, and heard that some of the boys had turned out bad, and had been in prison and whipped. I never said that five or six boys went out together to thieve after school-time. He said this himself. My master was present when I answered the gentleman's questions, and heard all I said."

As the boy referred me to his master, I now give his evidence. He first corroborated all that the boy had stated. I then read to him the following sentence from your Correspondent's letter, which is contained in the boy's statement:—"He had known four or five boys who were good when first sent to the school led away to be thieves by their vicious schoolfellows." On hearing this he said, "It's not true, it's false, I was here all the time, and the boy never said such a thing. He put questions to the boy in such a manner as would have made him say anything, by merely getting him to assent to it." These statements, sir, are not mine, they are those of the boy and his master.

The master of the other boy says that, "He had a strong objection in his mind at the time as to the propriety of any person putting questions to his boy in the manner which he did."

Since writing the above I have received accounts from one of the policemen in Lambeth respecting the interview he had with your Correspondent. I shall first give a few extracts from the evidence of that officer as given in your columns, and then a brief statement which he lately gave as to the manner in which the questions were put and answered. The following is your Correspondent's version:—

"They would burst out into nigger songs at school, and would sing vulgar songs instead of the hymns."

"When the boys leave they halloo, cat-call, swear, and make a great disturbance. Their language is most obscene."

"I know the boys who are better disposed, by their appearance and by their bringing their bibles with them."

"I don't see any improvement in the neighbourhood in going or returning on a Sunday evening. There is as much gambling, cursing, swearing, and mixing together of boys and girls as ever."

In giving the officer's account of the interview I must give both question and answer. The questions are those of your Correspondent, the answers those of the policeman:—"Do they sing? Yes.—Have you not sometimes heard them sing songs while the hymns have been singing, such as nigger songs?" The policeman says that his answer was distinctly "No, I never heard them do this."—"Don't they make a great noise when they leave the school, and swear and use bad language?" "They make a noise like boys always do when they leave school; but I never hear them swear, or use very bad language."—"The neighbourhood is not much improved, is it; I suppose there is just as much swearing, cursing, and gambling as ever, is there not?" "It is impossible for me to answer that, as I am only in the neighbourhood on a Sunday for about an hour and a half or two hours. My beat is some distance from here."—"Are the boys and girls any better than they were?" "Yes."—"How do you know?" "Because a great many of them buy bibles for themselves."—"But don't you think they buy them to sell again?" "No; because I see them bring the bibles with them every Sunday evening—last Sunday I should think there were about five or six stopped to pay off bibles."

Here the policeman was interrupted by your Correspondent, who said—"Ah, well—never mind that; we don't want to put that down." All I have to say respecting the above statement is, that it was made by the policeman. It is either true or false. If true, it must form a sufficient reply to every questionable statement your Correspondent has made, and afford the clearest evidence that the course he has pursued, and the misrepresentations he has made respecting Ragged Schools, have been such as neither the force of prejudice nor the influence of peculiar principles could ever excuse. If, on the other hand, it is false, it may assist the public in ascertaining how far they can depend upon the "exterior" evidence he has furnished, and also show how fruitless has been his painstaking in collecting it from such sources.

I shall only mention one other case. It is that of a boy found in Tothill-fields prison, who states that "he shouldn't have been a thief but for the Ragged School." As this is the only real case in proof which your Correspondent furnishes, I have been at considerable pains to ascertain how far it is correct. I have not depended, as he did, on the boy's own statement, but as he happens to be well known as a notorious thief, both in Knightsbridge and Westminster, I had no great difficulty in obtaining accurate information. The history of the boy may be summed up in few words, all of which, if doubted, I am prepared to prove. His father and mother are both drunkards. The schoolmaster of the Tothill-fields prison lately found the mother lying in her own room in a state of intoxication. The eldest son is at present in Coldbath-fields prison, the next eldest your Correspondent found in Tothill-fields. A third and younger boy is living at present in a thieves' lodging-house, kept by a notoriously abandoned woman, in

Westminster. Here the other boy also lived before he was committed to Tothill-fields. He was once sent to a National School, at Knightsbridge, for six months, but did not attend more than one month in the six. About this time he joined "The Brass Band," a notorious gang of young thieves, with whom, after committing several robberies, he went to Chatham. There he was detected stealing, and was committed to prison. *After he returned from Chatham*, he went for a very short time to Exeter-buildings Ragged School. The boy has now confessed the lie, and excuses himself by saying that the gentleman asked if he did not learn to steal at the Ragged School, and, supposing he would give him something, or speak a good word to the governor, he said, "I shouldn't have been a thief but for the Ragged School, I know I shouldn't." I shall not enter further into the details furnished from the statements of those children. No one can read them without perceiving that children could never have given such answers unless they had been prompted by leading questions. Even the poor girl who was examined, seems to have been teazed with the most indelicate questions, until she is forced to blush, and, with the view of getting rid of her unwelcome visitor, she proposes to call in her brother from the street to answer for her.

The zeal of your Correspondent in getting up a case against the Ragged Schools seems very much to have exceeded his prudence, or he would not have expected the public to believe that the best information he could obtain was from the testimony of ragged boys, especially when asked, as was stated by one of their mothers, if they had anything to say *against* the Ragged Schools.

It were easy on such testimony to prove that all the schools and seminaries in London "are nurseries for criminals," especially as some of those who have even attended them may occasionally be found in prison.

I shall now add one word respecting the Industrial School in Westminster. That school is open to the public for inspection, and hundreds of noblemen and gentlemen who have visited it can testify, that there is no secrecy in regard to the mode of its operations, or the history of the children who attend it. Nothing is said by your Correspondent respecting the reformation of the children, nor am I aware that this formed part of the inquiry. It is statements "against" the school that are sought—as little as possible in favour of it. The testimony of two tradesmen are brought into the service, who complain bitterly against the poor children being taught to make or repair their own clothes, as they will grow up to be "sweaters" or slopworkmen, and thereby "add to the poverty, and perhaps the crime, of the country."

A very slight inquiry at some experienced person would have saved much of this trouble, and secured more correct information. It was never intended to make the boys tailors or shoemakers unless in the case of those who have been regularly apprenticed to those trades, which in every instance is by indentures for a term of six or seven years. The simple object is to inculcate habits of industry, by means of which, to remove the children's rags and supply them with better clothing. It yet remains to be proved that ever a single boy who was taught tailoring or shoemaking at a Ragged School became either a "sweater or slopworker." Those who emigrate to Australia invariably go to the bush as shepherds, and in such cases the ability to repair their own clothes will be extremely valuable.

I shall not trespass much further on your pages; by your Correspondent's own figures I have shown that his statistical conclusions are erroneous. As to the value of the evidence he furnishes to prove that children are led astray by attending Ragged Schools, I leave the public to judge. The greater portion of that evidence is mere theory, and the very questionable statements of a few ragged children. Not one of the policemen, or the other parties referred to, could instance a single case in proof. As I am prepared to prove that the history I have given of the boy in Tothill-fields prison is correct, and that he was imprisoned for theft *before* he went to a Ragged School, we are therefore left without a single instance by which the charges can be substantiated. On the contrary, we have the testimony of 60 fathers and 130 mothers of Ragged School children, who attended the meeting in Westminster, all raising their voices in favour of the benefits their children derived at the schools; and not one could state a single instance they had ever known to the contrary. Might not your Correspondent have obtained more correct information by assembling such meetings for himself? He did so on other occasions, why not on this? I am prepared to call other such meetings in any part of London where schools have been established, and give him due notice to come and judge for himself, and put to the meeting what questions he pleases. If the testimony of those parents is not sufficient, I offer further— that for every case he can produce of a child having been led astray in the manner he describes, I produce three reformed thieves, and prove they have been reformed through the agency of Ragged Schools. I will not depend in either case on the mere statements of children, nor on the testimony of drunken mothers who would rather see their children begging or stealing in the streets than being educated at school. Every one must know who has ever been in a Ragged School that it is impossible for children, when sitting in class under the superintendence of their teachers, to corrupt each other in the manner your Correspondent has described. A slight acquaintance with the habits and condition of the children who swarm in the filthy courts and alleys of the metropolis will soon show that they require not to attend a Ragged School in order to get acquainted. They are acquainted from childhood, and that intimacy is generally increased at the gambling sweet-shops, the evening dances, and the penny theatres, before they come within the precincts of a Ragged School.

In conclusion, I may state that those schools are not perfect. We never said they were, nor could we expect them to be so, considering the brief period they have been in operation, the rough and peculiar material on which they operate, and the many obstacles against which they have to contend—obstacles that lie not within their power to remove. That they have done much good we are prepared to prove. That they have done more harm, we are as ready to deny. We must look upon those who assail us, as your Correspondent has done, as we would upon the infidel who would deprive us of the Word of God. While we cling more to the one as the charter of our hopes, we shall never shrink from the other as a means of blessing to the poor so long as in either case our opponents merely seek to demolish what we have, *and leave us nothing in their stead.*

I am, sir, your obedient servant,

ALEXANDER ANDERSON.

Ragged School Union, 15, Exeter-hall, April 16.

[The answer of our Special Correspondent to Mr. Anderson's letter shall appear to-morrow, if possible.]

LABOUR AND THE POOR.

——◆——

THE METROPOLITAN DISTRICTS.

[FROM OUR SPECIAL CORRESPONDENT.]

REPLY TO THE SECRETARY OF THE RAGGED SCHOOL UNION.

Letter XLIX.

In answer to the assertions contained in Mr. Anderson's letter which appeared in your columns on Monday, I must first recapitulate as briefly as possible the nature of the facts that I collected concerning the influence of Ragged Schools.

Those facts were of two kinds—statistics and the testimony of individuals. I showed by reference to the Government returns—

1. That the number of juvenile offenders in the metropolis had been steadily increasing every year since the institution of the Ragged School Union.

2. That whereas the number of criminals who *cannot* read and write has *decreased* from 24,856 (in 1844) to 22,968 (in 1848)—or no less than 1,888 in that period—the number of those who *can* read and write imperfectly has *increased* from 33,337 to 36,229—or 2,857—in the same time.

3. That the connection which was usually supposed to exist between an increase of education and a decrease of crime was a fallacy; for I proved by tables showing the relative amount of education and crime in the different counties of England and Wales, that Middlesex contained not only the greatest number of persons who could read and write, but the greatest number of criminals; whereas North Wales, which was the least criminal country of all, ranked among the least instructed.

The ability to read and write, I would observe, was taken as a type of the kind of education received at Ragged Schools.

"So vast an educational machinery as the Ragged Schools," I said at the time of citing the above statistics, "cannot have been entirely

powerless. A thousand teachers instructing seventeen thousand scholars of the lowest and most depraved propensities and habits, must
have produced *some* effect." If they had not been *reforming*, at least
they must have been *educating* the juvenile criminals of London. Of
this, I added, the returns for the metropolis afford us positive proof;
the number of those who *cannot* read and write have decreased nearly
2,000, and those who *can* read and write imperfectly have increased
nearly 3,000 since the institution of the Union. Then, as a further
demonstration of the non-reforming power of such an education as
that received at Ragged Schools, I proved by statistical facts that the
most highly criminal county is the least ignorant, and that the least
criminal county is one of the most ignorant, in England and Wales.

I wish the reader to bear in mind the last two facts especially,
as I consider the mere circumstance of the increase of the juvenile
offenders of the metropolis a matter of comparatively little weight
against the Ragged Schools. The evidence that I believe to be conclusive against those institutions, viewed as *correctives of crime*, is the
co-existence of that fact with the decreased ignorance and increased
education of the criminal class, as well as with the equally important
fact, that the ignorance and crime of different counties bear no relation to one another. He therefore who seeks to account for the
increase of juvenile offenders since 1844, must—in order to do so
successfully—be likewise able to account for the increased education
of the class.

The testimony that I obtained concerning the influence of Ragged
Schools consisted of the evidence of Ragged School boys, Ragged
School apprentices (*to whom I was expressly referred by the secretary
of the Union*), tradesmen living in the neighbourhood of Ragged
Schools, policemen on duty in the districts of Ragged Schools (to
whom I was directed by the police authorities as officers having
the greatest experience concerning the influence of the Schools
in their particular localities), juvenile criminals who had attended
Ragged Schools and were then in prison, and lastly, the Governor of
Tothill-fields Prison and his officers.

Surely this was the best possible testimony that could be obtained
exterior to the Ragged Schools. In order that I might do the institutions no injustice, I was particularly anxious to collect information
from those parties only who had the best means of judging. Accordingly I applied to the Commissioners of Police to be permitted to avail
myself of the evidence of their most experienced officers concerning

the effects of Ragged Schools upon the boys in particular districts, and to Lieutenant Tracy, the governor of Tothill-fields Prison, to be allowed to interrogate, *in his presence*, some of the Ragged School boys that he had under his charge.

The result of my inquiries was, that *the indiscriminate association of boys of the most vicious nature with children of better dispositions, but who, from their extreme poverty, were the most liable of all persons to temptation, was fraught with great and almost inconceivable evil.*

In my remarks appended to a letter recently addressed to you by Mr. Doulton, I stated that the facts I had collected were either true or false. If true, I said that Ragged School teachers should feel grateful for having such things made known to them for the first time; but if they were false, and could be proved to be so, I added that no man would be more ready than myself to acknowledge my error in the most public manner possible. This I here repeat.

The Secretary of the Ragged School Union, seeing the dilemma in which I had placed the Society, and feeling that the only thing left to be done was to throw discredit upon my statements, endeavours to do so in a long letter, by four means:—1st. He questions my statistics; 2nd. He asserts that I obtained the statements I received in answer to unfair leading questions put by me to the witnesses; 3rd. He charges me with publishing downright falsities; and 4th. He impugns my motives, declaring that he looks upon me "as an infidel who would deprive society of the Word of God." Mr. Anderson's arguments in reply to my letters, therefore, may be said to be of three kinds— counter-statistics, counter-testimony, and personal abuse. The first two I shall endeavour to disprove; to the last I shall of course pay no heed.

I shall first deal with the *statistical* part of the subject.

The increase in the number of juvenile offenders, which has occurred since the institution of the Ragged-School Union, has been referred to a variety of causes by the speakers at the recent Ragged-School meetings. One gentleman attributes it to the increased vigilance of the police though he forgets to tell us how it is that the police have had to arrest, every year since the institution of the Ragged-School Union, a *greater* number of those who can read and write imperfectly, and a *less* number of those who cannot read and write at all. Another thinks the increase is due to bad harvests. A third ascribes the difference of crime in the several counties to the difference in the amount of property they contain, declaring that the crime of robbery

is in proportion to the temptation, and to the property exposed to it.
This, if tested by the Government returns, will be found to be untrue.
But Mr. Anderson takes a bolder and wider range than all. He is
not contented with merely one cause, but—determined to be right
somehow—he refers the increase of juvenile offenders to no less than
four distinct phenomena—viz., the Irish famine, the Larceny Act, the
railway panic, and the French revolution. To no one of these surmises,
however, is any test whatever applied. All is mere vague conjecture,
and to show how wide such guesses come short of the truth, we will
now put to the proof the most plausible of all the above theories—
viz., that which attributes the increase of crime to seasons of unusual
distress or the greater scarcity of food. The following table exhibits
the average price of corn and the number of criminals committed for
a series of years:—

TABLE SHOWING THE PRICE OF CORN ACCORDING TO THE LONDON GAZETTE,
AND ITS INCREASE AND DECREASE PER CENT. IN EACH OF THE YEARS FROM
1839 TO 1848; ALSO THE NUMBER OF PERSONS COMMITTED FOR TRIAL,
THROUGHOUT ENGLAND AND WALES, AND THEIR INCREASE AND DECREASE
PER CENT. IN THE SAME YEARS.

Year	Price of Wheat per Quar.	Number of Persons committed for trial.	Corn.		Persons committed.	
			Increase per Cent.	Decrease per Cent.	Increase per Cent.	Decrease per Cent.
1839	70s.	24,443				
1839-40	66s.	27,187	—	5.7	11.2	
1840-41	64s.	27,760	—	3.0	2.1	
1841-42	57s.	31,309	—	10.9	12.7	
1842-43	50s.	29,591	—	12.2	—	5.4
1843-44	51s.	26,542	2.0	—	—	10.3
1844-45	50s.	24,403	—	1.9	—	8.0
1845-46	54s.	25,107	8.0	—	2.8	
1846-47	69s.	28,833	9.2	—	14.8	
1847-48	50s.	30,349	—	27.5	5.2	
1839-48	—	—	—	28.5	24.1	

The above table shows that from 1839 to 1842 the price of wheat
decreased gradually from 70s. to 57s. per quarter, whereas, the number
of persons committed for trial in England and Wales *increased just as
gradually* from 24,443 to 31,309 in the same period. On the other
hand, it will be seen that from 1843-44 the price of wheat *increased*
from 50s. to 51s. the quarter, whereas the number of criminals committed *decreased* from 29,591 to 26,542. Again, in 1847-48 the price
fell from 69s. to 50s. the quarter, or as much as 27.5 per cent. Crime,

however, instead of *decreasing* in a like proportion, rose from 28,833 to 30,349, or 5.2 per cent. In the last ten years, it will be observed, wheat has *decreased* in price from 70s. to 50s. the quarter, or 28.5 per cent., whereas crime has *increased* in the same time from 24,443 to 30,349, or 24.1 per cent.

In all the theories which have yet been advanced as a means of accounting for the increase of juvenile offenders, *since* the establishment of the Ragged School Union, none pay the least regard to the increased education of the criminal class; and upon this subject in particular—as well as the fact that the least criminal counties are some of the most ignorant, while those that are the least ignorant are the most criminal—the matter mainly hinges. This, as I said before, appears to be the most important point of all; but concerning it Mr. Anderson is silent. The question simply is whether such an education as is received at Ragged Schools is likely to prove a corrective of crime. That the facts are against such a conclusion I proved by tables which I constructed expressly, as a means of demonstrating the point. These, however, Mr. Anderson does not even notice, but advances four distinct theories to account for the increase of crime, not one of which does he consider it necessary to put to the least practical test, though it certainly would have been very easy for him to do so, before making his assertions. As yet I have seen but one theory advanced on this subject, that is in any way consistent with the facts, and that is the one propounded by the Constabulary Commissioners, who, after patiently investigating a large variety of cases, declare that crime is *mostly* the result of a desire to obtain property with a less degree of labour than by regular industry. Whether we are likely to overcome this indisposition on the part of the criminal class to labour for their living, by giving them a knowledge of reading, writing, and arithmetic, I leave men of common sense to decide. I would not, however, have it inferred from the above remarks that I am adverse to the diffusion of a knowledge of reading and writing among the poor. I am but desirous of impressing upon the minds of zealous persons that reading and writing are no more education than (as Dr. Cooke Taylor used to say) a knife and fork is a good dinner; in a word the ability to read and write is not knowledge, but merely the means of knowledge, and may be used for the acquirement of bad as well as good principles. The thief who is taught to read may as easily apply his learning to the perusal of "Jack Sheppard" as of the Holy Scriptures, and my experience of the class convinces me that our juvenile criminals are far more likely to devote themselves to the study of the one than the other. Those who believe that criminal practices are induced by want, will find it distinctly stated by the most experienced persons who were examined under the Constabulary Commission that *poverty is seldom the cause of crime.*

"*The notion that any considerable proportion of the crimes against property are caused by blameless poverty or destitution, we find,*" say the Constabulary Commissioners, in their first report, "*disproved at every step.* The tenor of the evidence on this subject is conveyed in such testimony as that of the following. We cite that of Mr. Wontner, the late governor of Newgate:—'Of the criminals who came under your care, what proportion, so far as your experience will enable you to state, were by the *immediate pressure of want* impelled to the commission of crime? By want is meant the absence of the means of subsistence, and not the want arising from indolence and an impatience of steady labour?—*According to the best of my observation scarcely one-eighth.*'"

Mr. Anderson, in disproof of my statistics, constructs the following table, wherein he shows that there has been no increase in the number of juvenile offenders *since* the institution of the Ragged-School Union:—

METROPOLITAN JUVENILE OFFENDERS.

Taken into Custody.	Number of persons under twenty years taken into custody during the five years preceding the establishment of the Ragged School Union in 1844.	Taken into Custody.	Number of persons under twenty years taken into custody during five years since the establishment of the Ragged School Union in 1844.
In 1839 ..	13,587	In 1844 ..	13,600
1840 ..	14,031	1845 ..	15,128
1841 ..	17,425	1846 ..	15,552
1842 ..	16,987	1847 ..	15,698
1843 ..	16,316	1848 ..	16,917
Total	78,346	Total	76,895
Average ..	15,669	Average ..	15,379

The Ragged School Union, be it observed, was instituted in April, 1844; and yet Mr. Anderson does not hesitate to ascribe the decrease in the number of criminals which occurred in that year—a decrease of no less than 2,716—to the influence of the Ragged Schools, though the funds at their disposal were then only £61 per annum; whereas, in 1848, when the number of juvenile offenders was nearly 17,000, those funds had increased to upwards of £4,000! "It would be absurd to say," acknowledges Mr. Gordon (a Ragged School teacher), in a letter in reply to the facts advanced by me, that in the year 1844 any effect was produced by Ragged Schools, "that being the year in which the Union was formed, *and little or nothing done.*" Mr. Anderson, however, does not think it absurd to do so—nor to credit the Ragged Schools with the entire decrease of "the number of persons under 20 years taken into custody *since* the establishment of the Ragged School Union in 1844." Such are Mr. Anderson's own words, though at the very time he wrote down the figures against the year 1844, he must have known that it was not until the April of that year, when four months had already elapsed, that the Union was even founded.

Now concerning Mr. Anderson's attempted disproof of the *testimony* advanced by me. This Mr. Anderson attacks in several ways. He charges me, as I said before, with publishing statements that were positively false, and with obtaining others by means of leading questions put to the parties whose evidence I adduced, as well as being animated by a disposition to seek out only the worst cases. For myself, I can but declare most emphatically and unequivocally that such assertions, and the evidence by which they are attempted to be supported, are utterly destitute of truth. I am anxious, however, that the contradiction to these accusations should not rest upon my own statement, and I beg, therefore, to subjoin the following letters:—

To THE EDITOR OF THE MORNING CHRONICLE.

SIR—I was directed by your Special Correspondent to obtain for him the addresses of some of the boys and girls who attended the Ragged School in Westminster, so that he might be able to visit them at their own homes. Your Correspondent desired me to take the names of the first parties that came to hand, so that neither particularly good nor bad cases might be selected, but such as might be presumed to be fair average examples of the practical tendency of the school in question; and I now solemnly assert that each of the cases I met with were obtained quite promiscuously, and that they were not chosen by me for him as instances to bear out any particular opinion. Indeed, it was your Correspondent's express wish, that "all selections of cases might be avoided." The parties with whose addresses I furnished your Correspondent are those whose statements have appeared in your paper. This I can positively assert from my own knowledge, because I was afterwards requested by your Correspondent to inquire into the characters of the parents of the children, before he printed their statements. I did so, and found that the parties were worthy of credit.

In conclusion, I beg to be permitted to state, that, having been engaged in performing the same office for him for these several months past, it never has been his practice either to select his cases or to publish the statements of individuals without previously obtaining some voucher for their credibility. I can conscientiously declare that I have never received instruction from him to furnish him with the addresses of such parties as might not be justly considered fair types of the class into whose condition he has been inquiring at the time.

I am, sir, yours obediently,   R. KNIGHT,
Late of the "City Mission."
18, Great Warner-street, Clerkenwell.

To the EDITOR of the MORNING CHRONICLE.

Sir—My attention has been called to a letter addressed to you by Mr. A. Anderson, impugning the veracity of your Metropolitan Correspondent on the subject of Ragged Schools. I beg to say that I myself took the statements of the apprentices alluded to by Mr. Anderson, and gave my notes to your Correspondent for publication. These notes contained a simple report of the facts narrated to me by the apprentices— facts *not* narrated in answer to "leading questions," but in the course of inquiry as to the general character of Ragged School boys. I perfectly well remember being impressed at the time with the conviction that these boys were understating the truth, and that they merely told what they knew to be *notorious* facts. This understating is not imputable to any improper motive on the part of the boys; they naturally may look for further aid in their course through life from the supporters of Ragged Schools; or they might feel gratitude for their having been apprenticed to good masters, and be unwilling to tell the whole truth of institutions from which *they* at least had derived benefit. To suppose, as Mr. Anderson does, that the facts detailed to me were in any way twisted or perverted by me or your Correspondent to answer any purpose whatever, is ridiculous. Previously to the inquiry my predilections were decidedly in favour of Ragged Schools; nor, considering the benevolent aim of these institutions, can I wonder at my having been so short-sighted, for we are prone to think good is done where good is purposed.

I may add that I was also present when the statements of all the policemen were taken, and they spoke most guardedly, and with an evident desire to tell as little as possible that might hurt the feelings of so good a man as they all represented Lord Ashley to be, as well as to avoid anything, in the way of a statement or opinion, that might lead to their being further questioned on the subject. They frequently said as their words were taken down before them: "I think you had better leave that out; let us be on the safe side," or words to that effect. The especial statement (of a policeman) which Mr. Anderson has endeavoured to upset was printed as the policeman gave it to your Correspondent in my presence, and the officer spoke with the official guardedness of the others, and evidently wished to say all he could, with truth, in favour of Ragged Schools. I perfectly remember the policeman stating that he heard the Ragged School boys sing Nigger songs when the hymns were being sung, and that the lads swore and used bad language on leaving school. These two truths, indeed, pervaded, incidentally, his whole course of conversation, guarded as he was. Nothing like the course of leading question and answer (such as it has pleased Mr. Anderson to detail) took place between your Correspondent and the policeman in question, nor was a word said about "five or six boys stopping on the previous Sunday to pay off their bibles." Neither did your Correspondent say, "Never mind that; we don't want to put that down." In fact, I never heard him say so on any occasion—unless, indeed, concerning some statement too personal, or utterly irrelevant. The statements made by Mr. Anderson, to impugn your Correspondent's veracity, are altogether false. The matter which was printed in *The Morning Chronicle* was, to my knowledge, detailed as it appeared, and obtained and checked with every care to ensure even minute accuracy.

As to Nigger-song singing in Ragged Schools, permit me to refer you to the January number of the *English Journal of Education*, and, indeed, to the subsequent numbers. They contain a very excellent series of articles—"The Diary of the Master of a London Ragged School"— which fully accord with the evidence collected for your journal on the same subject. Of the existence of these articles I was not aware until Tuesday last, when my attention was called to them by the publisher.

I may add, that many unprejudiced persons, some not knowing the purport of the statements that had appeared in *The Morning Chronicle*, have expressed to your Correspondent, in my hearing, their opinion of the great danger to the community of institutions like Ragged Schools, because the association of bad children with good *must*, through emulation and other causes, be prejudicial to the good. Among experienced persons holding this opinion, I may instance a very intelligent schoolmaster, teaching a great number of children in one of Mr. Green's excellent preparatory schools, who dared not, he said, unwilling as he would be to stand in the way of any child's being taught and possibly reformed, admit a boy or girl known to be a thief among his pupils.

A schoolmistress (also one of Mr. Green's teachers) made a similar avowal.

In conclusion, I will merely remark that your Correspondent's instructions to me have invariably been, to take average cases and to test their truthfulness by all possible means. His whole endeavour, so long as I have been connected with him in his inquiry, has been to elicit the plain truth—no matter what theory was upset or confirmed.

I am, sir, your obedient servant,

HENRY WOOD.

4, Woronzow-road, St. John's-wood, April 19, 1850.

Mr. Anderson, endeavouring to disprove the statement of one of the lads in prison who declared that he had been first taught to thieve by the boys whom he met at the Ragged School, says:—"I shall not enter further into the details furnished from the statements of those children. No one can read them *without perceiving that children could never have given such answers unless they had been promoted by leading questions.*"

The following letter (addressed to myself), is from Lieutenant Tracy, the governor of Tothill-fields House of Correction, in whose presence the boys were examined:—

"Tothill-fields, Westminster, April 20.

"Dear Sir—My attention having been directed to a statement in one of the papers, wherein it is asserted that two boys, inmates of this prison, had furnished some information in reference to a Ragged School in this district, and also commenting on the mode in which such information was obtained, I shall feel obliged, if the opportunity is given you, by your showing to the parties who seem to question its accuracy, the course adopted when you visited this establishment about a month since, by the authority of the Secretary of State. It will be within your recollection, I think, that two boys, named Cook and Blandford, who had been very frequently at the Ragged School in Westminster (Old Pye-street), were questioned with my concurrence, and in my presence, on the manner in which they disposed of their time throughout each day that they were attached to this school. And I deny most emphatically that leading questions were put to them. They were enjoined by me to speak the truth, and only examined in the ordinary way that all juveniles are on being sent here, with a view of ascertaining their habits and course of life, without prejudice to the school before named. Their replies were given in a straightforward manner, in their own usually plain language; and the boy Cook finished, when about to

be removed by the officer, by voluntarily observing, that he had been *first taught to thieve whilst belonging to the Ragged School.*
"Very faithfully yours, dear sir,
"A. F. TRACY."

The passage printed in italics was underscored in Lieutenant Tracy's note.

The above letters afford full and ample contradiction to the various assertions contained in Mr. Anderson's communication, which, before leaving the subject, I must repeat, is not merely unfounded in one point alone, but in every particular from beginning to end.

To assure myself, however, that I had not been deceived concerning the evil effects arising from the indiscriminate association of the bad with the good children at Ragged Schools, and that I had not been guilty of an injustice which I should ever regret, I determined to pay a visit to the House of Correction in Coldbath-fields, where I had been informed a number of Ragged-School boys were then imprisoned.

Here I saw Captain Chesterton, the governor, and the Rev. Mr. Illingworth, the chaplain of the gaol, both of whom I found strongly impressed with a sense of the evils likely to arise from the *indiscriminate* association of the bad and good at Ragged Schools. Captain Chesterton said: "I was deeply impressed at one time in favour of such schools—indeed, so much so, that I was indirectly a subscriber to them. But on making an inquiry here very recently as to the number of Ragged-School boys that we had in the prison, and finding that we had upwards of 60, out of 170 youths, *the fact of the evil tendency of such institutions appeared to me to be quite conclusive.*" I then asked Captain Chesterton whether I was at liberty to state publicly that such was his opinion; when he gave me full permission to say that he considered Ragged Schools, from the indiscriminate mingling of the bad and good boys together, calculated to have a pernicious rather than a beneficial effect. The Rev. Mr. Illingworth, the chaplain, said "My *impression* is, that to bring the children of the poorest people, and consequently the children most liable to be tempted, into connection with boys known to be of decidedly vicious habits, *cannot but be attended with evil effects.* Until lately I have paid no attention to the subject. I fancied at first that Ragged Schools would do good—if they did nothing else, I thought they would at least keep the poor creatures out of mischief; but upon reconsideration, *I do not doubt about the danger of Ragged Schools; but unequivocally condemn the indiscriminate mingling of good and bad children practised in those establishments.*" Captain Chesterton here again expressed a similar opinion, saying that such was evidently the common-sense view of the matter. "The great difficulty we have to contend with here," continued the chaplain, "is to *prevent* the association of the prisoners. Our chief object is to keep them separate, and so to guard against evil communications among them." "We are obliged," observed the governor, "even to place steady men between vicious boys, to avoid corruption." "We consider the system of Ragged Schools," observed the chaplain, "as a step back towards that indiscriminate association of thieves, which was formerly permitted in prisons, and from which so much evil is known to have arisen. To prevent this association all our efforts here, of late years, have been specially directed. But if the association of vicious persons is found to be fraught with evil inside a prison, how much more pernicious must it be outside one, in institutions where no supervision and little or no discipline are maintained. A boy may come to the school for the express purpose of seducing others, and our experience here teaches us it is a common practice among expert thieves to decoy boys not previously known to the police as being safer instruments for the perpetration of their crimes. Upon good and poor girls the effect of association with bad ones must be more pernicious still." "It is hardly possible," remarked Captain Chesterton, "to conceive the depravity of exceedingly young bad girls." "I wish you to say," added the chaplain, "that I am speaking from my general impression and experience of human nature, and not from any attention that I have given expressly to the subject of Ragged Schools. My opinions are formed not from any investigation of the matter, but simply from the experience I have had here as to the nature and habit of criminals." I then inquired of Captain Chesterton whether, on making the inquiry as to the number of Ragged-School boys that he had in his custody, he had found the youths who had received instruction at those establishments were a better class than the other delinquents. His answer was, that they were *altogether as depraved as the rest.* The chaplain then informed me, that until he had seen the subject noticed in the morning papers he had given little or no attention to it. "What I saw in *The Morning Chronicle* I must say certainly convinced me of the great danger of such indiscriminate association as appeared to be allowed at the

Ragged Schools." "Of that," said Captain Chesterton, "there cannot be a doubt in the mind of any one practically acquainted with the subject."

After this I requested permission of the Governor to see the boys in his custody who had been instructed at Ragged Schools, so that I might ascertain how many times they had been in prison *previously* to attending a Ragged School, and how many times *afterwards*. I was desirous of obtaining an answer to these questions, because in a circular which had been "privately and confidentially" sent out by the Ragged-School Union, and which had been forwarded to me by one of the teachers, the same interrogatories had been proposed as a test of the efficacy of those institutions, and I thought that I could not deal more fairly with the society than by adopting the very means that they themselves had used. The Governor gave me permission to do as I requested, and, in company with the chief warder, I proceeded round the prison.

The officer, when we entered the several wards, desired the boys who had been to Ragged Schools to stand up, and told them merely to answer all questions truly. They were then asked how many times they had been in prison *before* they had been at a Ragged School, and how many times *after*. They were asked also if they had been members of gangs of young thieves who resorted to Ragged Schools; some boys hesitated in giving an answer, and whenever they did so, the question was not pressed. The following are the results, the warder believing them (unless where I have expressly stated so) to be correctly given. I have placed a cipher (0) where there was no committal to prison prior to the boy's having been to a Ragged School, and have placed the word "gang" where the boy avowed his having belonged to a band of young thieves at the school. The average age of the boys, whose years are not specified, the officer considered to be thirteen:—

ROGUES AND VAGABONDS.

	Times in Prison before going to a Ragged School.	Times in Prison after going to a Ragged School.
Boy	1	2
„	1	1
„	0	1
„	1	1
„ (gang)	0	1
„	1	1
„	1	2
„	0	3
„	0	1
„	2	1
„	0	2
„	2	1
„	1	3
„	0	2
„	0	1
„	2	1
„ (gang)	0	1

FELONS.

	Before.	After.
Boy	0	2
„	0	1
„ (gang)	1	1
„	1	2

[The warder said that instead of twice, six times would be a truer statement.]

Boy (gang)	3	2
„ (gang)	0	10

[All these 10 committals for felony].

Boy	2	2
„	0	1
„	0	1
„	0	2
„	0	1
„	0	2
„	0	1
„	0	1
„	1	4
„	0	2
„	0	1
„ (12 years old)	0	1
„	0	1

I thought it best, as I proceeded with this inquiry, to give the ages of the individual prisoners: the preceding list, as I have stated, gives an average of boys of 13 years.

FELONS.

	Age.	Before.	After.
Boy	12	0	4
„	18	0	10
„	19	0	1
„	20	1	1
„	18	0	1
„	17	0	3
„ (misdemeanant)	30	0	1
„	20	0	2
„	20	1	1

[The warder said this boy had been far more times in prison.]

FELONS.

	Age.	Before.	After.
Boy (gang)	20	0	1
„	22	0	1
„	13	0	3
„	13	0	2
„	21	0	2
„	20	2	2
„	21	0	4
„	21	0	3
„	17	1	4
„	40	-	4

[Many times in prison—couldn't tell how often; was to have been sent out as an emigrant from the Ragged School, but got into prison at the very time.]

	Age.	Before.	After.
Boy (gang)	17	5	2

[Was connected with a gang of young thieves meeting at Pye-street School, Westminster.]

	Age.	Before.	After.
Boy (gang)	15	1	2
„	19	3	2
„ (gang)	16	0	5
„	24	1	3
„ (gang)	17	1	2
„	17	1	1
„	22	1	1
„	16	0	2
„	15	0	2
„ (gang)	17	0	3
„ (gang)	13	0	2
„ (gang)	11	1	2
„ (gang)	17	0	2

MISDEMEANANTS AND FELONS.

	Age.	Before.	After.
Boy	19 ...	4 ...	1
„	15 ...	1 ...	2
„ .... (felon)	15 ...	0 ...	3
„	20 ...	1 ...	1
„ .... (felon)	21 ...	0 ...	2

MISDEMEANANTS.

	Age.	Before.	After.
Boy	18 ...	1 ...	1
„	20 ...	0 ...	1
„ .... (gang)	22 ...	0 ...	2
„ .... (gang)	18 ...	3 ...	1
„	14 ...	0 ...	4
„	11 ...	0 ...	1
„	9 ...	1 ...	1

[Was first taken out to steal from a Ragged School, in George-street, Lisson-grove.]

	Age.	Before.	After.
Boy .... (gang)	13 ...	1 ...	2
„ .... (gang)	13 ...	1 ...	2
„ .... (gang)	13 ...	0 ...	2
„ .... (gang)	12 ...	0 ...	1
„ .... (gang)	16 ...	0 ...	1

[Was first tempted to steal by boys he met at the Ragged School in Old Gravel-lane, Wapping.]

	Age.	Before.	After.
Boy	14 ...	0 ...	2
„ .... (gang)	11 ...	0 ...	1
„ .... (gang)	13 ...	0 ...	1

[Was first tempted to steal by Ragged School boys in White Horse-street School, Poplar.]

	Age.	Before.	After.
Boy .... (gang)	16 ...	2 ...	7

On the day of my visit there were in Coldbath-fields Prison 793 male prisoners of all ages, 170 of them being boys of sixteen and under. Of the 170 youths in Coldbath-fields Prison, 90—*or more than one-half*—had been instructed in Ragged Schools, and among this number there had been 34 imprisonments before going to the Ragged Schools, and no less than 185 after. *As many as nineteen boys confessed to having belonged to gangs of young thieves at Ragged Schools.*

In order to complete my inquiry, I also applied to Lieutenant Tracy, the governor of Tothill-fields, to be allowed to put the same questions to the Ragged-School boys in his prison as I had done at Coldbath-fields. He immediately granted me permission to do so, and gave directions that all those youths who had attended Ragged Schools should be mustered in the school-room of the prison. Here they were interrogated in precisely the same manner. The inquiry was conducted in the presence of the officers of the prison, and the Rev. Mr. Rogers, the assistant chaplain, who gave me permission to state that he considered the *indiscriminate association of the good and bad children at Ragged Schools to be fraught with great danger.* The opinion of Lieutenant Tracy upon this subject is as decisive as that of Captain Chesterton. The following results were obtained at this prison. I have placed an "*f*" where the whole of the imprisonments have been for felony; where no letter appears against the number of imprisonments, they have been generally for misdemeanors as well as theft:—

	Age.	No. of times in prison before going to a Ragged School.	No. of times in prison after going to a Ragged School.
Boy	17	2	1 f.
„	14	0	1 f.
„	16	0	2 f.
„	16	0	2
„	15	0	2
„	15	1 f.	2
„	17	0	2 f.
„	16	0	1 f.
„	15	1	2 f.
„	15	1	1 f.
„	16	1	2 f.
„	14	0	4 f.
„	13	0	2
„	16	0	3 f.
„	15	0	1 f.
„	16	0	6
„	12	0	4 f.
„	12	0	2
„	14	0	1 f.
„	13	3 f.	2 f.
„	13	0	1 f.
„	13	0	2 f.
„	11	0	11
„	13	13*	—

[* This lad could not remember how many times he had been imprisoned before going to a Ragged School, and how many times after. I have, therefore, so as to err on the right side, set down the whole of his imprisonments as occurring before.]

	Age.	No. of times in prison before going to a Ragged School.	No. of times in prison after going to a Ragged School.
Boy	7	0	1
„	12	12	2 f.
„	12	0	2 f.
„	15	0	2 f.
„	14	0	1 f.
„	15	0	3
„	14	0	7
„	14	1	8
„	15	0	2 f.
„	17	0	2 f.
„	15	2th	1 f.
„	17	0	6
„	16	0	4
„	17	2	1 f.
„	17	0	2 f.
„	17	0	2 f.
„	17	0	1 f.
„	17	0	1 f.
„	16	0	3
„	15	0	4 f.
„	10	4	1 f.
„	13	3f	2 f.
„	12	0	1 f.
„	14	0	1 f.
„	16	0	1 f.
„	14	0	2 f.
„	17	4th	2 f.
„	17	0	2 f.
„	16	1	1 f.

There are 117 boys at present confined in Tothill-fields Prison, and of this number it appears 52—*or nearly one-half*—have been instructed at Ragged Schools. Among these there had been 33 imprisonments before attending the schools, and no less than 128 afterwards. Twenty-three of the fifty-two boys confessed to having heard the boys planning robberies outside the school doors; 5 knew good boys who had been led away by young thieves that they had met at the schools; 9 declared that they themselves had first been taught to thieve at a Ragged School; and 13 protested that they knew many of the boys went thieving after attending school. The addresses given by the boys in prison, as well as the principal circumstances detailed by them, proved to be quite correct, so that there appears every reason to place credence in their narratives.

From Tothill-fields and Coldbath-fields Houses of Correction then, we have the following facts:—In the two prisons there were altogether 287 boys confined. Of these, 142, *or within a fraction of one-half*, had received instruction in a Ragged School. Among this latter number there had only been 92 imprisonments before attending Ragged Schools, *and no less than* 313 *imprisonments afterwards*. Surely no persons, in the teeth of such overwhelming facts as these, will now maintain that Ragged Schools are unattended with evil.

To make assurance doubly sure, however, I sought out a boy whom I knew to have attended a Ragged School in the vicinity of Wapping, and whom I had met while inquiring into the condition of "the mudlarks." This lad, whose history has been already described in this paper in a letter from a lady, was kindly provided with a situation by Messrs. Bradbury and Evans, and has now for some months past been earning an honest living. Before printing the statement I received from the boy I applied to his employers to know how he had conducted himself in their service, and was favoured with the following answer:—

"Whitefriars, April 22.
"Messrs. Bradbury and Evans beg to say that the boy J.C. has conducted himself in a very satisfactory manner since he has been in their employment."

With this preamble, I now give the statement of the lad himself:—

"I am getting on for fourteen years. My mother used to go out washing. My father has been dead nine years. He was a coal-porter, and died from falling down between the barges in the river. After his death my mother was left without any means of living, with myself and two sisters to keep. My eldest sister is now sixteen, and the young-est twelve. After my father died my mother went out washing, and when she couldn't get that to do, she used to go selling fruit—apples and oranges, and gooseberries and cherries—in the street. When I was nine years old, my mother sent me to Red Lion School, which is in Greenbank, near Old Gravel-lane, Ratcliffe-highway. She paid a penny a week for my schooling. I didn't learn much there, and couldn't write at all, though I could read a little when I left. I was there a year altogether. There were 200 boys in the school. My mother got so poor and distressed after I had been a twelvemonth at the school that she couldn't afford to pay the penny a week for me any longer, so I was forced to go out with my sister selling fish about the streets. I was kept at this for three months, but after that my mother's stock-money was all gone, and we had nothing to eat until I went down to the shore to pick up a potful or two of coals. Before this I had been down to the water-side to pick up bits of wood for my mother's fire, and there I saw the boys picking up coals. I told my mother, and she bid me do the same. I had been picking up things along shore for three months before I went to the Ragged School. One night when I came up off the shore, I went and washed my feet, and I heard the boys talking about the Ragged School in High-street, Wapping. They was saying what they used to learn there. They asked me to come along with them, and said it was great fun. They told me that all the boys used to be laughing and making game of the master. They said they used to put out the gas, and chuck the slates all about everywhere. They told me too there was a good fire there; so I went to have a warm, and see what it was like. When I got there the masters was very kind to me. They used to give us tea parties; and to keep us all quiet, they used to show us the magic lantern. I soon got to like going there, and went every night for six months. We used to begin school at seven o'clock at night, and come out at nine. There was about forty or fifty boys in the school. The most of them was thieves. They used to go thieving coals out of the barges alongshore, and cutting the ropes off the ships, and going and selling it at the rag-shops. They used to get three farthings a pound for the rope dry, and a halfpenny a pound wet. There was no pickpockets—the boys was no good at that. Some used to steal pudding out of shops, and hand it to those outside, and the last boy it was handed to would go off with it. They used to steal bacon and bread sometimes out of the shops. About half of the boys at the Ragged School I went to were thieves, and the rest of the boys were honest. Some had work to do at iron-mongers, lead factories, engineers, soap-boilers, and so on; and some had no work to do, but were good boys still. After we came out of school at nine o'clock at night, some of the bad boys would go thieving—perhaps half-a-dozen, and from that to eight, would go out in a gang together. There was one big boy of the name of C——, he was 18 years old—and is in prison now for stealing some bacon. I think he's in the House of Correction. This C—— used to go out of the school before any of us, and wait outside the door as the other boys came out. Then he would call the boys he wanted for his gangs on one side, and tell them where to go and steal. He used to look out in the daytime for the shops where things could be prigged, and at night he would tell the boys to go to them. He was called the captain of the gangs. He had about three gangs altogether with him, and there were from 6 to 8 boys in each gang. The boys used to bring what they stole to C—— and he used to share it with them. I belonged to one of these gangs. There were six boys altogether in my gang. The biggest lad, that knowed all about the thieving, was the captain of the gang that I was in, and C—— was captain over him and over all of us. The name of the captain of my gang was C——. There was two brothers of them. You seed them, sir, on the night that you first met me at Mr. ——'s house. The other boys who was in my gang was B— B—— and B— L——, and D— B——, and a boy we used to call Tim. These with myself made up one of the gangs—and we all of us used to go thieving every night after school hours. And when the tide would be right up, and we had nothing to do along shore, we used to go thieving in the daytime as well. It was B— B—— and B— L—— that first put me up to go thieving. They took me with them one night up the lane (New Gravel-lane), and I see them take some bread out of a baker's, and they wasn't found out, and after that I used to go with them regular. Then I joined C——'s gang, and after that C—— came and told us that his gang could do better than ourn, and he asked us to join our gang with his'n, and we did so. Sometimes we used to make three and four shillings a day, or about sixpence a piece. Sometimes C—— used to try and entice the good boys at the Ragged School to come thieving with his gang, but I never knew him to take a boy from there. But we often used to plan up our robberies while waiting outside the school doors before they were opened. We used to plan up where we would go to after school was over. All the whole of the gang would be together while wait-ing outside the school, and we'd talk over where we would go to that night. I think I learnt more good than harm at the school, but I have planned up many times at the Ragged School to go thieving with our gang. If it hadn't been for the school we shouldn't have met together so often of a night, and I don't think we should have stolen so much. I didn't know not one boy out of our gangs that left off thieving after going to the school. I know that C—— and the captain of my gang (C——) are both in prison. C—— has got six months, and C——, I think, fourteen days of it, or a month, I can't be sure which. I was taken up once for thieving coals myself, but I was let go again. C—— was taken for stealing bacon in Wapping-wall; it was about half-past nine at night, and after he had been at the Ragged School. C——

was taken for coals one morning. C—— has been in prison twice, and C—— three times."

This statement was afterwards shown to the mother of the boy, who assured me that it was true in every part of it; and she, moreover, told me, that she herself has known the old thieves come down from Ratcliffe-highway and Rosemary-lane to teach the young boys how to steal; and if the young ones would not go with the old thieves they used to make up a gang themselves to go and do the same as the old ones had told them they wanted them for. "The school was a great nuisance at night with the boys both going and coming, and from what I have heard," she said, "from my son, since you saw him, sir, it appears to have been a regular practice with the bad boys in the neighbourhood to meet at the school and plan up their robberies. I know my son has spoken the truth to you, because he told me so quite privately, after you had wrote down what he said, and if he had deceived you I am sure he would have confessed it to me. He has thought of several other things since he saw you, and among the rest that about the old thieves coming down from Rosemary-lane to the school, to get hold of the young ones. The boy C——, at the school, was 18 years, and another boy of the name of M^cG—— was 18 too. M^cG—— had been a dozen and more times in prison, and these two used to lead the young boys astray. I can swear from what I have since heard from my son, that he learnt more harm than good at the school. It is true he was taught how to read and write there, and Mr. G——, the teacher, was very good to him; all the boys would have done well if they only had followed the good advice he used to give them; but directly they were out of his sight they used to be off thieving all the same, and the big thieves would put the little ones up to things they would never have thought of if they hadn't met one another at the school."

[Since receiving the above statement I have endeavoured to trace the lad, but, owing to a boy, when arrested, seldom giving the same name twice, I have met with considerable difficulty. I am induced to believe, however, from information received at the Thames police-office, that he is now under sentence of transportation for seven years, under another name.]

Now for the evidence of Ragged School Teachers themselves. I have before refrained from making any application for information from this source, because I was impressed with the idea that the teachers believed Ragged Schools to be productive of pure unalloyed good.

From the silence of the annual reports concerning the evil, or even danger, of the indiscriminate association of the virtuous with the vicious, I considered it idle to make any application in such quarters. I gave the teachers every credit for being honest, benevolent, and zealous men, and felt quite satisfied that were they acquainted with the injurious tendency of those institutions, they would no longer remain connected with them. It appears, however, that several of the teachers have long been impressed with the injurious tendency of such institutions, and have not hesitated to speak out their sentiments upon the subject. The opinions of these gentlemen agree mainly with what I have advanced, and go far to corroborate the very facts which Mr. Anderson seeks not only to deny, but even to brand me as an infidel for daring to publish. The following extracts from the Diary of a Ragged School Teacher, printed in the *English Journal of Education* for January, March, and April, will afford the reader further proof of the truth of what has been asserted in these letters:—

"Oct. 29, 1849.— ... We prepared the school by placing benches in situations for the division of the scholars into four classes, and as they came tumbling and bawling up the stairs, we directed them to seats. ... In mere schooling they are not behindhand, but in decency of behaviour or in respect for the teacher, or in discipline of any kind, they are totally unparalleled. No school can be possibly worse than this. It were an easier task to get attention from savages. ... Without one exception, these boys are precocious. *They require more training than teaching.* The great city has been their book, and they have read men as such boys alone can do. ... To compose the children, I proposed that we should have a little music, and —— sang very sweetly the first verse of the Evening Hymn. We then invited the children to follow us, and we got through the first line or two very well, but a blackguard boy thought proper to set up on his own account, and he led off a song in this strain—

> " ' O, Susannah, don't you cry for me;
> I'm off to Alabama,
> With a banjo on my knee!'

I need scarcely add that every boy followed this leader—aye, girls and all—and I could not check them. ... In the midst of the Lord's Prayer, several shrill cries of 'cat's meat,' and 'mew, mew,' added another fact to the history of this school. ... *All our copy-books have been stolen,* and proofs exist that the school is used at night as a sleeping-room. We must get a stronger door to it.

"31st Oct., 1849.— ... They have had a great deal of good school-ing in a certain sense, or rather *much labour has been expended in teaching them to read, write, and cipher well. But I cannot believe that any attention has been bestowed in making this knowledge useful. They are ut-terly destitute of feeling or propriety;* and their technical education, such as it has been, has not made them more civilized or better children. After all, the school must be looked upon as secondary to home teach-ing. *It is apparently worse than useless to expect a man to be made better by merely learning to read and write. Those of our scholars who can do so best are decidedly the most depraved.* One boy, who is quite as well schooled as the average number of boys at his age are schooled—(say twelve years of age)—said to me to-day, 'Please, sir, I'll go down on my knees and say the Lord Jesus Christ and the Fellowship of the Holy Ghost for a halfpenny.' Another, as we went along the lanes from school, called after us, 'Glory be to the Father,' &c. ... Any careful observer would come to another conclusion; and that is, that *these people do not require the schoolmaster so much as they need some mu-nicipal act for the regulation of lodging-houses and dwelling-houses gen-erally. Preaching and teaching can never fructify in the heart or mind of a man who is never alone.* It is almost cruelty to talk of *virtue* or de-cency to a being who is doomed to sleep and do everything else in a crowd. ... *There is a boy in my first class who has made as much as four-teen pence a week by writing 'begging letters' for his neighbours, for which he charged one penny a piece;* and he also receives a few coppers now and then from the costermongers, who employ him to conduct their business correspondence. His moral tone is exceedingly low. ... Are we educating these boys for the purpose of confusing honest men, or for making them more expert in the prosecution of unlawful callings? Surely, the latter is not our object; but it will be the result of our ef-forts, unless we can find *employment* for those who are ready and able to do *useful work.*"

I shall now conclude with the evidence of a gentleman—a Ragged School teacher of great experience—who, it will be seen, cites facts far more appalling than any that I have yet published concerning the injurious tendency of those institutions.

"Could the full and minute particulars concerning Ragged Schools be made public—but many of those particulars could not, without outraging all decency—the world," he said, "would be shocked and surprised." He had read my letters on the subject of Ragged Schools, and knew, from his own intimate knowledge of those schools, that the facts given, and the inferences drawn, were undeniably correct, but that they were understated. Oaths were very common among the boys, who smoked their short pipes, and laughed at every precept of religion or morality. The language of these boys could not be printed in any newspaper, and their example, when, as is common in Ragged Schools, they came into contact with honest boys, *was most contagious and ruinous. My informant knew three previously honest boys who had been taught or tempted to steal in a Ragged School, containing then about forty boys.* Neither could all the children whom the benevolent and sanguine supporters of Ragged Schools pronounced reclaimed characters be considered reclaimed. One boy picked a pocket on the very eve of emigration as a reclaimed boy; a girl, selected as a reclaimed character for emigration, refused to emigrate when the time arrived, and was soon after convicted of having stolen a pair of boots from a child's feet, stopping the child in the street for the purpose. Young prostitutes resorted to the school; and of *their* corrupting influence upon all coming into contact with them in the school there can be no doubt whatever. My informant once asked an excellent gentleman, who expressed an opinion of the good to be accomplished by Ragged Schools, if he would allow his daughter to teach a girls' class in that school? The gentleman said certainly not, for it was his duty to take care that his daughter's ears should not be assailed by such language as some of those girls used so shamelessly. My informant then asked him if it were not safe or proper to expose a virtuous young lady, with all the safeguards of Christian principles and the comforts of a good home to ensure her against harm or temptation to such influences, how could it be safe or proper to expose poor, and ignorant, and little cared-for children to those influences? Five bad boys, he said, were enough to corrupt fifty good boys in a school, and so convinced was he of this, so certain of the mischief done by evil communications, which the teachers could not check, at Ragged Schools, that, could it be matter of proof, *far more children it would be found had been contaminated than had been reclaimed or benefited by these institutions.* Even some boys who were sent out as emigrants, on account of their being reformed characters, had conducted themselves so badly on shipboard, that stocks had to be set up for their punishment and coercion. Some of these young emigrants had sent the strangest letters home. When gentlemen or ladies visited the school—and my informant often was in fear for ladies who might be shocked by hearing language such as they never heard before—the vicious children, either in hope or in possession of a gift, or in expectation of some benefit to themselves or their parents, would behave tolerably well, but indulged in their usual coarseness when the visitors had left. The wit and sharpness of the replies of some of the boys was remarkable, and often exercised in ridicule of religious or moral precepts. Discipline was hopeless, and so was any good and lasting effect among Ragged School pupils. On my asking for proofs of the correctness of his conclusions as to the mischief done, my informant described one Ragged School with which he was acquainted—and all these schools were, more or less, alike—as a perfect nest of corruption and depravity. Boys in the school would expose their persons before the female class, and commit gross acts of indecency before the tittering girls. The boys occupied one end of the school-room, and the girls the other. The girls would, at one period, make any excuse to go into the yard, or would walk out without any excuse; and my informant once detected a boy and girl in criminal intercourse in the water-closet.

That the facts and opinions above adduced have more than confirmed what was previously advanced in these letters, I think the public—and even Mr. Anderson himself—will readily acknowledge. It cannot be said in justice that, in making these disclosures, I have been actuated by any feeling of prejudice against Ragged Schools, or the upholders of them. For myself, I would refer such as may still believe that I entered upon the inquiry with a preconceived aversion to these institutions, to a work entitled "The Magic of Kindness," published last June, and in which I spoke approvingly of them. Subsequent investigation, however, has compelled me to change my opinion. That no other motive has induced me to do so, it is due to myself and the proprietors of this Journal most unequivocally to declare. Our sole object has been—not only in this investigation, but in all our other inquiries—the development of the truth—and it has caused us no little pain to be compelled to denounce institutions that were admitted by all to have been designed and sustained by the purest and most benevolent feelings. We are thoroughly convinced, however, that the facts which have been elicited in the course of this inquiry must be productive of great good, and lead to the immediate reformation of the Ragged Schools; and we feel assured, that the supporters of these institutions will *then* do us the justice to rank us among their best friends. It is admitted by us that free schools for the children of the *honest* poor are much needed. These we are ready to advocate most heartily; for though we have felt ourselves called upon to expose the hopelessness of attempting to check crime by a diffusion of the knowledge of reading and writing, we are in no way adverse to the education of the people. We are merely opposed to the instruction of the honest poor *in connection* with the dishonest, believing that any attempt to educate *the two together* must necessarily, from the force of association, be productive of more harm than good to the community.

LABOUR AND THE POOR.

—◆—

THE METROPOLITAN DISTRICTS.

[FROM OUR SPECIAL CORRESPONDENT.]

LETTER L.

I return to the condition and treatment of the *Merchant Seaman ashore*.

In my last Letters upon this subject I gave an account of the Sailors' Home, in Well-street—"Green's Home," in the East India-road—and the lodging-houses of the more respectable boarding-masters. In my present Letter I shall treat of the worst class of boarding-masters, known by the name of "*Crimps*."

Concerning the practices of these persons I had the following account from one well acquainted with the subject:—

"The men who keep the worst class of lodging-houses for sailors are often lumpers—men who are employed by the stevedores to stow the cargo of a ship. They are not fully employed, and, having idle time, look out for lodgers. Those who supply them with lodgers are often runners or touters, but some tout for themselves. The keepers of these low houses are generally of the lower order of the Irish. They hang about the docks, infesting the bridges as ships come in, and getting hold of men who have come home from a voyage. If these men haven't houses of their own to take seamen to, they take them to the lower lodging-houses for seamen, kept by others. For taking men to these lodging-houses they will receive from 5s. to 20s.—as much as 30s. I have known given—but the price varies according to the voyage, for on this depends the amount the sailor has to receive, and this the crimps always endeavour to find out. They are generally dressed in the garb of a rigger—that is, a canvas jumper (a sort of spencer slipped on over the head), canvas trowsers—both so dirty that you can't tell what was their colour when new—and a sou'-wester. That sort of dress doesn't attract the notice of the officers. The lumper, or whoever keeps the low lodging-house, asks for the cook, and inquires if he has any fat to dispose of. This they do as a pretence, as it's against the act of Parliament for them to go aboard; so they get into the galley, and inquire as to the sums the seamen have to receive, and pump as to the 'green uns' (men who have not been in London before). They look out for stupid fellows—though some of the old ones are worse than the young ones. These crimps often take a drop of rum or gin in a bottle in their pockets, and treat Jack, who thinks them good fellows, and will go with them. They offer to carry the men's clothes, or to do anything to recommend themselves, or will lend a hand on deck to pull or haul, or help the ship's service as she comes into the dock. This sort of going on further removes the suspicion of the captain or his officers. Suppose they offer to act as a sailor's porter, and to carry his clothes anywhere, the sailor may say, 'But I've no place to go to.' Then the crimp—or whatever he is called—says, 'I'll take you to a good boarding-house,' and he takes him to some boarding-master who will pay him—if the crimp has no house of his own. The crimps' lodging-houses are chiefly in courts and alleys in the lower part of Shadwell, Wapping, St. George's, and East Smithfield. The courts are unpaved; they have been better cleansed lately, but they are very bad still; and a sensible seaman might be frightened at the look of them; but they don't want sensible seamen there, and so don't look out for them. The beds are bad. Men, women, and children pig together. I have known smart-looking young fellows go there, but they are generally frequented by men who haven't much money. Such boarding-masters soon get rid of their lodgers. They say:—'By dad, they'll eat their heads off; we must quit them in a jiffy.' Most of the men lodging in these houses come from St. John's, New Brunswick—some are from Nova Scotia, and some from Newfoundland; but they are from North America mainly. The sailors have the character of being soft, and think themselves cunning. They are often fine-looking fellows. They charge these men 14s. a week for their board and lodging, and give them very frequently red herrings or a bit of coarse beef for their dinner, or a bit of salt fish—not much fresh meat—but only what they can get cheap. Once a man went home drunk to one of these places—I've heard it from a person who couldn't be deceived—and when the man recovered from his drink he felt hungry and asked for his supper. The boarding-master, however, had greased his lips when asleep, and on hearing the seaman on waking ask for his supper, said, 'Well, by J——, havn't you supped already? Arn't your lips greased with the fat of the good meat you tucked in, and isn't the bones alongside of you!' The bones had been put there accordingly. This I know for a fact. Tricks of that kind are not uncommon when men have been drinking, and the men are encouraged to drunkenness and all kinds of debauchery. Another class of the lowest boarding-masters keep women in the house who live with the seamen, or they more generally have a house next door, where the women live, with a communication to the lodging-house. These houses are far more decent than the others as to cleanliness. A girl pays for a furnished room on the ground floor from 6s. to 9s. a week; upstairs from 4s. to 7s. for front rooms. For the ground floor back room from 4s. to 5s.; for the upstairs back room from 3s. to 4s. In these places a sailor's money is gone before he knows well where he is. If the lady be in arrear £2 or £3 for rent, he has to pay it, and to meet every expense for himself and his 'wife,' as she is called, besides a new cap for the mistress of the house, and some clothing for the children, and other expenses into the bargain, if the seaman be at all flush of money. As soon as his money and clothes are gone (he very seldom saves his clothes), he must go; and then he must resort to his shipmates at the more respectable boarding-masters'. I never heard of men being hocussed in those places. The girls are not of that class. These sort of houses are not so numerous as they have been. Some are carried on by a man and his wife; others by girls on their own account; and some of these girls keep lodging-houses for seamen as well, but they are getting very cautious about it, and I know but four or five of such places. There are more, no doubt. If a man have a good deal of money when he goes there, the people in the house never lose sight of him. If he wants to go to any place of amusement, 'Jack and his mistress go,' or somebody's got to go with him, and he's stuck to until he hasn't a farthing left. I know some women who keep beer-shops—along with lodgings for sailors—which are of the character I have described. The women keeping these beer-shops act as the men's wives; and indeed some have been married in church three or four times. The sailors often marry such people for the spree of the thing."

Three young men, employed as "*porters for seamen*" (so they described themselves), gave me the following statement concerning the tricks practiced by ships' porters generally, in which they all concurred:—

"It would be much better if such as we were licensed; we look after porter's work, carrying sailors' luggage ashore. Last ship we were aboard some coalwhippers were there, and were sarcy, and were turned out, and we were turned out as well. We go aboard to carry the sailors' goods ashore; but some porters—for there's two classes of us—go aboard for thieving, or to take men away. We work two or three together that we may save the goods from thieves by keeping watch. Perhaps if a ship comes into dock there'll be more porters go on board than there are seamen; twenty-five we've seen on board one ship, but not more than six were regular porters. There are regular porters at each dock—perhaps nearer forty than fifty in all. Four times that number do it for jobs. People that work about the dock, work as ships' porters. Dock labourers often leave their work to go on board a ship. If they hadn't done so this afternoon, we should have had a dinner tomorrow (Sunday). The coal-whippers look out as well as the dock labourers. When we get goods ashore one must always keep watch; we can't work singly. If nobody watched, somebody would sling the chest on his back and walk off with it. Besides, there's often so many things, that we can hardly keep watch enough. I saw a man the other day on board a ship pull off a pair of old boots, and slip on a new pair, that was put on the deck to be carried ashore. Such practices are common with jackets. The seamen look to us to be honest with them in bringing their things on shore."

One man, who said that he had been 25 years at the trade, off and on, gave me the following account:—

"From the West India Dock to Shadwell or Ratcliff-highway, a porter will receive 2s. or 2s. 6d.—2s. from the West India Docks will satisfy us, and 2s. 6d. from the East. The worst class of porters will do it at 1s., making up the difference by cribbing. Besides, they'll run away with the seaman, if they can, and sell him. They sell him to anybody—to any bad boarding-master. The price of the man depends upon what money he may have. One man was sold the other day by the porters; there was a good power of them, and they took him—he was a black man—to one of his countrymen, but he wouldn't buy him, but Mr. —— bought him at 6s. 6d. If we take a man to a decent boarding-house, we get 1s. or so for our trouble. A bad boarding-master will regulate his price to the porters according to what clothes the seaman may want, for one thing. We've heard of £1 being given for a 'Chinaman.' A two years' voyage man will fetch £1 at ——, or ——, or ——, or any crimp's. If we took a man to a respectable house, we might get 1s. for beer; so, to be paid, we must take men to lower lodging-houses, who will pay us. The way to stop this sort of thing is to license men like us. Men who are employed by the low boarding-masters will knock you down if you interfere with them. They treat the men if they get them ashore, and carry gin and rum aboard with them. Ashore they run off with the chests and things in a truck, and the sailor may follow. They go where the boarding-masters pay best, and the boarding-masters that keep half-brothels, or find women for the men, can afford to give higher prices for seamen than the respectable houses. We know a boarding-master who has, we believe, fourteen brothels. He may buy his sailors at £1 a piece, but he employs his own men. He has five cabs; we saw one at the West India Dock to-day, taking two men's things away, and hindering regular porters of a job. It's hard to say how many porters or runners he has, but we know two of his constant hands. His men are allowed in the dock, for they dress respectable, with gold chains as thick as your finger, and rings on their fingers; so these runners get in when we can't. The brothels for sailors are chiefly in East Smithfield. A man who went to a low boarding-master's with near £40 in his pocket—he was a ship's carpenter who had been away some eight or nine months—wasn't a fortnight before he was cleaned out—regularly 'skinned' of his clothes and all—and we found him in the streets without a shilling. He is a quiet, nice fellow, too. The boarding-master pretended to read the list of payments and money that the man had before he left, and the carpenter said, 'Yes, that's it,' and he was turned out directly. He was drunk all the time, and they give him shillings or fourpenny bits, and said they were sovereigns. He didn't care as long as he had gin. He used to take a farthing for a shilling to spend at a public-house. One boarding-master furnishes rooms for prostitutes, and recommends them to the seamen who lodge with him. The low boarding-masters usually buy the sailors' clothes for them, getting them second-hand often, and charging them as new, or else putting down for them—as much as the Sailors' Home tailors, who have to pay lots of money to their runners, and so you know must put on a little extra. The Sailors' Home tailors have many runners, who do us harm by getting jobs from us. There are two classes of boarding-masters—good and bad; the good treat their lodgers as well as the others use them badly. One boarding-master kept a man six months once, after his money was out. Scores of times we've heard seamen say, when the runners have asked them to go to the Sailors' Home, 'Go there, to be sent to the straw-house when our money's done? No! No! A boarding-master will keep us when it is done.' By licensing the porters and boarding-masters good must be done, for then half that carry on those trades would never get a license. None of the bad class of porters like to hear of a license. The worst sort of boarding-masters are Irish, and foreigners more than others. There are not many Jews. There may not be more than twelve regular boarding-houses of the worst class. More than fifty take occasional boarders—two or three; but they are generally the very worst of all. The charge is 2s. a day with all of them."

A well-spoken and good-looking sailor told the following story of the proceedings as regards himself in a low boarding-house:—

"I came to London last Wednesday," he said, "and was on my way to Mr. B——'s, a respectable boarding-master, whom I have known for eleven years. He had changed his residence in the five years that I had been away in India, China, New Zealand, Sydney, and other places. [The man, I ascertained, bore a good character.] Well, I was going along the Highway, with a little drop of drink in my head, sailor-like, you know, sir—half seas over, that's about the size of it—excited quite on getting ashore, and thinking how I would surprise them at home (that's what I always call Mr. B——'s), when I met with a young woman, and she asked me if I was looking out for anybody? I told her I wanted Mr. B——, and she said, 'You had best come to my house; he's gone away.' I answered, 'Well, I don't mind; short reckonings make long friends.' If I hadn't been tipsy I shouldn't have been carried off by such a craft. She took me to a house—I remember it was up a dark passage—there's plenty of ins and outs in the streets about here—and we had something more to drink. Next morning I found myself 'skinned'—that's about the size of it; and about 50s. was the value of the 'skin' I lost. A pair of old canvass trousers was left for my own good cloth ones, but all the rest of my clothes were gone, and the young woman was gone too. I never got served out so before, but I was catched on the hip this time. About Bluecoat-fields—that's the name of the place where I was taken to—is called 'Skinner's Bay,' because men are mostly served there as I was. When I awoke in the morning I thought at first I was at Mr. B——'s, but I soon found the difference. Instead of a comfortable bed-room, I was in a small, poor, dirty room, with a few halfpenny pictures over the mantel, and two or three broken cups or saucers in the room. The young woman told me overnight that I might as well stay at her house as at Mr. B——'s, for that I should only be charged 14s. all the same. In the morning I met with an old woman, when I looked out for the master of the house or somebody, and I soon found her a countrywoman of mine. She would give me no information, but wanted me to board there at 14s. a week, saying I might save money by it; and meaning, I suppose, that the people there would supply women or drink regularly, or any foolery a sailor was after, and all for the fourteen shillings. But I said—feeling I was a fool in the morning, though I thought myself a smart man overnight—'No, no, none of that; I'll be off.' So I walked away in my canvass trowsers and blue shirt, like a collier going nor'ard, bucket on one side and broom on the other. I got to my old boarding-master's, and then got clothes and help. If I'd stayed, as I'd money coming, I might have lost another skin. It's no use prosecuting the people. I shan't be any poorer a twelvemonth's hence."

I was told by an experienced person that seamen are not robbed in this manner so frequently as they used to be—or so frequently, perhaps, as people generally imagine. It is commoner to pawn the man's clothes than to steal them. The police warn a seaman if they see him led to a boarding-house that is known to be half a brothel, and so will the better sort of sailors' porters. Often, however, seamen will not state where they have been "skinned," having a greater feeling of shame in the matter now than they once had.

Concerning the practice known as *kidnapping*, among the worst class of boarding-masters, I had the subjoined statement from a person intimately acquainted with the subject:—

"The desertion of foreign seamen in this port is very great, particularly among the Prussian and Russian ships. The system is this. On the arrival of a Prussian or Russian vessel it is closely watched by certain lodging-house keepers, about half-a-dozen in number, who entice the foreign seamen to leave their vessels, the lodging-house keepers pretending that they will get them berths in English ships with better wages. Two of these lodging-house keepers are foreigners, and they can all express themselves so as to be understood by a Prussian or Russian. One of these men can make himself understood in four or five languages. They assist the foreign seamen to smuggle their clothes out of the ship, generally at night; or, as the principal place for this traffic is at the Commercial Dock, the clothes are sometimes taken out piecemeal, in the daytime, hid in some adjacent by-place—perhaps under a hedge—and then carried away at night, or early in the morning, to the lodging-house. One of those houses had a place fitted up in the back yard for the reception of the seamen to be concealed, and the place was so contrived by sliding pannels as to present the appearance of a dead wall, or of some building unconnected with the lodging-house. Here, and in similar places, the kidnapped people were detained until the sailing of their vessel—that is, if no reward had been offered for their apprehension by the master. By the laws of many foreign countries the master of a merchant ship is under a heavy bond to return the seamen to their native country. If the reward be offered, the man is restored to the ship, and the money paid as the reward is deducted by the captain from his wages. Should no reward be offered, the lodging-house keepers, knowing from what ship they have stolen the sailors, wait upon the master, telling him that they have heard his men are missing (much after the fashion of the street dog-stealers). Ultimately, perhaps, the captain will agree to pay some-thing to have his men sent back to the ship. This is only done when the seamen kidnapped are penniless, and the lodging-house keeper thinks it better to try to get £5 from the foreign captain than wait for a £2 advance note from a British ship. When the lodging-house keeper has bargained in this way with a foreign captain, he returns home and informs the poor fellows whom he has deluded that he has got them a British ship, with good wages, good living, and all the rest of it. The seamen are then taken to some convenient river-stairs, where the assistance of the Thames police inspector has been secured; he at once places the men in his boat and conveys them as prisoners to their own ship. Sometimes the men have been rowed right into the river without knowing they were in custody. When the men are returned to their own ship the crimp receives an order on the broker for the reward, or the amount agreed to be paid. In order to convince myself of these facts I called at a broker's office, and saw in the books an entry of £31 odd having been paid to a crimp, who had returned some foreign seamen to their ship; one of these men (there were six in all, £5 a piece being the money paid) was seen in the crimp's house, but no one had any power to interfere and compel the man to return to his duty. One of these lodging-house keepers was lately summoned at the Thames Police Court, at the instance of the Swedish Consul, charged with kidnapping a foreign seaman. The man was enticed away from his ship (a Swedish vessel) by a lodging-house keeper, and placed on board an English ship. He received an advance note for about £4, and the whole of this was taken posses-sion of by the crimp. At Gravesend the Swede's own vessel dropped down at the time the British ship that he was on board of was at an-chor there. The man swam, during the night, from the British ship to his own. He appeared as a witness at the police-court for the prosecution, and detailed these circumstances with the aid of an inter-preter. After much discussion between the solicitors employed, the case was dismissed, the magistrate having no jurisdiction—the Mer-chant Seamen's Act applying only to 'subjects of her Majesty,' and the Merchant Seamen's Protection Act to the 'seamen of this kingdom.'"

I have already given the opinion of an intelligent and experienced officer on the necessity of improved *sanitary regulations* on board ship. I now give three narratives, bearing closely on that important subject. At the time the statements were taken (ten days ago), R— and C—, the two seamen, were confined to the Dreadnought Hospital ship, both having been carried there from the ——, on Sunday, the 7th April. R— was able to move about with the assistance of a stick, but C— was still confined to his bed, being unable to bend his legs, or raise himself in his bed. R— stated:—

"I joined the —— as seaman, at Bombay, on the 15th of October, 1849, and sailed from that place about the 22d of that month for Lon-don; no spirits were allowed. I have been in temperance ships before, and no cases of scurvy have arisen. The lime-juice was served out gen-erally daily, and was always taken by the crew. Sheep and pigs were taken on board at Bombay; one sheep died, and one was killed to save its life. The one that died was cooked for the pigs, the one that was killed was made into a sea-pie; some of the crew eat it. I tasted the dough, but could not eat the meat. The pigs were all kept for the cap-tain's table. About the 27th of November we had some bad weather, and the long-boat, containing the pigs, sheep, and poultry, was filled with water. From that time they were removed into the forecastle, in which we slept; the stench from them was very bad—particularly from the pigs and the dead ducks. They all remained there till they were required to be killed. The captain did not have the same water as we had, which was very bad; but after all the cuddy water was gone, himself and mates were obliged to turn to ours. One man died with the venereal and scurvy; he only worked a month and ten days after he joined. An apprentice boy was the next who was taken ill. He first caught cold. He was kept up in the cross-trees all day naked in the wet and cold by the captain, who said he was too long over his work when aloft. The scurvy afterwards came on. The apprentice boy died first, then the man, and three others shortly after. They all com-plained of hunger. The salt meat was stopped, and no substitute was given to us. Two pigs were then left, one of which we brought to Eng-land; so there was enough and to spare. The sugar was stopped when any of us were taken ill, because, as the captain said, it was getting short; but those who could work had their proper allowance, for the captain always said we were shamming sick, and he would starve us out. He refused to give us anything but what we signed articles for. The vessel was built of iron. We felt the cold very much; out of the sixteen bunks (sleeping places) eight only were fit for use; the water ran into the others; they were never cleaned out from the time we left Bombay, neither were they touched there. Not even a drop of vinegar was given to us, to sprinkle the bunks with, when the men died. We clubbed together, and out of our allowance we used to get a little for that purpose. In the forecastle it was very close; there were no ventilators. Before the pigs were put into the place amidships, there was a door on the starboard side that we could open, but it was afterwards fastened up; the door on the larboard side was never opened. The hawser-holes run in amidships, so we did not even get the air that would have come through them. On arrival in the channel we had but three of the foremast hands who could do duty, and I think the master ought to have sent on shore and obtained other hands, at Scilly or Falmouth; he did take in six fresh hands in the Downs, about three hours before the steam-tug took us, but then none of the crew could stand on their feet."

C——, another of the sick men, corroborated the foregoing statement, adding, that if the pig brought to England had been killed, the fresh meat might have saved two or three men's lives. The men's gums were so sore that they could not eat the hard biscuits given to them, and they went on starving.

B——, an apprentice, was in a worse state than the seaman C——; but being younger, and a stout-made lad, the sickness had not taken that serious hold upon him which it would have done upon a less robust constitution. He was at home at his father's, in Deptford. The father complained that when his son came home he was covered with thousands of lice, and did not look as if he had been washed since he left home. The lad stated:—"I was bound an apprentice to Captain ——, and this was my first voyage. I went out and home in the vessel. Many of the crew were discharged at Bombay, after going before a magistrate. I do not know upon what grounds, but there was much grumbling all the voyage out. When we were in Bombay harbour, the rain-water was caught in sails and bucketed out into the casks; some of the water was the washings of the poop. At this time the boys and mates were painting the ship, and during the voyage, when the water was served out, it was quite yellow. When filling the water casks, I had to walk the poop one night for two hours naked, because I fell asleep while on duty. I was kept at work all day, and had to stop up of a night to catch rain-water, to save paying for water from the shore. When we left Bombay we had 5 pigs, 8 sheep, 28 ducks, and 28 fowls, all of which were stowed in the long-boat." [The boy here mentioned the removal of the pigs, &c., into the forecastle.] "They stunk very bad," he continued; "the pigs slept upon the top of the meat casks; the meat was all kept there. One sheep died, which was given to us for a Christmas dinner, but we could not eat it. Another was to say killed, but if it had not been it would have died, and was made into a mess. Some would not eat it. I did. That was all the fresh food I had all the passage home, until we arrived in the Downs; yet we brought one pig home, the largest of the lot. When we passed the Cape of Good Hope we were within sight of land, but when we were off St. Helena we were so close to it that we could easily see all the objects on shore. The water was as smooth as the river Thames, and though one man and an apprentice were both very bad, and unable to do duty, no attempt was made to obtain assistance from the shore. Between St. Helena and England five persons died. I cannot give dates." [Another party stated that all the deaths occurred since the 19th of March.] "Sundays or week days were all alike to us. A few prayers were read by the master when a man was buried. As soon as a man was taken ill the salt provisions were no longer served out, and nothing extra was given. We all complained of hunger and thirst. The master would ask one or so occasionally how they were. He did not visit the sick daily. The mate gave us the medicine. The forecastle was not cleaned from the previous voyage, for the mud is at the bulkheads now, which got there when she upset in the river going out of St. Katherine's into dry dock. This you may see. When we left Bombay the crew consisted of master, two mates, carpenter, cook, ten foremast hands, and four boys; in all nineteen hands. When we arrived off Falmouth only seven, including the master and mates, were able to do duty, yet we did not take in any fresh hands until we arrived in the Downs, and then only about three hours before the steamer came alongside, at which time none of the foremast hands could stand. We arrived in the West India Docks on Sunday morning, the 7th of April, before daylight. I was confined to my bed. I could not move. I remained there all Sunday. I never saw the captain; I was told that he had been on board and had gone on shore again. No victuals was brought to me. The Custom-house officer kindly gave me two pieces of bread and some fresh beef. On Monday I got no food from the ship. One of the Custom-house officers, who works on shore in a small house, came on board and gave me some pudding and other provisions. I did not see the master that day, and in the evening I was removed from the ship to the dock gates in a truck, and from thence to my father's house in a cart. This is my first voyage to sea, and I do not want to go again. The master would not give me any of my wages to buy soap to wash with. I have only had a small piece (and this I took with me) all the voyage. There was no regular day for washing clothes, and no time was allowed for that purpose. We towed them overboard to cleanse them."

I now give the opinion of a gentleman who has for a long time observed and studied the condition of seamen, and who has the best possible opportunities for observation:—

"I have known the seamen in the port of London," he said, "for twenty years, and am satisfied that there is a great improvement in their character since I first knew them. They are less drunken, I am sure of that—*much* less. Many of them have now a pride in keeping a good character, and twenty years ago they thought nothing about keeping a character at all; in fact, a character was hardly ever asked for. They swear less than when I first knew them, and there are far fewer blackguards among them. They are better educated too. Very few of them but what can read and write, and some of them to my knowledge write very good and entertaining letters from foreign ports. They don't fling their money about as they used to do— that's principally confined now-a-days to the stage-seamen. I have often known and heard of seamen who were inclined to fling their money about them foolishly, checked by their shipmates, and even their money or watches taken from them by their friends, to be restored to them when sober. A seaman, when doubtful of his power to withstand temptation, will oft enough leave his money or watch in the hands of some trusty person. There is not near so much marrying of many wives as there used to be. At one time a seaman would marry wives in different ports, and in London here would make a grand hackney-coach concern of it. Now seamen's marriages are as private as any landsman's. They may, perhaps, be still the same men as regards spending money on the women of the town—if the women may be called so, as they importune none but sailors. I am of opinion that, for the further improvement of seamen generally, the improvement of their officers on board merchant ships is most decidedly necessary. The common ignorance of masters and mates causes the loss of many a ship, and the drowning of many a fine fellow. Seamen will readily enough find out their officer's ignorance, and they will say one among another, 'He doesn't know where he's going; we must tell him.' Nothing causes greater dissatisfaction—nothing, as a natural consequence, tends more to introduce bad discipline—and so nothing can very well be worse. A drunken master is about as bad as an ignorant one. He will blackguard his men in the lowest terms—I am sorry to say there are many of that sort—and his men will blackguard back again, and will say, 'He's drunk, and doesn't know what he's talking about—who cares?' So, again, the want of discipline is bad and full of danger. I knew a captain who lost his life in the Bay of Honduras through drunkenness; indeed, he was never sober. He would go ashore in a small Spanish schooner, and though the mate and his seamen told him that she could never pass the bar—the sea runs very heavy there—the Spaniard was foolish and the captain was drunk, and they ventured, and the schooner was capsized, and they were all drowned. I think that the institution of a shipping-office for the engagement and payment of the seamen (as proposed by the bill now before the House) will work well. It will work well, in my opinion, for good seamen, in this way:—A captain will have the shipping of his own men, and good men will be preferred. That will be of advantage another way. When good seamen are sought after, more men will aim at the character of good seamen. Men, too, are generally better satisfied at being shipped by the captain than by a shipping-master. I think that when men are shipped from Sailors' Homes, a Government officer, acting quite independently of the establishment, should be present to see that the shipping is strictly according to the regulations, so that all men may be treated alike, and under one impartial system. It is of great importance, that all the seamen should be convinced of this. I hear now so many complaints of the treatment of the men at the Home, as regards turning them out when penniless and such like, that I think men would feel an unpleasantness if they thought the Sailors' Home, or any similar institution, had any exclusive privilege with the shipping of men, such as I think the proposed Act contemplates. I think a shipping-office would also be advantageous to the shipowner, as the captain would get good men, and the navigation of the ship would be better; as it is, a captain gets often enough a lot of worthless men foisted on to him. The superintendent of a shipping-office, too, might be very useful as an umpire between captain and men. In nine cases out of ten a dispute between master and men, when the owners are fairly disposed, might be decided by a party on whose disinterestedness both could depend—and so delays, and law expenses, and bad feeling caused thereby would be avoided. Of the necessity of allowing a deceased seaman's representatives to become possessed of what might be due to him at the time of his death there can be no doubt whatever." [My informant then expressed a similar opinion, as to advance notes, to what was stated at the meeting of the boarding-house masters.] "I consider," he continued, "the 53d clause of the proposed bill will act as badly for the seaman as for his boarding-master. The man, through its working, may be turned into the street, and the boarding-master may be cheated enormously." [The opinion given at the meeting of the boarding-masters was again confirmed by my present informant.] "It is now a great grievance that sailors may be kept ashore for an indefinite term—even longer than three weeks I have known it—after the signing of the articles, and for all that time they receive no wages, and must run into debt nine cases out of ten—unless, indeed, they prefer starving, and can stand it a bit. Why, I have known men turned out of the Sailors' Home, after they had actually signed articles and were waiting for their ship, because their money wouldn't spin out to let them wait long enough. I find it now proposed to limit such waiting, unpaid, to four days, which I consider a just and necessary change. As to characters and discharges, I have known men—and I have known it done five or six times in a day—one man lives by it—write characters for seamen, and discharges as well. I have known a character or a discharge written in a public-house for a pint of beer, or even for a penny. The seamen ask one another, 'Do you want a character or a discharge? I know a man will do it.' Hundreds of such documents have been so made to my knowledge. The man 'doing' the discharges, &c., knows all the ships' and captains' names—indeed I know a broken-down captain who now carries on the 'discharge' and 'character' trade. A shipping-office will very properly ruin these 'character' men's trade. An ensurement of more room in the men's berths on board ship will be a great good, as it must tend to health and decency, and bad accommodation makes even the decenter sort of men desert. The berths ought certainly to be kept dry by the better caulking of the deck. Many a forecastle now is like a shower bath, or a cold bath in winter, or some sort of bath just when it's not wanted. This bad accommodation causes sleeplessness, and the want of needful rest makes men dissatisfied and surly, and is a great incentive to their running away. I have given some attention lately to the Merchant Seamen's Fund. I have often heard sailors say, 'Why are we to pay 1s. a month to the Merchant Seamen's Fund; we never get any good from it, and now we hear that we may be called upon to pay 1s. 6d. a month instead of 1s.' I have said to them, 'So you will have to pay 1s. 6d.; and all the better for you, as by that payment you will be entitled to an extra pension in old age or infirmity—and a very good arrangement too.' As the Merchant Seamen's Fund is now conducted, it seems to me very bad. In some ports the pensioners receive 7s. or 8s. a month, in others only 1s. 6d. or 2s., a month—recollect that's as low as 4½d. a week, or something better than a halfpenny a day. In many cases the money due by law to the Merchant Seamen's Fund never reaches the men, especially in the coasting trade. A coaster sends in one muster-roll, as to the number of his men and of his voyages, to the Custom-house, and another to the Merchant Seamen's Fund, which is quite different from that furnished to the Custom-house. It shows fewer men and fewer voyages; so that the Fund may be bilked, and the shipowner pocket the difference. An experienced gentleman, on whose information I can rely, told me that these coasters paid only two-thirds of what was legally due from them. As to allotment or half-pay notes, they are often now made the means of robbing the seamen. An allotment note is quite different from an advance note. The allotment note is made payable at the owner's, or his agent's, commencing generally two months after date. It is intended to insure an allowance to a sailor's wife, mother, or any relative during a voyage, and the wrong done is often this—When the ship gets to sea and an application is made for payment of the note, the answer may be 'We can pay no money' (or 'no more money' as the case may be) 'for there's been a disturbance on board the ship, and there'll be no wages due to the man.' Very likely there has been no disturbance at all; but this is a trick shifty owners resort to—an attempt to save their money. If a man returns, say from a two years' voyage, some owners will pay his wages, deducting allotment note payments, as if discharged by them, though they may not have paid a penny. Besides, the stoppage on any plea drives, or may drive, a man's wife to the parish or worse. While a seaman is away, his wife, or any holder of the allotment note, has no remedy. If the man returns he may have a remedy, if he knows it, or is told of it, but just conceive what mischief may have been done in the meantime."

I shall conclude my present letter with the annexed table of the crimes committed by sailors during the last ten years. This table has been made out from the metropolitan police returns, and shows the number of sailors taken into custody for different offences in the years below cited. The last column but one gives the total number of offences committed from 1839 to 1848; and the last column of all shows the yearly average of the different kinds of offences committed by seamen in the Port of London. How many of the crimes indicated below are the result of the iniquities practised upon sailors by crimps, &c., I leave others to decide.

	1840.	1841.	1842.	1843.	1844.	1845.	1846.	1847.	1848.	1849.	Total for 10 Years.	Average per year, for 10 yrs.
Murder	1	3	4	1	1	1	…	…	1	…	12	1·2
Shooting at, stabbing, administering poison, &c.	12	…	6	…	3	…	3	…	…	3	27	2·7
Cutting and wounding with intent, &c.	5	12	4	1	10	2	8	8	7	7	64	6·4
Manslaughter	1	2	1	1	1	…	1	…	…	…	7	·7
Sodomy	…	…	1	1	3	…	…	1	…	4	10	1·0
,, Assaults with intent to commit, &c.	…	…	1	1	…	…	…	1	…	1	4	·4
,, Extorting money under threats, &c.	1	2	2	…	…	…	…	…	…	…	5	·5
Rape	…	…	…	…	…	1	1	4	1	…	6	·6
,, Assaults with intent to commit, &c.	…	1	1	…	2	2	…	…	1	1	8	·8
Bestiality	…	…	…	…	1	…	…	…	1	1	3	·3
Bigamy	…	…	2	…	…	2	…	1	1	1	7	·7
Assaults, common	22	106	92	79	171	167	121	157	125	215	1,255	125·5
,, on police	19	21	17	30	63	78	66	45	51	89	479	47·9
Attempting to rescue from custody	3	2	4	16	6	2	2	5	5	5	50	5·0
Obstructing police constables on duty	4	6	3	4	3	5	2	4	3	2	36	3·6
Total of offences against the person	68	155	138	134	264	260	204	226	195	329	1,973	197·3

	1840.	1841.	1842.	1843.	1844.	1845.	1846.	1847.	1848.	1849.	Total.	Average.
Burglary	1		1	3	3	2	3	4	5	2	24	2·4
Breaking into dwelling-house and stealing	1			6	2	2	2		7		20	2·0
,, into shops, warehouses, counting-houses, &c.		1				2					3	·3
Robbery			1	1	4		1	2	4		13	1·3
Assaults with intent to rob		1		1							2	·2
Total of offences against property, committed with violence	2	2	2	11	9	6	6	6	16	2	62	6·2
Larceny in a dwelling-house to the value of 5l.		1		3	10	2	3	2	3	5	29	2·9
,, in a dwelling-house			7	1	4	8	6	3	5	3	37	3·7
,, from the person	4		6	1	10	15	8	13	17	23	97	9·7
,, by servants			1				8	1	4	13	27	2·7
,, from letters containing Bank-notes						1					1	·1
,, simple	63	33	84	53	144	151	136	205	195	179	1,243	124·3
Misdemeanour with intent to steal	26	14	9	5	19	12	35	23	12	9	164	16·4
Embezzlement					1			1		2	4	·4
Receiving stolen goods						1		3	4	7	15	1·5
Frauds	3	5	17	6	17	13	30	22	20	15	148	14·8
Conspiracy with intent to defraud					1	5		1	1		8	·8
Dog stealing											1	·1

	1840.	1841.	1842.	1843.	1844.	1845.	1846.	1847.	1848.	1849.	Total.	Average.
Illegally pawning	...	...	...	...	1	1	1	...	4	5	12	1·2
Unlawful possession of goods	31	19	8	3	35	21	60	44	79	72	372	37·2
Total of offences against property, committed without violence	127	72	133	72	242	229	287	319	344	333	2,158	215·8
Arson	...	...	1	...	...	1	...	...	...	...	2	·2
Trespasses, malicious	...	1	...	...	...	2	...	...	...	...	3	·3
Wilful damage	32	36	52	48	98	63	51	53	40	67	540	54·0
Total of malicious offences against property	32	37	53	48	98	66	51	53	40	67	545	54·5
Forging and uttering forged instruments	1	1	1	...	2	2	3	3	6	...	19	1·9
Coin (counterfeit), putting off, uttering, &c.	5	3	1	2	7	4	8	8	20	14	72	7·2
Total of forgery and offences against the currency	6	4	2	2	9	6	11	11	26	14	91	9·1
Being at large under sentence of transportation	...	1	...	...	...	...	...	...	...	...	1	·1
Apprentices, runaway	53	35	54	45	46	41	27	21	25	41	388	38·8
Attempting to commit suicide	...	1	...	...	6	3	3	1	1	7	22	2·2
Cruelty to animals	...	...	...	...	1	...	...	2	3	2	8	·8
Deserting their families	...	...	...	...	4	...	2	1	...	...	8	·8
Deserters	...	...	1	...	2	...	1	9	16	24	52	5·2
Disorderly characters	372	205	220	194	120	37	41	54	69	161	1,473	147·3

	1840.	1841.	1842.	1843.	1844.	1845.	1846.	1847.	1848.	1849.	Total.	Average.
Drunk and disorderly ditto	··	··	··	··	194	294	378	194	119	398	1,577	157·7
Drunkenness	856	746	639	584	444	550	618	538	310	443	5,728	572·8
Furious driving	··	··	··	··	1	··	··	··	··	··	1	·1
Gambling	··	··	··	··	1	··	··	··	3	3	7	·7
Hawking without license	··	··	··	1	1	1	··	··	··	··	3	·3
Illicit distillation	1	··	··	··	··	··	··	··	··	··	1	·1
Indecently exposing the person	··	··	··	3	4	4	··	1	2	3	17	1·7
Nuisances	··	··	··	··	1	··	6	11	6	5	29	2·9
Offences under Hackney Crrge. Act	··	··	··	··	··	··	1	··	··	··	1	·1
" Metropolitan Police Act, sewers, &c.	3	··	··	··	··	2	··	··	··	··	5	·5
Poaching	··	··	··	··	1	··	··	1	··	··	2	·2
Reputed thieves	··	2	1	2	4	3	3	6	11	12	44	4·4
Smuggling	89	76	92	78	112	145	244	282	229	230	1,577	157·7
Suspicious characters	23	11	8	3	22	25	23	26	57	67	265	26·5
Unlawful assemblages	1	··	··	··	··	··	··	··	··	··	1	·1
Vagrants	48	71	89	64	110	116	130	89	195	133	1,045	104·5
Mutiny	··	··	14	··	2	16	5	1	··	4	42	4·2
Offences under Registered Seamen's Act	··	··	··	··	··	··	4	··	··	2	6	·6
Ditto, Railway Act	··	··	··	··	··	··	··	1	1	··	2	·2
Sending threatening letter	··	··	··	1	··	··	··	··	··	··	1	·1
Juvenile Offenders Act	··	··	··	··	··	··	··	··	2	··	2	·2
Total of other offences not included in the above classes	··	··	··	··	··	··	··	··	··	··		
	1,446	1,149	1,118	972	1,076	1,238	1,485	1,240	1,049	1,535	12,308	1,230·8

The general summary of the above table is as follows:—

Offences.	Total offences for sailors in 10 years.	Average per year for 10 yrs for sailors.	Number of sailors to one offender.	Number of population to one offender.
Offences against the person ...	1,973	197.3	1 in 38	1 in 226
Offences against property, committed with violence	62	6.2	„ 1,276	„ 7,328
Offences against property, committed without violence	2,158	215.8	„ 35	„ 140
Malicious offences against property	545	54.5	„ 141	„ 720
Forgery and offences against the currency	91	9.1	„ 850	„ 2,090
Other offences not included in the above classes	12,308	1,230.8	„ 6	„ 52
Total	17,137	1,713.7	„ 4	„ 30

The crimes for which the sailors belonging to the Port of London are particularly distinguished, are given below.

Offences.	Number of Sailors to one Offender.	Number of Population to one Offender.
Drunk and disorderly	1 in 10	1 in 122
Assaults	„ 44	„ 250
Smuggling	„ 48	„ 7,580
Disorderly characters	„ 52	„ 261
Simple larceny	„ 61	„ 324
Vagrancy	„ 73	„ 412
Wilful damage	„ 141	„ 729
Runaway apprentices	„ 196	„ 1,552
Unlawful possession of goods ...	„ 206	„ 835
Suspicious characters	„ 294	„ 610
Misdemeanors with intent to steal	„ 478	„ 1,254
Fraud	„ 510	„ 5,411
Uttering counterfeit coin	„ 1,093	„ 2,204
Murder	„ 7,657	„ 94,576

Hence it appears that drunkenness and disorderly conduct are vices to which sailors are peculiarly addicted. The next offence for which they are more particularly distinguished is that of assault; then comes smuggling; if the number of smugglers amongst the sailors be compared with the amount in the population, we shall find that they exceed the average in this case to a far greater extent than in any other.

This is easily accounted for by the nature of their occupation affording to them a facility for the commission of it.

As regards simple larceny, it will be seen that the number of sailors taken into custody for this offence, is one in every 61. This is considerably above the average, which is no more than one in 324 of the whole metropolitan population. In the more flagrant crime of murder they rank almost as high, the average number of murderers among the sailors being one in 7,657; whereas the average for the whole population of London is only one in 94,576.

The Morning Chronicle, Thursday, May 2, 1850.

SAILORS' HOME, WELL-STREET, LONDON DOCKS.

————◆————

To THE EDITOR of THE MORNING CHRONICLE.

SIR—The directors having examined the statements made by your Special Correspondent, in his 48th Letter, published in *The Morning Chronicle* of the 19th instant, referring to the Sailors' Home, Well-street, London Docks, deem it their duty to lay before the public some observations on the disparaging remarks he has thought proper to make respecting that institution. Previous to their so doing, they think it right to state that your Correspondent, with his companion, has during the last two or three weeks paid several visits to the Sailors' Home, where every opportunity was given them of instituting the fullest inquiry into all the details of the establishment: the cashbooks, ledgers, and accounts were examined by them, and the fullest explanations afforded; copies of statistics were prepared for them, and they had also the opportunity of conversing with the boarders privately. The result of their inquiries was published in *The Morning Chronicle* of the 11th of April last (Letter 47). Of that report the directors do not complain, for though some of the statements are inaccurate, still it is generally correct, and appears to be written in a spirit of truth and justice.

Your Correspondent commences his 48th Letter with a description of Mr. Green's Sailors' Home, in the East India-road, and speaks in commendable language of that useful establishment, to the value and excellence of which the directors cheerfully bear their testimony. It was built by the late Mr. Green, with the full concurrence of their honoured colleague, the late Captain Elliot, who was consulted on the subject, and the rules and regulations of the "Home" in Well-street were introduced by Mr. Green into his own institution. Your Correspondent states the following to be the number of men received into Mr. Green's "Home":—

1846	392	men
1847	383	"
1848	406	"
1849	487	"

and then he expresses his belief (but of this he has no proof) that the amount paid to the superintendent and his assistants is scarcely a tithe of the sum annually expended in salaries at the "Home" in Well-street. We therefore, by way of comparison, give the number of boarders received into the Sailors' Home, Well-street, during the same period:—

1846	3,760 boarders
1847	4,567 „
1848	4,932 „
1849	4,633 „

A glance at these figures will at once prove that the institution in Well-street receives ten times as many boarders as Mr. Green's "Home," and that, therefore, a much larger number of officers and servants is absolutely required to carry on the work. It should also be remembered that Mr. Green's "Home" is a private establishment, where he only receives such men as his captains recommend to that privilege; while, on the contrary, the Sailors' Home in Well-street is a public institution, where all men returning from sea are received without any reference to character or previous conduct, the great object the founders had in view having been to benefit all the sailors of the port of London. At Mr. Green's, his men are paid off from and are re-shipped in his own vessels, so that no pecuniary loss can possibly be sustained; whereas in Well-street, it is necessary to employ agents to attend the various pay tables—to get the men shipped—and, when possible, to board the ships on arrival and assist in bringing the men to the institution. The cashing and receiving the advance notes—the collection of the apprentices' bills for board, &c., from their various captains and owners—the Post-office orders—the remittances to the country, to benefit men who are going home—an extensive correspondence; all these transactions require an amount of agency which can be understood by those only who are conversant with the accounts which are kept at the Sailors' Home, a department, perhaps, as well and correctly managed as any in the metropolis. The sum of 25,960*l.* belonging to the boarders, a large portion of it in small sums, passed through the institution during the last year. But your Correspondent complains that 4,500 boarders pay 14s. a week at Well-street, while 12s. is the charge at Mr. Green's. In the first place, the statement is not correct that all the boarders pay 14s.; the apprentices—one-fifth of the number—pay only 10s. 6d., while the lads, or ordinary seamen, pay 12s. At Mr. Green's bad debts are not likely to occur, while in Well-street they occur frequently. Some men receive their 1*l.* advance and a week or ten days' board, and never pay a farthing. There are unworthy characters in all walks of life, though we believe among sailors they are less in number than in many other classes.

Your Correspondent is made the vehicle of a statement which is untrue, that "no man is allowed to remain at the Sailors' Home when his funds are exhausted." The directors are anxious that seamen should become provident men, and not waste their ample pecuniary resources in riot and debauchery; they, therefore, by every means in their power, urge them to place their money in the savings bank for their own use and benefit, or else to assist their families, should they be in want of such assistance; and to insure such results they are always advised to ship before they have spent their wages. But when no ships are to be obtained, it has frequently happened that men remain at the "Home" a long time after their resources have been expended, and during the last twelve months a considerable number have left the institution more or less in debt; but the directors feel confident that on their return these men will cheerfully repay the institution the sums now standing against their names. But it appears your Correspondent has met with some cases of men, who, being debtors to the "Home," have been urged by the officers, instead of increasing their debt, to go to the "Destitute Sailors' Asylum," a most comfortable institution in Well-street, for the express benefit of seamen who are in distress from any cause, and from whence they are shipped whenever opportunity offers. As the epithet "straw-yard," "straw-house," &c., is applied to the asylum in several parts of your Correspondent's letter, the directors deem it their duty to give the following extract from the annual report of 1848; and they would respectfully invite the public to visit the Destitute Sailors' Asylum, and form their own opinion as to the value and usefulness of that institution, in which every reasonable comfort is provided for them:—

"In order to form an adequate idea of the amount of good already conferred on this once neglected class of men, it may be well to tell you of the daily routine of duty at the asylum. In the evening, when you are enjoying the tranquil comforts of home, the wandering sailor rings the bell at the Asylum: he has not been long on shore; but during that short interval, sin and riot, or sickness, or calamity have reduced him to abject want. He is admitted within the house; as is too often the case, his person is cleansed from outward defilement; plain and clean clothes are put on him; a plain frugal meal is given him. This is succeeded by the hour of instruction and prayer. Words of eternal life fall with peculiar freshness and beauty on the mind too long accustomed to blasphemy and ribaldry; he listens, and when the instruction is over, he unites in the hymn and prayer which follow. He retires to his hammock. At an early hour he is roused from sleep, and, by a wise provision, which blends discipline with comfort, he is obliged to leave his hammock, and join with the others in the early meal, and in morning prayer. He is then sent out to look for a ship, and pains are taken to make his search successful, and to procure him a berth on board some sea-going vessel."

Your Correspondent also alludes to certain tailors, who are allowed the privilege of entering the Sailors' Home, for the purpose of supplying the men with clothes. The directors, in this, as in all their other arrangements, have only had the benefit of the sailor in view, their object being to insure to them clothes of good quality on the most reasonable terms; and so far from the seamen suffering from this system, the directors feel confident they are greatly benefited, by being enabled to deal with parties who are to some extent amenable to their authority, and whose proceedings may be made the subject of investigation. But your Correspondent has been grossly misinformed with reference to these transactions, as the bill of *any tailor* to whom the men choose to go is *readily* paid by the cashier. The importance of using every exertion to protect the sailor from the machinations of unprincipled dealers in slops cannot be better illustrated than by an extract from the minute book of the Sailors' Home, dated Sept. 18, 1848.

"The secretary brought to the notice of the board a case of fraud practised by ——, a slopseller, living at ——, who, having received from an old boarder, G. F. ——, a 20*l.* bank note, in payment for some clothes, afterwards declared that it was only a 5*l.* note he had received. The secretary having obtained a summons for him to appear at the police-court, he there admitted that he had received 20*l.*, and then paid the sailor the balance due to him."

Your Correspondent also alludes to the steps taken by the tailors, or their assistants, when the ships arrive, to obtain custom, and therefore to induce the men to board at the Sailors' Home. The directors are not aware of any evil consequences that can arise to seamen from such a course; they feel confident that sailors are greatly benefited by becoming inmates of the Sailors' Home, in preference to the abodes of iniquity into which they are too often inveigled by the crimps.

With reference to the remarks in your Correspondent's letter respecting the disposal of clothes left behind by the boarders, the directors introduce a copy of the rules, which, after ten years' experience, have been found to work exceedingly well, and no case has occurred during that period in which a sailor has sustained any inconvenience by these regulations; for whenever an application has been made, requesting the clothes to be kept longer than two years, it has always been complied with:—

"If a man, on quitting the institution, after the settlement of his accounts, wishes to deposit any property in charge of the institution, he is carefully to lock or lash it up, place his name and number on it, and give the superintendent the necessary information respecting it, when it will be placed in safe custody until his return.

"Should a man, on quitting the institution, leave any property in his cabin, or in the hands of the washerman, without informing the superintendent, the institution cannot be answerable for it, and it will be sold at the expiration of two years, and the money will be carried to an account for 'unclaimed property.'

"If a boarder goes away in debt to the institution, leaving property, it will be sold after the expiration of two years in liquidation of the debt."

It appears that your Correspondent has been informed that some persons in the employ of the Sailors' Home are in the habit of selling watches or clothes to the boarders. The directors most emphatically assert that they believe this charge to be false and malicious, and that the following regulations, which are publicly exhibited in the institution, are strictly adhered to:—

"All private money transactions with the officers, and all money dealings in any way with the servants, is strictly prohibited.

"The boarders are hereby informed that no agent or other person belonging to the Sailors' Home is permitted to receive any gratuity for shipping them, attending with them at the pay-table to receive their wages, or for any other assistance rendered to them while living at the institution.

"The boarders are hereby informed that all the servants of the Sailors' Home are strictly forbidden to solicit any money or other gratuity from them, and they are requested, should any such application be made, to report it immediately to the superintendent."

The Sailors' Home has been in operation fifteen years, and the directors have found it necessary on some occasions in the course of that period to remove persons who have been connected with the institution, and to prevent others from entering it for various improper acts. If your Correspondent has obtained any of his information from such parties, or alludes to any such transactions, it would have been more just and honourable for him to have stated it in his letter. The directors have reason to believe that many of his statements emanate from such a source.

Your Correspondent does not appear to be aware that seamen who require medical aid are gratuitously received on board the Dreadnought, lying off Deptford; and that for shipwrecked men there is a society in London ready and willing to afford prompt assistance. In all cases the Sailors' Home makes these benefits known to seamen, and the directors feel assured that the sick and the shipwrecked men to whom he refers were informed of those useful charities, and recommended to apply to them for relief. Your Correspondent has also omitted any mention of St. Paul's Church for seamen, with its 800 free seats, which communicates with the Sailors' Home, and must have been seen by him when he visited the institution.

With reference to the remarks of your Correspondent respecting the salaries and wages, the directors think it right to state that the following officers and servants compose the staff of the establishment, and that many of their duties are of a very onerous and responsible character, the accounts voluminous, and the labour great. It sometimes happens that 300 boarders are at one time in the "Home," and to insure order and regularity an efficient superintendence is necessary. The directors feel quite assured that 1,071*l.* per annum cannot be considered too large a remuneration for such services.

Secretary, cashier, accountant, superintendent, schoolmaster, examiner of accounts, two agents, cook, storekeeper, messenger, doorkeeper, night watchman, steward, porter, steward's mate, cook's mate, and six waiters.

The directors have, in the above list, omitted all reference to the valuable and important services of the chaplain and the Scripture readers—their duties are of too important a character to be introduced into this discussion, for all will admit the necessity of imparting religious instruction to our seamen and their families.

In conclusion, it only appears necessary to remark that the Sailors' Home is an object of the constant personal attention of some portion of the board of directors, who feel a deep interest in an institution which they believe to be effecting much good for our seamen; and they rejoice at being enabled to state that since its opening, in 1835, 44,788 boarders have been received into the institution, of which number 12,656 were old boarders returning again and again to enjoy its comforts and share in its advantages. This must be considered the best proof of the estimation in which the Sailors' Home is held by seamen, and is in itself an *overwhelming refutation* of the charges brought against the establishment by the persons who supplied your Correspondent with a large portion of his information.

The directors have now only earnestly to request those who feel an interest in the sailor's welfare to visit the "Home," and judge for themselves how far the institution is deserving of public support and patronage.

I have the honour to be, sir, your obedient servant,

H. HOPE, Chairman, Rear-Admiral.
Sailors' Home, Well-street, April 26.

―――――

[The above letter requires little comment. It admits the touting of the tailors' runners, and—tacitly—allows the iniquities practised by that class of persons upon the sailor. It urges nothing against the dishonest advances of money made by the tailors belonging to the Sailors' Home, nor does it attempt to rebut the assertion that it is usual among the touters for that Institution to plant a seaman who arrives late at night upon a woman of the town, so that he may be secured for it until the morning. An attempt is made to justify, rather than to deny, the sale of the effects of those seamen whose clothes have been detained by the conductors of the Home after the funds of the men have been exhausted. The sole assertion that the Chairman ventures to gainsay is the statement that watches and other articles are sold to the men by the servants of the Institution. The directors, it is said, "believe this charge to be false and malicious," and they complain of me for not making known the sources whence I obtained my information. All I can say in answer is, I gave the fact as it came to me, *authenticated by persons of credit*, and that it is not my custom to publish either the names or standing of the persons furnishing me with information. Concerning the enormous sum of 1,200*l.*, expended annually in salaries and wages among the officers and servants of the Home, there is not a word said; nor is any attempt made to explain how it is that an institution, receiving annually as many as from 4,000 to 5,000 boarders, should require to be supported by charitable subscriptions and donations to the extent of 2,000*l.* per annum. If the respectable boarding-masters can feed and lodge the seamen at the same price as the Home, and pay rent besides, and still make a profit by the transaction, surely the conductors of the Sailors' Home, who have no rent to pay, and who have hundreds to supply where the boarding-masters have one, should be able to pay their way without calling upon the public to subscribe a couple of thousand pounds a year to make up the deficiency. If the sum charged by the directors for the board and lodging of the seamen is not sufficient to meet the expenses of that institution, then either the charges should be raised or the expenses lowered; but to carry on such an institution by charitable subscriptions appears to me to be trading upon false principles. Concerning the regulations at Green's Home, we are told that that institution was originally built upon the plan of the Sailors' Home in Well-street. All I have to say in answer is, that the Home in Well-street would do well now to adapt itself to Green's Home, the rules of which appear to me to be far more considerate to the comfort and welfare of the men.—*The Metropolitan Correspondent.*]

LABOUR AND THE POOR.

———◆———

THE METROPOLITAN DISTRICTS.

[FROM OUR SPECIAL CORRESPONDENT.]

LETTER LI.

In the present letter, which is the last that I shall devote to the Seamen of the Port of London, I shall give an account of the principal charitable institutions for sailors in the vicinity of the Metropolis.

Before proceeding, however, to treat of the several establishments that have been designed with the view of alleviating the ills to which seamen are especially liable, let us endeavour to arrive at some idea as to the number of lives annually lost by shipwreck. The Government Returns upon this subject, though by no means so full as could be wished, still enable us to form some rough notion of the result. The following table is copied from the Report on Shipwrecks:—

TABLE SHOWING THE EXTENT OF THE LOSS OF PROPERTY
AND LIVES AT SEA.

Year.	Number of vessels stranded or wrecked.	Number of vessels missing or lost.	Number of vessels of which the entire crews were drowned.	Number of persons drowned in each year by vessels known.
1816	343	19	15	945
1817	362	40	19	499
1818	409	30	15	256
Total	1,114	89	49	1,700
1833	595	56	38	572
1834	454	43	24	578
1835	524	30	19	564
Total	1,573	129	81	1,714

The returns since the year 1835 are less particular. The following table is copied from the Shipping Returns; in this, it will be seen, no account is given of the number of vessels missing, nor of the number of persons drowned:—

A RETURN OF VESSELS AND THEIR TONNAGE WRECKED, ETC., IN THE UNDER-MENTIONED YEARS (BELONGING TO THE UNITED KINGDOM).

Year.	Number of Sailing Vessels.	Tonnage.	Number of Steam Vessels.	Tonnage.	Total Vessels.	Total Tonnage.
1846	529	91,221	8	678	537	91,899
1847	533	95,590	4	1,037	537	96,627
1848	501	93,848	13	3,072	514	96,920
Total.	1,563	280,659	25	4,787	1,588	285,446

By referring to the preceding tables, we find that in the first period of three years (1816-18), the number of vessels wrecked was 1,114; in the second period of three years (1833-35), 1,573; and the third triennial period (1846-48), 1,588.

The number of vessels wrecked during the last period of three years is fifteen more than those wrecked in 1833-35. If, however, we take into consideration the increase in the number of vessels since that period, we shall find that the proportionate number of shipwrecks has diminished to a considerable extent.

Calculating the vessels wrecked and missing in the three periods above named to have been of the average value of £5,000 for each ship and cargo (this is the estimate given in the Report on Shipwrecks), the loss of property occasioned by these wrecks would amount in the first three years to £6,015,000, being an average of £2,005,000 per annum; in the second three years to £8,510,000, being an average of £2,836,666 per annum; and in the last three years assuming the number of ships missing to be 130 (which bears the same proportion to the number wrecked as those in 1833-1835), to £8,590,000, being an average of £2,863,333 per annum.

The number of ships of which the entire crews were drowned will be seen to have been in the first period 49, and in the second period 81—while for the third period there are no returns. Reckoning the average number of persons in each of the vessels of which the entire crews were lost to consist of twelve individuals, including officers, seamen, and passengers, it would appear that in the first three years the total number of persons drowned at sea was 2,288, or 763 per annum; in the second three years, the total number of persons drowned at sea was 2,682, or 894 per annum; and in the last three years—assuming the proportion between the vessels wrecked and lost to have been the same as in the previous three years—the total number of persons drowned at sea would be 2,707, or 902 per annum.

But these results do not embrace the whole extent of the loss of property and lives occasioned by shipwrecks, among the vessels which belong to the United Kingdom; for the returns include only the losses entered in Lloyd's books; whereas it is well known that many vessels and lives are lost by wreck or foundering at sea of which no entry is made at Lloyd's, and of which, as no record is kept, no return can be given.

The whole loss of property in British shipping, wrecked or foundered at sea, may therefore be assumed as amounting to nearly *three millions of pounds sterling per annum.* The value of this property, though covered by insurance to the parties immediately concerned, is not the less absolutely lost to the nation.

The annual loss of life occasioned by the wreck or foundering of British vessels at sea may, on the same grounds, be fairly estimated at not less than *one thousand souls in each year*—which loss is also attended with increased pecuniary burdens to the British public, on whom the support of many of the widows and orphans thus left destitute must ultimately fall.

From the foregoing calculations we arrive at the conclusion that the annual loss by shipwreck amongst the vessels belonging to the United Kingdom is, on an average, one vessel in every 42; and the annual loss of property engaged therein, £1 in every £42. The average number of sailors drowned amounts to one in every 203 persons engaged in navigation.

The principal causes of shipwreck which are susceptible of removal or diminution appear, from the Report of the Select Committee on Shipwrecks, to be the following:—

1. Defective construction of ships. 2. Inadequacy of equipment. 3. Imperfect state of repair. 4. Improper or excessive loading. 5. Inappropriateness of form. 6. Incompetency of masters and officers. 7. Drunkenness of officers and men. 8. Operation of marine insurance. 9. Want of harbours of refuge. 10. Imperfection of charts.

Concerning shipwrecked men's wages, I was informed that, in the case of a total wreck with all hands lost, the widows or personal representatives of the dead seamen cannot legally recover one farthing of the wages due from the owner; because a certificate of the seaman's having exerted himself properly up to the time of the wreck is required by law for the receipt of the wages, and there is no survivor to give such certificate. When a vessel is reported at Lloyd's as "not since heard of"—dates being given—it is concluded that the vessel is lost. *The insurances are paid; but the lost seamen's representatives have no remedy.* From the subject of shipwrecks to that of marine insurance the transition is easy and natural. I have been at some pains to obtain an account of the number of vessels, as well as of the value of marine property insured, but to no avail. There are no direct means of ascertaining either the one point or the other. The sole mode by which the information can be arrived at is through the duty paid to the Government upon the amount of the premiums. Subjoined is a statement of the gross sums received annually since 1839, by way of duty on Marine Insurance.

AN ACCOUNT OF THE GROSS RECEIPT OF THE REVENUE DERIVED FROM THE DUTY COLLECTED FROM THE MARINE INSURANCE.

Year.	England.			Scotland.			Great Britain.			Ireland.			United Kingdom.		
	£	s.	d.	£	s.	d.	£	s.	d.	£	s.	d.	£	s.	d.
1838-39	264,906	15	3	29,897	13	9	294,804	9	0	1,539	10	8	296,343	19	8
1839-40	269,623	6	9	32,001	10	0	301,624	16	9	1,326	15	9	302,951	12	6
1840-41	254,493	13	6	31,794	13	3	286,288	7	0	1,475	10	0	287,763	17	3
1841-42	224,072	5	6	28,626	11	6	252,698	17	0	1,638	6	3	254,337	3	3
1842-43	226,449	18	9	28,879	10	0	255,329	8	9	968	3	9	256,297	12	6
1843-44	174,492	0	9	18,663	17	9	193,155	18	6	1,632	2	3	194,788	0	9
1844-45	131,945	18	6	14,876	11	3	146,822	9	9	1,898	6	6	148,720	16	3
1845-46	132,121	12	6	17,064	19	0	149,186	11	6	2,355	0	3	151,531	11	9
1846-47	160,949	4	3	19,303	19	0	180,253	3	3	2,079	17	3	182,333	0	6
1847-48	149,661	8	6	14,090	9	0	163,751	17	6	1,667	10	6	165,419	8	0

It is difficult, from the above table, to arrive at any correct conclusion concerning the value of the property insured, as the premiums paid on the different classes of vessels and cargoes vary to a considerable extent, and the duty varies with the premiums. Thus the rate of insurance for some vessels is only 10s. per cent., and then the duty is as low as 3d. for every £100 insured. When the rate of insurance is 20s. per cent., the duty amounts to 6d.; for an insurance at the rate of 30s. per cent. the duty is 1s.; for 40s. per cent., 2s.; for 50s. per cent., 3s.; and for 60s. per cent., 4s. If, however, we take an average of the whole, and assume the entire amount of property at sea to have been insured at 30s. per cent., and the duty consequently to have been 1s. on every £100 insured, we shall find that in 1839 the total value of the vessels and cargoes insured amounted to the enormous sum of £592,688,000—very considerably more than half of the National Debt. In the year 1847-48 it will be seen that the duty on marine insurance amounted to only £165,419 8s., whereas in 1839-40 it was nearly twice that amount. According to the preceding supposition the value of the property insured in the first-named year would have been only £330,838,800. This decrease is the more extraordinary as the number of vessels, as well as the maritime commerce of the country, had increased considerably since 1840. I am informed, however, that now colliers very rarely insure; while coasters insure only at intervals, in winter or stormy weather, and seldom or never when the weather is settled.

The principal institutions for the relief of the seamen belonging to the mercantile marine, are—1, the Merchant Seamen's Fund; 2, the Asylum for Destitute Sailors; and 3, the Dreadnought Hospital for Seamen of all Nations.

First, of the Fund:—

In the course of my present inquiry I heard many complaints from the seamen concerning the *Merchant Seamen's Fund.* Many of the men seemed to know nothing about it, beyond the fact of 1s. a month being deducted from their wages towards it. (The masters in the merchant service pay 2s. a month, and are entitled to twice the amount of pension granted to the seamen.) The Fund dates its existence from the year 1747, the 20 Geo. II., c. 82, incorporated "the President and Governors for the relief and support of sick, maimed, and disabled seamen, and of the widows and children of such as shall be killed, slain, or drowned in the merchant service." But widows whose husbands were neither killed, slain, nor drowned, in the service, are now entitled to pensions, *provided their husbands have contributed to the fund for 21 years.* The provisions of the act of Geo. II. are mainly in force still; but the collection and appropriation of the funds have been regulated, and, in some respects, materially altered, by the 4 and 5 Wm. IV., c. 52. Previously to the passing of the last-mentioned act (in 1834) the payment of the sailors to the fund was 6d. a month; but no additional impost is now levied on them, as they previously paid 6d. a month to Greenwich Hospital—a charge which was then abolished, or, rather, (virtually) transferred to the Merchant Seamen's Fund—£20,000 in lieu being charged on the Consolidated Fund as compensation to the Hospital. The same act also abolished the payment to the Fund by apprentices, they having previously paid at the same rate as adult seamen. The average payment of each seaman is computed at 9s. a year, and the yearly amount realised throughout the country was assumed—no full and precise returns for the whole kingdom being given—before a Select Parliamentary Committee in 1844, to be in round numbers £50,000. The payment is collected wherever the vessel unloads, and until it has been made a certificate of clearance is not granted. The corporation of the President and Governors of the Merchant Seamen's Fund comprises above one hundred merchants and shipowners. The act does not require any precise number. A committee of the body meets every fortnight. In addition to the port of London there are the following thirty-nine out-ports under the immediate management of the London board or corporation:—Aberystwith, Aldborough, Beaumaris, Bridport and Lyme, Boness, Baltimore, Carnarvon, Chester, Chichester, Cowes, Chepstow, Deal, Dublin, Dundalk, Faversham, Fleetwood-on-Wyre, Gloucester, Gweek, Galway, Grangemouth, Harwich, Inverness, Ipswich, Kirkcudbright, Kirkaldy, Leigh, Llanelly, Newry, Rochester, Ross, Ramsgate, Scilly, Sligo, Stornoway, Stranraer, Woodbridge, Waterford, Wick and Thurso, and Wigtown.

The greatest number of recipients among the men in the Port of London were, according to the Parliamentary return, from 60 to 64 years of age, the number being 226; the smallest number were from 20 to 26, being only 12; the greatest number of widows in receipt of pensions were from 50 to 56 years old, numbering 310; of widows whose age was from 20 to 26, there were 28; of the men, there were 44 pensioners who were 80 and upwards; of the widows of the same

years, there were 24. The following was the average yearly rate paid
in London in 1843:—

1,269 men, each £4   8   0
1,805 widows, do. 2 11   5
1,378 children, do.   1   3   7

At the out-ports enumerated the average was lower.

341 men £4   4   5
741 widows 2 10   4
1,109 children   1   2   3

The fund, in other out-ports, is managed by local trustees. In
his evidence before the committee, Lieut. Brown, R.N., the registrar
of seamen, expressed an opinion that these trifling pensions were of
little value to the seamen. If a seaman became disabled, and had
to accept parish relief, he was in no better situation than if he had
never contributed to the fund. Seven hundred seamen, in 1847, were
chargeable to the poor-rate. If however (Lieutenant Brown stated)
compulsory payments from the seamen brought them pensions of not
less than 10d. a day, such a circumstance would be a strong check
against desertion, and would make the men anxious to preserve their
character and the evidence of their identity—an anxiety not called
into existence by the prospect of £4 a year.

The average age of the male pensioners on the fund is 55; the rate
of pension for superannuation, which is from 55 to 60 years of age, is
£4 a year in London; the loss of a limb ensures £5 a year; blindness,
£7; and the loss of both arms, £7. No man who has not contributed
five years to the fund is entitled to assistance from it. Many Swedes
and Danes are pensioners.

The inequality of the pensions is a fertile source of dissatisfaction.
The amount is often dependent upon local arrangements, and upon
the state of the fund. According to a return laid before Parliament the
highest annual pensions awarded to mariners are £13 17s. 6d. in Cork,
£13 in Belfast, £13 in Liverpool, £12 10s. in Hull, £12 in Aberdeen,
£10 in Bristol; while the highest rate at Ulverston and at Weymouth
is 10s. The seaman is entitled to a pension from the fund at the port
from which he has sailed for the longest period during the last five
years; and thus he may have been contributing to the Liverpool fund,
and yet from accident, or from circumstances beyond his control, he
may only become entitled to a pension from Ulverston.

The subjoined table of the annual Receipts and Expenditure of the Fund is everyway deserving of attention:—

RECEIPTS.

	1838. £ s. d.	1839. £ s. d.	1840. £ s. d.	1841. £ s. d.	1842. £ s. d.	1843. £ s. d.	1849. £ s. d.
Duties received	9,523 19 3	10,696 11 9	10,076 7 0	10,058 17 6	8,945 4 7	10,253 18 0	10,454 11 7
Dead Men's wages	122 6 7	232 6 0	222 16 3	426 1 11	531 16 2	596 18 2	620 7 1
Benefactions	3 0 0	915 5 0	10 0 0	128 15 5	5 8 3	384 2 3	... 0 0
Interest on capital	1,782 0 0	1,905 0 0	1,980 0 0	2,010 0 0	2,013 4 2	2,031 4 6	1,404 0 0
Total	11,431 5 10	13,748 18 6	12,229 3 3	12,623 14 10	11,495 13 2	13,266 2 11	12,478 18 8

EXPENDITURE.

	1838. £ s. d.	1839. £ s. d.	1840. £ s. d.	1841. £ s. d.	1842. £ s. d.	1843. £ s. d.	1849. £ s. d.
Pensions and gratuities	8,407 19 0	9,091 15 0	10,021 13 6	10,599 8 0	11,874 15 0	12,842 7 4	13,843 14 0
Expenses of management	1,670 0 10	1,444 17 10	1,432 11 4	1,451 8 2	1,449 0 8	1,427 16 5	1,713 13 6
Other unenumerated expenses	...	...	1,498 19 0	...	...	...	487 18 3
Total	10,077 19 10	10,536 12 10	12,953 3 10	12,050 16 2	13,173 15 8	14,270 3 8	16,045 5 9

The salaries included in the expenses of management for each of the years 1841-2-3, amounted to £924 12s.

It will be seen that in the year 1842 the expenditure exceeded the receipts by £1,678 2s. 6d.; in 1843 the outgoings were £1,004 0s. 9d. more than the incomings; while in 1849 the sums paid were as much as £3,566 7s. 1d. beyond those received. It will therefore surprise no one who is at all acquainted with the defective and unscientific data on which annuities were calculated until of late years, to learn that Messrs. Finlayson and Ansell, the eminent actuaries, have shown that the Fund cannot continue to meet the demands upon it; and this conviction induced the Commissioners to recommend "that the required addition to the Merchant Seamen's Fund be raised by the imposition of a tonnage duty of 1s. a ton by the year, upon all vessels belonging to the United Kingdom entering or clearing out, such duty being imposed upon the owners, and the owners being permitted, in part reimbursement of this charge, to appropriate to their own use the dues now payable by seamen and masters to the fund." The allowance to widows and orphans is disproportionately great:—"From the 31st December, 1837," say the Commissioners, "to the 31st December, 1846, the pensions increased from £28,912 to £55,257, the present value of these pensions having been, at the first of these dates, £264,858; at the latter date, £506,586; while, after deducting in each case from these sums the amount of invested capital, the balance against the fund was at the former date, £131,833; and at the latter date, £333,826." Of the £506,586 no less than £354,547 was for pensions to widows and children.

The matter is now before Parliament. The principal provisions of the proposed measure, in order to relieve the fund from its embarrassments, are that 1s. 6d., instead of 1s. per month, be paid by each seaman, and twice that sum by masters; and that pensions be granted of not less than £9 a year to seamen, and £18 to masters. These pensions have been calculated on the scientific data of assurance companies; while Government will give £30,000, so that the fund may be placed on a durable and equitable footing.

Concerning the *Pensions given by the Fund*, I received the following statement from an old sailor, who had contributed his shilling per month to it for thirty-five years, and who is now in the receipt of the munificent pension of 9s. a quarter:—"I am a Swede, but I have been at sea 35 years, in different services, in the English trade; to the West Indies, North America, Hamburg, and North Shields and other coasting voyages. For that time I have paid 1s. a month, and I'm now 63 years old. That is, I didn't pay it, but my captain always stopped it out of my wages. I paid it without asking what it was about, because I knew it was the rule. Eight or nine years ago, I applied for a pension on account of my age and services. At the Fund-office they told me to write to Whitby, according to the rules, as the ship that I last belonged to hailed from that port, though she sailed from London to North America. I told them I couldn't write, and a clerk said, 'I'll write for you; come in a fortnight.' I went in a fortnight, and was told that there was an answer from Whitby with 9s. a quarter for me, as the Whitby fund was not so large as the London fund. I said to the clerk, 'Give me back the money I paid, that's all I ask;' but he said, 'I can't do that.' And what's a poor man to do? I'm now forced to work at the London Dock. I suppose—indeed I'm sure of it—that I paid 1s. a month for 35 years. I shall never live long enough to receive a quarter of it back again."

Within a few doors of the Sailors' Home is the *Asylum for Destitute Sailors*. It was established prior to the Home, and in last year's Report of the Institution there is the following statement relative to its establishment:—

"The war which stained the early growth of this century, ... had no sooner ceased, than the absence of the unusual demand for seamen immediately threw upon the country a large number of men unfit for any other profession; and each winter brought with it intense suffering to the sailors. ... It was in the years 1825 and 1826 that the attention of a few good men was invited by the distress to seek its alleviation. They found often, at night, groups of poor men lying huddled together near the sugar-houses, to gather a little heat, without shelter and without food. First, those kind benefactors employed an agent to distribute money to the outcasts, and afterwards they fitted up a room for their reception. This was the commencement of the Destitute Sailors' Asylum. In about nine years a commodious building was erected in Well-street, and the establishment placed on a proper footing. Since the period of its commencement the miseries of 27,855 seamen have been relieved; vast numbers of these have been sent to sea. The sick have been sent to the hospital, and convalescents from the hospital have been received into the Asylum, from whence they have procured berths on board sea-going vessels. During the last year 1,350 have been received into the institution, of whom 130 came from the hospital-ship. This number has exceeded that of last year by 193."

The Asylum is under the management of the same president, directors (with two or three exceptions), chaplain, general secretary, cashier, and collector as the Home. The institutions, however, as regards funds, are—as it was described to me at the Asylum—as independent, one from another, "as if the one were in London and the other in Liverpool." The Asylum is for the reception of seamen who are destitute; the Home is for those who are able to maintain themselves. The rules of the Asylum (which have not been printed) exclude all who have not been to sea upwards of a year, or who have not served as seamen in the course of the twelve months previous to the application for admission. Beyond this, no other test is asked for but destitution. Any foreigner is admissible. "Indeed," said Mr. Partridge, the superintendent, "we sometimes have men of all sorts of countries here—north, east, south, and west—speaking all sorts of tongues."

When I visited the Asylum only five men had been inmates on the preceding evening, so small a number being rarely known. As many as 165 had been admitted, 160 being the number undertaken to be accommodated; but there was overcrowding, and sickness resulted. The superintendent would now be unwilling to admit more than 100, as more than that number, he considered, could not be comfortably lodged. On the ground floor are the kitchen and proper offices, and a large room, or hall, in which the destitute seamen have their meals. These consist of thick oatmeal gruel and sea biscuit in the morning, and soup and biscuit in the evening. During the day the men are required to absent themselves to "look out for ships," and they are not allowed to remain in doors, unless they are sick, or the weather is such as to present an obstacle to any out-door inquiry being made by destitute or ill-clad seamen. I was told by a gentleman, familiar for some years with the matter, that at very slack times the inmates of the Asylum may be seen sitting—as many as thirty at a time perhaps— on a wooden rail in front of a piece of ground rendered waste by the pulling down of some houses, and known as "the rail." "It's called so," said a boarding-master to me, "and it's looked on as 'the rail' where the poor fellows are to be found." Here boarding and sailing masters may find them. The limitation of a sailor's reception in the Asylum is six weeks; but the managers exercise a discretion as to a longer or shorter period. Men have been—under peculiar circumstances—as long as six months, and some of the men admitted are employed in cleaning the place. Above the room where the men have their meals, is the dormitory. There is but one, as the men sleep in hammocks swung singly from a frame; this consists of a light transverse beam, on which the hammock is slung, resting on two upright poles, with the usual feet and props. The sleeping apartment is lofty, and all is scrupulously clean. Among the regulations of the establishment are the following:—

> "Any man who swears, uses improper language, or quarrels with another in the Asylum, must expect to be immediately sent out. No man shall leave the house before prayers in the morning, or after prayers at night, without the permission of the superintendent. The men are to attend Divine service on Sundays and Thursdays at St. Paul's-church for seamen, Dock-street, and the evening service at the Asylum. Any man refusing to go into the Queen's service, or take any employment that may offer, will not be allowed to remain in the Asylum. Men who get any work about the docks while in the Asylum, will be expected to purchase clothing with whatever money they may earn. Any man neglecting to be clean in his person, as far as the condition of his clothes will admit, must expect to be discharged from the institution. Every man in his turn will have to assist in the work necessary to be done at the Asylum."

The following is the return of the receipts and expenditure from April 30, 1848, to April 28, 1849:

RECEIPTS.

To balance at last audit	£185	14 7
Donations	266	11 2
Annual subscriptions	214	13 0
Collection at public meeting	2	9 0
West of London Auxiliary	20	0 0
Bath Association	11	6 6
Derby do.	1	15 0
Edinburgh do.	2	5 0
Guernsey do.	11	9 8
Norwich do.	19	19 0
Newcastle do.	3	1 0
Ryde do.	20	10 0
Torquay do.	18	6 7
	£778	0 5

EXPENDITURE.

By advertisements	£2	14	11
Biscuits	32	11	0
Coals	25	12	6
Clothing and shoes	19	5	0
Collector's poundage	8	16	4
Cleaning, scrubbing, hammocks, rugs, &c.	6	7	6
Carriage of parcels and waterage	0	14	2
Expenses of sick men at hospitals, and tea, sugar, &c., for patients	5	11	8
Exchange upon Guernsey currency	1	3	10
Gas	4	13	6
Insurance	2	15	0
Oatmeal, barley, and peas	50	17	9
Ox-heads	50	12	0
Printing	8	3	0
Petty cash and postage	8	4	9
Rent	35	0	0
Rates and taxes	6	6	8
Repairs, improvements, and furniture	20	1	0
Soap, candles, and oilman's account	10	18	9
Salaries to chaplain, secretary, surgeon, and cashier	150	0	0
Vegetables	4	3	8
Wages to superintendent, cook, porter, and night watchman	96	4	0
Savings Bank	100	0	0
Balance at Messrs. Williams, Deacon, and Co.	127	3	5
	£778	0	5

From this account it will be seen that the cost of the domestic arrangements of the Asylum, including the maintenance of the inmates, and the lighting, heating, cleaning, and the insurance of the institution, come to only £207 16s. 8d.—while the salaries and wages of the officers and servants for the year are no less than £246 4s.; or, in other words, that the sum paid to the officials is very nearly *one-fifth more* than the amount disbursed in charity to the destitute inmates. This is the more glaring as the officers of the Asylum are, with the exception of the superintendent, the officers of the Sailors' Home, where the salaries, as we have already seen, amount every year to no less than £1,200! If the receipts of the asylum are but £778 per annum, surely the salaries should not be allowed to swallow up very nearly one-third of the charity, especially when those salaries are principally paid to persons who are already in receipt of an income from the Home.

Men discharged as convalescent from the Dreadnought Hospital have in many cases to resort to the Asylum, and, so in some cases have men who must leave the Home (according to the regulations), when unable any longer to defray the cost of their board, as well as those destitute from other causes. The officers of the Asylum endeavour to find ships for the men under their care, which is generally a very difficult thing to accomplish, as the poor destitute fellows are usually in debt and in want of clothes.

From a man who had been an inmate in the Asylum I had this statement:—

"I was once in the Straw-yard (Asylum) for a few days. Men generally consider going to the Asylum a degradation, far more than landsmen think of going to a workhouse. We pay 1s. a month to the Merchant Seamen's Fund, and—isn't it shameful?—we have no benefit from it that I know of. All the men I know complain of this fund, as no benefit to them. I was once cast away, and applied to the Merchant Seamen's Fund—it was when the Mary Anne struck on St. Mary's, Scilly—and the people at the Fund-office gave me an order, as I understood it, to the Sailor's Society; and I went to the Sailors' Home, in Wells-street, and the people there sent me to the Straw-house (Asylum)."

This man represented the victuals dispensed at the Asylum as being of an inferior description, but other seamen whom I saw and interrogated upon this subject made no complaint upon this head; they said the Asylum was a sort of workhouse for them, and described the food as of that character. Indeed, with the exception of the salaries paid to the officers of the Home, the Asylum appears to be not only well conducted, but especially worthy of the support of the benevolent. Were the £2,000 subscription and donations that are devoted to the Sailors' Home, given to the Asylum, and the Home made to support itself entirely by a decrease of expenses, or an increase of the charges, a vast amount of good would be effected.

Any account of the state of the seamen of the Port of London would be incomplete without some description of the *Dreadnought, or Hospital for Seamen of all Nations*, an institution which has no parallel in any foreign land. All who have travelled by water from London to Greenwich have remarked the huge hull of a man-of-war, with her black deep sides relieved by numerous windows, bordered with white lines. On her deck, on a fine day, may often be seen night-capped and feeble-looking men, of all climes and complexions—white, black, and the many shades between white and black—patients sufficiently convalescent to breathe the air of the river. The *Dreadnought* is moored near Greenwich, on the Deptford side, and close in shore. She has been employed in this capacity since the 31st October, 1831. She was a 104-gun ship, and was launched in 1802, and during the war was employed in cruising off Toulon and off Cadiz. She was Lord Collingwood's ship, and was one of the vessels engaged in the momentous battle of Trafalgar. The Dreadnought was a heavy sailer, and together with the Prince, a 98-gun ship, was late in the action, but was serviceable not only in completing the victory, but in rendering aid to the crippled ships, and in rescuing the wounded, or others afloat on the spars or timbers of the battered vessels. She was afterwards one of the Channel squadron ships, but nothing notable is known of her after Trafalgar, until her present capacity presented so beautiful a contrast to her warlike career.

The Dreadnought, Deptford

On board the ship some relics of her former condition are preserved. Among these one of the most curious is an old pane from one of the skylight windows, on which the master of the ship wrote with his diamond ring nineteen names, chiefly the names of officers. There is preserved on board, also, the *Times* of Nov. 7, 1805, No. 6,572, containing the *Gazette*, and the account of Nelson's last fight. The paper is of four pages—the page the present size of the *Examiner*.

The Dreadnought was not the first vessel devoted to the purposes of a hospital.

"A public meeting was held on the 8th of March, 1821, at the City of London Tavern, at which it was determined that a permanent Floating Hospital should be established on the River Thames, for the use of sick and diseased seamen only; to be supported by voluntary subscriptions, under the management of a committee; and the present hospital was accordingly established on board the Grampus (a 50-gun ship), moored off Greenwich. But the committee finding, in 1830, that the Grampus was not large enough to accommodate the numerous applicants for admission, represented the same to his Majesty's Government, who, in consequence, exchanged her for the Dreadnought (104-gun ship), which the committee fitted up for that purpose in 1831."

The Grampus was broken up in 1832.

The first three patients received on board the Grampus were, I was told, an Englishman, an Irishman, and a Scotchman.

But it was not until 1833—eleven years after the first establishment of the floating hospital—that an act of incorporation was obtained. In 1832 died Mr. John Lydekker, a shipowner. He had risen from a very humble condition as a worker in whalebone to great opulence. He had not unfrequently visited the hospital ship when some of his own seamen, ill after a South Sea voyage, were patients aboard. He was struck with the excellence of the institution, and was cognizant of its wants. A few hours before his death, when he felt himself struck by mortal illness, he bequeathed to the hospital the residue of his estate, which realised, from 1833 to 1841, the sums of £48,434 16s. 11d. in the Three per Cents., and £10,295 11s. 4d. in money. After this munificent bequest, the committee of management, in 1833, applied to Parliament for an act of incorporation, which they obtained, and by which they are empowered either to build an hospital on shore or to continue their establishment afloat. That it is politic, not to say indispensable, to continue the establishment afloat, is maintained in the latest report. It says:—

"If informed of, or directed to, hospitals, asylums, or other places of relief, on shore, which do not bear the title of 'Seamen's,' they (sailors) are unwilling to approach them, and submit to be driven to such receptacles only by extreme anguish and misery. A sailor, rather than repair to an hospital on shore, will strip almost the last rag from his back, for the means of obtaining a cure; and it is well known to every person acquainted with the habits of these extraordinary beings, that they will at any time prefer remaining on board their ship, even on approaching death, to being taken to an hospital on shore, although with a prospect of returning health. This prejudice may appear unaccountable, but is nevertheless general and powerful."

Concerning the character of the Seamen's Hospital the Report of 1850 says:—

"The establishment on board the Dreadnought is placed precisely on the footing of other hospitals; with a superintendent, surgeons, assistant-surgeon, apothecary, visiting physicians, chaplain, &c. The ship is moored off Greenwich, being the most central and eligible situation that could be found, contiguous to the bulk of the shipping in the docks and in the stream, where accidents of every description are continually happening; it is the only place provided for the reception of sick seamen arriving from abroad, or to whom accidents may happen on the water, between the mouth of the river and London-bridge. The Royal Humane Society have presented a complete apparatus for the recovery of suspended animation, which is kept in constant readiness. Sick seamen, of every nation, on presenting themselves alongside, are immediately received, without the necessity of any recommendatory letters; their own apparent condition being sufficient to obtain their admission. This peculiar facility of reception is in itself productive of greater benefit than may be imagined by the public in general, as the cases are immediately attended to; the consequence of which is, that the patients are effectually relieved in a much shorter period than would otherwise have been necessary. It frequently happens, that vessels coming into the Thames from long voyages have most distressing cases of sickness, disease, or accident on board; the subjects of which, being now sent to the Dreadnought, are restored with astonishing rapidity, and who, but for this institution, must have waited some days before admission could have been procured for them into hospitals on shore, with the hazard of becoming incurable, from the effect of delay in applying a remedy. The rules and regulations by which other hospitals are governed limit the period which the patients are permitted to remain in them to that of their requiring medical treatment; and which is generally sufficient, as the objects to whom their beneficence is extended have homes to receive them after cure, and friends to support and comfort them; whilst, on the contrary, a sailor, who, having been relieved from his complaint, is discharged in a weak condition, is without a home to go to, or a place to yield him a night's repose, and is compelled to wander about the streets or fields. In this respect the regulations of the Seamen's Hospital are essentially different;

every person being allowed to remain on board in a state of convales-
cence, until he has completely regained his health and strength; and in
the interim, an opportunity is afforded him of obtaining employment,
in which pursuit he is aided by the personal influence of the committee with their friends connected with the shipping interests; by which
means many men are speedily embarked for climates most congenial
to their constitutions."

The following is the account of the receipts and expenses of the
establishment for the last year:—

STATEMENT OF RECEIPTS AND EXPENDITURE OF THE SEA-
MEN'S HOSPITAL SOCIETY, FROM THE 1ST JANUARY, TO THE
31ST DECEMBER, 1849.

DR.

	£	s	d
To Balance of last year's account	152	7	4
Amount of donations	1,613	8	2
„ of annual subscriptions	1,284	10	6
„ of interest upon stock	2,654	17	6
„ of per centage upon merchant sea-men's money from ships belonging to the port of London	487	18	3
„ of penalties and forfeitures under 7th and 8th Vict., cap 112	939	13	11
„ of bequest of R. N. Hunt, Esq.	500	0	0
„ of unclaimed property	3	0	3
Balance	628	8	7
	£8,264	4	6

CR. CHARGES ON SHORE—VIZ.:

	£	s	d		
By advertising annual proceedings, &c.	78	8	9		
Stationery, printing 750 books of the annual reports and list of subscribers, periodical returns, &c.	75	9	5		
Salaries to secretary and his clerk	160	0	0		
Commission on collections and gratuity to late secretary	137	8	7		
Gratuity to family of late secretary, and funeral bill	173	0	0		
Rent of office, coals, &c.	105	0	0		
Postage and porterage	25	11	3		
Law expenses	130	17	9		
				£885 15	9

CHARGES AFLOAT

By victualling, patients, officers, and crew, and necessaries for the sick 1,987 17 1

Salaries to superintendent, surgeons, assistant-surgeon and apothecary, chaplain, steward, petty officers, and nurses ... 1,595 10 5

Coals, oil, paint, rope, and other stores, for ship's use and hospital wards 184 11 11

Medicines, medical stores, and surgical instruments 450 4 1

Washing hospital bedding and clothing 265 6 3

Burials 167 2 0

Plumber's work 57 14 2

Engineer's work 38 12 0

Labour on removal of stores, furniture, and patients, on repair of the ship, carpenters' work, and sundry fittings 259 3 8

Sundries, viz., physician's coach-hire, insurance from fire, boat and coach hire, and other incidental expenses ... 182 19 8

Gratuity to servants 26 0 0

5,215 1 3

Donation to Small-pox Hospital 30 10 0

Cash paid Sarah Gray, one year's annuity .. 12 0 0

„　　for £400 Stock, Three per Cent. Consols 361 10 0

„　　for £400 Stock, Three per Cent. Reduced 359 10 0

„　　for £500 Stock, three-and-a-Quarter per Cents. 470 0 0

„　　for £1000 Stock, ditto 926 17 6

£8,264 4 6

The subjoined table gives the receipts (including the balance of the preceding year)—the expenditure (including the investments) being equivalent—with larger or smaller balances, up to the balance in hand at the close of the last year:—

1839	£7,213	4	3
1840	7,320	9	11
1841	7,201	12	9
1842	7,487	9	1
1843	7,317	10	0
1844	9,741	8	0
1845	9,045	1	10
1846	8,893	14	8
1847	9,025	13	9
1848	6,957	12	8
1849	8,264	4	6

The difference in the receipts is mainly owing to the greater or smaller amounts of the bequests. Among the bequests some are noticeable; the following for instance:—

One-third of an *intended bequest* of the late Joseph Somes, Esq. (per his widow), £333 6s. 8d.; Christian Thornstedt, a patient, £6. Dreadnought, subscription box on board the, £19 12s. 10d.; Enterprise, proceeds of sale of blubber, given by officers of her Majesty's ship, £4 18s. 4d.; Gizzard, Francis, a patient, bequest of, 10s.; Wellesley, sacrament collection on board the, £1 4s. 6d.; ditto, proceeds of a play performed on board the, £4; ditto, proceeds of a lottery on board the, £10; White, Charles, a patient, bequest of, £1.

I ought to mention that the institution fulfils the office of a dispensary as well as a hospital, administering to the necessities of those seamen in the vessels in the River, whose cases are not so urgent as to require removal into an hospital. In 1849 the number of patients in the ship was 2,239; and the number of out-patients 2,099.

According to the last report, I find that no less than 61,250 seamen have been admitted as patients into the floating hospital since its formation in March, 1821. The annexed table shows the nations to which the seamen belonged. It will be seen that but little more than one-half of the number are Englishmen—the Swedes and Norwegians admitted into the ship being nearly 2,000, and the Prussians, East Indians and West Indians, and Americans more than 1,000 respectively.

STATEMENT OF THE NUMBER OF PATIENTS RECEIVED ON BOARD
THE SEAMEN'S HOSPITAL SHIPS, GRAMPUS, FROM MARCH,
1821, TO 30TH OCTOBER, 1831, AND DREADNOUGHT, FROM
THE 31ST OCTOBER, 1831, TO THE 31ST JANUARY, 1850,
SHOWING THE DIFFERENT NATIONS TO WHICH THEY BELONG,
AND THE LAST SERVICE IN WHICH THEY HAVE BEEN EM-
PLOYED.

	No.		No.
Englishmen	36,014	West Indians	1,055
Scotchmen	7,479	British Americans	804
Irishmen	5,537	United States	1,123
Frenchmen	226	South Americans	126
Germans	820	Africans	368
Russians	762	Turks	16
Prussians	1,191	Greeks	49
Dutchmen	195	New Zealanders	29
Danes	834	New South Wales	29
Swedes and Norwegians	1,934	South Sea Islanders	179
Italians	554	Chinese	37
Portugese	469	Born at Sea	128
Spaniards	268		
East Indians	1,024	Total	61,250

IN WHAT SERVICE EMPLOYED.

	No.
Her Majesty's navy	3,038
Hon. East India Company's Service	1,797
Merchant vessels of different nations	56,415
Total	61,250

Of the 61,250 patients admitted into the Dreadnought, only 3,489,
or scarcely 6 per cent. died; 32,394 were discharged cured; 14,222
were sent away convalescent; 1,311 were relieved, and 993 dismissed
not cured; 1,228 had ships found them by the Society; 240 were conveyed to their homes; 32,060 were admitted as out-patients; 2,446
were completely clothed after being cured, and 3,086 supplied with
shoes and stockings.

LABOUR AND THE POOR.

—◆—

THE METROPOLITAN DISTRICTS.

[FROM OUR SPECIAL CORRESPONDENT.]

LETTER LII.

It is no easy matter to classify the different kinds of labour scientifically. To arrange the several varieties of work into "orders," and to group the manifold species of arts under a few comprehensive genera—so that the mind may grasp the whole at one effort—is a task attended with considerable difficulty. The first attempt to bring any number of diverse phenomena within the rules of logical division is not only laborious, but generally unsuccessful. It is impossible, however, to proceed with the present inquiry without making some attempt at systematic arrangement. Crude and illogical as the result may be, still it is essential to the proper conduct of the present investigation that I should seek to give some method to it. I shall therefore, before proceeding to the immediate subject of the present Letter, endeavour to arrange the several kinds of labour into their different classes.

In my first communication I stated that the poorer classes appeared to be divisible into (1) those that *will* work—as artisans, labourers, servants, &c.; (2) those that *cannot* work—as paupers, almspeople, and the inmates of our hospitals and asylums; (3) those that *will not* work—as professional beggars, vagrants, criminals, and prostitutes. These three classes seem to comprise the whole of the humbler portion of the community; and every individual belonging to the poorer class of society must, therefore, fall under one or other of the above divisions.

The people that cannot or will not work, are neither a very various, nor, compared with the artisans and labourers, are they a very numerous class. They form, however, a most important section, living upon the earnings or the property of the more industrious or wealthy. Hence it is essential that we should know all we can about them, so that we may learn how at least to check their increase, if not to bring about a positive diminution of their numbers. The paupers alone cost the country seven millions a year; the sum dispensed in charities to almspeople, mendicants, the inmates of asylums and hospitals, amounts at least to three millions (the income derived from property bequeathed for charitable purposes is very nearly half the amount); and the cost of maintenance of the thirty thousand criminals that enter our gaols every year, together with the value of the property stolen, is upwards of a million—making the entire expense of supporting those that either cannot or will not work come to little less than twelve millions sterling per annum.

The class that will work, however, is far more complex. The branches of industry are so multifarious, the divisions of labour so minute and manifold, that it seems almost impossible to reduce them to any system. Moreover, the crude generalizations expressed in the names of the several arts render the subject still more perplexing. Some kinds of workmen are called after the *articles they make*—as saddlers, hatters, boot-makers, dress-makers, breeches-makers, stay-makers, lace-makers, button-makers, glovers, cabinet-makers, artificial-flower-makers, ship-builders, organ-builders, boat-builders, nailers, pin-makers, basket-makers, pump-makers, clock and watch makers, wheelwrights, shipwrights, and so forth. Some operatives, on the other hand, take their names not from what they make, but from the *kind of work they perform.* Hence we have carvers, joiners, bricklayers, weavers, knitters, engravers, embroiderers, tanners, curriers, bleachers, thatchers, lime-burners, seamstresses, assayers, refiners, embossers, chasers, painters, paperhangers, printers, bookbinders, and so on. Other artisans, again, are styled after the *materials upon which they work*, such as tinmen, jewellers, lapidaries, goldsmiths, braziers, plumbers, pewterers, glass workers, glaziers, &c. &c.; while a few operatives are named after the *tools they use;* thus we have ploughmen, sawyers, and needlewomen.

But these divisions, it is evident, are as unscientific as they are arbitrary; nor would it be possible by adopting such a classification to arrive at any practical result. We must therefore take a wholly different view of the subject. The first grand division that naturally presents itself is, according to the skill of the operative, into *artisans* and *labourers*—an artisan being a skilled workman, and a labourer an unskilled one. That is to say, an artisan is an educated handicraftsman, following a calling that requires an apprenticeship of greater or less duration in order to arrive at perfection in it; whereas a labourer's occupation needs no education whatever. Many years must be spent in practising before a man can acquire sufficient manual dexterity to make a pair of boots or a coat; dock labour or porter's work, however, needs neither teaching nor learning, for any man can carry a load or turn a wheel. The artisan, therefore, is literally a handicraftsman—one who by practice has acquired manual dexterity enough to perform a particular class of work, which is consequently called "skilled." But both artisans and labourers work for masters who make a profit out of their labour. Hence they belong to the class of workmen called operatives—whereas *servants* who are not employed with a view to profit constitute a different order. Under the term servants, clerks and shopmen are included, as well as those who perform the ordinary domestic duties, for though both the former are engaged in business, still the tradesman makes no profit directly out of their labours. His gains are derived from his goods, the making of which is expressed in the price of the articles he sells, and out of those gains the clerks and shopmen are paid. Strictly speaking, the wages of the latter enter no more into the price of the goods than the money he pays to his domestic servants, which must also be derived from his profits.

There are, then, three classes of workpeople—artisans, labourers, and servants. Of these the artisans are not only the most numerous, but the most varied in their occupations. The natural classification of artisans or skilled labourers appears to be according to the materials upon which they work, for this circumstance seems to constitute the peculiar quality of the art more than the tool used—indeed, it appears to be the principal cause of the modification of the implements in different handicrafts. The tailor who stitches woollen materials together would make but a poor hand at sewing leather. The two substances are joined by the same means, but in a different manner, and with different instruments. So the turner, who has been accustomed to turn wood, is unable to fashion metals by the same method. Hence we may divide the artisans into two classes, according as they pursue some *mechanical* or *chemical* occupation. The former are literally mechanics or handicraftsmen—the latter chemical manufacturers. The handicraftsmen consist of (1) the workers in wood, as the carpenters, the cabinet-makers, &c.; (2) the workers in metals, as braziers, tinmen, plumbers, goldsmiths, pewterers, coppersmiths, iron-founders, blacksmiths, whitesmiths, anchor-smiths, locksmiths, &c. (3) The workers in brick and stones—as bricklayers, masons, &c. (4) The workers in glass and earthenware—as potters, glass-blowers, glass-cutters, bottle-makers, glaziers, &c. (5) The workers in silk, cotton, wool, flax, and hemp—as weavers, spinners, knitters, carpet-makers, lace-makers, tailors, seamstresses, embroiderers, milliners, dress-makers, stay-stitchers, rope-makers, canvass-weavers, &c. (6) The workers in skin, hair, and feathers—as tanners, curriers, boot and shoe makers, glove-makers, furriers, brush and broom makers, hair-manufacturers, feather dressers, &c. The chemical manufacturers come next—as powder-makers, white-lead-makers, alkali and acid manufacturers, lucifer-match makers, blacking-makers, ink-makers, soap-boilers, tallow-chandlers, &c. Then follow the mixed arts—as the paper-makers, cardboard-makers, printers, bookbinders. After these come the occupations connected with shipping—as shipwrights, boat and barge builders, block, mast, and oar makers, &c; and next to those, the saddlers, coach-makers, whip-makers, wheelwrights, &c. Then come the several occupations in connection with provisions—as millers, bakers, butchers, drovers, provision curers, market-gardeners, maltsters, brewers, vinegar-makers, and mustard-makers.

But these callings are mostly pursued in-doors, and there is still a large number of individuals who obtain their livelihood in the street. They consist of three classes—hucksters, or those who live by selling something in the street; showmen, or those who exhibit or perform something in the street; and working pedlars, or those who make or mend something in the street.

Of the Hucksters I have already treated at considerable length. As we have seen, they include the street vendors of provisions—as fish, vegetables, fruit, pea-soup, hot eels, spice-cakes, sweetmeats, coffee, baked potatoes, water-cresses, ham sandwiches, cats' and dogs' meat, pickled-whelks—and the street vendors of domestic articles, as blacking, crockery-ware, lucifers, hearthstones, cutlery, sand and gravel, tea-trays, slippers, sponges and washleathers, sheeting and table covers, &c., &c.

Of the Street Showmen and Performers it is my intention to treat at present. They are not a numerous but an extremely curious class, and are worthy of attention, as affording us another instance of the love of "a roving life," and of the irksomeness of labour among certain individuals. The same characteristics as were found to prevail among the hucksters and the vagrants will be found generally to distinguish the street performers. There is the same improvidence—the same intemperance—the same objection to pursue any regular occupation.

Some I have met with who appear to be more soberly and industriously inclined than the rest, and anxious to abandon their vagabond life. For the most part it will be seen that the Street Performers have been induced to take to the business, not only from an indisposition to follow any settled employment, but from the gains of the business having been, a few years back, considerably more than could be obtained by any of the present arts or handicrafts. It will be seen that, not very long since, £10 a week was the ordinary income of an attractive street exhibition. From all I can gather now, even the best street performance affords but a scanty subsistence; and indeed I have found, among all the members of the "purfession" (for so it is invariably called), a strong desire to emigrate—or to do anything that will procure them a more certain subsistence. But they all agree that after they have once taken to the streets, it is almost impossible to get any other employment; they are too well known to be engaged by any one, and they are generally too old and their habits too unsettled to learn any new craft. Some, however, who are far advanced in years, I have found practising shoemaking as a means of emancipating themselves from the streets. Altogether the inquiry into the condition of these men has a saddening effect upon one.

The class has several divisions and subdivisions. First, there are the street actors—their performances consist of four different kinds: (1) Street puppet-shows—as Punch, Fantoccini, Chinese shades, and Galantee shows; (2) Street-feats of strength or sleight-of-hand, including the performances of jugglers, conjurors, balancers, posturers, stiff tumblers, pole balancers, salamanders or fire-eaters, and sword and snake swallowers; (3) Street-dances—as street hornpipes and street highland flings; (4) Street performances of trained animals—as dancing dogs, performing birds, and mice. Besides these several kinds of street actors, there are the street musicians, and their different classes—as street bands—brass and mixed—street Ethiopians, farm-yard fiddlers, horse organs, Italian organ boys, hurdy-gurdy players, blind and crippled fiddlers, and violoncello and clarionet-players. Then there are the street artists—as the artist upon the pavement in coloured chalks, the black profile cutters, and the proprietors of peep-shows; and after these the various street exhibitions and curiosities—as shows of giants, dwarfs, industrious fleas, alligators, happy families, glass ships, together with street telescopes, microscopes, thaumascopes, and weighing, lifting, and measuring machines. These constitute the chief varieties of the class.

I shall begin with the street actors, and first with the performances of the street puppets.

The performer of Punch that I saw was a short, dark, pleasant-looking man, dressed in a very greasy and very shiny green shooting-jacket. This was fastened together by one button in front, all the other button-holes having been burst through. Protruding from his bosom, a corner of the Pandæan pipes was just visible, and as he told me the story of his adventures he kept playing with the band of his very limp and very rusty old beaver hat. He had formerly been a gentleman's servant, and was especially civil in his manners. He came to me with his hair tidily brushed for the occasion, but apologized for his appearance on entering the room. He was very communicative, and took great delight in talking like Punch, with his call in his mouth, while some young children were in the room, and who, hearing the well-known sound of Punch's voice, looked all about for the figure. Not seeing the show, they fancied the man had the figure in his pocket, and that the sounds came from it. The change from Punch's voice to the man's natural tone was managed without an effort, and instantaneously. It had a very peculiar effect:—

"I am the properietor of a Punch's show," he said. "I goes about with it myself, and performs inside the frame behind the green baize. I have a pardner what plays the music—the pipes and drum—him as you seed with me. I have been five and twenty year now at the business. I wish I'd never seen it, though it's been a money-taking business—the best of all the street hexhibitions I may say. I am fifty year old. I took to it for money gains—that was what I done it for. I formerly lived in service—was a footman in a gennelman's family. When I first took to it I could take two and three pounds a day—I could so. You see the way in which I took first to the business was this here—there was a party used to come and 'cheer' for us at my master's house, and her son having a hexhibition of his own, and being in want of a pardner, axed me if so be as I'd go out, which was a thing that I degraded at at the time. He gave me information as to what the money taking was, and it seemed to me that good that it would pay me better nor service. I had £20 a year in my place, and my board and lodging and two suits of clothes; but the young man told me as how I could make £1 a day at the Punch and Judy business after a little practice. It took a deal of persuasion, though, before I'd jine him—it was beneath my dignity to fall from a footman to a showman. But, you see, the French gennelman as I lived with (he were a merchant in the City, and had fourteen clerks at work for him) went back to his own country to reside, and left me with a written kerackter—but that was no use to me, though I'd five recommendations at the back of it—no one would look at it—so I was five months out of employment, knocking about—living first on my wages and then on my clothes, till all was gone but the few rags on my back. So I began to think that the Punch and Judy business was better than starving after all. Yes, I should think any thing were better than that—though it's a business that, after you've once took to, you never can get out of—people fancies you know too much, and won't have nothing to say to you. If I got a situation at a tradesman's, why the boys would be sure to recognize me behind the counter, and begin a shouting into the shop (they *must* shout, you know), 'Oh, there's Punch and Judy—there's Punch a sarving out the customers.' Ah, it's great annoyance being a public kerackter, I can assure you sir—go where you will it's 'Punchy, Punchy!' As for the boys they'll never leave me alone till I die, I know; and I suppose in my old age I shall have to take to the parish broom. All our forefathers died in the workhouse. I don't know a Punch's showman what hasn't. One of my pardners was buried by the workhouse; and even old Pike, the most noted showman as ever was, died in the workhouse. Pike and Porsini—Porsini was the first original street Punch, and Pike was his apprentice—their names is handed down to prosperity among the noblemen and footmen of the land. They both died in the workhouse, and, in course, I shall do the same. Something else *might* turn up, to be sure. We can't say what this luck of the world is. I'm obliged to strive wery hard—wery hard indeed, sir—now, to get a living, and then not get it after all at times—compelled to go short often. Punch, you know, sir, is a dramatic performance, in two hacts. It's a play, you may say. I don't think it can be called a tragedy hexactly: a drama is what we names it. There is tragic parts, and comic and sentimental parts too. Some families where I performs will have it most sentimental—in the original style—them families is generally sentimental theirselves. Others is all for the comic, and then I has to kick up all the games I can. To the sentimental folk I am obliged to perform werry steady and werry slow, and leave out all comic words and business. They won't have no ghost, no coffin, and no devil; and that's what I call spiling the performance entirely. It's the march of hintellect wots a doing all this ere—it is sir. But I was a-going to tell you about my first jining the business. Well, you see, after a good deal of persuading, and being druv to it, I may say, I consented to go out with the young man as I were a speaking about. He was to give me 12s. a week and my keep, for two years certain, till I could get my own show things together, and for that I was to carry the show and go round and *collect*—collecting, you know, sounds better than begging, the pronounciation's better like. Sometimes the people says, when they sees us a coming round, 'Oh, here they comes a-begging'—but it can't be begging, you know, when you're a hexerting yourselves. I couldn't play the drum and pipes, so the young man used to do that himself, to call the people together before he got into the show. I used to stand outside, and patter to the figures. The first time that ever I went out with Punch was in the beginning of August, 1825. I did all I could to awoid being seen. My dignity was hurt at being hobligated to take to the streets for a living. At fust I fought shy, and used to feel queer—somehow you don't know how like—whenever the people used to look at me. I remember werry well the first street as ever I performed in. It was off Gray's-inn, one of them quiet, genteel streets, and when the mob began to gather round, I felt all overish, and I turned my head to the frame instead of the people. We hadn't had no rehearsals aforehand, and I did the patter quite permiscuous. There was not much talk to be sure, required then; and what little there was consisted of merely calling out the names of the figures as they came up, and these my master prompted me with from inside the frame. But little as there was for me to do, I know I never could have done it if it hadn't been for the spirits—the false spirits, you see (a little drop of gin)—as my master guv me in the morning. The fust time as ever I made my appearance in public, I collected as much as eight shillings, and my master said, after the performance was over, 'You'll do!' You see, I was partly in livery and looked a little bit decent like. After this was over I kept on going out with my master for two year, as I had agreed, and at the end of that time I had saved enough to start a show of my own. I bought the show of old Porsini, the man as first brought Punch into the streets of England. To be sure there was a woman over here with it before him. Her name was —, I can't think of it just now, but she never performed in the streets, so we consider Porsini to be our real forefather. It isn't much more nor seventy year since Porsini—he was a wery old man when he died, and blind—showed the hexhibition in the streets of London. I've heerd tell that old Porsini used to take very often as much as £10 a day, and he used to sit down to his fowls and wine, and the very best of everything, like the first gennelman in the land—indeed he made enough money at the business to be quite a tip-top gennelman, that he did. But he never took care of a halfpenny he got. He was that independent that if he was wanted to perform, sir, he'd come at *his* time, not your'n. At last he reduced himself to want, and died in St. Giles's workhouse. Ah, poor fellow! he oughtn't to have been allowed to die where he did, after amusing the public for so many years. Every one in London knowed him. Lords, dukes, princes, squires and wagabonds—all used to stop to laugh at his performance, and a funny clever old fellow he was. He was past performing when I bought my show of him, and werry poor. He was living in the Coal-yard, Drury-lane, and had scarcely a bit of food to eat. He had spent all he had got in drink, and in treating friends—aye, any one, no matter who. He didn't study the world, nor himself neither. As fast as the money came it went, and when it was gone why he'd go to work and get more. His show was a werry inferior one, though it were the fust—nothing at all like them about now—nothing near as good. If you only had four sticks then, it was quite enough to make plenty of money out of, so long as it was Punch. I gave him 35s. for the stand, figures and all. I bought it cheap you see, for it was thrown on one side, and was of no use to any one but such as myself. There was twelve figures and the other happyratus, such as the gallows, ladder, horse, bell, and stuffed dog. The characters were—Punch, Judy, Child, Beadle, Scaramouch, Nobody, Jack Ketch, the Grand Senoor, the Doctor, the Devil (there was no ghost used then), Merry Andrew, and the Blind Man. These last two keracters are quite done with now. The heads of the keracters was all carved on wood, and dressed in the proper costume of the country. There was, at that time, and is now, a real carver for the Punch business. He was dear, but werry good and hexcellent. His Punch's head was the best as I ever seed. The nose and chin used to meet quite close together. A set of new figures, dressed and all, would come to about £15. Each head costs 5s. for the bare carving alone, and every figure that we has takes at least a yard of cloth to dress him, besides ornaments and things that comes werry expensive. A good show at the present time will cost £3 odd for the stand alone—that's including baize, the frontispiece, the back scene, the cottage, and the letter cloth, or what is called the drop-scene at the theatres. In the old ancient style the back scene used to pull up and change into a gaol scene, but that's all altered now. We've got more upon the comic business, and tries to do more with Toby than with the prison scene. The prison is what we calls the sentimental style. Formerly Toby was only a stuffed figure. It was Pike who first hit upon hinterducing a live dog, and a great hit it were, it made a grand alteration in the exhibition, for now the performance is called that of Punch and Toby *as well*. There is one Punch about the streets at present that tries it on with three dogs, but that ain't much of a go—too much of a good thing I calls it. Punch, as I said before, is a drama in two hacts. We don't drop the scene at the hend of the fust—the drum and pipes strikes up instead. The first act we consider to end with Punch being taken to prison for the murder of his wife and child. The great difficulty in performing Punch consists in the speaking, which is done by a 'call,' or whistle in the mouth such as this here." [He then produced the call from his waistcoat pocket. It was a small flat instrument, made of two curved pieces of metal about the size of a knee-buckle, bound together with black thread. Between these was a thin plate of some substance (apparently silk) which he said was a secret. The call, he told me, was tuned to a musical instrument, and took a considerable time to learn. He afterwards took from his pocket two of the small metallic plates unbound. He said the composition they were made of was also one of the "secrets of the purfession." They were not tin nor zinc, because "both of them metals were pisons in the mouth, and hinjurious to the constitution."] "These calls," he continued, "we often sell to gennel-men for a sovereign a-piece, and for that we give 'em a receipt how to use them. They ain't whistles, but calls, or unknown tongues, as we sometimes names 'em, because with them in the mouth we can pronounce each word as plain as any parson. We have two or three kinds—one for out-of-doors, one for indoors, one for speaking and for singing, and another for selling. I've sold many a one to gennel-men going along, so I generally keeps a hextra one with me. Porsini brought the calls into this country with him from Italy, and we who are now in the purfession have all larnt how to make and use them, either from him or those as he had taught 'em to. I larnt the use of mine from Porsini himself. My master whom I went out with at first would never teach me, and was wery particklar in keeping it all secret from me. Porsini taught me the call at the time I bought his show of him. I was six months in perfecting myself in the use of it. I kept practising away night and morning with it until I got it quite perfect. It was no use trying at home—'cause it sounds quite different in the hopen hair. Often when I've made 'em at home I'm obliged to take the calls to pieces, after trying 'em out in the streets—they've been made upon too weak a scale. When I was a practising I used to go into the parks and fields and out-of-the-way places, so as to get to know how to use it in the hopen hair. Now I'm reckoned one of the best speakers in the whole purfession. When I made my first appearance as a regular performer of Punch, on my own account, I did feel uncommon narvous to be sure; though I knowed the people couldn't see me behind the baize, still I felt as if all the eyes of the country were upon me. It was as much as hever I could do to get the words out and keep the figures from shaking. When I struck up the fust song my woice trembled so as I thought I should never be able to get to the hend of the fust hact. I soon, however, got over that there, and at present I'd play before the whole bench of bishops as cool as a cowcumber. We always have a pardner now to play the drum and pipes, and collect the money. This, however, is only a recent dodge. In older times we used to go about with a trumpet—that was Porsini's ancient style; but now that's stopped. Only her Majesty's mails may blow trumpets in the streets at present. The fust person who went out with me was my wife. She used to stand outside and keep the boys from peeping through the baize whilst I was a performing behind it, and she used to collect the money arterwards as well. I carried the show and trumpet, and she the box. She's been dead these five year now. Take one week with another all through the year, I should say I made then £5 regular. I *have* taken as much as £2 10s. in one day in the streets, and I used to think it a bad day's business at that time if I took only £1. You can see Punch has been good work—a money-making business—and beat all mechanics right out. If I could take as much as I did when I first began, what must my forefathers have done when the business was five times as good as ever it were in my time. Why I leaves you to judge what old Porsini and Pike must have made. Twenty year ago I've often and often got 7s. and 8s. for one hexhibition in the streets—2s. and 3s. I used to think low to get at one collection—and many times I'd perform eight or ten times in a day. We didn't care much about work then, for we could get money fast enough, but now I often show twenty times in the day and get scarcely a bare living at it arter all. That shows the times you know, sir—what things was and is now. Arter performing in the streets of a day we used to attend private parties in the hevening, and get sometimes as much as £2 for the hexhibition. This used to be at the juvenile parties of the nobility, and the performance lasted about an hour and a half. For a short performance of half an hour at a gennel-man's house we never had less than £1. A performance houtside the

house was 2s. 6d., but we often got as much as 10s. for it. I have performed afore almost all the nobility. Lord —— was particular partial
to us, and one of our greatest patroniziers. At the time of the Police
Bill I met him at Cheltenham on my travels, and he told me as he
had saved Punch's neck once more; and it's through him principally
that we are allowed to hexhibit in the streets. Punch is exempt from
the Police Act. If you read the hact throughout you won't find Punch
mentioned in it. But all I've been telling you is about the business as
it was. What it *is* is a werry different consarn. A good day for us now
seldom gets beyond five shillings, and that's between myself and my
pardner, who plays the drum and pipes. Often we are out all day, and
get a mere nuffing. Many days we have been out and taken nuffing at
all—that's wery common when we dwells upon horders. By dwelling
on horders I mean looking out for gennelmen what want us to play
in front of their houses. When we strike up in the open street we
take upon a haverage only 3d. a show. In course, we *may* do more,
but that's about the sum, take one street performance with another.
Them kind of performances is what we calls 'short showing.' We gets
the halfpence and hooks it. A long pitch is the name we gives to performances that lasts about half an hour or more. Them long pitches
we confine solely to street corners in public thoroughfares, and then
we take about a shilling upon a haverage, and more if it's to be got—
we never turns away nuffing. 'Boys, look up your fardens,' says the
houtside man, 'it ain't half over yet, we'll show it all through.' The
short shows we do only in private bye streets, and of them we can get
through about twenty in the day—that's as much as we can tackle—
ten in the morning and ten in the arternoon. Of the long pitches, we
can only do eight in the day. We start on our rounds at nine in the
morning, and remain out till dark at night. We gets a snack at the
publics on our road. The best hours for Punch are in the morning
from nine till ten, because then the children are at home. Arter that,
you know, they goes out with the maids for a walk. From twelve till
three is good again, and, then, from six till nine—that's because the
children are mostly at home at them hours. We make much more
by horders for performance houtside the gennelmen's houses than we
do by performing in public in the hopen streets. Monday is the best
day for street business; Friday is no day at all, because then the poor
people has spent all their money. If we was to pitch on a Friday we
shouldn't take a halfpenny in the streets, so we in generall on that day
goes round for horders. Wednesday, Thursday, and Friday is the best

days for us with horders at gennelmen's houses. We do much better in the spring than at any other time in the year, excepting holiday time, at Midsummer and Christmas. That's what we calls Punch's season. We do most at evening parties in the holiday time, and if there's a pin to choose between them, I should say Christmas holidays was the best. For attending hevening parties now we generally get £1 and our refreshments—as much more as they like to give us. But the business gets slacker and slacker every season. Where I went to ten parties twenty year ago, I don't go to two now. People isn't getting tired of our performances, but stingier—that's it. Everybody looks at their money now afore they parts with it, and gennelfolks haggles and cheapens us down to shillings and sixpences, as if they was guineas in the holden time. Our business is werry much like hackney-coach work; we do best in vet veather. It looks like rain this evening, and I'm uncommon glad on it to be sure. You see the vet keeps the children in doors all day, and then they wants something to quiet 'em a bit, and the mothers and fathers, to pacify the dears, gives us a horder to perform. It musn't rain cats and dogs—that's as bad as no vet at all. What we likes is a regular good steady Scotch mist, for then we takes double what we does on other days. In summer we does little or nothing; the children are out all day enjoying themselves in the Parks. The best pitch of all in London is Leicester-square; there's all sorts of classes, you see, passing there. Then comes Regent-street (the corner of Burlington-street is uncommon good, and there's a good publican there besides). Bond-street an't no good now. Oxford-street, up by Old Cavendish-street, or Oxford-market, or Wells-street, are all favourite pitches for Punch. We don't do much in the City. People has their heads all full of business there, and them as is greedy after the money an't no friend of Punch's. Tottenham-court-road, the New-road, and all the *henwirons* of London is pretty good. Hampstead, though, an't no good; they've got too poor there. I'd sooner not go out at all than to Hampstead. Belgrave-square, and all about that part, is uncommon good; but where there's many chapels Punch won't do at all. I did once, though, strike up hopposition to a street preacher wot was a holding forth in the New-road, and did uncommon well. All his flock, as he called 'em, left him and come over to look at me. Punch and preaching is two different creeds—hopposition parties, I may say. We in generally walks from twelve to twenty mile every day, and carries the show, which weighs a good half-hundred at least. Arter great exertion our woice werry often fails us; for speaking all day through the 'call' is werry trying, specially when we are chirrupping up so as to bring the children to the vinders. The boys is the greatest nuisances we has to contend with. Wherever we goes we are sure of plenty of boys for a haudience; but they've got no money, bother 'em, and they'll follow us for miles, so that we're often compelled to go miles to awoid 'em. Many parts is swarming with boys—such as Vhitechapel—Spitalfields; that's the worst place of all for boys I ever come anear—they're like flies in summer there, only much more thicker. I never shows my face within miles of them parts. Chelsea, again, has an uncommon lot of boys, and wherever we know the children swarm, them's the spots we makes a point of awoiding. Why, the boys is such a hobstruction to our performance that often we are obliged to drop the curtain for 'em. They'll throw one another's caps into the frame while I'm inside on it, and do what we will we can't keep 'em from poking their fingers through the baize and making holes to peep through. Then they *will* keep tapping the drum—but the worst of all is, the most of 'em a'n't got a farden to bless themselves with, and they *will* shove into the best places. Soldiers again we don't like, they've got no money—no, not even so much as pockets, sir. Nusses a'n't no good. Even if the mothers of the dear little children has given 'em a penny to spend, why the nusses takes it from 'em and keeps it for ribbins. Sometimes we can coax a penny out of the children, but the nusses knows too much to be gammoned by us. Indeed servants in generally don't do the thing what's right to us—some is good to us, but the most of 'em will have poundage out of what we gets. About sixpence out of every halfcrown is what the footman takes from us. We in generally goes into the country in the summer time for two or three months. Watering-places is wery good in July and August. Punch mostly goes down to the sea-side with the quality. Brighton, though, a'n't no account: the Pavilion's done up with, and therefore Punch has discontinued his wisits. We don't put up at the trampers' houses on our travels, but in generally inns is where we stays, because we consider ourselves to be above the other showmen and medicants. At one lodging-house as I stopped at once in Warwick there was as many as fifty staying there what got their living by street performances—the greater part were Italian boys and girls. There are altogether as many as sixteen Punch and Judy frames in England. Eight of these is at work in London, and the other eight in the country, and to each of these frames there are two men. We are all acquainted with one another; are all sociable together, and know where each other is, and what they are doing on. When one comes home another goes out—that's the way we proceed through life. It wouldn't do for two to go to the same place. If two on us happens to meet at one town, we jine and shift pardners, and share the money. One goes one way and the other another, and we meet at night and reckon up over a sociable pint or a glass. We shift pardners so as each may know how much the other has taken. It's the common practice for the man what performs Punch to share with the one what plays the drum and pipes—each has half of what is collected; but if the pardner can't play the drum and pipes, and only carries the frame and collects, then his share is but a third of what is taken until he larns how to perform himself. The street performers in London lives mostly in little rooms of their own; they has generally wives and one or two children, who are brought up to the business. Some lives about the Westminster-road and St. George's in the East. A great many are in Lock's-fields; they are all the old school that way. Then some, or rather the principal part of the showmen, are to be found up about Lisson Grove. In this neighbourhood there is a house of call, where they all assembles in the evening. There are a very few in Brick-lane, Spitalfields, that is mostly deserted now by showmen. The West-end is the great resort of all, for it's there the money lays, and there the showmen abound. We all know one another, and we can tell in what part of the country the others are. We have intelligence, by letters, from all parts. There's a Punch I know on now is either in the Isle of Man, or on his way to it."

The proprietor of the Fantoccini was less communicative than that of Punch. "He was afraid," he told me, "that telling so much would do the purfession harm. It was letting the public know too much—and they were quite 'cute enough already." He spoke all throughout very guardedly. He said, it looked quite fearful-like to have every word as he uttered written down. On inquiry, however, I found that he had spoken nothing but the truth. He was a short, spare man, with sharp features. His dress consisted of an old blue pilot coat, that had turned to a bright plum-colour with age, and two waistcoats—one an old shiny black satin "vest" that almost covered what appeared to be the remains of a crimson plush. His trowsers were corduroy, and very greasy down the front of the thigh, apparently with the friction of the big drum. He appeared to be a well-meaning man, and particularly anxious not to say anything that could be taken amiss by the nobility and gentry, who, he said, were

Punch, 1841

his best customers. He "didn't care about the streets; but the houses," he said—he "wouldn't offend for a good deal."

"I go out with the *Fantoccini* sometimes," he said, "and sometimes with the *Chinese Shades*. The Shades I work in the winter season, and the Fantoccini in the summer. The Shades don't do in the summer, because it is a night exhibition, and the days are long then. I was originally brought up to the artificial flower business, and had, as a boy, 3s. 6d. a week for veining the leaves. I was then ten years old. I stopped working at this after five years, during which time my wages had risen to 7s. 6d. per week, and I had learnt myself to play the Pandæan pipes, and after that to beat the drum, much to the annoyance of my mother, who was a religious kerackter. At last I made acquaintance with a person belonging to a street band, and he proposed that I should go out with him of an evening to play at the hotels. I thought I would try, and I got for my first night's share 7s. 6d.; there were four of us in the band, and all played the pipes. Street bands then were very different to what they are now. They were much worse, but thought a great deal better of than at present. I considered the 7s. 6d. that I got by playing the pipes for one evening in the street was much easier arned than the 7s. 6d. that I got for working the whole week through at the artificial flower business, so I knocked off work, and took to the street band altogether. My share at that time (I am speaking of thirty years ago) used very often to come to 15s. and 18s. per night, and there were three of us who had as much as myself. We used to play outside the hotels chiefly. Sometimes we took as much as a sovereign from one house, sometimes 5s., and sometimes only 2s. 6d. Soon after this I saw a Fantoccini show, and was so much taken with it that I made up my mind to get a set of the figures, and start in the business. I bought a common set for practice, and those I larnt myself upon. After that I went to a regular maker, and had a good set made on purpose for me. I gave him 7s. 6d. a figure. I had seven of them to start with. There was the Sailor for the hornpipe dancer—that was one; the Pole-andrew, to perform backwards and forwards over two chairs with a pole; the Magic Turk, who danced the fandango; then there was the Clown, the Indian Juggler with the balls, the Skeleton that tumbles all to pieces, and Tom and Jerry's larks, which consisted of four figures—African Sal, Dusty Bob, Billy Waters, and Tom and Jerry. Each of these figures were about a foot high, and were made for me by a pupil of Mr. Gray's, who was the first that introduced the Fantoccini into the streets; and that is just upon 25 years ago. Before Mr. Gray's time the same figures, upon a larger scale, were shown by Mr. Myddleton in a booth, and called 'the Puppets.' Myddleton worked his figures in a different way to those in the Fantoccini, and being much larger, they were not near so nimble. My stock in trade, puppets and all, cost me about £10. The frame was £3 of the money. The heads of the figures were carved in wood, and the bodies dressed so as to be supple and easy. The working of them is a secret, and requires a great deal of practice; they are moved principally by the fingers. It would not do for a person with the gout or rheumatism to try his hand at it. The Sailor dances as nat'ral as T. P. Cooke, and the Indian Juggler flings the balls about as nimbly as Rammy Sammy. The exhibition is the same as it was in Gray's time, with the exception of some new figures, such as the maid with the milking-pails and the enchanted Turk, whose limbs come all to pieces. The skeleton is the most difficult to work, but, perhaps, the Pole-andrew requires the greatest practice and nimbleness in the fingers. When the Fantoccini first came up, a great deal of money was taken by it. Gray could not attend at the gentlemen's houses fast enough. Very often he would have to perform at two or three different parties in the course of the evening, and get a pound or more at each. He gave his musician who played the pipes 7s. a day, and the man that carried his frame 5s. When I first took to the Fantoccini business I used to make £5 a week throughout the Christmas and Midsummer holidays. After that I used to take about £3 a week. Some weeks of course was bad, but take it altogether I got on very well till about eight years after I started. There are only four regular Fantoccini men in the country, and these seldom work that alone. If you can't change your hand in the street-exhibition line from one thing to another, it won't do now-a-days. People grows tired of seeing the same thing, and they want something fresh. When I goes round to the gentlemen's houses with the Fantoccini, if I am not wanted I comes home. I charge half-a-crown if ordered to play in front of a house. Sometimes I play at the corners of the streets, like Punch. We depend more upon the orders from gentlemen's houses than we do on the streets. Take it upon an average we make about the same as Punch. *The Chinese Shades* is a different affair—it is a night exhibition. It consists of a frame like Punch's, with a transparent curtain in front. Behind this the shadows of movable figures are shown. There are about six of these in London, and there may be more in different parts of the country. They were first brought into the public streets by a man named Brown, who used to show them in a waggon forty years ago. In former years they were shown at Astley's Theatre, upon a much larger scale; at least, I know the Broken-bridge and Billy Button was, which are both parts of our entertainment to the present day. Since its first introduction into the streets we have added the female dancer on the tight-rope, as well as the performance of the west-country Bull-bait, Spring-heel Jack, and Monsieur Kline. In the Chinese Shades there is a great deal of talking, but in the Fantoccini nothing is said. The nights of the fore part of the week are much the best. We seldom go out in the latter part if things pay us in the day—except one gets an order to 'tend a gentleman's house. Our audience in the streets consist chiefly of working-men, but the Shades pleases the children a great deal. Last Christmas night, as ever was, I performed in St. Giles's Union. I showed the parish boys and girls the Fantoccini, the Chinese Shades, and Mr. Punch as well. It was the clergyman of the parish as engaged me, and it seemed to be a treat to the poor children. Each of them had an orange in their hand; and you should have heard them laugh—good Lord! Fine evenings we do pretty well, but in wet weather it is no use to show our faces in the streets. We go out with the Shades about six in the evening, and come home about ten; we manage to show about four long performances during that time. The Chinese Shades is a deal more labour and exertion for the lungs than the Fantoccini. I don't know that we make more money at it. I should say, taking it all the year round, I make upon an average from 15s. to 20s. a week, but in former times I could make more in a day than I can in a week now. I had two guineas a week about twenty years back along with Diavolo Antonio, at Norwich, for playing half an hour of a night at the Assembly Rooms. I also performed at the Royal Gardens at Vauxhall, and there I exhibited the Shades, Fantoccini, and Punch, for many years. Nobody but Mr. Pike and myself have ever shown there of late years; our business is all gone to the dogs now. To show you the impression our street performances makes on some folks, I will just tell you about one party who was so struck with Punch that wherever the exhibition went there he was at our heels. Miles upon miles he travelled after us; he never lost a performance; day after day, and week after week, he stuck to us as close as wax. He was a dealer in books, and used to hawk them from house to house, but he was so struck with the performance of Punch that he gave up his business to follow the show wherever it went. Among our profession he was nicknamed the Ghost, because he positively haunted us. If we told him to go away, he would disappear for a short time, and then shoot into sight again the very next performance. From our first exhibition in the morning till our last at night he was at our heels; and if we were ordered to play before a gentleman's house, there he was sure to be standing in the front. Not so much as a farthing did he ever give us; and if we went into a public house to dinner, we should find him waiting outside for us when we came away, let us stay as long as we would. It was quite a hinfatuation. We used to tell him to go about his business, or hold horses; but no, he would never leave us. At last his friends, finding how he was taken up with the show, and that he would not do anything else, purchased a frame and a set of figures for him from one of our regular men. Then he had to be taught the performance before he could make any use of it. He is now travelling the country with this same show, but he is not much of a hand at it to this day. You see, sir, he has great taste for Punch, but no lungs."

A short thick-set man, with small puckered-up eyes, and dressed in an old brown velveteen shooting jacket, gave me an account of some by-gone exhibitions and the *Galantee Show:*—

"My father was a soldier," he said, "and was away in foreign parts, and I and a sister lived with my mother in St. Martin's workhouse. I was 55 last New Year's-day. My uncle, a bootmaker in St. Martin's-lane, took my mother out of the workhouse, that she might do a little washing and pick up a living for herself, and we children went to live with my grandfather, a tailor. After his death, and after many changes, we had a lodging in the Dials, and there —— the sweep coaxed me with pudding one day, and encouraged me so well, that I didn't like to go back to my mother; and at last I was apprenticed to him from Hatton-garden, on a month's trial. I liked chimley sweeping for that month; but it was quite different when I was regularly indentured. I was cruelly treated then, and poorly fed, and had to turn out barefooted between three and four many a morning in frost and snow. In first climbing the chimleys, a man stood beneath me and pushed me up, telling me how to use my elbows and knees: if I slipped he was beneath me, and ketched me, and shoved me up again. The skin came off my knees and elbows; here's the marks still you see. I suffered a great deal as well as Dan Duff, a fellow sweep, a boy who died. I've been to Mrs. Montagu's dinner in the square, on the 1st May, when I was a sweep boy; it was a dinner in honour of her son having been stolen away by a sweep" (the man's own words). "I suppose there was more than 300 of us sweeps there in a large green at the back of her house. I ran away from my master once; but was carried back, and was rather better used. My master then got me knee and elbow pads, and bathed my joints in salt and water, and I managed to drag on seven sorrowful years with him. I was glad to be my own man at last, and I cut the sweep trade, bought Pandean pipes, and started with an organ man as his mate. I saved money with the organ man, and then bought a drum. He gave me 5s. a week and my wittles, drink, washing, and lodging; but there wasn't so much music afloat then. I left the organ man and went out with 'Michael, the Italy bear.' Michael was the man's name that brought over the bear from somewhere abroad. He was a Italy man; and he used to beat the bear and manage her. They called her Jenny; but Michael was not to say roughish with her, unless she was obstropolous. If she were he showed her the large mopstick and beat her with it—hard sometimes—'specially when she wouldn't let the monkey get a top of her head, for that was part of the performance. The monkey was dressed the same as a soldier, but the bear had no dress but her muzzle and chain. The monkey—a clever fellow he was, and could jump over sticks like a Christian—was called Billy. He jumped up and down the bear too, and on to his master's shoulders, where he sat as Michael walked down the street. The bear had been taught to roll and tumble—she rolled right over her head all round a stick, and then she danced round it. She did it to the word of command. Michael said to her, 'Round and round again.' We fed her on bread; a quartern loaf every night, after her work, in half a pail of water; the same every morning; never any meat, nothing but bread, boiled tatoes, or raw carrots; meat would have made her savage. The monkey was fed on nuts, apples, gingerbread, or anything. Besides them we had two dancing dogs. The bear didn't like them, and they were kept on one side in performing. The dogs jumped through hoops and danced on their hind legs; they're easyish enough trained. Sometimes the butchers set bull-dogs—two or three at a time—at Jenny, and Michael and me had to beat them off, as well as the two other men that were with us. Those two men collected the money, and I played the pipes and drums, and Michael minded the bear, and the dogs, and monkey. In London we did very well. The West-end was the best; Whitechapel was crowded for us, but only with coppers. I don't know what Michael made, but I had 7s. a week, with my wittles and lodging. Michael did well; he generally had 20s. to 30s. every night in ha'pence, and used to give 21s. worth of it for a one-pound note; for they was in then. He must have taken £12 week by week, or more. When we've travelled in the country we've sometimes had trouble to get lodgings for the bear. We've had to sleep in outhouses with her, and have sometimes frightened people that didn't know we were there, but nothing serious. Bears is well-behaved enough, if they're not aggrawated. Perhaps no one but me is left in England now, what properly understands a dancing bear. Jenny wasn't ever baited, but offers were made for it by sporting characters. The country was better than London when the weather allowed; but in Gloucester, Cheltenham, and a good many places, we weren't let in the high streets. The gentlefolk in the balconies, both in town and country, where they had a good sight, were our best friends. It's more than thirty years ago— yes a good bit more now. At Chester races one year, we were all taken and put into prison—bear, and dogs, and musicianers and all—every one—because we played a day after the races; that was Saturday. We were all in quod until Monday morning. I don't know how the authorities fed the bear. We were each in a separate cell, and I had bread, cheese, and gruel. On Monday we were discharged, and the bear was shot by the magistrates' orders. They wanted to hang poor Jenny at first, but she was shot and sold to the hairdressers. I couldn't stay to see her shot, and had to go into an alehouse on the road. I don't know what her carcase sold for; it wasn't very fat. Michael and me then parted at Chester, and he afterwards went home, rich, to Italy, taking his monkey and dogs with him, I believe. He lived very careful, chiefly on rice and cabbage, and a very little meat with it, which he called manesta. He was a very old man. I had manesta sometimes, but didn't like it much. I drummed and piped my way from Chester to London, and there took up with another foreigner named Green, in the clock-work figure line. The figures were a Turk called Bluebeard, a Sailor, a lady called Lady Catarina, and Neptune's car, which we called Nelson's car as well—but it was Neptune's by rights. These figures danced on a table when taken out of a box. Each had its own dance after being wound up. First came my Lady Catarina. She, and the others of them, was full two feet high. She had a cork body, and a very handsome silk dress, or muslin, according to the fashion and the season—black in Lent, or whatever the nobility wore. Lady Catarina, when wound up, danced a reel for seven minutes, the Sailor a hornpipe, and Bluebeard shook his head, rolled his eyes, and moved his sword, just as natural as life. Neptune's car went either straight or round the table, as it was set. We often showed our performance in the houses of the nobility, and would get 10s. or 12s. at a good house where there was children. I had a third share, and in town and country we cleared 50s. a week at least, every week, among the three of us, after all our keep and expenses had been paid. At Doncaster races we have taken £3 in a day, and £4 at Lincoln races. Country, in summer, was better than town. There's no such exhibition now, barring one I have, but that's pledged. It cost £20 at Mr. ——'s, for the four figures without dresses. I saved money, which went in an illness of rheumatic-gout. There's no bears at all allowed now—times is changed, and all for the worser. I stuck to this clock-work concern sixteen years, and knows all parts of the country—Ireland, Scotland, Guernsey, Jersey, and the Isle of Wight. A month before Christmas we used to put the figures by, for the weather didn't suit, and then we went with a galantee show of a magic lantern. We showed it on a white sheet, or on the ceiling, big or little, in the houses of the gentlefolk and the schools where there was a breaking-up; it was shown by way of a treat to the scholars. There was Harlequin, and Billy Button, and such like. We had 10s. 6d. and 15s., for each performance, and did very well indeed. I have that galantee show still, but it brings in little now. Green's dead, and all in the line's dead but me. The galantee show don't answer, because magic lanterns are so cheap in the shops. When we started, magic lanterns wasn't common, but we can't keep hold of a good thing long in these times. It was a regular Christmas thing once—the galantee show. I can make, in a holiday time, 20s. a week at present; but that's only at holiday times, and is just a mere casualty a few times a year. I do other jobs when I can get them—at other times I delivers bills, carries boards, and helps at funerals."

The Morning Chronicle, Saturday, May 25, 1850.

LABOUR AND THE POOR.

—◆—

THE METROPOLITAN DISTRICTS.

[FROM OUR SPECIAL CORRESPONDENT.]

LETTER LIII.

In my last Letter I commenced an account of the street performers and showmen. There are a large class of individuals, I said, who obtain their living in the open air. Some sell something—others perform or show something—others do something (as sweep crossings, deliver bills, hold horses, carry boards, &c.)—and others, again, mend or make something—by way of gaining a subsistence. The first are *Hucksters*, or street tradesmen; the second are *Mountebanks*, or street performers; the third *Working Pedlars*, or street artisans; and the fourth, street *Labourers or Jobbers*.

The Mountebanks appear to arrange themselves into five classes, viz.—the street performers, or exhibitors of puppet shows, peep shows, feats of strength and sleight of hand, and trained animals, together with dancers and musicians. I have already given an account of the puppet shows. In my present Letter I purpose describing the condition and earnings of the street performers of feats of strength and manual dexterity.

These consist of many distinct varieties. First, there are the "Acrobats," or posturers; second, the "Equilibrists," or balancers; third, the "stiff" and "bending" tumblers; fourth, the jugglers; fifth, the conjurors; and sixth, the sword swallowers, and "salamanders" or fire-eaters. Each of these is generally a distinct branch of the "profession," requiring a separate education; in some cases, the same individual will combine in himself two or three of the different "lines," but this is by no means usual. A stiff and bending tumbler is a very distinct character from either an equilibrist or a conjuror; in the one the muscles of the back and limbs have been educated, whereas, in the others, the eye and hand have acquired especial quickness from long practice and training. Indeed, the essential difference between the several branches of these arts appears to be in the cultivation of a different set of muscles or organs. In the sword-swallower, the throat—in the equilibrist, the eye—in the tumbler, the back and limbs—and in the conjuror, the hands—have been trained to the performance of feats that to uneducated muscles are utterly impossible. The marvel lies not so much in what the performers do, as it does in what first led them to adopt so strange a means of subsistence, and why they should continue to pursue a calling in which the perils are so great, and the gains so limited and uncertain. To see a man bend backwards, and pick up pins from the ground with his eyes—to behold another balance the heaviest and lightest substances on his chin—now a donkey and then the ashes of a burnt paper bag—to witness another swallow swords and live snakes, and all for the sake of a few pence—is wonderful enough; but surely it is more wonderful still to think what could have originally induced these people to give up the ordinary means of subsistence, and adopt a mode of life which appears to require a longer apprenticeship than the common handicrafts, and after all to yield a far more precarious support. The explanation is to be found partly in that love of the marvellous, and of exciting admiration, which is more or less innate with us all, and partly—or rather principally—in the irksomeness of labour, as well as the incapacity for steady and continuous employment, which appears to be a distinctive feature of the vagabond class. It is this irksomeness of labour and this indisposition for any settled occupation, together with a love of novelty and amusement, and an objection to restraint (all of which are implied in the desire for "a roving life" of which the class themselves so often speak), which, as I have before pointed out, constitute the main characteristics of the vagrants and hucksters; and that similar tastes and propensities are among the most notable traits in the moral physiognomy of the beggars and criminals, we shall see when I come to treat of them specially. Another of the main causes of the prevalence of street performers and street tradesmen, is to be found not only in the irksomeness of labour, but in the small remuneration to be obtained from many industrial occupations. Costermongering is easier work—and far more profitable, even now, overstocked as the business appears to be—than toiling at any handicraft; and juggling, conjuring, balancing, posturing, and even sword-swallowing, with all their attendant perils and casualties, are better than starving by the sweat of the brow. The sword-swallower whom I saw assured me that he had tried to get his bread by slipper-making for some two or three years; but as he could only obtain 3s. 6d. a dozen from the slopsellers, and out of this he had to give 1s. 6d. for materials, and could make only 6s. a week at it, he was obliged to return to swallowing swords and snakes, and eating fire in the streets, as a means of getting something more substantial for his family to swallow and eat at home.

The habits and character of the street performers of feats of strength and dexterity present some curious moral and social phenomena, and they are the more curious as the posturers, balancers, conjurors, jugglers, and others who may be considered as the "skilled labourers" of the streets, represent their calling as "dying out." I have met with few old men among street performers, and the class generally seem to look on fifty as a great age. "The original Billy Barlow" (a kind of street clown or fool), said one man to me, "died quite an old man in St. Giles's workhouse—I dare say he was fifty." The prevailing age among street performers appears to be from eighteen to thirty, which I have before shown is the vagabond period of life. Among the whole class I observed two characteristics—intelligence and poverty. By intelligence, I mean that quickness of perception which is commonly called "cunning," a readiness of expression, and a familiarity (more or less) with the topics of the day—the latter picked up probably in public-houses. I found very few of the class unable to read and write; they were naturally quick, and among the whole body there was little of what is understood as vulgar manners. In some few instances I discovered a taste for reading, and almost all expressed a strong desire to leave the streets for some more reputable and certain livelihood. The poverty of many of these people—even of the more skilful—is great, and in some few cases extreme. It is the more irksome too, as most of them have known what they call "better times," by which they naturally mean better earnings. One of the most dexterous of the street conjurors—and that in the opinion of "the profession"—is very poor, and living in a wretched place. His landlady, a tidy, well-behaved woman, gave me (not knowing who I was) an excellent character of her lodger—a single man. He was very quiet, she said, and not irregular in his habits. This poverty is doubly injurious to the street performers, as, from the nature of their "profession," they have necessarily acquired a habit of begging, and it makes them even more servile and importunate for money where there is any expression of sympathy than they might otherwise be. With one or two exceptions, the class seem to have lost all pride of independence, and to consent to subsist on the "generosity" of others, without the least sense of shame. But if they are deficient in pride, they assuredly make it up in vanity—for, according to their own accounts, they are one and all the best and only regular performers in their respective lines. One of the poorest men that I met with seemed to be one of the most deserving. He lived with his family in a small room, and was indignant at the supposition of its being a common lodging-house. The furniture was a turn-up bed, one table, and two chairs, both of the chairs being without bottoms, where rags and fragments of old clothes were so disposed about the framework as to give the semblance of a seat. Above and upon the poor man's mantelpiece was a profusion of small pictures and common china ornaments (his notion of the beautiful), among which his crucifix (for he was a Roman Catholic) was not wanting; and his small German pipe—"his pipe," he said, "was often a meal to him"—held a conspicuous position. The same improvidence—which is the invariable concomitant of every kind of labour that is *uncertain*—prevails among this class as among all others where the income is of a precarious character.

The street performers do not appear to be habitually intemperate. That they indulge in those excesses which great gains at uncertain periods naturally engender, they themselves allow; but they seem rather to have a *habit* than a *love* of drinking. Indeed it is a peculiar feature in the character of the vagrant class that they generally exhibit little taste for fermented liquors. They are libidinous, but not drunken—and this is to be accounted for, in most cases, by the comparatively youthful age to which the vagabond period of life is confined. Drunkenness is the vice of the old rather than the young. The intemperance of the street performers is more acquired than natural, being begotten not only by the love of excess which comes of excessive gain, but by the sociality of their natures, and that "love of company" which is the ordinary concomitant of a desire for approbation. The public tap-room is the arena for display with such people as much as the public streets. Again, it is usual for the performers to put on their street costumes in public-houses, for which accommodation a certain amount of drink is expected to be taken, as well as to dine in such places, and to retire thither during wet weather; so that, after discovering the many inducements that there are among the class to drink, a stranger is struck with the little intoxication that is to be found among them. The older members of the profession certainly appear to have acquired *habits* of drinking; but speaking of the street performers generally, I must say they seem to be far less intemperate than labouring people. Improvidence appears to be their great failing. Let them make what they will in the summer, it is all squandered as soon as got, and they starve in the winter. Let their gains be as large as they may in their youth, not one penny is laid by, and they die in the workhouse in their old age.

Some performers, it will be seen, have been "regularly born and bred" to the street business, while others have been brought up to handicrafts, but preferred a "roving life" to a settled occupation. Some, again, it will be found, have, according to their own statements, been forced into the streets by harsh treatment at home. "Their home," to use their own words, "was no home to them." It should be remembered, however, that one of the most marked characteristics of the vagrant class is an objection to control, so that such people are likely to look upon the mildest form of domestic government as positive tyranny. I do not mean to imply that the severity of parents has not driven many a youth to resort to a vagabond life, who might, with kind conduct, have been brought up to some reputable calling; but, in many cases, I believe that the love of amusement and the irksomeness of restraint are so strong in these individuals, that they desire greater liberty and licence than is consistent with parental care, while they are so "self-willed" that they are ready on every occasion to rebel at authority, and to leave their homes whenever any attempt is made to control them.

A tall, stalwart young man, dressed in a faded blue surtout and trousers patched at the knees, beneath which he wore the elastic cotton dress, with short spangled velvet drawers, that constitutes the ordinary street costume of the class, gave me the following account as to the calling of an "*Acrobat*," or *posturer*. He was of ready speech, good manners, and almost respectable in his appearance:—

"I am the son of a man moving in a superior sphere of life to mine. I left home to follow my fancy for a public life, though it was partly compulsion, as my home was no home. I took to the nigger business at first—about eight years ago, but not in any band of niggers. I began not long after Jem Crow came out, and before there were any Ethiopian serenaders. It was pretty good then, but it's turned about and wheeled about backwards since that time. I have long wished to leave public life, and wish it still more now, for I have a wife and child; and I *would* leave it too, if I could get anything better to do—but 'half a loaf' you know, sir. I have no ambition to stop in it. After my coming out as a street nigger I was a balancer. This I acquired by practice, and after that I picked up balancing with the pole. I was never taught anything in my life. I picked every thing up by practice and assiduity. I balance the pole sometimes now. I lie on my back in the streets (the streets and fine weather is all I have to depend upon) with a cushion under my loins, and I balance and dance the pole with my feet. It's called 'pole-dancing.' It's very hard work to the muscles, and trying to the nerves. I learned pole-dancing, or rather perfected myself in it, in private, after twelve months' pains, at Bristol. I had often a rap on the head, while learning, by the pole's falling, and it *will* slip occasionally still with the best feet, though I flatter myself, that I can perform it, with any man in England. I joined the acrobats three or four years ago. I make my pole performance part of our acrobat business. It's done generally to 'keep the pitch up,' as we term it, that is to keep the people together until we can get the ha'pence from them. We have six in our company of acrobats, including a boy. The man who stands at the bottom is called '*the bearer*,' and is generally a strong man; but there's as much tact as strength in his part of the business. Another man jumps upon his shoulders and is called '*the second*.' I am a second (and occasionally a bearer, too). The man who stands on the second's shoulder is called '*the top-mounter*.' He gets first on the shoulder of the bearer, and so up to the back of the second, then he takes hold of the second's left hand and raises himself up to stand on the second's shoulders—each assists the other. As the top-mounter leans or inclines, the bearer walks forward—he must follow the inclining of the top-mounter as he feels it communicated to him by the second, who just projects his chest a little, the slightest motion is sufficient. If he (the bearer) did not move on we should all come down together—nothing could prevent it. He must bend forward, for we who are up above use our shins and legs as stays against the bearer's or second's heads, and if there be any backward movement the bearer loses his command over the men upon him. Sometimes there is a fall; I once was hurt from one. I never knew any one killed in the acrobat performance, but a young performer has broken his arm twice by falling as an acrobat. Accidents, though, are not common, and we have ways of saving ourselves by a cat-like agility. If the top-mounter finds he is falling by leaning too far forward, he must jump down. He says 'go,' and the second puts his hand up to help the top man in the jump. If he lights on the ball of his foot there is no great hurt, but come down flat-footed and your foot's jarred all to pieces. Learners generally practise at a place in ——, St. Pancras, where they form 'a school.' Sunday mornings is the chief time. In practising there are terrible falls sometimes. There is no particular tuition. Young men have a turn for it and try it one with another. All classes and all grades are in the profession, but the general of us have been pretty well educated. I don't know a dishonest man among us. We ought of all men to be temperate; but still some of us drink hard. I don't care about drink myself, but men pick up a taste for it by being treated when performing at public houses. I felt rather nervous the first time I was 'a second' in public, for fear of 'making a mull of it' (a slip in private's nothing). I got through very well though. I once left off acrobating for six weeks. On rejoining the acrobats as a second I was too confident the first time, and slipped; the 'top mounter' was thrown down and slightly hurt. There are now thirteen acrobats in London, and two London 'schools' numbering four or five each, are in the country and Scotland. We generally know where one another is, by letters to wives and such like. The West-end is the best for acrobating in the London season of fashion—the summer; but it's an aggravating place often, for we *have* got only 2d. for a performance, and some few times nothing. Gentlemen have looked on and walked away without giving a farthing. In the other parts of the year the East-end is the best. Mechanics are our best friends—indeed our principal dependence. We, that is all 'the school,' share alike. I said there were six persons in our company—but besides these, who are all posturers, there is the musician and a negro singer and dancer. Thirty shillings a week is the most I ever got for my share, and that was in the height of summer when the days are longest; but take the year through, we acrobats can't make 12s. a week a piece, and out of that, too, we must find our dresses for performing in. It costs us 1s. a week for our pumps: our dresses are a close suit of strong elastic wove cotton; they cost generally 8s. 6d. We usually have a deep girdle round our waists, and a fillet of spangled velvet round our heads. Some have their dresses dyed flesh-colour—but that I hate; it looks so much like nudity that, on a sudden, it might startle any one. I have been well educated, and should like to get out of such a business; it is as disagreeable to me as it is dangerous. My wife has to work with her needle to help to keep the family—but what can a woman earn that way, when there are so many slop shops? The acrobats, and people of that class, differ perhaps in their tastes from ordinary mechanics. We have some very intellectual men among us. I've travelled with one young man, who was what I call 'a fanatic' for Shakespeare. He is the son of a tradesman. On our way into the country in an acrobat school, he used always to carry Mansell's penny Shakespeare, and he and I would recite Othello and Iago and such like, to while away the time on the road, and in our lodgings. My pipe, however, is my chief solace, for I can't get books enough to read, though I pick up a twopenny volume at a stall now and then. I've exhausted all my neighbours' libraries, too, but that was soon done. The best of the acrobats are fondest of theatricals by way of amusement—a good tragedian, or a comedian—when there's a shilling in the locker. Acrobats sometimes get into theatres, and are sprites, and even harlequins. [He mentioned some.] The dull fellows of Acrobats—and there are such—have no amusements out of a public house. Our living is generally a meat dinner in summer, when performing. Against my will, beer and dinner have cost me far more, when out performing, than I have had to take home to my family. Only four acrobats (including myself) are, I believe, legally married. Our wives are all compelled to work at something. One man's wife earns 6s.—as 'a topper' in the shirt business, and that is a great help. Among the acrobats that I know some have been glass-cutters, hod-carriers, errand boys, shoemakers, and paper block cutters, before taking to the street business. I can hardly say what the others were. We all have an inkling of shoemaking, because we have to mend our own shoes. I consider all are acrobats who stand on each others' shoulders. The acrobats are generally tumblers or posturers as well. A tumbler is one who throws somersaults, head-springs, fore-springs, lion's leaps, and such like. A posturer is a man who puts his leg behind his head, or does what we call 'the frog;' namely, he puts his two legs over his shoulders, and hops along on his hands; some posturers put their legs behind their backs down to their hips; they are what we term limp posturers. The tumblers are either stiff or bending tumblers. The stiff tumbler performs such feats as I have described, as somersaults, head springs, lion's leaps, and such like. The bending tumbler is one who can bend his head back down to his feet and pick up a sixpence, or such like. We have a man with our school whose body seems all joints and bendable everywhere; he fairly sits on his own head, bringing it down his back, his chin resting on the ground, and he looks out from between the top of his thighs. A juggler I consider a man who balances plates, throws balls, and feats of that kind; whereas a conjuror is a man who performs tricks of deception by sleight-of-hand, changing cards, coins, and so on. The acrobats don't reside in any particular part of the town—perhaps no body of men are more equally distributed through London. We settle over night where we are to meet next day—always with the uncomfortable proviso, weather permitting. I have read the letters in the *Morning Chronicle* on the costermongers. My lot once led me to live among that class, and the accounts I saw of them were perfectly true. I should like to emigrate to Australia, where I could get on by perseverance, for I have plenty of that. I wouldn't be an acrobat there, of course, but a labourer of some description. I should like it, but cannot even get on to the first step of the ladder. My wife also wishes to emigrate; but what's the use of such people as us wishing?"

A little boy, with an inanimate look, large sleepy eyes, and very high shoulders, so that he looked almost deformed, gave me the subjoined account:—

"I was twelve years old last March, and play with the acrobats. I have done so for the last three years. I stand on the hands of the 'top mounter,' who holds my feet and throws me about, catching me." [The 'second' here showed the way, even with the boy's thick shoes on, showing great agility, and a very quick eye.] "I was frightened at first," continued the lad, "but never am now. My father is dead. My mother—she has five of us—put me to this business. I'm allowed 1s. a day when performing, and get my dinner with the men. My master takes the money to keep and clothe me. I am very kindly treated. I'd sooner be a trade than this line of life, but if I am to be a tumbler, why I must stick to it; so I practise a few tricks now and then, and try to do something new. I was never let fall in performing so to be hurt. I am the only boy, except one, who plays with the street acrobats."

The next class of street performers are the tumblers. The man whom I saw had a quiet pleasant look and manner, but he was in no way remarkable for muscular development. He had, however, a very graceful bend in the back, and was exceedingly well proportioned, though short. He was dressed like a mechanic on a Sunday.

"I am *a tumbler—a stiff tumbler and a bending tumbler* too," he said. "I have been in this business since I was two years of age. My father was in the profession, and was my teacher. I tumbled at two years old, and have followed it until now, which is twenty-six years. I was compelled to tumble when a child, but my father wasn't cruel to me. He took up the trade of tumbling; he had been a soldier, a silversmith, and a shoemaker, before he became a tumbler. At two years I used to bend back and pick up pins with my eyes—four pins—and then drop them one by one. I do that still. It wasn't very painful to learn this, but I had the headache often, and my nose used to bleed. I used to tremble a good deal when doing it as a child, and so I do now if I leave it off and begin it again. As I grew up I learned other tricks. I can stand on my head, and walk round my head with my legs, while I keep my head standing still. It required a great deal of practice for me to get that perfect—two months perhaps—when I was seven or eight years old. It's a laborious thing, but not painful. We must begin tumbling young, before the bones get set. I can walk along on my elbows, with my legs over my head; it's not painful to me, but it would be to others. I learned that when I was 12 or 13. I have been in this trade all my life, and a very bad trade it is. Some days I may take 6d., some days 1s., some 1s. 6d., and the best day's work I ever had was 10s.; but it's all casualty, and depends greatly on the weather. I have taken as low as 1½d. A fine day like this I might make 7s. or 8s., with luck, in the streets; but on wet days I can do nothing but at the public-houses, and public-house work is very bad indeed. In summer the nights are very short, and night's the only time for tavern tumbling. In one public-house I was stooping back to pick up the pins with my eyelids, and a fellow, half drunk, kicked me, and the pins stuck about my eyes, and it's a mercy I wasn't blinded. I've had gin flung in my eyes, and snuff, and have been subjected to every kind of insult, perhaps for no money at all, when I've asked leave for to perform in the tap-room, and had it granted me. Sometimes I'm refused leave in a public-house and sometimes I'm kicked out of it. The street's the best for money, but there the boys heave stones at you, and the policemen order you on, and go you must. I do the best in the West-end streets—one's about as good as another, if it's only quiet. Regent-street's too busy; Portland-place is pretty good; and so is Grosvenor-square and the squares generally, but we're not often allowed to perform in them. Gentlefolks, both male and female, are my best patrons; the ladies are best generally. I'm never sent for to perform as Punch is. I don't go to any saloons to perform, but I go to fairs. Country is generally better than town for me, but only in summer. Some parts of the City are not so bad; but I'm only allowed in the back streets, such as Bartholomew-close and them places. I believe there are only two other men in London who are of the same profession as myself, a bending and a stiff tumbler at once; they're almost all posturers now, which is easier work. I suppose these two men average what I do, which may be 15s. a week the year through, and that's very little, because I find my own dresses, which come expensive. My dress is made of elastic cotton; it costs me 6s. 6d. or 7s. One dress lasts only six or seven weeks. In bending and tumbling it's strained all to pieces. I want to get out of this line of life, and get into shoemaking, of which I do know a little. To know how to make shoes well is better than all the tricks I know, for the profession is very bad. I owe a man 10s. for giving me instructions in making children's shoes, and I'm improving very much in the trade. Tumbling strains every nerve in the body. I ought to know what it does, for I can manage all these tricks:—I can walk on my hands; jump on my hands, nine feet in three jumps; put a penny under my toe, bend back and pick it up with my mouth without putting my hands to the ground; bend my body back and pick up four pins with my eyes. I can do lion's leaps, that's to jump over chairs like a cat, pitching on my hands and going on; I can bend backwards and bring my head and feet into a tea saucer; do head springs, or go on my head and turn over without using my hands. That's about all. I can't tell which trick is most admired, for I do them all at one performance, leaving the walking round my head to the last. I am a married man. My wife is a shoebinder. I have no children; and if I had I wouldn't like to bring them up to be tumblers. I nearly always play by myself, but I have played with Jim Crows and Highland fling and hornpipe dancers, and jugglers too. We all shared alike, but I do best by myself. I am very strong in the back, and in the muscles of my leg and thigh, but I have never tried all my strength." This man showed me one of his headsprings; he ran along for a few yards and then threw himself violently on his head, and so turned "head over heels" without using his hands. The fore part of the skull had a large callous lump on it, induced by the repeated performance of this trick. After this he stuck four pins upright in the carpet, two close together in one place, and two more about four inches from the others. He then stood with his back towards the pins, about two or three feet from them, and bending backwards brought his head gradually down to the ground, when he removed the pins from the floor by closing his eyelids. Then he raised himself slowly up, and advancing towards the table, with his eyelids still grasping the pins, he shook them one by one from his eyes. His next feat was to run round his head, his neck appearing to serve as a pivot on which his body turned, and he literally flinging his trunk round his head very rapidly. The sights were all painful enough, but done very deftly. He stated, however, that he was out of practice, neither was he in proper costume.

Concerning the street equilibrists or balancers, a spare wiry-looking man, and with an appearance of anything rather than surpassing strength in his body, stated the following:—

"My father was an equestrian and brought me up to his business, but my ancles failed me eight years back from somersaulting, &c. I then took to the *equilibrist* line. I am 40 years old. I liked equestrian-ing. I knew Ducrow, and know Mr. Batty and others in the business, and have performed in Belgium and France. I have been an equilibrist for eight years now, playing in the open air or in-doors. I am a slack wire dancer as well. As an equilibrist I balance poles and an 18-foot deal plank on my chin. Formerly I balanced a donkey on the top of a ladder. It's dreadfully hard work; it pulls you all to pieces. Over 30 years of age you feel it more and more. The donkey was strapped tight to the ladder; there was no training needed for the donkey; any young donkey would do. It was frightened at first generally, but got accustomed to it after a time—use is a great thing. The papers attacked the performance and I was taken to Union-hall for balancing my donkey in the streets. I was fined 7s. 6d., and they kept the donkey in default. I never let the donkey fall, and always put it down gently, for I have the use of my hands in that feat. I was the original of the saying, sir, 'Twopence more, and up goes the donkey.' It's a saying still, and a part of the language now. I sometimes stand on my head on the top of a pole, without the assistance of my hands, and drink a glass of ale in that position, and go through all sorts of postures while on my head. It's more tiring than painful. I've fallen off the pole, for sometimes I'm nervous; when I'm performing, I dare only take one glass of spirits and water. When I fell, I always lighted on my legs, though not so as to make it appear part of the performance—one can't. On the slack-wire I perform all kinds of balancing, spinning plates on sticks, and such like, and I stand on my head on the wire at full swing, holding it in my hands. The wire has broken with me—it was rusty. I fell, and dislocated my hip; that was at Epping. It's dangerous work. I think that I'm the only man now in London who is an equilibrist and slack-wire dancer, and there is only one in the country in my particular line. It's a bad trade; one day I may pick up 5s., that's a first-rate day for street work. In bad weather I can do nothing. It's all a casualty what I make. I couldn't undertake to depend upon 10s. 6d. a week if I confined myself to out-door performances. My trade is a bad one, and badly paid; and the jewels and spangles worn by performers like me are a sort of mockery. We are in general poor;

and it's difficult to get a rise, or even to leave the business, after you're once in it. When you're old you're like a worn-out horse, reckoned fit for nothing." The man's arms and limbs were hard and firm to the touch, though not remarkable for muscular development. He attributed his success as an equilibrist more to art, or "a way of doing it," than to mere bodily strength. He showed me some of his lighter feats, blowing from his mouth a piece of cinquefoil hay, and catching it on the balance, upright on the chin, and balancing a piece of paper rolled up into a conical bag (such as is used for moist sugar), which he placed alight on the bridge of his nose, and there allowed it to burn to the bottom, after which he balanced the black pile of ashes that remained with amazing dexterity—tossing them and catching them upright without breaking them, in a manner that made one positively wonder at the useless skill. He told me that he has balanced fireworks and ships—the Chesapeake and the Shannon, the Chesapeake blowing up and burning close to his chin. Gentlefolks he thought his best friends, if he had any *best*—but the City was perhaps as good as the West-end for money. Grooms and "people about horses" were very fair customers.

The following account of a street juggler's business I had from a grave looking man, of half dignified appearance both in face and figure, and with long well-oiled locks that seemed to be got up expressly for public display:—

"I have been twenty-eight years in the profession of a juggler. I was a plasterer born, as the saying is, and a citizen too, but family circumstances, such as I'd rather not state, led me to form a connection with old Mr. Saunders, the rider, a well-known mountebank. With Saunders's company I juggled on stilts, both in town and country. I believe no man in England but me ever juggled on stilts five feet high. When I started first I did well—most excellent, and never knew what it was to want money. I dare say I made my £5 every week, full that, when I began. I performed on the stilts, with brass balls, from one to five; throwing them up and down and catching them, like the Indian juggler, only he did it from the ground, and I on my stilts. After the brass balls, I threw large brass rings, catching them, and then linking them together. Then I threw three large daggers, or rather from one to three, I have thrown more, all round about my body, catching them as they came. I next took a wooden pole, and on the top of it a wash hand basin—the pole was 7 feet high, and on the top of the pole, still on my stilts, I kept the basin spinning round. I kept to the stilts until six or seven years ago, doing pretty well. After the stilts I performed on the ground, and now I carry a small box which stands on four legs, and with it I'm mostly to be seen at the West-end. I perform out of doors as well as at parties. The box is to hold my apparatus. In one of my tricks I appear to eat a quantity of shavings, and draw them afterwards, in the shape of an immense long barber's pole, out of my mouth. A little doll I make appear and disappear from the folds of a cloak. I show the cloak to be empty, and the next moment there's the doll in it. The shavings, the pole, and the doll are generally called for, if I try anything else. These are my juggling feats; as to conjuring, I do all sorts of things with cards. I make them do anything but speak. I do chiefly the old tricks, such as the shavings, which are not known in the toy-shops. These toy-shops, with their toy tricks, are the ruin of us. I teach conjuring and juggling, and am a professor of legerdemain. I have no pupils—worse luck. I had a natural turn for the profession myself, and didn't require teaching. I perfected myself by study and practice. There are, I believe, only eight persons whom I can rank with myself as regular professional men in London; but toy-shops send out their own conjurors now, and the number of chance conjurors—and they are half gamblers many of them—is uncertain. I don't reckon them professionals. This time of the year is the best of my seasons, but I can make nothing like what I used. I've been ailing too, or else I might make my £2 a week or even more, bad as it is. Private parties is a casualty business. The winter time is my slack time, except about Christmas. I juggled at Vauxhall in 1831, before the Queen. I find town the best for me, but common hands do best in the country; the people are not up to the town mark there. I've taught many an amateur conjuror, real gentlemen, who amuse their friends that way; some of them take to it very kindly, others slop it; but I make them perfect conjurors if I can."

A red-faced man, with what is called a "professional look," gave me the following account. He wore a black dress-coat that had seen better days, and had much the appearance of a third or fourth rate actor:—

"I have been thirty years a professor of conjuring," he said, "and was regularly brought up to the profession. My father was a sailor. I was seven years a clown to old Mr. Brown, known as 'the salt-box,' and known all over the world. He was the first Chinese shades man, and used to take them about in a waggon. He died latterly, very poor. Before Brown took to me I was destitute, and slept two nights in a

cart. When I left Brown, I joined a man named B—, in the theatrical way, I doing the conjuring for the concern. I then travelled five
years professionally, on my own account, in the country. I conjured
both in the open air and in rooms, and have conjured for ten years
in the open air in London. When I first knew the trade it was far
better than it is now, a great deal. I could take 20s. a night, in a London public-house; now I can't make a living by my tricks, dogs and
all, and I'm the first dog breaker in England. There's been a wonderful deal of change in the tricks. The old tricks were what I may call
a little indelicate. The amusements, generally, were more brutal in
those days; so were our tricks, as for instance cutting off a cock's head
and putting it on again—that's done by attaching a false head and
neck as you swing the cock round, but one man used actually to cut
the cock's head off and have a *fac simile* live cock under the table as a
substitute—that's an expensive way; but the people see the bird flutter
and die, and they like that, or rather they *did* like it once. Cups and
balls were fashionable then; they're lost now; but I play them in an improved manner. At present I'm the only man in all the profession can
do it in the style I do. I put three small potatoes, real potatoes, under
three cups, and conjure them into six good-sized balls, all brought to
light under the cups when lifted. [He showed me this trick, which
was done with remarkable neatness.] The egg bag was a popular trick
then; bringing a number of eggs from an empty bag. Frying pancakes
in any one's hat was all the rage too at that time; frying them over a
lamp or a candle, bringing them out of the hat, and then showing
that the hat was perfectly clean within. The batter really goes into the
hat, in an apparatus which is whisked into it for the purpose, and the
pancakes were eaten by the company, and were made of good stuff.
Cutting off a man's nose was common then. A gentleman was asked
to lend a conjuror his nose, and was placed in a chair to have it cut
off. The conjuror used a knife with a wire attached to the middle
round a vacant part of the blade, and this was pressed on the nose.
The conjuror first applied a cloth with rose pink on it, so that being
removed, it looked as if the nose were cut off, and a bloody mass remained. Afterwards the conjuror drew the cloth over the face, wiped
off the colouring, and the nose appeared as before. I've often seen
gentlemen put their fingers to their nose to feel if it was all right, and
that caused great laughter. We used to press the nose with the wire as
if there were a wound. Bringing a guinea-pig from under the hat was
an old trick. The guinea-pig was ready behind the conjuror, and was

got into the hat while some little tricks were being played with it. [He illustrated this by conjuring a doll into a hat.] A cabbage was used when a guinea-pig wasn't to be had. Conjuring now is revolutionised like other things. People weren't so enlightened formerly, and easier tricks passed. Now producing a bowl of gold fish from a shawl, and a quantity of bouquets from an empty hat are the rage. The inexhaustible bottle is popular now. The conjuror in the inexhaustible bottle has tubes in his sleeves, and other contrivances, to have sufficient of any liquor wanted; some of the glasses are prepared, too, as the bottle contains only five compartments, four of which are controlled by the fingers, and the fifth flows out naturally. In the palmy days of conjurors I've had £4 a week at a saloon, and now many a week I can't make more than 10s., both in the open air and the public-houses together. Money's a thing not easy to be conjured, sir. The West-end's the best for the open air. Leicester-square is pretty good; Grosvenor and Belgrave are no good—they're not thoroughfares—you wouldn't get a penny in a day there. Oxford-street and Piccadilly are pretty good. In open air conjuring children and women are small benefit. Mechanics and tradespeople are our best friends in 'pitching,' as we call it. One day I may get 3s., or 4s., or 5s.; next day almost nothing. I know but a dozen professed street conjurors—pure conjurors—in England; five of them are in London, and I believe that ten years ago there were three times as many, not reckoning the numbers of people that practise conjuring whom we call impostors, or 'shisers.' I break dogs to do conjurors' tricks." [He showed me one which picked up cards out of a ring, in answer to questions; such as how many days are in the week? The answer being a card with '7' marked on it. How many gentlemen are in the room? How many ladies? and such like. The dog never took a wrong answer.] "I have broken a dog in three days," he continued, "but that dog took me three months, he's a spaniel, but I believe one kind of dog is as tractable as another under a proper system. I've known the stupidest dogs as they were reckoned make the best conjuring dogs. I've broken at least 20. I perfect them by constant training, great petting, and a little bit of the whip. The trade gets worse and worse, and I don't know what it'll come to."

Concerning *sword swallowing*, I had the subjoined narrative from a fat-faced man, with what may be called a first-rate clown's look, and of grave manners. He and Ramo Samee are, I understand, the only sword swallowers now living—and both are old men. Ramo Samee is the once famous Indian juggler:—

"I have been connected with the conjuring and tumbling professions, and every branch of them for 46 years. I lost my mother when a child, and my father was a carpenter, and allowed me to go with the tumblers. I continued tumbling until my feet were knocked up. I tumbled twenty-three or twenty-four years. It was never what you may call a good business, only a living. I got £3 a week certainly, at one time, and sometimes £4; but you had to live up to it, or you were nothing thought of; that is to say, if you kept 'good company.' Now there's not a living to be made in the trade. Six and twenty years ago I began to practise sword swallowing against the celebrated Ramo Samee, who was then getting £25 and £30 a week. I first practised with a cane, and found it difficult to get the cane down. When I first did it with the cane, I thought I was a dead man. There's an aperture in the chest which opens and shuts; and it keeps opening and shutting, as I understand it; but I know nothing about what they call anatomy, and never thought about such things. Well, if the cane or sword go down upon this aperture when it's shut, it can go no further, and the pain is dreadful. If it's open, the weapon can go through, the aperture closing on the weapon. The first time I put down the cane, I got it back easily, but put my head on the table and was very sick, vomiting dreadfully. I tried again the same afternoon, however, three or four hours after, and did it without pain. I did it two or three times more, and next day boldly tried it with a sword and succeeded. The sword was blunt, and was 36 inches long, an inch wide, and perhaps a sixth of an inch thick. I felt frightened with the cane, but not with the sword. Before the sword was used, it was rubbed with a handkerchief and made warm by friction. I swallowed swords for 14 years. At one time I used to swallow three swords, a knife and two forks, of course keeping the handles in my mouth, and having all the blades in my stomach together. I felt no pain. No doubt many of the audience felt far more pain at seeing it than I in doing it. I wore a Turkish dress both in the streets and the theatres. I never saw ladies faint at my performance; no, there was no nonsense of that kind. Gentlemen often pulled the swords and knives by their handles out of my mouth, to convince themselves it was real, and they found it real, though people to this day generally believe it's not. I've sometimes seen people shudder at my performance, but I generally had loud applause. I used to hold my head back with the swords in my stomach for two or three minutes. I've had a guinea a day for sword-swallowing. This guinea a day was only for a few days at fair times. I was with old 'salt-box' Brown too, and swallowed swords and conjured with him. I swallowed swords with him thirty times a day—more than one each time, sometimes three or four. I had a third of the profits; Brown had two-thirds. We divided after all expenses were paid. My third might have been 30s. a week, but it wouldn't be half as much now if I could swallow swords still. If I could swallow a tea-kettle now the people would hardly look at me. Sometimes—indeed a great many times—say twenty—I have brought up oysters out of my stomach after eating them, just as I swallowed them, on the end of the sword. At other times there was blood on the end of the blade. I always felt faint after the blood, and used to take gin or anything I could get at hand to revive me, which it did for a time. At last I injured my health so much that I was obliged to go to the doctor's. I used to eat well, and drink too. When I felt myself injured by the swallowing I had lost my appetite, and the doctor advised me to take honey. I was three months on his hands, living on honey and liquids, tea, beer, and sometimes a drop of grog. At three months' end he told me, if I swallowed swords, it would be my death; but for all that I was forced to swallow the swords to get a meal to swallow. I kept swallowing swords three or four years after this, not feeling any great suffering. I then thought I would swallow a live snake. I'd never heard of any one, Indian or anybody, swallowing a live snake. It came into my head once by catching a grass snake in the fields in Norfolk. I said to myself, as I held it by the neck, 'there seems no harm in this fellow, I'll try if I can swallow him.' I tried then and there, and I *did* swallow him. It felt cold and slimy as it went down. I didn't feel afraid, for I kept tight hold of him by the tail; and no one has any business to be afraid of a grass snake. When I brought the snake up again, in about three minutes, it seemed dead. After that I introduced snake swallowing into my public performances, and did so for about four years. I have taken 5s., and as low as 1s. when I swallowed snakes in the streets of London. I catched my own snakes a few miles from London, and killed very few through swallowing on 'em. Six snakes, properly fed on milk, lasted me a-year. The snakes never injured me; and I shouldn't have given it up, but the performance grew stale, and people wouldn't give me anything for it. I have swallowed swords in the streets thirty to forty times a day, and snakes as often, both in town and country. I thought once I couldn't have followed any other sort of life; you see, I'd been so long accustomed to public life; besides I may have liked it far better than labour, as most young men do, but no labour can be harder than mine has been. If my father had been what he ought, he might have checked my childish doings and wishes. I *have* tried other things though, in the hopes of bettering myself. I have tried shoemaking, and for five or six years, but couldn't get a living at it. I wasn't competent for it—that's two years ago—so now I'm a musician to a 'school' of acrobats. Very many like me remain in the street business, because they can't get out of it; that's the fact. Whilst I swallowed swords and snakes I played the fire-eater. I did it once or twice last week. I eat red-hot cinders from the grate, at least I put them in my mouth; really red-hot cinders. I have had melted lead in my mouth. I only use a bit of chalk. I chalk my palate, tongue, and fingers; it hardens the skin of the tongue and palate, but that's all. Fire-eating affects the taste for a time, or rather it prevents one tasting anything very particularly. I've eaten fire for 20 years in the streets and in public places. It hasn't brought any money of late years. I wasn't afraid when I first tried it, and I first tried it by eating a lighted link—a small flambeau. I felt no inconvenience. The chalk did everything that was right. You may stroke a red hot poker with chalked hands, and not be burnt. I make the same as the acrobats; perhaps I average 12s. a week, and have a wife and six children, the oldest under eleven, to maintain out of that. Sometimes we're obliged to live upon nothing. When I was slipper-making I had from 3s. 6d. to 4s. a dozen, the grindery costing me 1s. 6d., leaving me 2s. for a dozen. I could only clear 6s. a week by it; that's all I could get out of the slop-shops. There's one good thing coming from sword swallowing that I ought to mention. I'm satisfied that Ramo Samee and I gave the doctors their notions about a stomach-pump."

Another class of out-door performers are the *street dancers*. These, I am informed by one who has had many years' experience at the business, are not so numerous as they were nine years back. It is about twelve years since dancing was introduced into the public thoroughfares as a source of amusement to the spectators, and of subsistence to the performers. The cause of this new kind of street performance being adopted, I am told, was the bad business and payment at the itinerant theatres. Before that time the lower order of dancers were confined to the travelling booths. The first dancer who made his appearance in the streets did only the sailor's hornpipe, dressed in character. It was very successful then, and produced about 9s. or 10s. on a fine day. From £2 5s. to £2 10s. per week was the regular income in the summer at that period. My informant had himself taken as much as 10s. a day in the streets only four years back. The success of the first street dancer soon spread among the tribe in the booths. The salary of a dancer at a booth only goes on during fair time, and was some few years ago 10s. a day for the three days that the fair usually lasted. (Now the price is from 3s. to 5s., the latter being the terms of the "very best" performers.) A booth dancer is generally at work three days in the week, there being fairs enough throughout the country to keep them half employed, and, indeed, fully employed if they could reach them in time. From the first introduction of dancing into the streets, up to the present time, performers have kept on leaving the booths for the streets, so that the street business is now quite overdone; and the average taking, I am credibly informed, does not amount to above 2s. a day. It requires a great deal of luck, says my informant, to raise it to 2s. 6d., and often they get only 1s. or 1s. 6d. The street dances are always performed on a small piece of board (about three feet long and two feet wide), placed in the middle of the road. The most popular dances are the Sailor's Hornpipe—in and out of fetters—the Lancashire Clog dance, the Highland Fling, and a comic medley dance. The street dancers at present in London are about a dozen or fifteen in number; many of these can only dance the sailor's hornpipe. Only one-third of the number, I am informed, can do the whole of the dances before mentioned. Included in the twelve London street-dancers are six children; these are girls from five to fifteen years of age. The fathers of these girls play the drum and pipes, and have brought them up to the business. The children make more money than the grown men. The takings of these people are, in fine weather, from 5s. to 10s. a day. The father takes the whole of the money collected, and gives but a halfpenny or a penny to the girls, and that not always. These children appear in the streets either in Scotch or ballet dresses. There is no female above 20 dancing in the streets of London. Stilt dancing has quite disappeared from the streets; the police will not allow it, I am told. The male dancers are between 20 and 30 years of age. The occupations of the men previously to taking to street dancing were of various kinds. One was a baker, another a coach-smith, another a cotton-spinner, another a street singer, and the rest have been brought up to the "profession" in booths. The men have mostly taken to the street business under the impression of doing better at it than at their trades. Some have gone to it from the love of a roving life, and objection to any settled occupation or continuous labour. It is thought to be easy work—dancing in the streets—"but," says my informant, "I find it to be much harder than even smith's work, which was the business I was brought up to; it strains the nerves of the legs and sinews, and is more tiring than the sledge-hammer. I was at smith's work five years, and got upon an average from 15s. to 22s. a week when I followed it. But I thought I could do better at dancing, and so I did at first; though now I don't make not a quarter of what I did at my trade, and have picked up habits that have quite unsettled me for following the business I was brought up to. Ah, I was young, sir, when I left it, and now I begin to see my folly. Had I stuck to my trade it would have been a good thing for me and my poor wife. I'd go to anything indeed rather than be as I am. Our life is so uncertain. There is no Saturday night you know, sir. You get your money in dribs and drabs, and being about we are obliged to drop into public-houses, and so a good part of even the little we do get goes in beer. We are obliged to have beer at the publics where we go and dress. I learnt my dancing in tap-rooms. I used to dance to my fellow-workmen of a night, and was thought a little of; that was why I took to it. The male dancers seldom go out alone, but usually with the Acrobats. Occasionally two dancers will join, one doing the Highland fling, and another the sailor's hornpipe. And sometimes one will go out alone with a clown or a Billy Barlow, to keep the pitch up. These all share equally. A small party generally does better than a large one. Sometimes two 'schools' will meet at a public-house, and, 'getting on the drink,' will agree together after they have spent all their morning's earnings in beer and gin, to go out together merely for the purpose of getting more drink. I have known," says my informant, "as many as ten acrobats, jugglers, dancers, clowns, and Jim Crows to go out altogether, and spend every halfpenny they brought back in drink, and even after that to pledge the big drum for more liquor. The wives of the street dancers are generally very poverty stricken, and very miserable. Some do a little needlework or washing, but many are dependent solely upon their husbands' exertions, and often they have neither food nor fire at home."

My informant had been for the last two years playing "my lord" in Jack-in-the-green, on May-day. He had been engaged at 5s. a day, and "plenty to drink" by the sweeps, who I am informed made a very good thing of it, having cleared £4 or £5 in the three days. This kind of street performance is generally got up by some master sweep in re-duced circumstances, who engages all the parties and finds the dresses. There was only one regular sweep in the school that my informant joined. Many of the Jacks-in-the-green are got up by costermongers.

"My Lady" generally has 3s. a day, and is mostly the sweep's or cost-ermonger's daughter or sister—anything, indeed, said my informant, so as she can shake a leg about a bit. The Clown gets 5s., the Jack 3s. or 4s., and the drum and pipes 6s. There are generally from five to six persons go out together, and the expenses (not including dresses) will be about 30s. a day, and the receipts about £3. Another street dancer, "in the general line," whom I saw, said, "I can't state how many there are in London like me—perhaps twenty. I dare say I make about 7s. or 8s. a week, take the year through—perhaps 9s. some years."

Among the street dancers, or performers, may be enumerated a soldier who dances, and goes through the manual exercise with con-siderable spirit and gesticulation. His appearance is that of an ordin-ary foot-soldier, well sunburnt. His dress is an artilleryman's blue jacket, and a pair of (patched, but clean) grey trowsers, with a dark blue undress military cap. His jacket, he told me, was not what he might be considered entitled to wear by right of his military service, but it was given to him at —— Barracks (he wouldn't like it to be known where), by soldiers who had a feeling for a comrade. The lodging-house at which he lived was of the better kind; only adults were admitted. He couldn't bear, he declared, to live in a house where there was boys and girls, and all sorts—"there was such carryings on." He said, "I was born in the town of Ballinrobe, county of Mayo, and when I was eighteen (I'm now thirty-six), I went to Liverpool to try to get work. My father was a carpenter, but I followed no trade. I think I could have given my mind to trade; but I don't know, for I wasn't tried, and I always thought of a soldier's life, and a roving one too. I used to look into the barracks at Ballinrobe to see the soldiers go to church, and I thought a soldier's life was a fine life; but God knows, then, it isn't; for I have seen men drop in Leuchistan for want of water—that was in Sir Charles Napier's campaign in 1845. I have been as near to Sir Charles as I am to you now. He's a good man to a private soldier, and would talk to them as to a staff-officer; there's no pride in him. I marched 100 miles barefoot over the hills and through the desert. I was all through the Seikh campaign, and suffered a good deal in forced marches, with just reasonable to eat, but the water was the worst. I served in Spain three years before I went to India. I was with General Evans, and for two years didn't sleep on a bed. I came home with a good character, and £9 2s. 6d. to receive, but never re-ceived it, no nor a fraction of it. I then listed for India, where I was discharged at Sebatho, in the Himala Mountains, and came down the Ganges (three months of it in boats) to Calcutta. When I got to the India House, on my return here, I received 3s.—that was all, sir. I kicked up a row at the India House for some employment, and was taken before the Lord Mayor, who was very civil to me, and sent me to prison because I was turned into the streets to starve. I was ill three months after that, and was in the Free Hospital, ill of fever and want. I had to beg next with matches, and met with all kinds of insult and contempt, till I thought dancing was better than begging, with a turn every now and then in prison for begging, for I never stole in my life. I was nervous the first time I tried it, but I've since done the soldier's exercise in the street, both broadsword and firelock. I dance anything that comes into my head. The exercise is better than the dancing; it pleases the people; they like the soldiers; they say, 'this poor man works hard, he deserves a halfpenny, and he sells a few books, we'll buy one.' I always do it in this uniform. I reckon 1s. a very good day's work for my exercise, but oftener get 8d. or 9d. It's hard work, killing work. I may dance half an hour, too, for a halfpenny and break my old boots to pieces. I would like to get out of this exercise, and exercise myself as an emigrant. I'm heart broken and foot-sore, for I walk from twenty to thirty miles every day, except Sunday, besides being hunted by the police to stop my gathering a crowd—I don't know why exactly; for if it's right to fight, it can't be so wrong to show how it's done. I never eat idle bread in my life, and would do anything for an honest living. I'm not a drinking man. I didn't drink in India, that's clear—or I shouldn't have been here exercising. I believe I have all the trade to myself. Quiet bye streets are my best places; one part of town is about as good as another; and ladies are my best customers."

LABOUR AND THE POOR.

---◆---

THE METROPOLITAN DISTRICTS.

[FROM OUR SPECIAL CORRESPONDENT.]

Letter LIV.

There are still a few of the class of Street Performers, connected with those indulging in feats of strength or sleight-of-hand, that remain to be treated of. They are the street Clowns, the street 'Billy Barlows,' and the players of the drum and pipes, all of whom appear to be essential parts of every street exhibition. I shall begin with the *Street Clown*.

The one whom I saw was a melancholy-looking man, with the sunken eyes and other characteristics of semi-starvation. His mouth was wide, and over his face were lines and wrinkles, telling of paint and premature age. I saw him performing in the street with a "school" of acrobats soon after I had been questioning him; and the readiness and business-like way with which he resumed his professional buffoonery was not a little remarkable. The tale he told was more pathetic than comic, and proved that the life of a street clown is perhaps the most wretched of all existences. Jest as he may in the street, his life is literally no joke at home:—

"I have been a Clown for sixteen years," he said, "having lived totally by it for that time. I was left motherless at two years of age, and my father died when I was nine. He was a carman, and his master took me as a stable boy, and I stayed with him until he failed in business. I was then left destitute again, and got employed as a supernumerary at Astley's, at 1s. a night; now the pay's less at some theatres. I was a 'super' some time, and got an insight into theatrical life. I got acquainted, too, with singing people, and could sing a good song, and came out at last on my own account in the streets in the Jim Crow line. My necessities forced me into a public line, which I'm far from liking. I'd pull trucks at 1s. a day rather than get 12s. a week at my business. I've tried to get out of the line. I've got a friend to advertise for me for any situation as groom. I've tried to get into the police, and I've tried other things, but somehow there seems an impossibility to get quit of the street business. Many times I have to play the Clown, and all kinds of buffoonery, with a very heavy heart. I have travelled very much, too, but I never did over well in the profession. At races I may have made 10s. for two or three days, but that was only occasional; and what is 10s. to keep a wife and family on, for a month may be? I have three children, one now only eight weeks old. You can't imagine, sir, what a curse the street business often becomes, with its insults and starvations. The day before my wife was confined, I jumped and laboured all day—a wet day too—and I earned 1s. 3d. and returned, after jumping Jim Crow—I'm known as Sambo—to a *home* without a bit of coal, and with only half-a-quartern loaf in it. I know it was 1s. 3d., for I keep a sort of log of my earnings and my expenses—here it is. It is what I've earned as clown, or the funny-man, with a party of acrobats since the beginning of this year." [He showed me this log as he called it, which was kept in small figures, on paper folded up as economically as possible. His latest weekly earnings were—12s. 6d., 1s. 10d., 7s. 7d., 2s. 5d., 3s. 11½d., 7s. 7½d., 7s. 9¼d., 6s. 4½d., 10s. 10½d., 9s. 7d., 6s. 1½d., 15s. 6¼d., 6s. 5d., 4s. 2d., 12s. 10¼d., 15s. 5½d., 14s. 4d. Against this there was the set-off of what the poor man had to expend for his dinner, &c., when out playing the clown, as he was away from home and could not dine with his family. The cyphers intimate the weeks when there was no such expense:—0, 0, 0, 0, 2s. 2½d., 3s. 9¼d., 4s. 2d., 4s. 5d., 5s. 8¼d., 5s. 11¼d., 4s. 10½d., 2s. 8¾d., 3s. 7¾d., 3s. 4¼d., 6s. 5¼d., 4s. 6¾d., 4s. 3d. The above gives an average of 8s. 6½d. a week as the earnings, while, if the expenses be deducted, not quite 6s. remained for wife, family, and all expenses at home.] "I dare say," continued the man, "that no persons think more of their dignity than persons in my way of life. I would rather starve than ask for parochial relief. Many a time I've gone to my labour without breaking my fast, and played clown until I could raise a dinner. I have to make jokes as clown, and could fill a volume with all I know." [He told me several of his jests; they were all of the most venerable kind, *e.g.* "A horse has ten legs: he has two fore legs and two hind ones. Two fores are eight, and two makes ten." The others were equally ancient, as "Why is the city of Rome" (he would have it Rome) "like a candle-wick? Because it's in the midst of Greece." "Old and young are both of one age: your son at twenty is young, and your horse at twenty is old; and so old and young are the same."] "The dress," he continued, "that I wear in the streets consists of red striped cotton stockings, with full trunks, which are striped red and dotted red and black. The body, which is dotted like the trunks, fits tight, like a woman's gown, and has full sleeves and frills. The wig or scalp is made of horsehair, which is sown on to a white cap, and is in the shape of a cock's comb. My face is painted with dried white lead. I grease my skin first, and then dab the white paint on (flake white is too dear for us street clowns). After that I colour my cheeks and mouth with vermillion. I never dress at home. We all dress at public-houses. In the street where I lodge only a very few know what I do for my living. I and my wife both strive to keep the business a secret from our neighbours. My wife does a little washing when able, and often works eight hours for sixpence. I go out at eight in the morning, and return at dark. My children hardly know what I do. They see my dresses lying about, but that is all. My eldest is a girl of thirteen. She has seen me dressed at Stepney Fair, where she brought me my tea (I live near there). She laughs when she sees me in my clown's dress, and wants to stay with me; but I would rather see her lay dead before me (and I had two dead in my place at one time, last Whitsun Monday was a twelvemonth) than she should ever belong to my profession." [I could see the tears start to the man's eyes as he said this.] "Frequently, when I am playing the fool in the street, I feel very sad at heart. I can't help thinking of the bare cupboard at home; but what's that to the world? I've often and often been at home all day, when it's been wet, with no food at all, either to give my children or take myself, and have gone out at night to the public-houses, to sing a comic song and play the fool for a meal—you can imagine with what feeling for the part, sir—and when I've come home I've called my children up from their beds, to share the loaf I had brought back with me. I know three or four more clowns, as miserable and bad off as myself. The way in which our profession is ruined is by the stragglers or outsiders, who are often men that are good tradesmen. They take to the clowns' business only at holiday or fair time, when there *is* a little money to be picked up at it, and after that they go back to their own trades; so that you see we, who are obliged to continue at it the year through, are deprived of even the little bit of luck that we should otherwise have. I know only of another regular street clown in London beside myself. Some schools of acrobats, to be sure, will have a comic character of some kind or other to keep the pitch up—that is, to amuse the people while the money is being collected; but these, in general, are not regular clowns. They are mostly dressed and got up for the occasion. They certainly don't do anything else except the street comic business, but they are not pantomimists by profession. The street clowns generally go out with dancers and tumblers. There are some street clowns, to be seen with the Jacks in the Greens, but they are mostly sweeps, who have hired their dress for the two or three days, as the case may be. I think there are three regular clowns in the metropolis, and one of these is not a professional: he never smelt the sawdust, I know, sir. I dare say there are as many as twenty other clowns strolling throughout the country. The most that I have known have been shoemakers before taking to the business. When I go out as a street clown, the first thing I do is a comic medley dance, and then after that I crack a few jokes, and that is the whole of my entertainment. The first part of the medley dance is called the Good St. Anthony (I was the first that ever danced the Polka in the street) then I do a waltz, and wind up with a hornpipe. After that I go through a little burlesque business. I fan myself, and one of the school asks me whether I am out of breath. I answer, 'No, the breath's out of me.' The leading questions for the jokes are all regularly prepared and understood beforehand. The old jokes always go the best with our audiences. The older the better for the streets. I know, indeed, of nothing new in the joking way; but even if there was, and it was in any way deep, it would not do for the public thoroughfares. I have read a great deal of 'Punch,' but the jokes are nearly all too high there; indeed, I can't say I think very much of them myself. The principal way in which I've got my jokes up is through associating with other clowns. We don't make our jokes ourselves; in fact, I never knew one who did. I must own that the street clowns like a little drop of spirits, and occasionally a good deal. They are in a measure obligated to it. I can't fancy a clown being funny on table beer, and I never in all my life knew one who was a teetotaller. I think such a person would be a curious character indeed. Most of the street clowns die in the workhouses. In their old age they are generally very wretched and poverty-stricken. I can't say what I expect will be the end of me. I daren't think of it, sir." A few minutes afterwards I saw this man dressed as Jim Crow, with his face blacked, dancing and singing in the street as if he was the lightest-hearted fellow in all London.

"*Billy Barlow*" is another supposed comic character that usually accompanies either the street dancers or acrobats in their peregrinations. The dress consists of a cocked hat and red feather, a soldier's coat (generally a sergeant's, with sash), white trousers with the bottoms tucked into Wellington boots, a large tin eye-glass, and an old broken and ragged umbrella. The nose and cheeks are coloured bright red with vermillion. The "comic business" consists of the songs of the "Merry month of May," and "Billy Barlow," together with a few old conundrums and jokes, and sometimes ("where the halfpence are very plentiful") a "comic" dance. The following statement concerning this peculiar means of obtaining a living, I had from a man whom I had seen performing in the streets, dressed up for the part, but who came to me so thoroughly altered in appearance that I could hardly recognize him. In plain clothes he had almost a respectable appearance, and was remarkably clean and neat in his attire. Altogether, in his undress, he might have been mistaken for a better kind of mechanic. There was a humorous expression, however, about his mouth, and a tendency to grimace, that told the professional buffoon. "I go about now as Billy Barlow," he said; "the character of Billy Barlow was originally played at the races by a man who is dead. He was about ten years at the street business doing nothing else than Billy Barlow in the public thoroughfares, and at fairs and races. He might have made a fortune had he took care on it, sir, but he was a great drunkard, and spent all he got in gin. He died seven years ago—where most of the street performers ends their days—in the workhouse. He was formerly a potman at some public-house, and got discharged, and then took to singing comic songs about the streets and fairs. The song of Billy Barlow (which was very popular then) was among the lot that he sung, and that gave his name. He used to sing, too, the song of 'I hope I don't intrude;' and for that he dressed up as Paul Pry, which is the reason of the old umbrella, the eye-glass, and the white trowsers tucked into the boots being part of the costume at present. Another of his songs was the 'Merry month of May, or follow the drum;' and for that he put on the soldier's coat and cocked hat and feather which we wears to this day. After this he was called 'General Barlow.' When he died one or two took to the same kerackter, and they died in the workhouse—like us all. Two months ago I thought I'd take to it myself, as there was a vacancy in the purfession. I have been for thirty years at the street business, off and on. I am 50 now. I was a muffin and biscuit baker by trade, but, like the rest on us, I got fond of a roving life. My father was a tailor by trade, but took to being a supernumerary at Covent-garden Theayter, where my uncle was a performer, and when I was nine years old I played the part of the child in *Pizarro*, and after that I was one of the devils what danced round my uncle in *Mother Goose*. When I was fourteen years old my uncle apprenticed me to the muffin business, and I stuck to it for five years, but when I was out of my time I made up my mind to cut it and take to performing. First I played clown at a booth, for I had always a taste for the comic, after I had played the devil and danced round my uncle in the Covent-garden pantomime. Some time after that I took to play the drum and pipes, and since then I have been chiefly performing as musicianer to different street exhibitions. When business is bad in the winter or wet weather, I make sweetmeats and go about the streets and sell them. I never made muffins since I left the business—you see I've no stove nor shop for that—and never had the means of raising them. Sweetmeats takes little capital—toffy, brandy-balls, and Albert rock isn't expensive to get up. Besides, I'm known well among the children in the streets, and they likes to patronize the purfession for sweetmeats, even though they won't give nothing while you're a performing. I've done much the same since I took to the Billy Barlow as I did before at the street business. We all share alike, and that's what I did as the drum and pipes. I never dress at home: my wife (I'm a married man) knows the part I play. She came to see me once, and laughed at me fit to bust. The landlord nor the fellow lodgers where I live—I have a room to myself—ain't aware of what I do. I sneaks my things out, and dresses at a public-house. It costs us a pot for dressing and a pot for undressing. We has the use of the tap-room for that. I'm like the rest of the world at home—or rather, more serious, maybe—though, thank God, I don't want for food; things is cheap enough now; and if I can't get a living at the buffoonery business, why I tries sweetmeats, and between the two I do manage to grub on somehow, and that's more than many of my purfession can do. My pardner (a street dancer whom he brought with him) must either dance or starve; and there's plenty like him in the streets of London. I only know of one other Barlow but me in the business, and he's only taken to it after me. Some jokes an't fit for ladies to listen to, but wot I says is the best approved jokes—such as has been fashionable for many years, and can't give no offence to no one. I say to the musician 'Well, master, can you tell me why are the Thames Tunnel and Hungerford Suspension Bridge like two joints badly done?' He'll say, 'No, Mr. Barlow,' and then I give him the answer: 'Because one is over-done and the other is under-done.' Then I raise my umbrella, saying, 'I think I'm purwided against the weather,' and as the umbrella is all torn and slit, it raises a laugh. Some days

I get 6s. or 7s. as my share; sometimes not a quarter of the money. Perhaps I may average full 18s. a week in the summer, or more, but not a pound. In the winter, if there's a subsistence, that's all. Joking is not natural to me, and I'm a steady man; it's only in the way of business, and I leave it on one side when I've got my private apparel on. I never think of my public character if I can help it until I get my show dress on, and I'm glad to get it off at night, and then I think of my home and children, and I struggle hard for them, and feel disgust oft enough at having been a Tom Fool to street fools."

A stout, reddish-faced man, who was familiar with all kinds of exhibitions, and had the coaxing, deferential manner of many persons who ply for money in the streets, gave me an account of what he called "his experience" as the "*drum and pipes*:"—

"I have played the pandean pipes and the drum for thirty years to street exhibitions of all kinds. I was a smith when a boy, serving seven years' apprenticeship; but after that I married a young woman that I fell in love with, in the music line. She played a hurdy-gurdy in the streets; so I bought pandean pipes, as I was always fond of practising music, and I joined her. Times for street musicianers were good then, but I was foolish. I'm aware of that now; but I wasn't particularly partial to hard work; besides, I could make more as a street musicianer. When I first started, my wife and I joined a Fantoccini; it did well. My wife and I made from 9s. to 10s. a day. We had half the profits. At that time the public exhibitions were different to what they are now. Gentlemen's houses were good then, but now the profession's sunk to street corners. Bear-dancing was in vogue then, and clock-work on the round board; and Jack-i'-the-Green was in all his glory every May, thirty years ago. Things is now very dead indeed. In the old times, only sweeps were allowed to take part with the Jack; they were very particular at that time; all were sweeps but the musicianers. Now it's anybody's money, when there's any money. Every sweep then showed his plate when performing. My Lady was anybody at all likely that they got hold of; she was generally a watercress seller, or something in the public way. My Lady had 2s. 6d. a day and her keep, for three days, that was the general hire. The boys, who were climbing-boys, had 1s., or 6d., or what the master gave them; and they generally went to the play of a night, after washing themselves in course. I had 6s. a day and a good dinner, shoulder of mutton, or something prime, and enough to drink. My Lord and the other characters shared and shared alike. They have taken, to my knowledge, £5 on the 1st of May. This year, one set, with two My Ladies, took £3 the first day. The master of the lot was a teetotaller, but the others drank as they liked. He turned teetotaller because drink always led him into trouble. The dress of the Jack is real ivy tied round hoops. The sweeps gather the ivy in the country and make the dresses at their homes. My Lord's and the other dresses are generally kept by the sweeps. My Lord's dress costs a mere trifle at the second-hand clothes shop, but it's gold-papered and ornamented up to the mark required. What I may call war tunes, such as 'The White Cockade,' 'The Downfall of Paris' (I've been asked for that five or six times a day—I don't remember the composer), 'Bonaparte's March,' and 'The Duke of York's March,' were in vogue in the old times. So was 'Scots wha hae' (very much), and 'Off she goes.' Now new tunes come up every day. I play waltzes and pokers now chiefly. They're not to compare to the old tunes; it's like playing at musicians, lots of the tunes now-a-days. I've played with Michael, the Italy bear. I played the fife and tabor with him. The tabor was a little drum about the size of my cap, and it was tapped with a little stick. There are no tabors about now. I made my 7s. or 8s. a day with Michael. He spoke broken English. A dromedary was about then, but I knew nothing of that or the people; they was all foreigners together. Swinging monkeys were in vogue at that time as well. I was with them, with Antonio, of Saffron-hill. He was the original of the swinging monkeys twenty years ago. They swing from a rope just like slack-wire dancers. Antonio made money, and went back to his own country. He sold his monkeys—there was three of them, and small animals they were—for £70, to another foreigner; but I don't know what became of them. Coarse jokes pleased people long ago wot don't now; people get more enlightened, and think more of chapel and church instead of amusements. My trade is a bad one now. Take the year through, I may make 12s. a week, or not so much; say 10s. I go out sometimes playing single—that's by myself—on the drum and pipes; but it's thought nothing of, for I'm not a German. It's the same at Brighton as in London; brass bands is all the go when they've Germans to play them. The Germans will work at 2s. a day at any fair, when an Englishman will expect 6s. The foreigners ruin this country, for they have far more privileges than the English. The Germans pull the bells and knock at the doors for money, which an Englishman has hardly face for. I'm now with a Fantoccini—figures from Canton brought over by a seaman. I can't form an exact notion of how many men there are in town who are musicianers to the street exhibitions, besides the exhibition's own people—I should say about 100. I don't think that they are more drunken than other people, but they're liable to get top-heavy at times. None that I know live with women of the town. They live in lodgings, and not in lodging-houses—oh! no, no, we're not come to that yet. Some of them succeeded their fathers as street musicianers; others took it up casalty-like by having learned different instruments; none that I know were ever theatrical performers. All the men I know in my line would object, I am sure, to hard work, if it was with confinement along with it. We can never stand being confined to work after having been used to the freedom of the streets. None of us save money; it goes either in a lump, if we get a lump, or in dribs and drabs, which is the way it mostly comes to us. I've known several in my way who have died in St. Giles's workhouse. In old age or sickness, we've nothing but the parish to look to. The newest thing I know is 'the singing dogs.' I was with that as musician, and it answers pretty well amongst the quality. The dogs is three Tobies to a Punch and Judy show, and they sing—that is, they make a noise; it's really a howl; but they keep time with Mr. Punch as he sings."

The next class of Mountebanks or Street Performers, or Showmen, are those who go about with animals trained to perform certain feats. These street performances consist of several kinds, viz., those of dancing dogs, performing monkeys—both of which are generally conducted by foreigners—and trained birds and mice. I shall conclude the present Letter with a specimen of each class.

First, of the trained birds and mice:—

A stout, acute-looking man, whom I found in a decently furnished room with his wife, gave me an account of this kind of street exhibition:—

"I perform," said he, "with birds and mice, in the open air, if needful. I was brought up to juggling by my family and friends, but colds and heats brought on rheumatism, and I left juggling for another branch of the profession; but I juggle a little still. My birds are nearly all canaries, a score of them sometimes—sometimes less. I have names for them all. I have Mr. and Mrs. Caudle, dressed quite in character; they quarrel at times, and that's self-taught with them. Mrs. Caudle is not noisy, and is quite amusing; they ride out in a chariot drawn by another bird, a goldfinch mule. I give him any name that comes into my head—the goldfinch harnesses himself to a little wire harness. Mr. and Mrs. Caudle and the mule is very much admired by people of taste. Then I have Marshal Ney in full uniform, and he fires a cannon to keep up the character. I can't say that he's bolder than others. I have a little canary called The Trumpeter, who jumps on to a trumpet when I sound it, and remains there until I've done sounding. Another canary goes up a pole, as if climbing for a leg of mutton, or any prize at the top, as they do at fairs, and when he gets to the top he answers me. He climbs fair, toe and heel, no props to help him along. These are the principal birds, and they all play by the word of command, and with the greatest satisfaction and ease to themselves. I use two things to train them—kindness and patience; and neither of these two things must be stinted. The grand difficulty is to get them to perform in the open air without flying away, when they've no tie upon them, as one may say. I lost one by its taking flight at Ramsgate, and another at Margate. They don't and can't do anything to teach one another; not in the least; every bird is on its own account; seeing another bird do a trick is no good whatever. I teach them all myself, beginning with them from the nest. I breed most of them myself. To teach them to sing at the word of command is very difficult. I whistle to the bird to make it sing, and then when it sings I feed, and pet, and fondle it, until it gets to sing without my whistling, understanding my motions. Harshness wouldn't educate any bird whatsomever. I pursue the same system all through. The bird used to jump to be fed on the trumpet, and got used to the sound. To train Marshal Ney to fire his cannon, I put the cannon first like a perch for the bird to fly to for his food; it's fired by stuff attached to the touch-hole that explodes when touched. The bird's generally frightened before he gets used to gunpowder, and flutters into the body of the cage, but after a few times he don't mind it. I train mice too, and my mice fetch and carry like dogs, and, three of the little things dance the tight-rope on their hind legs, with balance-poles in their mouths. They are hard to train, but I have a secret way, found out by myself, to educate them properly. They require great care, and are, if anything, tenderer than the birds. I have no particular names for the mice; they are all fancy mice, white or coloured. I've known four or five in my way in London. It's all a lottery what I get. For the open-air performance, the West-end may be the best, but there's little difference. I have been ill seven months, and am just starting again. Then I can't work in the air in bad weather. I call 21s. a very good week's work, and to get that every day must be fine—10s. 6d.

is nearer the mark, as an average for the year. An order to play at a private house may be extra; they give what they please. My birds come with a whistle, and come with a call, and come with a good will, or they won't do at all—for me. The police don't meddle with me, or nothing to notice. A good many of my birds and mice die before they reach any perfection—another expense and loss of time in my business. Town or country is pretty much the same to me, take it altogether. The watering-places are best in the country perhaps, for it's there people go for pleasure. I don't know any *best* place; if I did, I'd stick to it. Ladies and children are my best friends generally." The performance of the birds and mice, above described, is very clever. "Mr. and Mrs. Caudle" are dressed in red and blue cloaks, trimmed with silver lace and spangles; while Mr. Caudle, with an utter disregard of propriety, is adorned with a cocked hat.

I received the following narrative from the old man who has been so long known about the streets of London with a troop of performing dogs. He was especially picturesque in his appearance. His hair, which was grizzled rather than grey, was parted down the middle, and hung long and straight over his shoulders. He was dressed in a coachman's blue great coat, with many capes. His left hand was in a sling, made out of a dirty cotton pocket handkerchief; and in his other he held a stick, by means of which he could just manage to hobble along. He was very ill, and very poor, not having been out with his dogs for nearly two months. He appeared to speak in great pain. The civility, if not politeness, of his manner threw an air of refinement about him that struck me the more forcibly from its contrast to the manners of the English belonging to the same class. He began:—

"I have de dansing dogs for de street—now I have noting else. I have tree dogs, von is called Finette, anoder von Favorite, that is her nomme, and de udder von Ozore. Ah," he said with a shrug of the shoulders, in answer to my inquiry as to what the dogs did, "On dance, on valtz, on jomp a de stick, and troo de hoop—non, nothing else. Sometime I had de four dogs—I did lose de von. Ah, she had beaucoup d'esprit—plenty of vit you say—she did jomp a de hoop better dan all. Her nomme was Taborine. Taborine—she is dead dare is long time. All ma dogs have des habillements—de dress, and de leetel hat. Dey have a leetel jackette in divers couleures en etoffe—some de red, and some de green, some de bleu. Dare hats is de rouge et noir—red and black, wid a leetel plume—fedder you say. Dare is some ten or eleven year I have been in dis country. I come from Italie—Italie!

Oui, monsieur, oui. I did live in a little ville trente miglia, dirty miles de Parma. Je travaille dans le campagne. I vork out in de countree, je ne scais comment vous appellez le campagne. There is no commairce in de montagne. I am come in dis country here—I have leetel business to come. I thought to gaigner ma vie—to gain my life—wid ma leetel dogs in dis countree. I have dem déjà when I am come here from Parma. J'en avait dix. I did have de ten dogs. Je les ai porté—I have carried all de ten from Italie. I did learn, yes—yes, de dogs to danse in ma own countree. It did make de cold in de montagne in vinter, and I had not no work dere, and I must look for to gain my life some oder place. Apres ça I have instruit ma dogs to danse. Ils learn to danse, I play de moosic, and dey do jomp. Non, non! pas de tout! I did not never beat ma dogs; dare is a way to learn de dogs widout no vip. Premierement ven I am come here I have gained a leetel monnaie—plus que now—beaucoup d'avantage—plenty more. I am left ma logement—my lodging, you say—at nine hours in de morning, and I am stay avay vid ma dogs till seven or eight hours in de evening. Oh, I cannot count how many time de leetel dogs have danse in de day—twenty—dirty—forty—peut-être—all depend. Sometime I vould gain de tree shilling, sometime de couple, sometime not nothing—all depend. Ven it did make bad time I could not vork—de leetel dogs could not danse. I could not gain my life den. If it make cold, de dogs are ill—like tout le monde. I did pay plenty for de nourriture of de dogs. Sometime dey did get du pain (de bread) in de street—sometime I give dem de meat, and make de soup for dem. Ma dogs danse comme les chiens, mais dey valtz comme les dames, and dey stand on dare back legs like des gentilhommes. After I am come here to dis countree two day, I am terreeble malade. I am gone to hospital—to Sainte Bartolomé—the veek before the Jour de Noel (Christmas-day). In dat moment dere I have de fievre. I have rested in l'hôpital quatre semaine—four veek. Ma dogs vere at liberté all de time. Von compagnon of mine have promised me to take de care of ma dogs, and he have lose dem all—tout les dix. After dat I have bought tree oder dogs—one espanol, anoder qu'on appelle 'grifon,' and de oder was de dog ordinaire—non! non! not one 'pull-dog'— he no good. I must have one month, or six semaine, to instruite ma dogs. I have rested in a logement Italien at Saffron-hill, ven I am come here to London. Dare vas not much vant of Italians dare. It vas tout plein—quite full of étrangers. All come dare—dey are come from France, from Germany, from Italy. I have paid two shillan par semaine each veek—only pour le lit—for de bed. Every von make de kitchen for himself. Vot number dare vas dare, you say? Sometime dere vas twenty person dare, and sometime dere vas dirty persons in de logement—sometime more dan dat. It vas a very petite maison. Dare vas von dozen beds, dat is all; and two sleep demselves in each bed. Sometimes, ven dere arrive plenty, dey sleep demselves tree in von bed, but ordinairement dere vas only two. Dey vas all musicians dare—on play de organ—de piano—de guitar—de flute—yes dare vas some vot played it—and de viol too. De great part vas Italians. Some of dem have des monkeys, de oders des mice, white, and des pigs d'Indes (guinea pigs), and encore oders have des dolls vid de two heads, and des puppets vot danse vit de foot on de board. Des animals are in an apartment apart vit de moosek. Dare vas sometime tree monkeys, von dozen of mice, five or six pigs d'Indes, and ma dogs altogether, vid de moosek by demselves. Dare is all de actors vot vas there. Ma tree dogs gained me sometime two shillan, sometime von shillan, and sometime I vould rest on my feet all day and not gain two sous. Sometime de boys would ensoolt ma dogs vid de stones. Dare is long time I am rested in London. Dare is short time I vas in de campagne—de countree here—not much. London is better dan de campagne for ma dogs—dare is always de world in London—de city is large. Yes I am always rested at Saffron-hill for ten, eleven, years. I am malade at present—since the 15th of Mars. In ma arms, ma legs, ma tighs, I have de douleur. I have plenty of pains to march. Ma dogs are in de logement now. It is since the 15th of Mars dat I have not vent out vid ma dogs—yes, since de 15th of Mars I have not done no vork. Since dat time I have not pay no money for ma logement—it is due encore. Non, non. I have not gained ma life since the 15th of Mars. Plenty of time I have been vitout noting to eat. Des Italiens at de logement have give to me de pieces of bread and bouilli. Ah, it is very miserable to be poor like me. I have sixty and dirteen years. I cannot march now but with plenty of pains. Von doctor have give to me a letter for to present to de poor-house. He did give me my medicine for noting—grattis. He is obliged. He is de doctor of de paroisse. He is very brave and honest man dat doctor dare. At de poor-house dey have give to me a bread and six sous on Friday of de week dat is passed, and told to me to come de Vednesday next. But I am arrive dare too late, and dey give to me noting, and tell to me to come de Vednesday next encore. Ma dogs dey march now in de street, and eat someting dare. Oh, ma God non! dey eat noting but vot dey find in de street ven it makes good times; but ven it makes bad times, dey have noting at all, poor dogs. Ven I have it dey have it—but ven dare is noting for me to eat dare is noting for dem, and dey must go out in de street and get de nourriture for demselves. Des infants vot know ma dogs will give to dem to eat sometime. Oh yes, if I had de means I would return to Italie—ma countree. But I have not no silver, and not no legs to walk. Vat can I do? Oh yes, I am very sick at present. All my limbs have great douleur—oh yes, oh yes, plenty of pain."

An Italian, who went about with *trained monkeys*, furnished me with the following account. He had a peculiar boorish, and yet good-tempered, expression, especially when he laughed, which he did continually. He was dressed in a brown ragged cloth jacket, a long loose dirty drab waistcoat, with two or three brass buttons, and broad ribbed corduroy trousers. Round his neck was a plaid handkerchief. His shoes were of the extreme "strong men's" kind, and grey with dust and long want of blacking. He wore the Savoyard broad-brimmed felt hat, and, with it on his head, had a very pictur-esque appearance. The shadow of the brim falling on the upper part of his brown face, gave him an almost Murillo-like look. There was, however, an odour about him (half monkey, half dirt) that was far from agreeable, and which pervaded the apartment in which he sat.

"I have got monkey" he said, "but I musn't call in London—I goes out in countree. I was frightened to come here. I was frightened you give me months in prison. Some of my countrymen is very frightened what you do. Now sir, I never play de monkey in de town. I have been out vare dere is so many donkey up a-top at dat village—vot you call—I can't tell de name. Dey goes dere for pleasure—for pastime—ven it makes fine vether. Dere is two church and two large hotel—yes, I tink it is Blackheath—I goes dere sometime with my monkey. I have got only one monkey now—sometime I have got two. It is dressed—comme un soldat-rouge—like von soldier, vid a red jacket, and a Bonaparte's hat. My monkey only pull off his hat and take a de money. He used to ride a de dog, but dey stole a de dog—some of de tinkare, or man wid de ombrella going by, stole a him—dere is only tree months dat I got my monkey. It is my own; I gave dirty-five shilling for dis one I got. He did not know no tricks when he is come to me first. I did teash a him all he know. I teash him wid de kindness, do you see; I must look rough for tree or four time, but not to beat him, and den I look sweet upon him. If you beat him he can hardly stir about, he is afraid dat you go to hit him, you see. I mustn't feed him ven I am teashing him; sometimes I buy a haporth of nuts to give him after he has done vot I vant him to do. Dis one has not de force behind; he is weak in de back. Some monkey is like de children at de school; some is very hard to teash; and some larn de more quick, you see. De von I had before dis von could do many tings. He had not much esprit—pas grande chose—but he could play de drom, de fiddle, too—ah, but he don't play de fiddle like de Christian you know, but like de monkey. He used to fight wid de sword—not exactly same as de Christian but like de monkey, too—much better. I beg your pardon to laugh, sir. He used to move his leg and jomp. I call it danse, but he could not do de Polka like de Christian—I have seen de Christian though wot can't danse more dan de monkey. I beg your pardon to laugh. I did play valtz to him on de organ. Non! he had not mush ear for de mooseek, but I force him to keep de time by de jerk of de string. He commence to valtz vell ven he die. He is dead de vinter dat is passed, at Sheltenham. He eat some red-ee pant. I put him in de cupboard to go and fetsh ma loaf-ee bread, and some tea; and ven I am come home, I find he have eatee de red-ee paint. He is dead, perhaps, seven or eight hours after he eatee de red-ee paint. I give him some castor oil, but no good. He die in great deal pain, poor fellow; I rather lose six pound dan lose my monkey. I did cry. I cry because I have no money to go and buy anoder monkey. Yes, I did love my monkey. I did love him for the sake of my life. I give de raisin, and bile dem for him. He have every ting he like. I am come her from Parma, about fourteen or fifteen year ago. I used to vork in my countree. I used to go and look at de ship in de Montagnes; non! non!—pas des vasseaux—mais des moutons. I beg your pardon to laugh. De master did bring me up here. Dat master is gone to America now. He is come to me and tell me to come to Angleterre. He has tell me I make plenty money in dis country. Ah, I could get plenty money dat time in London, but now I get not mush. I vork for myself at present. My master give me nine—ten shillan each veek, and my food and my lodging—yes, every ting, ven I am first come here. I used to go out wid de organ, a good von, and I did get two, tree, and more shillan for my master each day. It was shance work; sometime I did get noting at all. De organ was my master's. He had no von else but me wid him. We use to travel about togeder; and he took all de money. He had one German piano, and play de mooseek. I can't tell how mush he did make—he never tell to me; but

I did sheat him sometime myself; sometime ven I take de two shillan I give him de eighteen pence—I beg your pardon to laugh. De man did bring up many Italians to dis country, but now it is difficult to get de passports for my countrymen. I was eighteen month wid my master; after dat I vent to farm house. I run away from my master; he gave me de slap a de face you know von time, so I don't like it and I run away. I beg your pardon to laugh. I used to do good many tings at de farm house; it was in Yorkshire. I used to look at de beast, and take a de vater. I don't get noting for my work, only for de sake of de belly I do it. I vas dere about tree year; dey behave to me very vell; dey give me de clothes and all I vant. After dat I go to Liverpool and I meet some of my countrymen dare, and dey lend me de money to buy de monkey, and I teash him to danse, fight, and jomp, mush as I could, and I go wid my monkey about de country. Sometime I make tree shillan wid my monkey, sometime only sixpence, sometime noting at all. When it rain or snow I can't get noting. I gain peut-être a doozan shillan a veek wid my monkey, sometime more, but not often. Dare is long time I have been in de environs of London, but I don't like to go in de streets here. I don't like to go to prison. Monkey is defended—defendu—vot you call, in London. But dare is many monkey in London still. Oh, non—not a doozan. Dare is not one doozan monkey vot play in Angleterre. I know dare is two monkey at Saffron-hill, and one go in London, but he do no harm. I don't know dat de monkey was train to go down de area and steal a de silver spoons out of de kishen. Dey would be great fool to tell dat, but every one must get a living de best dey can. Vot I tell you about de monkey I am frightened will hurt me. I tell you dey is defended in de streets, and dey take me up. I hope not. My monkey is very honest monkey, and get me de bread. I never was in prison, and I would not like to be. I play de mooseek, and please de people, and never steal noting—non, non; me no steal, nor my monkey too. De policemen never say nothing to me. I am not beggar, but artiste—everybody know dat—and my monkey he is artiste too. I beg your pardon to laugh."

The Morning Chronicle, Monday, June 3, 1850.

To THE EDITOR OF THE MORNING CHRONICLE.

SIR—I beg to enclose a Post-office order for one pound, which I request you to apply (through your Commissioner) to the relief of any deserving case that he may meet with in the course of his important labours. Will you kindly acknowledge the receipt of this in your paper, and thus confer an additional obligation on

Yours, &c.,

A FORMER CONTRIBUTOR.

LABOUR AND THE POOR.

◆

THE METROPOLITAN DISTRICTS.

[FROM OUR SPECIAL CORRESPONDENT.]

Letter LV.

I now come to the Street Musicians and Street Vocalists of London. These are a more numerous class than any other of the street performers that I have yet dealt with. The Musicians are estimated at 1,000, and the Ballad Singers at 250.

The Street Musicians are of two kinds—the skilful and the blind. The former obtain their money by the agreeableness of their performance, and the latter in pity for their affliction rather than admiration of their harmony. The blind Street Musicians, it must be confessed, belong generally to the rudest class of performers. Music is not used by them as a means of pleasing, but rather as a mode of soliciting attention. Such individuals are known in the "profession" by the name of "pensioners;" they have their regular rounds to make, and particular houses at which to call on certain days of the week, and from which they generally obtain a "small trifle." They form, however, a most peculiar class of individuals. They are mostly well-known characters, and many of them have been performing in the streets of London for many years. They are also remarkable for the religious cast of their thoughts, and the comparative refinement of their tastes and feelings.

I shall begin with the more skilful class of Street Musicians. Among these are the London Street Bands, English and German— the Highland Performers on the Bagpipes, and a few others. First of the English Street Bands:—

Concerning these, a respectable man gave me the following details:—

"I was brought up to the musical 'profession,' and have been a street performer twenty-two years, tho' I'm now only twenty-six. I sang and played the guitar in the streets with my mother when I was only four years old. We were greatly patronized by the nobility at that time. It was a good business when I was a child. A younger brother and I would go out into the streets for a few hours of an evening from five to eight, and make 7s. or 8s. the two of us. Ours was and is the highest class of street music. For the last ten years I have been a member of a street band. Our band is now four in number. I have been in bands of eight, and in some composed of as many as twenty-five; but a small band answers best for regularity. With eight in the band it's not easy to get 3s. a piece on a fine day, and play all day too. I consider that there are 1,000 musicians now performing in the streets of London; and as very few play singly, 1,000 performers, not reckoning persons who play with niggers or such like, will give not quite 250 street bands. Four in number is a fair average for a street band; but I think the greater number of bands have more than four in them. All the better sort of these bands play at concerts, balls, parties, processions, and water excursions, as well as in the streets. The class of men in the street bands is, very generally, those who can't read music, but play by the ear; and their being unable to read music prevents their obtaining employment in theatres or places where a musical education is necessary; and yet numbers of street musicians (playing by the ear) are better instrumentalists than many educated musicians in the theatres. I only know a few who have left other businesses to become musicians. The great majority—nineteen-twentieths of us—I should say, have been brought regularly up to be street performers. Children now are taught very early, and seldom leave the profession for any other business. Every year the street musicians increase. The better sort are, I think, prudent men, and struggle hard for a decent living. All the street performers of wind instruments are short-lived. Wind performers drink more, too, than the others. They must have their mouths wet, and they need some stimulant or restorative after blowing an hour in the streets. There are now twice as many wind as stringed instruments played in the streets; 15 or 16 years ago there used to be more stringed instruments. Within that time new wind instruments have been used in the streets. Cornopeans, or cornet-à-pistons, came into vogue about fourteen years ago; ophicleides about ten years ago (I'm speaking of the streets); and saxhorns about two years since. The cornopean has now quite superseded the bugle. The worst part of the street performers, in point of character, are those who play before or in public-houses. They drink a great deal, but I never heard of them being charged with dishonesty. In fact, I believe that there's no honester set of men breathing than street musicians. The better class of musicians are nearly all married men, and they generally dislike to teach their wives music; indeed, in my band, and in similar bands, we wouldn't employ a man who was teaching his wife music, that she might play in the streets, and so be exposed to every insult and every temptation, if she's young and pretty. Many of the musicians' wives have to work very hard with their needles for the slop-shops, and earn very little in such employ; 3s. a week is reckoned good earnings, but it all helps. The German bands injure our trade much. They'll play for half what we ask. They are very mean, feed dirtily, and the best band of them, whom I met at Dover, I know slept three in a bed in a common lodging-house, one of the very lowest. They now block us out of all the country places to which we used to go in the summer. The German bands have now possession of the whole coast of Kent and Sussex, and wherever there are watering places. I don't know anything about their morals excepting that they don't drink. An English street performer in a good and respectable band will now average 25s. a week the year through. Fifteen years ago he could have made £3 a week. Inferior performers make from 12s. to 15s. a week. I consider Regent-street and such places our best pitches. Our principal patrons in the parties line are tradesmen and professional men, such as attorneys. 10s. a night is our regular charge."

Next come the German Bands. I had the following statement concerning these from a young flaxen-haired and fresh-coloured German, who spoke English very fairly:—

"I am German, and have been six year in zis country. I was nearly fourteen when I come. I come from Oberfeld, eighteen miles from Hanover. I come because I would like to see how it was here. I heard zat London was a goot place for foreign music. London is as goot a place as I expect to find him. There was other six come over with me, boys and men. We come to Hull and play in ze country about half a year; we do middling, and zen we come to London. I didn't make money at first when I come; I had much to learn, but ze band, oh! it did well. We was seven. I play ze clarionet, and so did two others; two play French horns, one ze trombone, and one ze saxhorn. Sometime we make 7s. or 8s. a piece in a day now, but the business is not so goot. I reckon 6s. a day is goot now. We never play at fairs, not for caravans. We play at private parties or public ball-rooms, and are paid so much a dance—sixpence a dance for ze seven of us. If zare is many dances it is goot; if not it is bad. We play sheaper zan ze English, and we don't spend so much. Ze English players insult us, but we don't care about that. Zey abuse us for playing sheap. I don't know what zeir terms for dances are. I have saved money in zis country, but very little of it. I want to save enough to take me back to Hanover. We all live togezer, ze seven of us. We have three rooms to sleep in, and one to eat in. We are all single men but one; and his wife, a German woman, lives wis us, and cooks for us. She and her husband have a bedroom to zemselves. Anysing does for us to eat. We all join in housekeeping and lodging, and pay alike. Our lodging costs 2s. a week each; our board costs us about 15s. a week each; sometime rather less. But zat includes beer, and ze London beer is very goot, and sometime we drink a goot deal of it. We drink very little gin, but we live very well, and have goot meals every day. We play in ze streets, and I sink most places are alike to us. Ladies and gentlemen are our best frients; ze working people give us very little. We play opera tunes chiefly. We don't associate with any Englishmen. Zare are three public-houses kept by Germans, where we Germans meet. Sugar bakers and other trades are of ze number. There are now five German brass-bands, with thirty-seven performers in zem, reckoning our own, in London. Our band lives near Whitechapel. I sink zare is one or two more German bands in the country. I sink my countrymen, some of them, save money; but I have not saved much yet."

The Highlanders, with their bagpipes, are next in order. A well-looking young man, dressed in full Highland costume, with modest manners, and of slow speech, as if translating his words from the Gaelic before he uttered them, gave me these details:—

"I am a native of Inverness, and a Grant. My father was a soldier and a piper in the 42d. In my youth I was shepherd in the hills until my father was unable to support me any longer. He had 9d. a day pension for 17 years' service, and had been thrice wounded. He taught me and my brither the pipes; he was too poor to have us taught any trade, so we started on our own accounts. We travelled up to London, having only our pipes to depend upon. We came in full Highland dress. The tartan is cheap there, and we mak it up oursels. My dress as I sit here, without my pipes, would cost about £4 in London. Our mithers spin the tartan in Inverness-shire, and the dress comes to may-be 30s., and is better than the London. My pipes cost me three guineas new. It's between five and six years since I first came to London, and I was twenty-four last November. When I started I thought of making a fortune in London, there was such great talk of it in Inverness-shire, as a fine place with plenty of money; but when I came I found the difference. I was rather a novelty at first, and did pretty well. I could make £1 a week then; but now I can't make 2s. a day, not even in summer. There are so many Irishmen going about London and dressed as Scotch Highlanders, that I really think I could do better as a piper even in Scotland. A Scotch family will sometimes give me a shilling or two when they find out I am a Scotchman. Chelsea is my best place, where there are many Scotchmen. There are now only five real Scotch Highlanders playing the bagpipes in the streets of London, and seven or eight Irishmen that I know of. The Irishmen do better than I do because they have more face. We have our own rooms. I pay 4s. a week for an empty room, and have my ain furniture. We are all married men, and have no connection with any other street musicians. 'Tullochgorum,' 'Money-musk,' 'The Campbells are coming,' and 'Lord Macdonald's Reel,' are among the performances best liked in London. I'm very seldom insulted in the streets, and then mostly by being called an Irishman, which I don't like; but I pass it off just as weel as I can."

Of the Irish Pipes, a well-dressed, middle-aged man, of good appearance, wearing large green spectacles, led by a young girl, his daughter, gave me the following account:—

"I was eleven years old when I lost my sight from cold, and I was brought up to the musical profession, and practised it several years in Ireland, of which country I am a native. I was a man of private property—small property—and only played occasionally at the gentle-people's places; and then more as a guest—yes, more indeed than professionally. In 1838 I married, and began to give concerts regularly; I was the performer, and played only on the Union pipes at my concerts. I'm acknowledged to be the best performer in the world, even by my own craft—excuse what seems self-praise. The union pipes are the old Irish pipes improved. In former times there was no chromatic scale; now we have eight keys to the chanter, which produce the chromatic scale as on the flute, and so the pipes are improved in the melody, and more particularly in the harmony. We have had fine performers of old. I may mention Caroll O'Daly, who flourished in the fifteenth century, and was the composer of the air that the Scotch want to steal from us—Robin Adair, which is 'Aileen ma ruen,' or 'Ellen my dear.' My concerts in Ireland answered very well indeed, but the famine reduced me so much that I was fain to get to England with my family, wife and four children—and in this visit I have been disappointed, completely so. Now I'm reduced to play in the streets, and make very little by it. I may average 15s. in the week in summer, and not half that in winter. There are many of my countrymen now in England playing the pipes, but I don't know one respectable enough to associate with, so I keep to myself; and so I cannot tell how many there are."

A very handsome man, swarthy even for a native of Bengal, with his black glossy hair most picturesquely disposed, alike on his head and in his whiskers and moustache, gave me, after an oriental salute, the following statement. His teeth were exquisitely white, and his laugh or smile lighted up his countenance to an expression of great intelligence. His dress was a garb of dark brown cloth, fitting close to his body and extending to his knee. His trowsers were of the same coloured cloth, and he wore a girdle of black and white cotton round his waist. He was accompanied by his son (whom he sometimes addressed in Hindostanee), a round-faced boy, with large bright black eyes and rosy cheeks. The father said—

"I was born in Calcutta, and was Mussulman—my parents was Mussulman—but I Christian now. I have been in dis contree ten year. I come first as servant to military officer, an Englishman. I live wit him in Scotland six seven mont. He left Scotland, saying he come back, but he not, and in a mont I hear he dead, and den I come London. London is very great place, and Indian city little if you look upon London. I use tink it plenty pleasure look upon London, as de great Government place, but now I look upon London and it is plenty bad pleasure. I wish very often return to my own contree, where every ting sheap, living sheap, rice sheap. I suffer from climate in dis contree. I suffer dis winter more dan ever I did. I have no flannels, no drawer, no waistcoat, and have cold upon my chest. It is now near five year I come London. I try get service, but no get service. I have character, but not from my last master. He could not give me; he dead ven I want it. I put up many insult in dis contree. I struck sometime in street. Magistrate punish man gave me blow dat left mark on my chin here. Gentlemen sometime save me from harm, sometime not. De boys call me black dis or de oder. Wen I get no service I not live, and I not beg in street, so I buy tom-tom for 10s. De man want 30s. De 10s. my last money left, and I start to play in streets for daily bread. I beat tom-tom and sing song about greatness of God, in my own language. I had den wife, Engliswoman, and dis little boy. I done pretty well first wid tom-tom, but it is very bad to do it now. When I began first I make 3s., 4s., 5s., or 6s. a day. It was someting new den, but nine or ten monts it was something old, and I took less and less, until now I hardly get piece of bread. I sometime get few shilling from two or three picture-men, who draw me. It is call model. Anyting for honest bread. I must not be proud. I cannot make above 6s. a week of tom-tom in street. Dere is, well as I know, about fifty of my contreemen playing and begging in streets of London. Dose who sweep crossing are Malay; some Bengal. Many are impostor, and spoil spectable man. My contreemen live in lodging-house; often many are plenty blackguard lodging-houses, and dere respectable man is always insult. I have room for myself dis tree mont, and cost me tree shilling and six pennies a week; it is not own furniture; dey burn my coke, coal, and candle too. My wife would make work wid needle, but dere is no work for her, poor ting. She servant when I marry her. De little boy make jump in my contree's way wen I play tom-tom—he too little to dance—he six year. Most of my contreemen in street have come as Lascar, and not go back for bosen, and bosen mate, and flog. So dey stay for beg, or sweep, or anyting. Dey are never pickpocket dat I ever hear of."

I now come to the class of players on the harp and hurdy-gurdy, imitators of farm-yards on the fiddle, performers on bells, and on the bass viol. Among these the Blind Musicians will mostly be found.

A poor, feeble, half-witted looking man, with the appearance of far greater age than he represented himself (a common case with the very poor), told me of his sufferings in the streets. He was wretchedly clad, his clothes being old, patched, and greasy. He is well known in London, being frequently seen with a crowd of boys at his heels, who amuse themselves in playing all kinds of tricks upon him:—

"I play the harp in the streets," he said, "and have done so for the last two years, and should be very glad to give it up. My brother lives with me, we're both bachelors, and he's so dreadful lame, he can do nothing. He is a coach body-maker to his business. I was born blind, and was brought up to music, but my sight was restored by Dr. Ware, the old gentleman, in Bridge-street, Blackfriars, when I was nine years old, but it's a near sight now. I'm 49 in August. When I was young I taught the harp and the pianoforte, but that very soon fell off, and I have been teaching on or off these many years—I don't know how many. I had three guineas a quarter for teaching the harp at one time, and two guineas for the piano. My brother and I have 1s. and a loaf a piece from the parish, and the 2s. pays the rent. Mine's not a bad trade now, but it's bad in the streets. I've been torn to pieces; I'm torn to pieces every day I go out in the streets, and I'd be glad to get rid of the streets for 5s. a week. The streets are full of ruffians. The boys are ruffians. The men in the streets too are ruffians, and encourage the boys. The police protect me as much as they can. I should be killed every week but for them; they're very good people. I've known poor women of the town drive the boys away from me, or try to drive them. It's terrible persecution I suffer—terrible persecution. The boys push me down and hurt me badly, and my harp too. They yell and make noises so, that I can't be heard, nor my harp. The boys have cut off my harp-strings, three of them, the other day, which cost me 6½d. or 7d. I tell them it's a shame, but I might as well speak to the stones. I never go out that they miss me. I don't make more than 3s. a week in the streets, if I make that."

One of the long-remembered street performers in London is a blind woman, led by a female. She came to me scrupulously clean, and very tidily dressed; she was accompanied by her usual attendant in the streets, who was almost as clean and tidy as herself. Her countenance is cheerful, and her manners those of a well-contented old woman. She plays on an old hurdy-gurdy, or an instrument of that description, which she calls a cymbal. It has a battered, heavy look with it, and is grievously harsh and out of tune. She said:—

"I have been 43 years a public performer. My parents died when I was a child, and I was put into the poor-house, and left it before I was twenty, to earn my own living. The parish paid for my learning music, and bought me an instrument, and so started me in life, God bless them. I started with a cymbal, which some call a hurdy-gurdy, and have been playing it ever since; it's not the same instrument as I carry now, but I've had this one fifteen years last August. I have been blind since I was nine weeks old. When I started on my own account, a woman forty-one years of age, who had been in Bloomsbury poor-house with me, came out to lead me. We shared alike. She died, and I had several after that who didn't do me justice, for they didn't give me all the money. Forty years ago the two of us would get 6s. a day; now sometimes we can only make 2s. a day for the two of us on an average the summer through, and 1s. 6d. in winter. I have my regular rounds. My Monday's round is Marylebone; my Tuesday's is Kentish-town—they call me Mrs. Tuesday there—the people say, 'Ah, here's Mrs. Tuesday come;' Wednesday is Kensington way generally; Thursday is Brixton and that way; Friday, Hackney round, and

Saturday is Pimlico way. In some rounds I have friends who have given me a trifle every week (or nearly so) for twenty years."

A quiet-looking man, half-blind, and wrapped in a large old faded, black cotton great coat, made the following statement, having first given me some specimens of his art:—

"I imitate all the animals of the farm-yard on my fiddle. I imitate the bull, the calf, the dog, the cock, the hen when's she laid an egg, the peacock, and the ass. I have done this in the streets for nearly twelve years. I was brought up as a musician at my own desire. When a young man (I am now 53) I used to go out to play at parties, doing middling until my sight failed me. I then did the farm-yard on the fiddle for a living. Though I had never heard of such a thing before, by constant practice I made myself perfect. I studied from nature. I never was in a farm-yard in my life, but I went and listened to the poultry anywhere in town that I could meet with them, and I then imitated them on my instrument. The Smithfield cattle gave me the study for the bull and the calf. My peacock I got at the Belvidere-gardens in Islington. The ass is common, and so is the dog, and them I studied anywhere. It took me a month, not more, if so much, to acquire what I thought a sufficient skill in my undertaking, and then I started it in the streets. It was liked the very first time I tried it. I never say what animal I am going to give. I leave that to the judgment of the listeners. They could always tell what it was. I can make 12s. a week the year through. I play it in public houses as well as in the streets. My pitches are all over London, and I don't know that one is better than another. Working people are my best friends. Thursday and Friday are my worst days; Monday and Saturday my best, when I reckon 2s. 6d. a handsome taking. I am the only man who does the farm-yard."

A hale-looking blind man, with a cheerful look, poorly but not squalidly dressed, gave me the subjoined narrative. He was led by a strong, healthy-looking lad of 15, his step-son:—

"I have been blind since within a month of my birth," he said, "and have been twenty-three years a street performer. My parents were poor, but they managed to have me taught music. I am 55 years old. I was one of a street band in my youth, and could make my 15s. a week at it. I didn't like the band, for if you are steady yourself, you can't get others to be steady, and so no good can be done. I next started a piano in the streets; that was twenty-three years ago. I bought a chaise big enough for an invalid, and having had the body removed, my piano was fitted on the springs and the axle-tree. I carried a seat, and could play the instrument either sitting or standing, and so I travelled through London with it. It did pretty well; in the summer I took never less than 20s., and I have taken 40s. on rare occasions in a week; but the small takings in the winter would reduce my yearly average to 15s. a week at the utmost. I played the piano, more or less, until within these three or four years. I started the bells that I play now, as near as I can recollect, some eighteen years ago. When I first played them I had my fourteen bells arranged on a rail, and tapped them with my two leather hammers held in my hands in the usual way. I thought next I could introduce some novelty into the performance. The novelty I speak of was to play the violin with the bells. I had hammers fixed on a rail, so as each bell had its particular hammer; these hammers were connected with cords to a pedal acting with a spring to bring itself up, and so by playing the pedal with my feet, I had full command of the bells, and made them accompany the violin, so that I could give any tune almost with the power of a band. It was always my delight in my leisure moments, and is a good deal so still, to study improvements such as I have described. The bells and violin together brought me in about the same as the piano. I played the violoncello with my feet also, on a plan of my own, and the violin in my hand. I had the violoncello on a frame on the ground, so arranged that I could move the bow with my foot in harmony with the violin in my hands. The last thing I have introduced is the playing four accordions with my feet. The accordions are fixed in a frame, and I make them accompany the violin. Of all my plans, the piano and the bells and violin did the best, and are the best still for a standard. I can only average 12s. a week take the year through, which is very little for two."

I had the following narrative from a stout, blind woman, with a very grave and even meditative look, fifty-six years old, dressed in a clean cotton gown, the pattern of which was almost washed out. She was led by a very fine dog (a Scotch collie, she described it), a chain being affixed to the dog's leather collar. A boy, poor and destitute, she said, barefooted and wearing a greasy ragged jacket, with his bare skin showing through the many rents, accompanied her when I saw her. The boy had been with her a month, she supporting him. She said:—

"I have been blind twelve years. I was a servant in my youth, and in 1824 married a journeyman cabinet-maker. I went blind from an

inflammation two years before my husband died. We had five children, all dead now—the last died six years ago; and at my husband's
death I was left almost destitute. I used to sell a few laces in the street,
but couldn't clear 2s. 6d. a week by it. I had a little help from the parish, but very rarely; and at last I could get nothing but an order for the
house. A neighbour, a tradesman, then taught me at his leisure to play
the violin, but I'm not a great performer. I wish I was. I began to play
in the streets five years ago. I get halfpennies for charity, not for my
music. Some days I pick up 2s., some days only 6d., and on wet days
nothing. I've often had to pledge my fiddle for 2s.—I could never get
more on it, and sometimes not that. When my fiddle was in pledge I
used to sell matches and laces in the streets, and have had to borrow
1¼d. to lay in a stock. I've sometimes taken 4d. in eight hours. My
chief places when I've only the dog to lead me are Regent-street and
Portland-place, and really people are very kind and careful in guiding
and directing me—even the cabmen—may God bless them."

A stout, hale-looking blind man, dressed very decently in
coloured clothes, and scrupulously clean, gave me the following
details:—

"I am one of the three blind Scotchmen who go about the streets
in company, playing the violoncello, clarionet, and flute. We are really
Highlanders, and can all speak Gaelic; but a good many London
Highlandmen are Irish. I have been 30 years in the streets of London; one of my mates has been 40 years (he's 69); the other has been
30 years. I became partially blind, through an inflammation, when I
was 14, and was stone blind when I was 22. Before I was totally blind I
came to London, travelling up with the help of my bag-pipes, guided
by a little boy. I settled in London, finding it a big place, where a
man could do well (at that time), and I took a turn every now and
then into the country. I could make 14s. a week, winter and summer
through, 30 years ago, by playing in the streets. Now I can't make 6s.
a week, take winter and summer. I met my two mates, who are both
blind men—both came to England for the same reason as I did—in
my journeyings in London, and at last we agreed to go together—
that's twenty years ago. We've been together, on and off, ever since.
Sometimes one of us will take a turn round the coast of Kent, and
another round the coast of Devon; and then join again in London, or
meet by accident. We have always agreed very well, and never fought.
We—I mean the street blind—tried to maintain a burying and sick
club of our own; but we were always too poor. We live in rooms. I

don't know one blind musician who lives in a lodging-house. I myself know a dozen blind men now performing in the streets of London; these are not all exactly blind, but about as bad—the most are stone blind. The blind musicians are chiefly married men. I don't know one who lives with a woman unmarried. The loss of sight changes a man. He doesn't think of women, and women don't think of him. We are of a religious turn, too, generally. I am a Roman Catholic; but the other Scotch blind men here are Presbyterians. The Scotch in London are our good friends, because they give us a little sum altogether, perhaps; but the English working people are our main support; it is by them we live, and I always found them kind and liberal, the most liberal in the world as I know. Through Marylebone is our best round, and Saturday night our best time. We play all three together. 'Johnny Cope' is our best-liked tune. I think the blind Scotchmen don't come to play in London now. I can remember many blind Scotch musicians or pipers in London: they're all dead now. The trade's dead too; it is so. When we thought of forming the blind club there was never more than a dozen members. These were two basket-makers, one mat-maker, four violin players, myself, and my two mates, which was the number when it dropped for want of funds; that's now fifteen years ago. We were to pay 1s. a month, and sick members were to have 5s. a week when they'd paid two years. Our other rules were the same as other clubs, I believe. The blind musicians now in London are we three; C——, a Jew, who plays the violin; R——, an Englishman, who plays the violin elegantly; W——, a harp-player; T——, violin again; H——, violin (but he plays more in public-houses); R——, the flute; M^c——, bagpipes; C——, bagpipes; K——, violin: that's all I know myself. There's a good many blind who play at the sailors' dances, Wapping and Deptford way. We seldom hire children to lead us in the streets; we have plenty of our own, generally. I have five. Our wives are generally women that have their eyesight; but some blind men—I know one couple—marry blind women."

The *Street Vocalists* are almost as large a body as the street musicians. It will be seen that there are fifty Ethiopian serenaders, and above 250 who live by ballad singing alone. In my present letter I shall deal with the Ethiopian Serenaders and the better class of Ballad Singers:—

Two young men, who are of the former class, gave the following account. Both were dressed like decent mechanics, with perfectly clean faces, except that a little of the professional black remained at the root of the hairs on the forehead.

"We are niggers," said one man, "as it's commonly called; that is negro melodists. Nigger bands vary from four to seven, and have numbered as many as nine; *our* band is now six. We all share alike. I (said the same man) was the first who started the niggers in the streets about four years ago. I took the hint from the performance of Pell and the others at the St. James's. When I first started in the streets I had five performers, four and myself. There were the banjo-player, the bones, fiddle, and tambourine. We were regularly full-dressed in fashionable black coats and trowsers, open white waistcoats, pumps (bluchers some had, just as they could spring them), and wigs to imitate the real negro head of hair. Large white wrists or cuffs came out after. It was rather a venturesome 'spec, the street niggers, for I had to find all the clothes at first start, as I set the school a-going. Perhaps it cost me 6s. a head all round; all second-hand dress except the wigs, and each man made his own wig out of horse-hair died black, and sewn with black thread on to the skin of an old silk hat. Well, we first started at the top of the Liverpool-road, but it was no great success, as we wern't quite up in our parts, and didn't play exactly into one another's hands. None of us were perfect, we'd had so few rehearsals. One of us had been a street singer before, another a street fiddler, another had sung nigger songs in public-houses, the fourth was a mud-lark, and I had been a street singer. I was brought up to no trade regularly. When my father died I was left on the world, and I worked in Marylebone stone-yard, and afterwards sung about the streets, or shifted as I could. I first sung in the streets just before the Queen's coronation—and a hard life it was. But, to tell the truth, I didn't like the thoughts of hard labour—bringing a man in so little too—that's where it is; and as soon as I could make any sort of living in the streets, with singing and such like, I got to like it. The first debew, as I may say, of the niggers brought us in about 10s. among us, besides paying for our dinner and a pint of beer a piece. We were forced to be steady you see, sir, as we didn't know how it would answer. We sang from eleven in the morning till half-past ten at night, summer time. We kept on, day after day, not rehearsing, but practising in the streets, for rehearsing in private was of little use; voices are as different in private rooms and the public streets as is chalk from cheese. We got more confidence as we went along. To be sure we all had cheek enough to start with, but this was a fresh line of business. Times mended as we got better at our work. Last year was the best year I've known. We start generally about ten, and play till it's dark, in fine weather. We averaged £1 a week last year. The evenings are the best time. Regent-street, and Oxford-street, and the greater part of St. James's are our best places. The gentry are our best customers, but we get more from gentlemen than from ladies. The City is good, I fancy, but they won't let us work it; it's only the lower parts, Whitechapel and Smithfield ways, that we have a chance in. Business and nigger songs don't go well together. The first four days of the week are pretty much alike for our business. Friday is bad, and so is Saturday, until night comes, and we then get money from the working people. The markets, such as Cleveland-street, Fitzroy-square (Tottenham-court-road's no good at any time), Carnaby-market, Newport-market, Great Marylebone-street, and the Edgware-road, are good Saturday nights. Oxford-street is middling. The New Cut is as bad a place as can be. When we started, the songs we knew was 'Old Mr. Coon,' 'Buffalo Gals,' 'Going ober de Mountain,' 'Dandy Jim of Caroline,' 'Rowly Bowly, O,' and 'Old Johnny Booker.' We stuck to them a twelvemonth. The 'Buffalo Gals' was best liked. The 'bones'—we've real bones, rib-of-beef bones; but some have ebony bones, which sound better than rib bones—they toil best in 'Going ober de Mountain,' for there's a sym-phony between every line. It's rather difficult to play the bones well; it requires hard practice, and it brings the skin off, and some men have tried it, but with so little success that they broke their bones and flung them away. The banjo is the hardest to learn of the lot. We have kept changing our songs all along; but some of the old ones are still sung. The other favourites are, or were, 'Lucy Neale,' 'O, Susannah,' 'Uncle Ned,' 'Stop that Knocking,' 'Ginger Blue,' and 'Black-eyed Suseannah.' Things are not so good as they were. We can average £1 a-piece now in the week, but it's summer-time, and we can't make that in bad weather. Then, there's so many of us. There's the Somers-town 'mob' now in London; the King-street, the four St. Giles's mobs, the East End (but they're white Niggers), the two Westminster mobs, the Marylebone and the Whitechapel. We interfere with one another's beats sometimes, for we have no arrangement with each other, only we don't pitch near the others when they're at work. The ten mobs now in London will have fifty men in them at least; and there's plenty of stragglers, who are not regular niggers; there's so many dodges now to pick up a living, sir. The Marylebone and Whitechapel lots play at nights in penny theatres. I have played at the Haymarket in 'the

New Planet,' but there's no demand for us now at the theatres, except such as the Pavilion. There are all sorts of characters in the different schools, but I don't know any runaway gentleman, or any gentleman of any kind among us; not one; we're more of a poorer sort, if not to say a ragged sort, for some are without shoes or stockings. The 'niggers' that I know have been errand-boys, street-singers, turf-cutters, coalheavers, chandlers, paviours, mudlarks, tailors, shoemakers, tinmen, bricklayers' labourers, and people who have had no line in particular but their wits. I know of no connection with pickpockets, and don't believe there is any, though pickpockets go round the mobs; but the police fling it in our teeth that we're connected with pickpockets. It's a great injury to us is such a notion. A good many of the niggers—both of us here likes a little drop—drink as hard as they can, and a good many live with women of the town. A few are married. Some niggers are Irish; there's Scotch niggers too. I don't know a Welsh one, but one of the street nigger singers *is* a real black, an African."

Scene in a Gin Palace in the New Cut

An experienced street vocalist, of the better kind, upon whose statements I satisfied myself that every reliance might be placed, described to me the present condition of his calling. He was accompanied by his wife:—

"I have been in the profession of a vocalist," he said, "full twenty-five years. Before that I was a concert singer. I was not brought up to the profession; I was a shipping agent, but I married a concert-singer, and then followed the profession. I was young, and a little stage-struck." ("Rather," said his wife smiling, "he was struck with those who were on the stage"); "and so I abandoned the ship-agency. I have tried my fortune on the stage as a singer, and can't say but what I have succeeded. In fact, my wife and I have taken more than any two singers that have ever appeared in the humble way. We have been street vocalists for twenty-five years. We sing solos, duets, and glees, and only at night. When we started, the class of songs was very different to what it is now. We were styled 'the royal glee singers.' 'Cherry ripe,' 'Meet me by moonlight,' 'Sweet home,' were popular then. Haynes Bailey's ballads were popular, and much of Bishop's music, as, indeed, it is still. Barnett's or Lee's music, however, is now more approved in the concert-rooms than Bishop's. Our plan was and is to inquire at gentlemen's houses if they wished to hear glee, or solo singing, and to sing in the street, or in the halls, as well as at parties. When we first commenced we have made £3 and £3 10s. in a night this way; but that was on extraordinary occasions, and £3 a week might be the average earnings, take the year through. These earnings continued eight or ten years, and then fell off. Other amusements attracted attention. Now, my wife, my daughter, and I may make 25s. a week by open-air singing. Concert singing is extra, and the best payment is a crown per head a night for low-priced concerts. The inferior vocalists get 4s., 3s., 2s. 6d., and some as low as 2s. Very many who sing at the concerts have received a high musical education; but the profession is so overstocked, that excellent singers are compelled to take poor engagements." The better sort of cheap concert singers, the man and wife both agreed in stating, were a well-conducted body of people, often struggling for a very poor maintenance, the women rarely being improper characters. "But now (said the husband) John Bull's taste is inclined to the brutal and filthy. Some of the 'character songs,' such as 'Sam Hall,' 'Jack Sheppard,' and others, are so indelicate that a respectable man ought not to take his wife and daughters to see them. The men who sing character songs are the worst class of singers, both as regards character and skill; they are generally loose fellows; some are what is called 'fancy men;' persons supported, wholly or partly, by women of the town. I attempted once to give concerts without these low character-singings, but it did not succeed, for I was alone in the attempt. I believe there are not more than half-a-dozen street vocalists of the same class as ourselves. They are respectable persons; and certainly open-air singing, as we practise it, is more respectable than popular concert singing as now carried on. No one would be allowed to sing such songs in the streets. The 'character' concerts are attended, generally, by mechanics and their families; there are more males than females among the audiences."

The Morning Chronicle, Thursday, June 6, 1850.

J. D. H. has handed us half-a-crown for the poor Italian who had been in Bartholomew's Hospital, mentioned in the Letter of the 30th ult.

LABOUR AND THE POOR.

---◆---

THE METROPOLITAN DISTRICTS.

[FROM OUR SPECIAL CORRESPONDENT.]

Letter LVI.

In the present Letter I shall conclude my account of the Street Performers and Showmen. The classes that are still undescribed are the lower class of street singers—the street artists—the writers without hands—the blind readers—and the street exhibition keepers. I shall begin with the Street Singers.

Concerning the ordinary street ballad-singers, I received the following account from one of the class:—

"I am what may be termed a regular street ballad-singer—either sentimental or comic, sir, for I can take both branches. I have been, as near as I can guess, about five and twenty year at the business. My mother died when I was thirteen years old, and in consequence of a step-mother, home became too hot to hold me, and I turned into the streets on account of the harsh treatment I met with. My father had given me no education, and all I know now I have picked up in the streets. Well, at thirteen years I turned into the London streets, houseless, friendless. My father was a picture-frame gilder. I was never taught any business by him—neither his own nor any other. I never received any benefit from him that I know. Well, then, sir, there was I, a boy of thirteen—friendless, houseless, untaught, and without any means of getting a living—loose in the streets of London. At first I slept anywhere. Sometimes I passed the night in the Old Covent-garden Market; at others, in shutter-boxes; and at others, on door-steps near my father's house. I lived at this time upon the refuse that I picked up in the streets—cabbage stumps out of the market, orange peel, and the like. Well, sir, I was green then, and one of the Stamp-office spies got me to sell some of the '*Poor Man's Guardians*' (an unstamped paper of that time), so that his fellow-spy might take me up. This he did, and I had a month at Coldbath-fields for the business. After I had been in prison I got in a measure hardened to the frowns of the world, and didn't care what company I kept, or what I did for a living. I wouldn't have you to fancy though that I did anything dishonest. I mean I wasn't particular as to what I turned my hand to for a living, or where I lodged. I went to live in Church-lane, St. Giles's, at a threepenny house, and having a tidy voice of my own, I was there taught to go out ballad singing, and I have stuck to the business ever since. I was going on for fifteen when I first took to it. The first thing I did was to lead at glee singing. I took the air, and two others, old hands, did the second and the bass. We used to sing the 'Red Cross Knight,' 'Hail Smiling Morn,' and harmonize 'The Wolf,' and other popular songs. Excepting when we needed money, we rarely went out till the evening. Then our pitches were in quiet streets or squares, where we saw, by the lights at the windows, that some party was going on. Wedding parties was very good, in general quite a harvest. Public-houses we did little at, and then it was always with the parlour company; the tap-room people have no taste for glee singing. At times we took from 9s. to 10s. of an evening—the three of us. I am speaking of the business as it was about two or three and twenty years ago. Now glee singing is seldom practised in the streets of London. It is chiefly confined to the provinces at present. In London, concerts are so cheap now-a-days that no one will stop to listen to the street glee singers; so most of 'the schools' or sets have gone to sing at the cheap concerts held at the public-houses. Many of the glee singers have given up the business, and taken to the street Ethiopians instead. The street glee singers had been some of them brought up to a trade, though some had not. Few were so unfortunate as me—to have none at all. The two that I was with had been a ladies' shoemaker and a paper-hanger. Others that I knew had been blacksmiths, carpenters, linendrapers' shopmen, bakers, French polishers, pastrycooks, and such like. They mostly left their business and took to glee singing when they were young. The most that I knew were from nineteen to twenty-two years old. They had, in general, been a little racketty, and had got stage-struck or concert-struck at public-houses. They had got praised for their voices, and so their vanity led them to take to it for a living when they got hard-up. Twenty years ago there must have been at the east and west end at least fourteen different sets, good and bad, and in each set there was on an average three singers; now I don't think there is one set at work in London streets. After I had been three years glee singing in the streets, I took up with the ballad business, and found it more lucrative than the glee line. Sometimes I could take 5s. in the day, and not work heavily for it either—but at other times I couldn't take enough to pay my lodging. When any popular song came up that was our harvest—'Alice Gray,' 'the Sea,' 'Bridal Ring,' 'We met,' 'the Tartar Drum' (in which I was well known), 'The Banks of the Blue Moselle,' and such like—not forgetting 'The Mistletoe Bough;' these were all great things to the ballad singers. We looked at the bill of fare for the different concert rooms, and then went round the neighbourhood where these songs were being sung, because the airs being well known, you see it eased the way for us. The very best sentimental song that ever I had in my life, and which lasted me off and on for two years, was Byron's 'Isle of Beauty.' I could get a meal quicker with that than with any other. The 'Mistletoe Bough' got me many a Christmas dinner. We always works it at that time. It would puzzle any man, even the most exactest, to tell what they could make by ballad-singing in the street. Some nights it would be wet, and I should be hoarse, and then I'd take nothing. I should think that, take one week with another, my earnings were barely more than 10s. a week—12s. a week, on the average, I think, would be the very outside. Street ballad-singers never go out in costume. It is generally supposed that some who appear without shoes, and wretchedly clad, are made up for the purpose of exciting charity; but this the regular street ballad-singer never does. He is too independent to rank himself with the beggars. He *earns* his money, he fancies, and does not ask charity. Some of the ballad-singers may perhaps be called beggars, or rather pensioners— that is the term we give them; but these are of the worst description of singers, and have money given to them neither for their singing nor songs, but in pity for their age and infirmities. Of these there are about six in London. Of the regular ballad-singers, sentimental and comic, there are not less than 250 in and about London. Occasionally the number is greatly increased by an influx from the country. I should say that throughout England, Wales, and Scotland, there is not less than 700 who live solely by ballad singing, and selling ballads and song books. In London the ballad-singers generally work in couples—especially the comic singers. The sentimental more commonly go alone; but there are very few in London who are merely sentimental ballad-singers—not more than a dozen at the very outside. The rest sing whatever comes up. The tunes are mostly picked up from the street bands, and sometimes from the cheap concerts, or from the gallery of the theatre, where the street ballad-singers very often go, for the express purpose of learning the airs. They are mostly utterly ignorant of music, and some of them get their money by the noise they make, by being paid to move on. There is a house in the Blackfriars-road where the people has been ill for these last sixteen years, and where the street ballad-singer always goes, because he is sure of getting twopence there to move on. Some, too, make a point of beginning their songs outside of those houses where straw is laid down in front. Where the knockers are done up in an old glove the ballad-singer is sure to strike up. The comic songs that are popular in the street are never indecent, but are very often political. They are generally sung by two persons, one repeating the two first lines of a verse, and the other the two last. The street ballads are printed and published chiefly in the Seven Dials. There are four ballad publishers in that quarter and three at the East-end. Many ballads are written expressly for the Seven Dials press, especially the Newgate and the political ones, as well as those upon any topic of the day. There are five known authors for the Dials press, and they are all street ballad-singers. I am one of these myself. The little knowledge I have, I have picked up bit by bit, so that I hardly know how I have come by it. I certainly knew my letters before I left home, and I have got the rest off the dead walls and out of the ballads and papers I have been selling. I write most of the Newgate ballads now for the printers in the Dials, and, indeed, anything that turns up. I get a shilling for a 'copy of verses written by the wretched culprit the night previous to his execution.' I wrote Courvoisier's sorrowful lamentation. I called it 'A Woice from the Gaol.' I wrote a pathetic ballad on the respite of Annette Meyers. I did the helegy, too, on Rush's execution. It was supposed, like the rest, to be written by the culprit himself, and was particular penitent. I didn't write that to order—I knew they would want a copy of verses from the culprit. The publisher read it over, and said, 'That's the thing for the street public.' I only got 1s. for Rush. Indeed, they are all the same price, no matter how popular they may be. I wrote the life of Manning in verse. Besides these I have written the lament of Calcraft the Hangman on the decline of his trade, and many political songs. But song and Newgate ballad writing for the Dials is very poor work. I've got five times as much for writing a squib for a rag-shop as for a ballad that has taken me double the time."

I now come to the street artists. These include the artists in coloured chalks upon the pavements, the black profile-cutters, and the blind paper-cutters.

A spare sad-looking man, very poorly dressed, gave me the following statement. He is well-known by his coloured drawings upon the flag stones:—

"I was usher in a school for three years, and had a paralytic stroke, which lost me my employment, and was soon the cause of great poverty. I was fond of drawing, and colouring drawings, when a child, using sixpenny boxes of colours, or the best my parents could procure me, but I never had lessons. I am a self-taught man. When I was reduced to distress, and indeed to starvation, I thought of trying some mode of living, and remembering having seen a man draw mackerel on the flags in the streets of Bristol twenty years ago, I thought I would try what I could do that way. I first tried my hand in the New Kent-road, attempting a likeness of Napoleon, and it was passable, though I can do much better now. I made half-a-crown the first day. I saw a statement in one of your letters that I was making £1 a day, and was giving fourteen pence for a shilling. I never did. On the contrary, I've had a pint of beer given to me by publicans for supplying them with copper. It doesn't hurt me, so that you needn't contradict it unless you like. *The Morning Chronicle* letters about us are often talked over in the lodging-houses. It's fourteen or fifteen years since I started in the New Kent-road, and I've followed up 'screeving,' as it's sometimes called, or drawing in coloured chalks on the flag stones, until now. I improved with practice. It paid me well; but in wet weather I have made nothing, and have had to run into debt. A good day's work I reckoned 8s.—or 10s. a very good day's work. I should be glad to get it now. I have made 15s. in a day on an extraordinary occasion, but never more, except at Greenwich Fair, where I've practised these fourteen years. I don't suppose I ever cleared £1 a week all the year round at screeving. For £1 a week I would honestly work my hardest. I have a wife and two children. I would draw trucks or be a copying clerk, or do anything for £1 a week to get out of the streets. Or I would like regular employment as a painter in crayons. Of all my paintings the Christ's heads paid the best, but very little better than the Napoleon's heads. The Waterloo-bridge-road was a favourite spot of mine for a pitch. Euston-square is another. These two were my best. I never chalked 'starving' on the flags, or anything of that kind. There are two imitators of me, but they do badly. I don't do as well as I did ten years ago, but I'm making 15s. a week all the year through."

A cheerful blind man, well known to all crossing Waterloo or Hungerford Bridges, gave me the following account of his figure cutting:—

"I had the measles when I was seven, and became blind, but my sight was restored by Dr. Jeffrey, at Old St. George's Hospital. After that I had several relapses into total blindness in consequence of colds, and since 1840 I have been quite blind, excepting that I can partially distinguish the sun and the gas lights, and such like, with the left eye only. I am now 31, and was brought up to house painting. When I was last attacked with blindness I was obliged to go St. Martin's workhouse, where I underwent thirteen operations in two years. When I came out of the workhouse I played the German flute in the street, but it was only a noise, not music, sir. Then I sold boot-laces and tapes in the street, and averaged 5s. a week by it—certainly not more. Next I made little wooden tobacco stoppers in the street, in the shape of legs—they're called 'legs.' The first day I started in that line—it was in Tottenham-court-road—I was quite elated, for I made half-a-crown. I next tried it by St. Clement's Church, but I found that I cut my hands so with the knives and files, that I had to give it up, and I then took up with the trade of cutting out profiles of animals and birds, and grotesque human figures in card. I established myself soon after I began this trade by the Victoria-gate, Bayswater—that was the best pitch I ever had. One day I took 15s., and I averaged 30s. a week for six weeks. At last the inspector of police ordered me off. After that I was shoved about by the police, such crowds gathered round me, until I at length got leave to carry on my business by Waterloo-bridge—that's seven years ago. I remained there till the opening of Hungerford-bridge, in May, 1845. I sit there cold or fine, winter or summer, every day but Sunday, or if I'm ill. I often hear odd remarks from people crossing the bridge. In winter time, when I've been cold and hungry, and so poor that I couldn't get my clothes properly mended, one has said, 'Look at that poor blind man, there;' and another (and oft enough, too) has answered, 'Poor blind man! he has better clothes and more money than you or me; it's all done to excite pity.' I can generally tell a gentleman's or lady's voice, if they're the real thing. I can tell a purse-proud man's voice, too. He says, in a domineering, hectoring way, as an ancient Roman might speak to his slave, 'Ah, ha! my good fellow, how do you sell these things?' Since January last I may have averaged 8s. a week; that's the outside. The working and the middling classes are my best friends. I know of no other man in my particular line, and I've often inquired concerning any."

The next in order are the writers without hands, and the readers without eyes.

A man of 61, born in the crippled state he described, tall, and with an intelligent look and good manners, gave me this account:—

"I was born without hands, merely the elbow of the right arm and the joint of the wrist of the left. I have rounded stumps. I was born without feet also, merely the ankle and heel, just as if my feet were cut off close within the instep. My father was a farmer in Cavan county, Ireland, and gave me a fair education. He had me taught to write. I'll show you how, sir. [Here he put on a pair of spectacles, using his stumps, and then holding the pen on one stump, by means of the other he moved the two together, and so wrote his name in an old-fashioned hand.] I was taught by an ordinary schoolmaster. I served an apprenticeship of seven years to a turner, near Cavan, and could work well at the turning, but couldn't chop the wood very well. I handled my tools as I've shown you I do my pen. I came to London in 1814, having a prospect of getting a situation in the India-house, but I didn't get it, and waited for eighteen months until my funds and my father's help were exhausted, and I then took to making fancy screens, flower vases, and hand-racks in the streets. I did very well at them, making 15s. to 20s. a week in the summer, and not half that, perhaps not much more than a third, in the winter. I continue this work still when my health permits, and I now make handsome ornaments, flower vases, &c., for the quality, and have to work before them frequently to satisfy them. I could do very well but for ill health. I charge from 5s. to 8s. for hand-screens, and from 7s. 6d. to 15s. for flower vases. Some of the quality pay me handsomely—some are very near. I have done little work in the streets this way, except in very fine weather. Sometimes I write tickets in the street at a halfpenny each. The police never interfere unless the thoroughfare is obstructed badly. My most frequent writing is 'Naked came I into the world, and naked shall I return.' 'The Lord giveth and the Lord taketh away. Blessed be the name of the Lord.' To that I add my name, the date sometimes, and a memorandum that it was the writing of a man born without hands or feet. When I'm not disturbed I do pretty well, getting 1s. 6d. a day, but that's an extra day. The boys are a great worry to me. Working-people are my only friends at the writing, and women the best. My best pitches are Tottenham-court-road and the West-end thoroughfares. There's three men I know who write without hands. They're in the country chiefly, travelling. One man writes with his toes, but chiefly in the public-houses or with showmen. I consider that I am the only man in the world who is a handicraftsman without hands or feet. I am married, and have a grown-up family; two of my sons are in America, one in Australia, one a sailor, the others are emigrants on the coast of Africa, and one a cabinet maker in London—all fine fellows, well made. I had fifteen in all. My father and mother, too, were a handsome well-made couple."

An intelligent man gave me the following account of his experience as a *blind reader*. He was poorly dressed, but clean, and had not a vulgar look.

"My father died when I was ten years old, and my mother in the coronation year, 1838. I am now in my thirty-eighth year. I was a clerk in various offices. I was not born blind, but lost my sight four years ago, in consequence of aneurism. I was a fortnight in the Ophthalmic Hospital, and was an out-patient for three months. I am a married man with one child, and we did as well as we could, but that was very badly, until every bit of furniture (and I had a house full of good furniture up to that time) went. At last I thought I might earn a little by reading in the street. The Society for the Indigent Blind gave me the Gospel of St. John, after Mr. Freer's system, the price being 8s.; and a brother-in-law supplied me with the Gospel of St. Luke, which costs 9s. In Mr. Freer's system the regular alphabet letters are not used, but there are raised characters, 34 in number, including long and short vowels, and these characters express sounds, and a sound may comprise a short syllable. I learned to read by this system in four lessons. I first read in public in Mornington-crescent. For the first fortnight or three weeks I took from 2s. 6d. to 2s. 9d. a day— one day I took 3s. My receipts then fell to something less than 18d. a day, and have been gradually falling ever since. Since the 1st of January, this year, I haven't averaged more than 2s. 6d. a week by my street reading and writing. My wife earns 3s. or 4s. a week with her needle, slaving for a 'sweater' to a shirtmaker. I have never read anywhere but in Euston-square and Mornington-crescent. On Whit Monday I made 2s. 8½d., and on Whit-Tuesday, 2s. 0½d., and that I assure you I reckon really good holiday earnings, and I read until I was hoarse with it. Once at Mornington-crescent, I counted, as closely as I could, just out of curiosity, and to wile away the time, above 2,000 persons, who passed and repassed without giving me a halfpenny. The working people are my best friends, most decidedly. I am tired of the streets, besides being half starved. There are now five or six blind men about London, who read in the streets. We can read nothing but the Scriptures, as 'blind printing'—so it's sometimes called—has only been used in the Scriptures. I write also in the streets as well as read. I use Wedgwood's manifold writer. I write verses from Scripture. There was no teaching necessary for this. I trace the letters from my knowledge of them when I could see. I believe I am the only blind man who writes so in the streets."

After the street artists, readers, and writers, come the street exhibition men. These include the exhibitors of peep-shows, happy families, &c.

First of the peep-shows. Concerning these I received the subjoined narrative from a man of considerable experience in the "profession:"—

"Being a cripple I am obliged to exhibit a small peep-show. I lost the use of this arm ever since I was three months old. My mother died when I was ten years old, and after that my father took up with an Irishwoman, and turned me and my youngest sister (she was two years younger than me) out into the streets. My father had originally been a dyer, but was working at the fiddle-string business then. My youngest sister got employment at my father's trade, but I couldn't get no work because of my crippled arm. I walked about till I fell down in the streets for want. At last, a man, who had a sweetmeat-shop, took pity on me. His wife made the sweetmeats, and minded the shop while he went out a juggling in the streets, in the Ramo Samee line. He told me as how, if I would go round the country with him and sell a few prints while he was a juggling in the public-houses, he'd find me in wittles, and pay my lodging. I joined him and stopped with him two or three year. After that I went to work for a werry large waste paper dealer. He used to buy up all the old back numbers of the cheap periodicals and penny publications, and send me out with them to sell at a farden a piece. He used to give me 4d. out of every shilling, and I done very well with that, till the periodicals came so low and so many on 'em, that they wouldn't sell at all. Sometimes I could make 15s. on a Saturday night and a Sunday morning a-selling the odd numbers of periodicals, such as 'Tales of the Wars,' 'Lives of the Pirates,' 'Lives of the Highwaymen,' &c. I've often sold as many as 2,000 numbers on a Saturday night, in the New Cut, and the most of them was works about thieves and highwaymen and pirates. Besides me there was three others at the same business. Altogether, I dare say my master alone used to get rid of 10,000 copies of such works on a Saturday night and Sunday morning. Our principal customers was young men. My master made a good bit of money at it. He had been about 18 years in the business, and had begun with 2s. 6d. I was with him 15 year on and off, and at the best time. I used to earn my 30s. a week full at that time. But then I was foolish, and didn't take care of my money. When I was at the 'odd number business' I bought a peep-show. I gave £2 10s. for it. I had it second-hand. I was persuaded to buy it. A person as has got only one hand, you see, isn't like other folks, and the people said, it would always bring me a meal of victuals, and keep me from starving. The peep-shows was a doing very well then (that's about five or six years back), when the theaytres was all a shilling to go into them whole price, but now there's many at threepence and twopence, and a good lot at a penny. Before the theayters lowered, a peep-showman could make sure of his 3s. or 4s. a day, at the least, in fine weather, and on a Saturday night about double that money. At a fair he could take his 15s. to a £1 a day. Then there was about nine or ten peep-shows in London. These were all back-shows. There are two kinds of peep-shows, which we call 'back-shows' and 'caravan-shows.' The caravan-shows are much larger than the others, and are drawn by a horse or a donkey. They have a green baize curtain at the back, which shuts out them as don't pay. The showmen usually live in these caravans with their families. Often there will be a man, his wife, and three or four children living in one of these shows. These caravans mostly go into the country, and very seldom are seen in town. They exhibit principally at fairs and feasts or wakes in country villages. They generally go out of London between March and April, because some fairs begin at that time, but many wait for the fairs at May. Then they work their way right round, from willage to town. They tell one another what part they're a-going to, and they never interfere with one another's rounds. If a new hand comes into the business they're werry civil, and tells him what places to work. The carawans comes to London about October, after the fairs is over. The scenes of them carawan shows is mostly upon recent battles and murders. Anything in that way of late occurrence suits them. Theattical plays ain't no good for country towns, 'cause they don't understand such things there. People is werry fond of the battles in the country, but a murder wot is well known is worth more than all the fights. There was more took with Rush's murder than there has been even by the battle of Waterloo itself. Some of the carawan shows does werry well. Their average taking is 30s. a week for the summer months. At some fairs they'll take 5*l.* in the three days. They have been about town as long as ever we can recollect. I should say there is full 50 of these carawan shows throughout the country. Some never comes into London at all. There is about a dozen that comes to London regular every winter. The business in general goes from family to family. The cost of a carawan show, second-hand, is 40*l.*—that's without the glasses, and them runs from 10s. to 1*l.* a piece, because they're large. Why, I've knowed the front of a peep-show, with the glasses, cost £60; the front was mahogany, and had 36 glasses, with gilt carved mouldings round each on 'em. The scenes will cost about £6, if done by the best artist, and £3 if done by a common hand. The back-shows are peep-shows that stand on trussels, and are so small as to admit of being carried on the back. The scenery is about 18 inches to 2 foot in length, and about 15 inches high. They have been introduced about 15 or 16 years. The man as first brought 'em up was named Billy T——; he was lame of one leg, and used to exhibit little automaton figures in the New-cut. On their first coming out, the oldest back-showman as I know on has told me they could take their 15s. a day. But now we can't do more than 7s. a week, run Saturday and all the other days together— and that's through the theayters being so low. It's a regular starving life now. We has to put up with the hinsults of people so. The back-shows generally exhibits plays of different kinds wot been performed at the theayters lately. I've got many different plays to my show. I only hexhibit one at a time. There's 'Halonzer the Brave and the Fair Himogen,' 'The Dog of Montargis and the Forest of Bondy,' 'Hyder Halley, or the Lyons of Mysore,' 'The Forty Thieves' (that never done no good to me), 'The Devil and Doctor Faustus;' and at Christmas time we exhibits pantomimes. I has some battle scenes as well. I've 'Napoleon's Return from Helba,' 'Napoleon at Waterloo,' 'The Death of Lord Nelson,' and also 'The Queen embarking to start for Scotland, from the Dockyard at Voolich.' We takes more from children than grown people in London, and more from grown people than children in the country. You see grown people has such remarks made upon them while they're a-peeping through in London, as it makes it bad for us here. Lately, I have been hardly able to get a living, you may say. Some days I've taken 6d., others 8d., and sometimes 1s.—that's what I call a good day for any of the week days. On a Saturday it runs from 2s. to 2s. 6d. Of the week days, Monday or Tuesday is the best. If there's a fair on near London, such as Greenwich, we can go and take 3s. and 4s., or 5s. a day, so long as it lasts. But, after that, we comes back to the old business, and that's bad enough; for, after you've paid 1s. 6d. a week rent, and 6d. a week stand for your peep-show, and come to buy a bit of coal, why all one can get is a bit of bread and a cup of tea to live upon. As for meat, we don't see it from one month's end to the other. My old woman, when she is at work, only gets five fardens a pair for making a pair of drawers to send out for the conwicts, and three halfpence for a shirt; and out of that she has to find her own thread. There are from six to eight scenes in each of the plays that I shows; and if the scenes are a bit short, why I puts in a couple of battle-scenes; or I makes up a pannerrammer for 'em. The children *will* have so much for the money now. I charge a halfpenny for a hentire performance. There is characters and all—and I explains what they are supposed to be a talking about. There's about six back-shows in London. I don't think there's more. It don't pay now to get up a new play. We works the old ones over and over again, and sometimes we buys a fresh one of another showman if we can rise the money—the price is 2s. and 2s. 6d. I've been obligated to get rid on about twelve of my plays to get a bit of victuals at home. Formerly we used to give a hartist 1s. to go in the pit and sketch off the scenes and figures of any new play that was a doing well and we thought 'ud take, and arter that we used to give him from 1s. 6d. to 2s. for drawing and painting each scene, and 1d. and 1½d. each for the figures, according to the size. Each play costs us from 15s. to £1 for the inside scenes and figures, and the outside painting as well. The outside painting in general consists of the most attractive part of the performance. The New-cut is no good at all now on a Saturday night; that's through the cheap penny hexhibitions there. Tottenham-court-road a'nt much account either. The street markets is the best of a Saturday night. I'm often obliged to take bottles instead of money, and they don't fetch more than 3d. a dozen. Sometimes I take four dozen of bottles in a day. I lets 'em see a play for a bottle, and often two wants to see for one large bottle. The children is dreadful for cheapening things down. In the summer I goes out of London for a month at a stretch. In the country I works my battle pieces. They're most pleased there with my Lord Nelson's death at the battle of Trafalgar. 'That there is,' I tell 'em, 'a fine painting representing Lord Nelson at the battle of Trafalgar. In the centre is Lord Nelson in his last dying moments, supported by Captain Hardy and the chaplin. On the left is the hexplosion of one of the enemy's ships by fire. That represents a fine painting, representing the death of Lord Nelson at the battle of Trafalgar, wot was fought on the 12th of October, 1805.' I've got five glasses, they cost about 5s. a piece when new, and is about 3½ inches across, with a 3 foot focus."

"Happy Families," or assemblages of animals of diverse habits and propensities living amicably, or at least quietly, in one cage, are so well known as to need no further description here. Concerning them I received the following account:—

"I have been three years connected with Happy Families, living by such connection. These exhibitions were first started at Coventry, sixteen years ago, by a man who was my teacher. He was a stocking-weaver, and a fancier of animals and birds, having a good many in his place: hawks, owls, pigeons, starlings, cats, dogs, mice, rats, guinea-pigs, jack-daws, fowls, ravens, and monkeys. He used to keep them separate and for his own amusement, or would train them for sale, teaching the dogs tricks and such like. He found his animals agree so well together, that he had a notion—and a snake-charmer, an old In-dian, used to advise him on the subject—that he could show in public animals and birds, supposed to be one another's enemies and victims, living in quiet together. He did show them in public, beginning with cats, rats, and pigeons in one cage, and then kept adding by degrees all the other creatures I have mentioned. He did very well at Coventry, but I don't know what he took. His way of training the animals is a secret which he has taught to me. It's principally done, however, I may tell you, by continued kindness and petting, and studying the nature of the creatures. Hundreds have tried their hands at happy families and have failed. The cat has killed the mice, the hawks have killed the birds, the dogs the rats, and even the cats, the rats the birds, and even one another; indeed, it was anything but a Happy Family. By our system we never have a mishap, and have had animals eight or nine years in the cage—until they've died of age, indeed. In our present cage we have 54 birds and animals, and of 17 different kinds; 3 cats, 2 dogs (a terrier and a spaniel), 2 monkeys, 2 magpies, 2 jack-daws, 2 jays, 10 starlings (some of them talk), 6 pigeons, 2 hawks, 2 barn fowls, 1 screech owl, 5 common-sewer rats, 5 white rats (a nov-elty), 8 guinea pigs, 2 rabbits (1 wild and 1 tame), 1 hedgehog, and 1 tortoise. Of all these the rat is the most difficult animal to make a member of a 'Happy Family.' Among birds, the hawk. The easi-est trained animal is a monkey; and the easiest trained bird, a pigeon.

They live together in their cages all night, and sleep in a stable unattended by any one. They were once thirty-six hours, as a trial, without food—that was in Cambridge; and no creature was injured, but they were very peckish, especially the birds of prey. I wouldn't allow it to be tried (it was for a scientific gentleman) any longer, and I fed them well to begin upon. There are now in London five Happy Families, all belonging to two families of men. Mine, that is the one I have the care of, is the strongest, 54 creatures; the others will average 40 each, or 214 birds and beasts in Happy Families. Our only regular places now are Waterloo-bridge and the National Gallery. The expense of keeping my 54 is 12s. a week; and in a good week—indeed the best week—we take 30s., and in a bad week sometimes not 8s. It's only a poor trade, though there are more good weeks than bad; but the weather has so much to do with it. The middle class of society are our best supporters. When the Happy Family—only one—was first in London, fourteen years ago, the proprietor took £1 a day on Waterloo-bridge, and only showed in the summer. The second Happy Family was started eight years ago, and did as well for a short time as the first. Now there are too many Happy Families. There are none in the country."

Index

Titles Available in the Series

LABOUR AND THE POOR

Volumes I to IV: The Metropolitan Districts
Henry Mayhew

ISBN 978-1-913515-11-9, 978-1-913515-12-6, 978-1-913515-13-3, 978-1-913515-14-0

Volume V: The Manufacturing Districts
Angus B. Reach

ISBN 978-1-913515-15-7

Volumes VI & VII: The Rural Districts
Alexander Mackay & Shirley Brooks

ISBN 978-1-913515-16-4, 978-1-913515-17-1

Volume VIII: Wales
Special Correspondent

ISBN 978-1-913515-18-8

Volume IX: Birmingham
Charles Mackay

ISBN 978-1-913515-19-5

Volume X: Liverpool
Charles Mackay

ISBN 978-1-913515-20-1

For information on these and other titles available please visit:

DittoBooks.co.uk

www.ingramcontent.com/pod-product-compliance
Lightning Source LLC
Chambersburg PA
CBHW060304030426
42336CB00011B/923